P9-CKX-075

DATE DUE

DEMCO 38-296

Once the major success story of a troubled continent, Kenya came in the early 1990s to be regarded as its fallen star. This book challenges such images of reversal and the analytical polarities which sustain them. Based on several years of research in Kenya, the analysis ranges from telescopic to microscopic fields of vision – from national political culture, oratory, and the staging of politics to everyday struggles for livelihood among people in one rural locale during the past century. This sliding scale of analysis allows the author to experiment theoretically with a number of themes informed by contemporary analytical tensions among post-modernist "chaos," historical contingency, and structural regularities. The result is a study which combines many disciplines and perspectives to give a rich and varied picture of the culture of politics in twentieth-century Kenya.

The culture of politics in modern Kenya

African studies series 84

Editorial board
Naomi Chazan, *Hebrew University of Jerusalem*
Christopher Clapham, *University of Lancaster*
Peter Ekeh, *State University of New York, Buffalo*
John Lonsdale, *University of Cambridge*
Patrick Manning, *Northeastern University*

Published in collaboration with
THE AFRICAN STUDIES CENTRE, CAMBRIDGE

A list of books in this series will be found at the end of this volume

R

The culture of politics in modern Kenya

Angelique Haugerud

Yale University

CAMBRIDGE
UNIVERSITY PRESS

Riverside Community College
Library
SEP '96
4800 Magnolia Avenue
Riverside, California 92506

JQ 2947 .A2 H38 1995

Haugerud, Angelique, 1952-

The culture of politics in
modern Kenya

the University of Cambridge
et, Cambridge CB2 1RP
10011–4211, USA
urne 3166, Australia

© Cambridge University Press 1995

First published 1995

Printed in Great Britain at the University Press, Cambridge

A catalogue record for this book is available from the British Library

Library of Congress cataloguing in publication data

Haugerud, Angelique, 1952–
The culture of politics in modern Kenya 1890s–1990s / Angelique Haugerud.
    p.   cm. – (African studies series: 84)
Includes bibliographical references and index.
ISBN 0 521 47059 5
1. Kenya – Politics and government – 1978–
2. Political culture – Kenya.
3. Kenya – Economic conditions – 1963–
4. Kenya – Social conditions – 1963–
5. Embu (Kenya: District) – Economic conditions.
6. Embu (Kenya: District) – Social conditions.
I. Title. II. Series.
JQ2947.A2H38   1995
320.96762 – dc20   94–19810   CIP

ISBN 0 521 47059 5

CE

Contents

Maps

Tables

Preface

This book began as a brief diversion from my prior focus on social and economic change in the Kenyan countryside. The global and African political upheavals of the early 1990s drew my attention to Kenya's vigorous new political contests, and to the heterodox political voices that now stormed the public domain – through popular music, theatre, sermons, court battles by human rights lawyers, and politicians' speeches. This recent tumult is not the central focus of this work, though it is the theme of chapter 2, and it inevitably affects readings of earlier processes of social change. The shifting political winds of the 1990s caught my attention as I was taking a new look at inventions of national political culture in earlier times, in an effort to connect rural livelihood struggles to the spectacle or staging of politics, especially as it occurred through public gatherings or *baraza*. I attended many of these political rituals while doing field research in rural Embu District, though at the time I did not imagine them to be particularly central to my work. They have turned out to be so, for reasons discussed in chapter 1. As I note there, though *baraza* are not the exclusive focus of this study, I take them as a revealing point of entry into the cross-currents of Kenyan life. From that entry point, I adopt a shifting angle of vision that captures interpenetrating domains of the local, the national, and the international.

I first visited Kenya during the summer of 1977, and returned for doctoral fieldwork in Embu District from mid-1978 through mid-1981. A number of shorter stays followed (in 1984, 1985, 1986, 1989, and 1993). This book draws on experiences from all of these visits. The academic interests that first took me to Kenya are most apparent in chapter 5. During several years of field research in one locality in Kenya's central highlands (Embu District) I focused on issues of land tenure, rural wealth differences, and social changes associated with processes of agricultural commercialization and economic diversification – considering, for example, who is rich, who poor, and how did they come to be so? Those economic interests widened to include political culture, partly because I began my field research at the start of the Moi era, a transition that saw

xii   Preface

the invention and diffusion (especially through *baraza*) of new national political symbols and rhetoric. Over a decade later questions about convergences with and divergences from the earlier Kenyatta, colonial, and pre-colonial eras informed new readings of the Moi transition, whose celebratory early months I had experienced directly.

I thank the Kenyan government for granting me permission to conduct research in Embu District, and the University of Nairobi's Institute for Development Studies (IDS), where I was a Visiting Research Fellow, for a stimulating and collegial institutional sponsorship. Special thanks are due to several generous families in Nairobi who first offered intellectual, moral, and logistical support; I am particularly grateful to Patty and Bud Winans, Gail and John Gerhart, Audrey and David Smock, and Jean and Edgar Edwards. David Brokensha and Jack Glazier were helpful fellow researchers in Embu District. Arlene and David P. Shea provided invaluable assistance during the first months in the area. I thank my generous hosts in Embu District, as well as helpful administrative officers and talented research assistants.

Fieldwork in Kenya was funded by generous grants from the Social Science Research Council, American Council of Learned Societies, National Science Foundation (BNS 7902715), Northwestern University (Program of African Studies), Rockefeller Foundation, and Yale University (Center for International and Area Studies). Some audio-tape transcriptions were funded by a grant from the Social Science Faculty Research Fund of Yale University. I am grateful to Yale University for the Junior Faculty Fellowship that allowed me time to write the first draft of the manuscript.

I thank the following individuals for helpful comments and suggestions on portions of the manuscript: Charles Ambler; Sara Berry; Niko Besnier; Ann Biersteker; Ben Blount; David William Cohen; Ronald Cohen; Micaela di Leonardo; Donald Donham; Marc Edelman; Joseph Errington; Gillian Feeley-Harnik; Robert Harms; Frank Holmquist; Ivan Karp; Deborah Kaspin; William Kelly; Frederick Klaits; Corinne Kratz; Michael Lambek; Robert Launay; Kimani Njogu; David Nugent; Stephen Orvis; Donna Perry; Charles Piot; James C. Scott; Elizabeth Sheehan; Parker Shipton; Helen Siu; K. Sivaramakrishnan; Jacqueline Solway; Michel-Rolph Trouillot; and Diana Wylie. I am grateful to Donna L. Perry for skillfully preparing the maps. Thanks also to the three Press reviewers for their very helpful and perceptive comments. Senior editor Jessica Kuper provided welcome encouragement and assistance.

Portions of this work have been presented at annual meetings of the American Anthropological Association, African Studies Association, and Society for Economic Anthropology, and in seminars at Yale University, Johns Hopkins University, Boston University, Harvard University, and Northwestern University. I thank participants on each of these occasions for helpful comments and suggestions.

A previous version of parts of chapter 3 appeared in Haugerud and Njogu 1991, coauthored with linguist Kimani Njogu who transcribed audio-tapes of some *baraza* I had attended years earlier in rural Embu. Niko Besnier, Joe Errington, and Kimani Njogu drew my attention to some of the linguistic literature that informs chapter 3. Previous versions of portions of chapter 5 have appeared in: *Africa* in 1989 ("Land Tenure and Agrarian Change in Kenya," vol. 59); in Ronald Cohen's 1988 edited volume, *Satisfying Africa's Food Needs: Food Production and Commercialization in African Agriculture* ("Food Surplus Production, Wealth, and Farmers' Strategies"), copyright © 1988 by Lynne Rienner Publishers Inc.: used with permission of the publisher; and in Christina H. Gladwin's 1989 edited volume, *Food and Farm: Current Debates and Policies* ("Food Production and Rural Differentiation in the Kenya Highlands"). I thank Lynne Rienner Publishers and the University Press of America for permission to reproduce in chapter 5 tables and some text from my chapters in the volumes just cited.

I am pleased to dedicate this book to the many friends in Embu District who warmly welcomed me into their homes (and who asked and answered many questions). With generosity and grace, they taught me much.

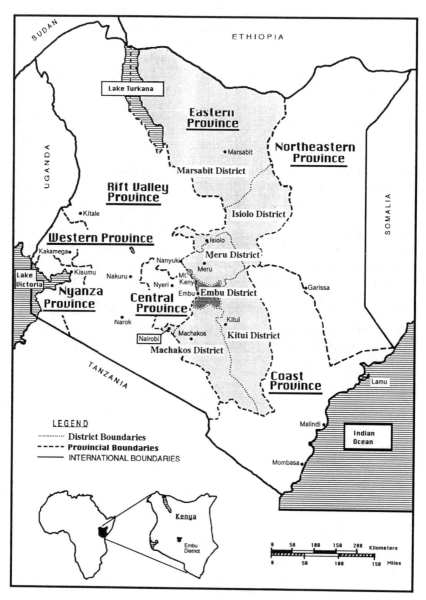

Map 1 Kenya (provinces, major towns, and districts in Eastern
Province, mid 1980s)

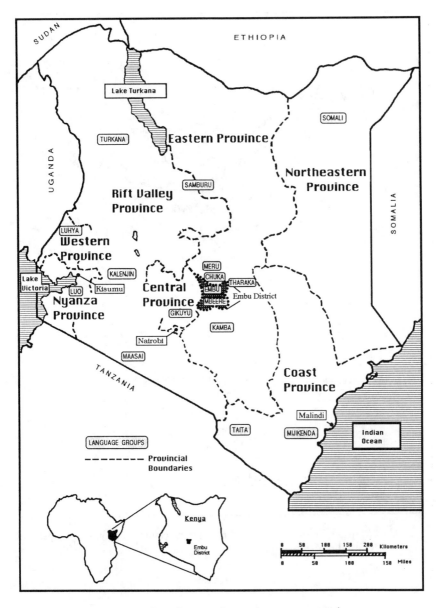

Map 2   Kenya (provinces and some language groups)

xvi

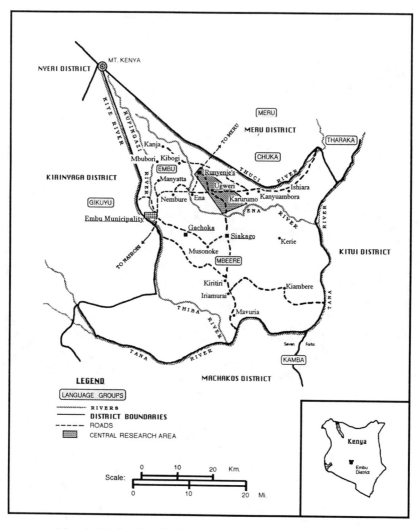

Map 3 Embu District (towns, market centers, language groups, and central research area)

1   Introduction: staging politics in Kenya[1]

> If this were played upon a stage now, I could condemn it as an improbable fiction.
>
> William Shakespeare, *Twelfth Night*

A political spectacle

Exuberant showmanship is one enduring face of Kenyan political life. A nineteenth-century European traveler records the scene his own party provoked at a Gikuyu assembly: "the speeches were rather screamed out than spoken, the meaning being emphasized with a club till it was reduced to splinters. The whole bearing of the speakers was aggressive and insolent."[2] A century later, on a more peaceful occasion, some two hundred people sit in a grassy clearing in Mt. Kenya's foothills. On this sunny day in March 1979, just months after the inauguration of President Moi, I heard a politician tell them: "Not long ago, before we had our new president, there were many things that were spoiling citizens here. There used to be a lot of drunkenness, bribery, corruption."[3] People have "spoiled the footsteps," fallen away from the path they should have followed, he went on to say. Now, however, Kenya is a nation "on the move," "on the run" toward rapid "development,"[4] asserts a fellow politician. He warns the crowd that those who cannot keep up with the new president's rapid footsteps will be left behind in a ditch.[5] The talk is emphatic, vigorous. Though clubs are absent, threats are not.

A great change had occurred, implied orators of the time. Gone were the days when a citizen must "cook tea" (pay a bribe) in return for routine government services. ("Tea," *chai* is a common metaphor for bribery in East Africa.) No longer would officers at the land registry delay farmers by demanding "tea" again and again from those who sought their assistance to settle boundary disputes. (So said one member of parliament who addressed the same ruling party rally in March 1979.)[6] No longer would home-brewed beer tempt men to spend cash their families badly needed.

Here was the public face of a fresh national political culture[7] – new traditions in the making. If successful, they might help to legitimize a new regime, and to sustain the nation-state as an "imagined community" (Anderson 1991). New slogans and catchwords circulated in gatherings in

1

town and countryside and re-echoed in national radio broadcasts and newspapers. But who was imagining what?[8]

The images were contradictory. A new head of state (Moi) pledged to end past evils, but simultaneously assured citizens he would follow the footsteps of his eminent predecessor (Jomo Kenyatta).[9] The new ruling regime included many faces from the old one. Citizens who earned incomes from home-brewed beer and who enjoyed consuming it heartily cheered its proposed prohibition. What realities lay beneath these appearances? Which renounced practices were actually to change? Was home-brewed beer now a thing of the past? Should citizens assume that their dealings with the land office would be straightforward and timely? Would the old cast of characters really adopt different standards and practices in a new political era?

These questions take us beneath the surface showmanship of a beguiling new political rhetoric. Oratory in public forums affords at best a cloudy view of political processes offstage, and the nontransparency itself is significant.[10] Indirect messages float between orators and hearers. Speakers maneuver within constraints on what is and is not publicly speakable. Listeners draw their own inferences, construct their own interpretations. Missteps on either side can be dangerous, even fatal. The possibilities for confusion, deception, ambiguity, and contradiction are endless. Epistemological difficulties for the analyst are as slippery as those of Geertz's (1973b: 6–7) and Gilbert Ryle's (1970) philosophical tale of winks and blinks. An ethnographer must pick his or her way through "piled-up structures of inference and implication," making sense of "twitches, winks, fake-winks, parodies, rehearsals of parodies" (Geertz 1973b: 7). As a foreign observer I cannot hope to decipher more than a fraction of the subtleties involved in Kenyan political theatre. But I do wish to suggest something of the spirit of those assemblies (or *baraza* in the Swahili language), large or small, where politicians and bureaucrats present themselves to citizens on a public stage.

Before defining the place of *baraza* in this study it is helpful to sketch the institution's contours. In this work I use the term *baraza* to refer to public assemblies that usually are held outdoors, are individually licensed by the state,[11] and range in size from huge rallies of several thousand women and men to smaller gatherings of a hundred or so individuals seated on grass in the countryside. The largest include gatherings in Nairobi held on patriotic national holidays and addressed by the president and other senior officials. Smaller assemblies in the countryside are addressed by chiefs, district officers, and other public servants and prominent individuals. A single gathering often includes dozens of speeches of varying length. "Traditional" dancers and singers and school choirs sometimes perform.

Flags and bunting in the national colors (red, green, and black) adorn speakers' platforms and roadsides at the larger assemblies in town and countryside. *Baraza* are held in soccer stadiums, chiefs' camps, or public spaces near markets or local council offices. The audience stands or sits on the ground, exposed to downpours or sunshine. Speakers are more comfortable, occupying chairs or a wood bench at the front, sometimes on a sheltered platform. This "VIP" section is shared by other local notables who do not address the assembly. In rural areas these might include school headmasters, chairs of school committees, coffee cooperative society officers, and church officials. Thus *baraza* are one of few occasions for the public display of elite group cohesion and exclusiveness.[12] Among the audience elder men often sit near the front (or on the "VIP" bench in small gatherings), and women near the back. Administrative police (*askari*) stand on the fringes of the crowd.

Nearby shops and markets must close during such meetings, which may last several hours. Attendance is "mandatory," but unevenly enforced and not openly sanctioned. Those who address these gatherings usually speak extemporaneously, rather than from written texts (with the exception of formal occasions such as presidential addresses on national holidays). Who shows up, who speaks, and who sits next to whom on the speakers' platform are all matters that attract keen interest among local observers. Such gatherings provide clues about factional shifts, about who is "in," who "out," and about what can and cannot be stated directly and publicly. From the organizers' perspective, a successful *baraza* keeps dissent offstage. Dissident voices, however, are not necessarily silent during these gatherings. Individuals in the audience sometimes shout out embarrassing questions or reminders of scandals associated with those on the speakers' platform (such as misuse of local funds collected for a development project). Rival leaders on the platform may enrage one another with direct and indirect attacks. In short, these assemblies are by no means utterly predictable rituals.

I take *baraza* as a point of entry into Kenyan politics and social life, and not as the exclusive focus of this study. *Baraza* are revealing because they are the principal meeting ground between ordinary citizens on the one hand, and state officials and bureaucrats on the other. A century ago these gatherings brought Gikuyu and other peoples face to face with European explorers, missionaries, and soldiers traversing or invading their territories. At *baraza* today, for a few hours farmers in patched clothing and bare feet encounter cabinet ministers in three-piece suits. Politicians park their Mercedes before people accustomed to miles of daily travel on foot. Leaders relax in chairs at the front of the assembly, sometimes under shelters, while the audience sits on the ground or stands in sun or rain. A status gulf on which a social order rests is here on very public display. Close inspection of the spectacle reveals schism and unity, danger and security. It is that volatile mix that demands attention.

Beyond images of reversal

An amalgam of danger and security, conflict and cohesion characterizes both *baraza* and the wider social order. These two faces of social life, however, are often counterposed rather than blended in social analysis.[13] They enter debates about Hobbes versus Rousseau, Durkheim versus Marx, 1950s functionalism versus 1980s political economy, and so on. At issue are fundamental questions about how to analyze social asymmetries that breed conflict and change, without neglecting or misrepresenting forces of cohesion and stability.

These analytical polarities have counterparts in both popular images and scholarly views of Kenya. Until the early 1990s Kenya was often portrayed in the West as a "beacon of success" and an "economic miracle." Western observers praised the country as a showpiece of economic prosperity and political stability. It was an appealing "success" to tourists in search of exotic animals and Indian Ocean beaches, to development economists impressed by high rates of post-independence economic growth and by sharp increases in marketed smallholder production, and to Western nations pursuing the "strategic" interests of superpower politics.

In the early 1990s, however, this burnished image suddenly was overturned. Prominent Western media voices asserted that political and other violence threatened Kenya's vital tourism industry, "corruption" threatened its economy, and government repression threatened its nascent "democracy" movement.[14] Post-cold-war geopolitics lessened the "strategic" imperative of Western support of rulers such as Moi. Once a favored recipient of foreign aid, part of Kenya's aid was suspended late in 1991, pending improvements in the management of its economy and political system.[15] By early 1992, many Western observers saw Kenya as a political holdout amidst apparent continental moves toward human rights improvements and democratic reforms.

Both burnished and tarnished images of Kenya are misleading. They recreate essentialist oppositions between "the West" ("us") and Kenya ("them"), as well as between Kenya and the rest of Africa. Prevalent myths assume that for "them" (Africa), but not for "us" ("the West"), coups, corruption, and violent "tribal" conflict are inevitable. Kenya's avoidance of these presumably endemic political and economic maladies until 1990 was thus construed as "miraculous."

Popular images and scholarly paradigms inform one another and are shaped by some of the same global forces. Much scholarly debate about processes of agrarian and economic change in Kenya also engages images of an economic and political "miracle" or "success story."[16] Some do so quite deliberately – for example, Michael Lofchie's article, "Kenya: Still an Economic Miracle?" (Lofchie 1990). The World Bank (1981: 51) drew in part on glowing academic accounts of the "success" of smallholder agriculture in Kenya to argue more generally that a policy focus on small farmers was crucial to alleviating Africa's economic "crisis." So too Kenya's political image was enhanced by the absence of a successful *coup d'état* during the country's first quarter-century of independence. This record struck both journalists and scholars as a sign of success in a continent where coups had become routine means of transferring power.[17]

Both images of Kenya – before and after its 1990 descent – should be questioned for two sets of reasons. First, each image emphasizes just one side of those polarities noted earlier: cohesion/conflict, order/disorder, security/danger. That is, an analytical opposition is transposed to pre-sumed historical sequence: from miracle to disaster. Instead of seeing Kenya's history as a sequence of contrary images, this study draws attention to the ways in which both sides of the 1990 historical divide contain seeds of the opposite image.

A second sense in which Kenya's contrary images are misleading is their emphasis on the nation-state as a discrete functional unit. Both burnished and tarnished images de-emphasize or overlook the intersec-ting streams of world history that constitute both "us" and "them." In Africa, for example, two continental processes – enlargement of state bureaucracies and attenuation of political expression[18] – emerged under colonial rule and re-emerged soon after independence, often with the support or acquiescence of the same Western powers that now advocate their reversal.[19] Africa's post-colonial states are successors to profoundly anti-democratic colonial forms of governing. Such historical continuities are lost in myths of individual nations' exceptionalism.

These exceptionalist myths resonate with colonial maps in which "each colony appeared like a detachable piece of a jigsaw puzzle. As this 'jigsaw' effect became normal, each 'piece' could be wholly detached from its geographic context" (Anderson 1991: 175). Such conceptions now are a familiar target of intellectual criticism. Tilly (1984: 11), for example, discusses the misleading notion that "'society' is a thing apart; the world as a whole divides into distinct 'societies,' each having its more or less autonomous culture, government, economy, and solidarity." Wolf's (1982: 6) analogy of sorting nations into differently colored "billiard balls" in a "global pool hall" supports a similar argument. This type of sorting and labeling fails to acknowledge that "their" history is analytically inseparable from "our" history (Wolf 1982, Roseberry 1989, O'Brien and Roseberry 1991). Such approaches draw attention away from the very different structural positions individual nations occupy in wider regional and global economies and power structures. If these criticisms have become familiar the influence of contrary assumptions persists nonetheless.

Kenya, for example, is not unique as the object of myths of exceptionalism. The Ivory Coast was West Africa's "economic miracle," Costa Rica is Central America's success story, and Taiwan, Singapore, Hong Kong, and South Korea are East Asia's "economic miracles." Indeed World Bank rhetoric advises Kenya to compare its economy to such East Asian nations, rather than to other African states. In addition, the official rhetoric of any African nation – including those which Western economists characterize as disasters – is likely to include myths of the nation's exceptional triumphs in meeting economic and political challenges. Within these fields of image and myth, however, Kenya is one of a handful of African nations to acquire relative prominence in Western media and scholarly circles as a point of reference against which observers assess the successes and failures of other African states. As both a scholarly and media showpiece, the case of Kenya offers a particularly rich example of how popular images and scholarly paradigms influence one another.

How did Kenya's image as an "island" of prosperity and stability in a troubled continent come to infuse the discourses of scholars, development practitioners, journalists, and Kenyan public figures? How might this case illuminate the more general question of how disciplinary concerns are locally transposed?[20] Appadurai (1986: 358) notes that "there is a tendency for places to become showcases for specific issues over time, and . . . the sources and implications of this tendency are poorly understood." He refers here to the historical creation of "classic" theoretical issues that become associated with particular fieldwork locales – for example, lineages in Africa or reciprocity in Polynesia.[21] To understand such historical processes, he notes, would require attention to a range of issues, such as the institutional prestige of the founding author, the theoretical power of the founding work, host government and elite responses to particular types of field research, the state of anthropology as a profession in the research locale, preferences of funding agencies, cross-disciplinary influences, and career pressures to stake claims to originality (see also Vincent 1990 and 1991).

A historical investigation of how Kenya came to be an academic and media showcase of the kind noted earlier might take into account a number of external linkages: colonial Kenya was advertised in England as a "winter home for aristocrats" and attracted European settlers in significant numbers; Jomo Kenyatta was a forceful and charismatic personality who attracted international attention; Nairobi is a principal continental base for many journalists, multinational firms, and development agencies; tourism contributes heavily to Kenya's foreign exchange earnings; Kenya often has offered a relatively hospitable climate for academic research; and Kenyan officials and scholars who screen applications for research permits have tended to favor studies oriented to economic and policy concerns and to discourage explicitly political research. A very heavy expatriate traffic to and from the country over many decades means that Kenya is better known in the West than are many other African nations.

What anthropologists find in Kenya, as elsewhere, is "a very complicated compound of local realities and the contingencies of metropolitan theory" (Appadurai 1986: 360). In Kenya scholarship one finds traces of a familiar parade of paradigms: from "lazy farmers" some decades ago to "poor but efficient farmers" more recently; from modernization to underdevelopment and dependency; from culture as unique life-ways to culture as obstacle to progress; and from "primordial" ethnic sentiments to invented ethnicities and nationalisms. Early 1990s political shifts in Africa and elsewhere accompany new academic searches for local political "spaces" where democracy might emerge. The quest now is for signs of new life in the associations or institutions of "civil society" that have been stifled by the state. One challenge for contemporary Kenyan ethnography is to explore how "local" cultures and histories provide the space for "global" ideologies of democracy. A continuing theme, however, and the starting point of the present study is the image of Kenya as a showpiece of political stability and of an economic prosperity that many assume rests in part on "progressive" small farmers.

To summarize thus far, I have drawn attention to two arenas of representation: (1) images of Kenya constructed in its own official rhetoric and conveyed through *baraza*; and (2) scholarly paradigms and media images that influence one another. I have suggested the need to move beyond images of reversal as historical narrative, and beyond analytical polarities that sustain such images. And I have introduced *baraza* as an institutional window on contending forces in Kenyan social and political life. These gatherings, like the wider social order, are an amalgam of security and danger, predictability and surprise, cohesion and conflict, conformity and creativity. To emphasize only the first element in each of these pairs is to paint a portrait as misleading as Kenya's pre-1990 popular stereotype. Missing from such a portrait is explicit attention to the social divisions and asymmetries that fuel change. It is to these that I turn next.

National political culture and local realities

National political culture, as conveyed through *baraza*, is a prism that refracts local realities. Official rhetoric does not necessarily "fool" citizens, though it sometimes symbolically neutralizes social divisions that might threaten the social order. Its capacity to do so, however, is historically contingent, as is its strategic balance between coercion and persuasion. *Baraza* do not convey an inevitably hegemonic ideology sustained through coercion and false consciousness, and reducible to material interests. *Baraza* do offer the state a grand opportunity to "naturalize" and rationalize the existing social order. But to portray *baraza* only in this way is to overplay both the state[22] and national political culture as coherent and monolithic entities. Such political culture is less rigid and monolithic than the literature on nationalism often suggests. It is, as Fox (1990: 4) puts it "malleable and mobile," a matter of "historical practice." Indeed, upon close inspection it may appear to dissolve into a confusing mass of contradictions and ambiguities.

National political culture, moreover, is not a disembodied entity overhanging discrete "local" cultures. There is cultural continuity as well as discontinuity between the worlds of small scale and large scale organization: between kin group elders, appointed chiefs, district and provincial commissioners, president, and foreign dignitaries; all of whom may encounter one another in *baraza*. The language of the state and that of localities are not discrete domains. As Parkin (1990: 195) notes more generally, "through the spread and negotiated use of oral language, people come to share many ideas in common while at the same time honing them to their own local requirements and practices."[23] That is, there is a "cross-fertilization of ideas transacted across constantly shifting cultural boundaries" (1990: 195).

Baraza, then, are a crossroads in two senses that are important to this analysis. First, they offer a window on processes occurring at multiple "levels" of social agency (from locality to nation-state, from assistant chief to cabinet minister or president). As political spectacle, these gatherings afford a view of an imposing vertical hierarchy of politicians and bureaucrats. They include baton-wielding district officers, district and provincial commissioners clad in starched khaki uniforms and pith helmets, as well as elected politicians, who range from local councillors likely to travel by *matatu* taxis, to members of parliament and cabinet ministers who own Mercedes Benzes. Second, as these last remarks indicate, *baraza* capture exchanges among individuals of widely different wealth and social status. Rich and poor, literate and illiterate, women and men, old and young, stranger and native – these are some of the social divisions mediated in *baraza*.

These two intersecting themes again draw attention to the challenge of understanding the interpenetration of "local," "national," and "global" domains. This is not a new problem in anthropology (cf. Wilson 1941, Wolf 1956, Mintz 1960, Mair 1965), but it is a focus of current experimentation in field research, analysis, and ethnographic writing. It has stimulated scholars to invent new language, as in the case of Appadurai's (1991) neologism "ethnoscape."[24] And it carries with it the challenge to avoid two extremes: (1) interpreting "all the minute observations of interaction seen in fieldwork ... only as they manifest signs of the operation of a postulated macrosystem"; and (2) interpreting "small-scale interaction ... primarily as a construct of the actors without systematic reference to some larger context" (S. F. Moore 1986: 328).[25] These challenges are carried forward in contemporary scholarship as analytic tensions among post-modernist "chaos," historical contingency, and structural regularities.

An emphasis on the "chaos" or flux of daily life is one possible outcome of recognizing that a number of processes once assumed to be linear and irreversible now look more complicated. For example, agricultural intensification and commercialization are neither inevitable nor irreversible (McCann 1991; Berry 1993). State formation is a result of historically uneven and uncertain processes of ascendancy and decline (Schatzberg 1988). So too patterns of exchange via reciprocity, redistribution, and markets exhibit historical pulsations rather than strictly linear trends. Such visions of "chaos" in social life contribute to scholarly suspicion about "ethnography's claim to provide a tidy picture of the Other," and help to inspire instead representations of the world as "decentered, fragmented, compressed, flexible, refractive, post-modern" (Fox 1991: 6,1).

The approach taken in the present study is not necessarily to assume the absence of structural regularities, but rather to try, as Comaroff and Comaroff (1991: 313) put it, "to capture the interplay of structural constraint and situational contingency." To explore the questions posed in this study requires a constantly shifting angle of vision: one that captures the interplay of local, national, and international forces,[26] and one that experiments theoretically with combined attention to strategy and constraint, conflict and cohesion, resistance and domination, and small scale and large scale processes.

I will note briefly two illustrations of this approach that are developed further in later chapters. First, I suggest that any particular *baraza* can be taken as an event that is not a simple reflex of an already existing and presumably coherent social or cultural system. Rather, as Gal (1989: 442) puts it in a different context, "such events are the means by which some groups make contingent claims to shore up a social order, in response to attempts by others to dismantle it." Indeed, rather than "an order" or "a structure," it is helpful to think in terms of "part-structures being built and torn down," "a complex mix of order, antiorder, and nonorder," and "contingencies of form" (S. F. Moore 1987: 730). Thus individual orators at particular *baraza* can be seen to create as much as to enact, political structures or "part-structures." National political culture is not a stable "text," but something these historical actors create, transform, and enact in everyday struggles and practices, starting from positions of unequal power and authority.

A second illustration of a theoretical argument developed later is to show how a crisis such as famine or social protest brings into sharper analytical focus the cohesive forces it threatens. Famine, for example, is a "revelatory crisis" that, as Sahlins (1972: 127–130) and Firth (1959: 77–105) demonstrate, can shed a suddenly bright light on previously obscured lines of structural conflict and competing interest. Tensions may center, for example, on competition between domestic welfare (feeding the immediate family) on the one hand and, on the other, wider obligations (some ceremonial) toward kin and neighbors, or between patrons and clients, elders and juniors, or chiefs and subjects. In Tikopia, in 1952–3, for example, hurricanes and famine strained the "norms of domestic conduct and of hospitality," and provoked competing explanations of spiritual agency and human moral failings (Firth 1959). In central Kenya, local famine names of past decades tell a story of moral crisis: "the famine of trickery," "the famine of hatred without cause," and "the famine that destroyed shame" (see chapter 4). Such crises draw attention both to lines of structural conflict, and to moral communities that bind farmers to one another and to better-off patrons. Again, the boundaries that define levels or scale of analysis are blurred. Moral communities with flexible boundaries tie localities into the political arena of the nation-state.

The "moral economy"[27] for which Kenyan citizens hold the state accountable is not that of an idealized unchanging village life. The rhetoric of governing elites – both colonial and post-colonial – implied protection of a rising subsistence standard, rather than a stable one. "Fire and light, lamps, oil, matches" were material improvements Africans should expect under colonial rule, in the words of a district official's 1925 welcoming speech to the Embu Local Native Council.[28] As Berry (1985:

4) argues in the case of Nigeria, farmers are likely to resent the state "because it constrains ... (their) ability to accumulate and to diversify their activities, rather than because it threatens to disrupt the stability and autonomy of village life." Amending Scott, then, this study of Kenya emphasizes the political importance of historical movement in subsistence expectations.[29] And again, that movement is captured in officials' own rhetoric in *baraza*.

As subsistence standards have risen, so too has the gap between rich and poor: a gulf that is culturally mediated at multiple levels of social agency. This is a terrain of cultural arguments over obligations between rich and poor: over, for example, how greedy or socially responsible are the wealthy, and how lazy or worthy are the poor. The rhetoric of elites, as noted, helps to define the state's moral bargain with citizens. As leaders stake claims to responsibility, they simultaneously publicize terms by which people may attempt to hold them accountable. Today's anti-corruption advocate may be tomorrow's exposed guilty party. Account-ability, however, is always ambiguous, and that indeed is its most useful characteristic for all political actors (Lonsdale 1986: 128). The ambiguity both emerges from and gives rise to cultural debates, to moral claims and attacks, to charges and counter-charges. These debates, with deep his-torical roots in smallscale communities, are reproduced and transformed beyond them. Accumulators and brokers who mediate relations between groups, and between state and locality, must be cultural bricoleurs – as were those wealthy nineteenth-century African traders, sometimes margi-nal in their own societies, who first collaborated with Europeans; and as is today's cabinet minister who addresses a *baraza* in a muddy field in the Kenyan countryside. Through claims of political accountability and social responsibility, then, the wealthy and powerful attempt to justify their positions to the less well-off. Debates over accountability both create new social divisions, and play into existing social asymmetries – hardening some, softening others.

Organization of the book

This study is ordered thematically rather than chronologically. Chapter 2 focuses on events in the early 1990s, chapters 3 and 4 consider much of the past century, chapter 5 focuses on the late 1970s and 1980s, and chapter 6 interweaves threads of past and present. In starting (in chapter 2) with the most contemporary political events, I draw attention to ways in which the present shapes (re)readings of the past. The early 1990s in Kenya might be construed as a time when violation of previous political norms confirms the existence of those norms, a time when "mechanisms" reveal their "secrets."

The swift shattering in the early 1990s of Kenya's burnished image is the subject of chapter 2. Here I place Kenya's early 1990s political upheavals in the context of global forces newly favorable to the rhetoric of democracy in Africa. Kenya in 1990 saw an escalating war of words between agents of authoritarian one-party rule and advocates of democratic and human rights reforms. Its economy was in decline, state coffers shrinking, and patronage networks therefore beginning to starve. This chapter's largely urban terrain of seditious music, social protest, and banned theatre performances might be read as a contemporary epilogue to the tale which follows it. To construct the narrative this way is to look consciously for seeds of the present in the past. In doing so, I argue that pre-1990 Kenya need not be seen as a "miracle." Nor must the unfortunate events of the early 1990s be read as Kenya's sudden infection by a fatal political disease peculiar to Africa.

Chapter 3 explores the "everyday forms of domination" that both structure and are shaped by resistance (while anthropologists of late have given more attention to resistance).[30] This chapter is a historical glance backward from 1990, as well as a change of physical setting. Here and in the chapters that follow, one countryside locale (Embu) moves to center stage. Historically people in Embu District (see maps 1–3) have been close to Kenya's political and economic "center," for reasons I discuss later. It was there that I carried out the field research upon which much of this study is based. I do not assume, however, that Embu constitutes a "natural" or discrete sociocultural unit. That particular locality offers one window on the intersecting "local" and "non-local" processes upon which this study is focused. Chapter 3 examines rural *baraza* as a key political ritual and state-building institution in both colonial and postcolonial eras. (Here I draw on both archival sources and on verbatim transcripts of *baraza* I attended in rural Embu.) The institution of *baraza* is one means by which the state attempts to preserve the public silences shattered by the events of the early 1990s. The state attempts this partly through persuasion, and partly through coercion and weapons of fear (such as a cabinet minister's *baraza* tale of helicopters dropping innocent people into Lake Victoria), and through warnings to avoid the "politics of the devil." One might expect *baraza* to create, in a Durkheimian sense, authorized representations of an imagined national community. But there is nothing inevitable about the ways in which the purveyors of national culture shape or constrain the lives of those in the countryside.

The second part of chapter 3 captures a new national political culture in the making. During the first months of Moi's presidency – a potentially treacherous political transition – new national symbols were invented, diffused, and "traditionalized" with remarkable rapidity through *baraza* across the country. How did Moi attempt to legitimize his own place in the nation's political history? With what symbolic weapons did he and his deputies get one locality after another to agree to ban home-brewed beer? What material interests did the ban overlook? In what ways is the *baraza* as ritual both socially integrative and an arena of political struggle? Under what circumstances do those attending express dissent? What are some of the unpredictabilities and dramas that appear upon a close inspection of the ritual that itself seems repetitive from a distance?

Chapters 4 and 5 take a closer look at social asymmetries noted in earlier chapters, and at the material interests at stake as individuals enact the drama of *baraza*. Here the focus shifts from the spectacle of political ritual to daily struggles for livelihood in the countryside. These include everyday contests within and between small farm households[31] over labor, crops, rent, loans, income, school fees, land titles, and bridewealth. Such struggles define relations between juniors and elders, women and men, wealthy and poor. What cultural understandings and moral principles enter these relationships? What material interests do farmers have in the patron–client networks on display during *baraza*?

Chapter Four is a historical sketch (1890–1980) of the quest for food and wealth in times of plenty and famine. Even in a region of apparent agricultural abundance, food production, exchange, and consumption are domains of political and cultural contest.[32] In this chapter, I consider some of the historical origins of contemporary wealth differences, as well as moral concepts associated with wealth and poverty (particularly obligations of the rich toward the poor). I suggest an analytic bridge between food crises of earlier decades and the contemporary state's cash crisis. To what extent does a state starved for cash place patrons in a position similar to that faced by their predecessors during pre-colonial and colonial famines?

Chapter 5 traces more particular expressions of the "large processes" and "big structures"[33] explored in the previous chapter. Here I focus on eighty-two farm households among whom I carried out field research from 1979 to mid-1981, and whom I revisited briefly in 1984, 1985, 1986, 1989, and 1993. How do personal relationships among individuals within and between households shape and reflect the character of social change? Who is rich, who poor, and how did they come to be so? How does interpersonal conflict affect material security? How is production organized, and how is household wealth related to patterns of food and labor exchange among households? To what extent are wealth differences among farm households attributable to "random oscillations" (Shanin 1982), to household demographic cycles (Chayanov 1966), or to long-term polarization into classes of rich farmers and landless laborers (Lenin

1964)? Are such assertions of structural regularities misleading representations of historical processes that are neither inevitable nor irreversible? How does the *baraza* as institution silence, rationalize, or naturalize such asymmetries?

Improbable fiction?

In the dramaturgical metaphor suggested in this chapter's Shakespearean epigraph, in the opening examples of *baraza* rhetoric, and in the subsequent discussion, I have drawn attention to possible gaps between lines spoken and lives lived. Some argue that lines spoken *are* lives lived. Murray Edelman (1988: 104), for example, states that "political language *is* political reality." Whatever complex sentiments lie behind public actions often are less important than the public display itself – "so that the public social order can continue, despite what anyone may privately believe" (Irvine 1982: 35; Bailey 1991). A successful *baraza* – from the vantage point of the state – confirms its preferred image of order, stability, unity, and popular good will. Indeed when the spectacle succeeds, it accords with that burnished pre-1990 image of Kenya defined earlier.

Even if the spectacle succeeds as public display, however, discrepant private beliefs do matter. The subtle boundary between "false" and "genuine" deference, between mockery and "sincere" praise is one subordinate groups learn to negotiate skillfully (Scott 1985, 1990). The powerful too deploy their own forms of feigned ignorance, flattery, foot-dragging, and false compliance. Their targets include fellow elites as well as subordinates. In short, there is always a darker underside both to the unifying claims of leaders seeking legitimacy, and to the cheering of their audiences. Leaders publicly construe displays of apparent enthusiasm by *baraza* crowds as support for the ruling regime. In the early 1990s Kenyan dissidents drew attention to what had been an open secret when they stated publicly that crowds who cheered the regime and chanted official slogans were "out to entertain themselves" or to "flatter their leaders" (Imanyara and Maina 1991: 17). In that respect, *baraza* are a perilous mix of ostensible respect and jocular disregard.

2 Shattered silences: political culture and "democracy" in the early 1990s

As some day it may happen
that a victim must be found,
I've got a little list,
I've got a little list
of society offenders
who might well be underground
who never would be missed
who never would be missed ...

There's the highly paid expatriate
who tells us we're all wrong,
and the biased journalist
I've got him on the list!
And the expert who knows Africa
but is never here for long
he never would be missed,
he never would be missed.
Then the idiot who praises
with enthusiastic tones
everything that's foreign,
every country but his own.

Gilbert and Sullivan, *The Mikado*, as performed by the Phoenix Players,
Nairobi, 1991[1]

Introduction

A lively opposition political culture stormed Kenya's public domain during the early 1990s. Carefully preserved silences were shattered, though the immediate outcome was not the "democracy"[2] some expected. This chapter examines the emergent political culture[3] and its intensified war of words. The theme beckons us into what one observer terms "the no-man's land between political science and anthropology which has fragmented our understanding of African politics" (Young 1993: 307). In negotiating this terrain, I combine attention to political economy and political culture.

Analytical challenges here include how to mediate a number of familiar oppositions: resistance versus domination; "politics from below" versus instruments of state; "subaltern" groups versus elites; informal versus formal institutions; and indeterminate versus linear processes. Among the pitfalls to be avoided are romanticizing resistance, aestheticizing politics,

15

homogenizing subaltern groups, or overdrawing distinctions between public and hidden transcripts, national and local culture. I make no attempt to "resolve" such polarities, or even to address each of them explicitly, but they do inform this chapter and the next in ways that will become apparent below.

What is the place of this work's keynote institution – the *baraza* – in Kenya's early 1990s upheavals? *Baraza*, which for decades had diffused an invented national political culture, became a crucial arena in which the rhetorical clashes of the 1990s were played out. In 1992 these public gatherings suddenly became a forum for open challenges to the invented traditions of the state. President Moi, under international and domestic pressure to democratize, began to allow new opposition political parties to convene their own public rallies. Among the first was a large, politically-charged gathering held by the Forum for the Restoration of Democracy (FORD) at Nairobi's historic Kamukunji grounds in January 1992. Estimates of the size of the attending crowd ranged from well over 100,000 (Barkan 1993: 91) to 500,000 people.[4] Local newspapers gave it prominent coverage under headlines such as "Record crowd at epic FORD rally," "Odinga condemns Nyayo era," and "Festive and carnival mood at epic rally."[5] Placards at the rally announced the death of the ruling party (KANU or the Kenya African National Union), and people spoke of the slaughter of the rooster (KANU's symbol).[6] In short, words that previously were publicly unspeakable suddenly took the limelight.

Selective denials, delays, and cancellations of the official permits required to hold such gatherings, however, remained a crucial regime tool. Gertzel's (1970: 147) comment on the brief period of multipartyism during the 1960s was again true when it re-emerged three decades later: "Executive control over meetings was undeniably a powerful advantage since it enabled the Government to determine the scope of the conflict and the extent to which the inter-party debate should take place in public."[7] Opposition politicians in the early 1990s, like those under Kenyatta's rule during the 1960s (with the short-lived opposition party, the Kenya People's Union or KPU), publicly protested when officials refused them permits to hold their own *baraza*. In the 1990s, with the end of the cold war, such protests were likely to stir more sympathy and attention in Europe and the USA than could Kenyan dissidents of the 1960s. Executive controls in the early 1990s did not as effectively marginalize some opposition discourses. Kenya's national political culture for a time became a public battleground; a zone of fierce contestation, rather than outward compliance. At the same time, the new 1990s opposition party politics brought its own displays of compliance in rituals of public dissimulation, flattery, pomp, and indifference.

While the Kenyan state had eliminated or eroded the independence of most formal "civil society"[8] organizations by the late 1980s (see below), a rich informal associational life continued to thrive. Subordinate or oppositional groups carved out "their own democratic space" in bars, football matches, religious organizations, courts, *matatu* taxis, markets, and funerals (Atieno-Odhiambo 1987: 200–201). In the late 1960s, for example, when opposition party (KPU) leaders could not obtain permits to hold public rallies, "they adopted the habit of attending traditional funeral ceremonies, which they were alleged to use for political propaganda" (Gertzel 1970: 147). Their opponents also used funerals for political purposes. So, too, in the early 1990s clergy and others addressing funerals used that "shelter" to make political statements that would be more risky in other contexts.[9] These are among the "popular spaces that can serve as the crucibles for the development of the habits of democracy" (Keller 1991: 52). They are not, however, spaces easily colonized by any official political parties, and by 1993 they contained perhaps as much antagonism toward many opposition party leaders as they did toward the ruling party.

Opposition to the ruling regime in the early 1990s was expressed not just in *baraza*, but also in theatre and popular culture, including widely circulated audio-cassettes of music and sermons which the state termed "seditious" and attempted to ban. One successful Nairobi theatre production that evaded the censors and that played for weeks was the Gilbert and Sullivan operetta, *The Mikado*. Why might a political executioner's list be taken as potent satire in contemporary Nairobi performances of *The Mikado*? With what alternative readings of the past and present does this satire resonate?

In addressing such questions this chapter's focus on upheavals in national political culture includes particular attention to the language of contestation. Here and in the next chapter, I build on a view of language as social action (Malinowski 1965, Burke 1966), and explore how such action constitutes social relations (Firth 1975). Power enters these processes in the manner noted by Bourdieu (1977: 21): "the constitutive power which is granted to ordinary language lies not in the language itself but in the group which authorizes it and invests it with authority." What global and national changes, then, contributed to the new authority vested in rhetorics of democracy in Africa during the early 1990s?

The "democracy" label was not necessarily more than a convenient cover term or legitimizing symbol for widely varying local political struggles. It is not easy to distinguish pressures for democracy *per se* from "demands for an increased standard of living, a direct attempt by a political elite to gain power, simply opposition to the incumbent administration, or sectional grievances" (Young 1993: 424–425). That is, ostensible moves toward democracy must be interpreted with these other struggles in view as well.

This chapter is organized as follows. (Readers who are already well acquainted with Kenya's recent political history may wish to skim through it.) First, the momentous events of the early 1990s are placed in the context of two wider streams of current history: (1) the (re-)emergence in Africa of multiparty politics, and (2) foreign aid donors' new focus on "governance" and their call for political reforms as a condition of assistance to African nations. I then focus on Kenya's lively new political culture of the early 1990s (with a look at protests, music, and theatre); the upheaval's origins and material ramifications; newly ethnicized forms of conflict; and the growing stresses and flux of patronage politics.

The shattered silences of the early 1990s tell us something about the workings of everyday forms of domination in earlier decades. (The latter theme is taken up in chapter 3.) That is, as suggested in the previous chapter, the early 1990s are analytically useful as a time when "mechanisms" reveal their "secrets." This metaphor would be misleading if it were taken to imply that the mechanisms are timeless rather than mutable, even fickle. Here the challenge is to read the ephemeral surface images of daily politics for signs of deeper changes and continuities.

Winds of change: Africa's re-emergent multiparty politics

As Africa in the early 1990s witnessed the sudden visibility of dissidents and the sudden vulnerability of entrenched rulers, to whom were dissidents newly visible? Much of the political satire and forms of political resistance now attracting international attention express meanings that have long been vital to the African communities from which they spring. The survival of these sentiments did not require that they be easily intelligible to outsiders. To disguise such messages was often essential to their authors' survival. Thus Kenya's early political struggles in the 1990s spring in part from opposition political cultures that have been sporadically visible in the past, and that have deep historical roots both within Kenya and across its borders.[10] They are part of what Isaacman (1990: 49) more generally terms "a long oppositional history which over time took many shapes and forms, part of a larger engagement in the political world." Kenya's upheavals had historical resonances with earlier struggles over land, political authority, and ideology. Kenyans appealed for democracy during the nation's anti-colonial struggle, and populist opponents of Kenyatta's policies did so in the 1960s. The 1990s calls for democracy, unlike those of the 1950s and 1960s, focused on democratic procedure or political process, rather than on a democracy-of-content that might favor, for example, radical social and economic reforms (Holmquist et al. 1993). The most audible 1990s calls for democracy at this time did not go beyond rhetorics attacking corruption and promoting accountability and economic efficiency.

Opponents of the Moi regime, who in the early 1990s advocated that the state adopt a multiparty political system, formed fragile, shifting coalitions that had quite disparate ideological and historical roots. They included, for example, intellectuals (some with sympathies toward the left) and politicians from the colonial, Kenyatta, and Moi eras; clergy; lawyers; and conservative disaffected businessmen and women who had lost ground under the Moi regime. Though ideological differences seldom entered public debate, they remained subtle subtexts rooted, for example, in individuals' varying colonial political affiliations, in their experiences as students and university lecturers, and in historical struggles over land. Public debate in the early 1990s centered on personal competition and factional struggles, rather than on social policy alternatives. Democracy's radical social and economic potential "was diluted if not completely repudiated" (Holmquist et al. 1993: 33).[11]

International observers, inspired by the fall of the Berlin Wall, saw 1990 as the start of changes of equal magnitude in Africa.[12] Events in Africa that fed such optimism included Nelson Mandela's release from prison, Namibia's independence and multiparty elections, new negotiations to end apartheid in South Africa, and popular protests and moves toward political liberalization in many African nations. Some observers suggested that Africa was on the verge of a "second liberation" – invoking again the optimism of the early 1960s.[13] Kenya's multiparty advocates themselves adopted in their rhetoric the theme of "democracy" as a "second liberation." The seeds of political change evident in the early 1990s, however, include new forms of authoritarianism, as well as democratization and liberalization.

Africa's recent political protests produced reforms that included changes in constitutions, in the rules of political party competition, and in bureaucratic practices (see Bratton and Van de Walle 1991; Chazan et al. 1992; Newbury 1994; Widner 1994). Though few would suggest that foreign events were the main cause of Africa's 1990 protests, political changes such as those in Eastern Europe and elsewhere may have "shape(d) the politicization and timing of protests" in some sub-Saharan African nations (Bratton and Van de Walle 1991: 42),[14] helping to legitimize some local calls for democratization and attacks on one-party states. The end of the cold war helped to reshape the fate of marginalized and submerged African political discourses (though those of the left remained largely submerged in the early 1990s), conferring on some of them new attention and authority. Rhetorics of democracy became newly convenient for dissident elites vying for power. By 1992, authoritarian one-party states began to seem a surprisingly mutable rather than inevitable feature of Africa's political landscape, though many nations had made only tentative or cosmetic moves toward liberal democracy.[15]

As African intellectuals in the 1990s became more likely to adopt liberal democratic language, new contests arose over what political values and practices were "indigenous" and what "foreign." Unlike the struggle for independence, the call for a "second liberation" in the early 1990s ostensibly criticizes the oppressiveness and inadequacies of domestic rather than foreign forces (Hyden and Bratton 1991: x). But today many African scholars and public figures struggle with issues such as how to "become advocates for democratic rights without appearing to merely echo the voices of the international donor community," and how to "perform their role without alienating the 'masses'" (Hyden 1991a: 11). Some insist that reforms must come from within Africa. At the same time, the effectiveness of pro-democracy voices in Kenya and elsewhere is strengthened by ties with the international press and with international church and human rights organizations such as Amnesty International and Human Rights Watch. As African advocates of democracy appeal simultaneously to international and domestic audiences, they must perform delicate balancing acts. Missteps can provoke criticisms such as those aimed at "the highly paid expatriate who tells us we're all wrong," or "the idiot who praises with enthusiastic tones everything that's foreign, every country but his own," as Gilbert and Sullivan put it.

Aid donors rediscover politics

Accompanying the striking changes in Africa's early political landscape were shifts in the rhetoric of development institutions such as the World Bank and bilateral aid agencies. With post-cold war cuts in aid to Africa and increases in assistance to Eastern Europe came a new rhetorical emphasis on human rights improvements and political liberalization as conditions of aid to Africa. Western banks became increasingly concerned with debt recovery rather than lending increases (see Amin 1994), and donors hoped that political liberalization would improve economic management, debt repayment, and political legitimacy (Holmquist et al. 1993: 34). For the World Bank and other aid agencies, however, solutions to development dilemmas were still cast in apolitical terms, disguising the fundamental political questions at stake in common interventions in agriculture, health, education, or population planning (see Ferguson 1990a, Mitchell 1991). The World Bank operates by the fiction that it is a neutral external body assisting neutral governments. Bank staff members now charged with implementing politically explosive reforms in public sector management in African nations are themselves formally prohibited by the Bank's mandate from influencing a country's political orientation.[16]

Aid donors in the early 1990s treated politics as a technical and management issue addressed under the antiseptic label "governance," by which the Bank means "the exercise of political power to manage a nation's affairs" (World Bank 1989: 60). The Bank attributed Africa's development problems to a "crisis of governance," and called for external aid agencies to insist on the following improvements: "Leaders must become more accountable to their peoples. Transactions must become more transparent, and funds must be seen to be properly administered, with audit reports made public and procurement procedures overhauled" (World Bank 1989: 60, 15). Without addressing its own historical role and that of foreign firms and governments in the problem, the Bank notes that "because countervailing power has been lacking, state officials in many countries have served their own interests without fear of being called to account" (World Bank 1989: 60).

Such rhetoric is part of the wider tendency, noted in the previous chapter, to imagine the nation-state as an ahistorical, discrete object. The advisory and planning reports of development agencies, for example, usually focus on national statistics and "country studies," taking for granted the nation-state as a functional unit susceptible to econometric modeling (Mitchell 1991). Such literature implicitly adopts the convention of "imagining countries as empirical objects," de-emphasizing or overlooking the ways in which "the value of what people produce, the cost of what they consume, and the purchasing power of their currency depend on global relationships of exchange" (Mitchell 1991: 28). Seldom publicly acknowledged by development agencies is the historical irony that the same Western powers and foreign aid donors who in the early 1990s tied their assistance to political reform requirements provided military hardware and economic assistance as the leaders of Africa's newly independent nations dismantled democratic institutions during the 1960s and 1970s.[17] Moreover, subject to debate is the question: under what historical circumstances does structural adjustment constitute a basis for democratization, and under what circumstances does it help to legitimize a return to authoritarian rule?

Some African politicians were quick to adopt the World Bank's new rhetoric. Kenyan multiparty advocates in 1991–2, for example, directly incorporated into their rhetoric the World Bank's new language of good governance, accountability and transparency,[18] asserting the absence of these principles in the ruling regime. (Moi, on the other hand, blamed the faltering economy on cruel donor policies unsuited to Africa's particular problems.) The language of accountability, transparency, and good governance also merged easily with that Kenyan lawyers employed during the 1980s and 1990s as they worked for human rights reforms. Their efforts contributed to a "culture of political justice" that (re-)emerged during the 1980s with efforts to decriminalize politics, and free civil society institutions from cooptation by the ruling party (see Githu 1992).

In short, the early 1990s saw disaffected elites and earlier authors of submerged political discourses suddenly command wider and more public audiences (both domestic and international) as they adopted the "democracy" banner and the language of political reform sanctioned by powerful foreign aid donors. With what local struggles and meanings were the re-emergence of multiparty politics and the foreign term "democracy" (*demokrasi* in Swahili) associated? It is to this theme that I turn next.

Political upheavals: Kenya, 1990–3

What events inspired Kenya's early protests in the 1990s? 1990 was a year of rising political tensions, which exploded in violent social protest on July 7. Cars were stoned, drivers beaten, buses burned, automobile windscreens smashed, and shops looted. The police fired on and beat people in crowds. Death estimates range from a few dozen to several hundred.[19] The nation had not seen such violence since the aftermath of an unsuccessful coup attempt in August 1982. President Moi blamed the looting and rioting on "hooligans and drug addicts."[20] In reality, protesters and sympathizers came from a wide cross-section of society, including dissident intellectuals, elites, the poor and middle classes.

Among the immediate events that sparked the July 1990 violence were the arrests early that month of two former cabinet ministers (Charles Rubia[21] and Kenneth Matiba[22]), and the government's denial of permission for these two multiparty advocates to hold a public rally[23] at Nairobi's historic Kamukunji grounds (the site of earlier anti-colonial protests) on July 7. Matiba and Rubia had advocated repeal of the 1982 constitutional amendment that made Kenya a one-party state.[24] They also urged the dissolution of Parliament, and a public referendum to decide the country's future. In spite of the arrests of Matiba, Rubia, and other government critics, many people did gather at Kamukunji on the day the political rally was to have been held. Violent clashes followed, between citizens and security forces there and in secondary towns such as Nakuru, Nyeri, Murang'a, Thika, and Naivasha. These were covered in the domestic and international press.

The day of the prohibited rally – July 7 – became known as "saba saba" day (since it fell on the seventh day of the seventh month; "saba" is Swahili for the number seven). The phrase became a kind of "celebratory nationalist metaphor" (Biersteker, in a personal communication), preserving in public consciousness a particular significance for a public rally the government had forbidden. The original "saba saba" day was July 7, 1954: the founding date of Tanzania's national political party (TANU, Tanganyika African National Union). This slogan's link to Tanzania's struggle for independence from colonial rule illustrates both the historical depth and cross-national resonances of contemporary opposition political cultures. The ruling regime found "saba saba" threatening enough for President Moi to announce that the use of this politically charged phrase was officially prohibited.

Such pronouncements are a reminder of the state's vulnerability as well as its capacity for violent retribution. They point to the symbolic means by which citizens can undermine as well as affirm state power and authority. To negotiate these realities, advocates of political reform adopt inventive strategies. For example, before opposition parties were legalized, Kenyan lawyers and clergy teamed up to organize special nation-wide prayer meetings: large public symposia to discuss "justice and peace in a free and democratic Kenya." These plans received front-page coverage in Nairobi newspapers.[25] A few days later, after politicians criticized this as a ploy to form an (illegal) opposition party, the prayer meetings were called off, though church leaders asserted that they would continue to work peacefully for political reforms.[26] An editorial cartoon in Nairobi's *Daily Nation* captures some of the associated ambivalences; it carries the caption "They want to make a meal out of you!," beneath a sketch of an elderly man who has an image of a machete in his mind and who is holding a KANU rooster, as he stands fearfully some distance from a throng of people holding LSK (Law Society of Kenya), NCCK, and CPK placards (the latter two are religious organizations: the National Council of Churches of Kenya and the Church of the Province of Kenya).[27] Not long afterwards, in August 1991, Odinga and other opposition leaders avoided the legal requirement to register the new Forum for the Restoration of Democracy (FORD) as an association under the Societies Act by limiting their number to nine (Barkan 1993: 91).[28]

Such ploys and their prominent press coverage escalated the confrontation between state officials and multiparty advocates. Kenyan human rights lawyers,[29] clergy,[30] intellectuals, politicians, and popular musicians joined in criticism of the Moi regime. When politicians such as Matiba and Rubia in 1990 campaigned publicly for a multiparty system, and became litigants or defendants in court, Muite and other lawyers took on their controversial cases. When the lawyers' vocal support of multipartyism led the state to bring charges against many of them as well, their appearances in law courts began to draw large crowds and shows of popular support for multipartyism. At the conclusion of one court case in Nairobi in September 1991, for example, "cheering crowds carried (Muite) . . . shoulder-high in Nairobi's streets."[31] This prominent lawyer later became a vice-presidential candidate in FORD-Kenya, the opposition party headed by Odinga: fueling administration complaints that some lawyers were politicians in disguise.

Women played a visible role in political opposition in the early 1990s, as well as in earlier colonial struggles (see, for example, Presley 1986; Kanogo 1987; and White 1990a). In early March 1992, for example, mothers of political prisoners staged a hunger strike in a corner of downtown Nairobi's Uhuru Park. When police brutally evicted these peaceful demonstrators, some of the women stripped and shouted Gikuyu curses at the officers who had beaten members of their group. (Such action against elder women was an obvious violation of cultural norms.) Among those injured was Professor Wangari Maathai, leader of the Green Belt Movement. The local press gave prominent coverage to the incident, including front-page photos of the women who had shed most of their clothing. The following day, as news of the brutality and eviction spread, riots broke out in many parts of Nairobi.[32]

Political conditions that contributed to the unrest included the growing concentration of power in the executive branch, and shrinking possibilities for political association and expression of opposition views (see Barkan 1991, 1993; Leonard 1991; Widner 1992). In a cold war context, these changes entailed a narrowing of the range of public ideological debate and increasing marginalization of leftist or populist views. Constitutional changes during the 1980s extended modifications begun in the 1960s, as politicians suspicious of the original document amended it to build up authoritarian administrative structures like those of the colonial era.[33] They did so not only to protect their own political longevity, but also because most "genuinely believed" that the independence constitution was an obstacle to "necessary development and national goals" (Githu 1992: 7). The latter was an argument made soon after independence in nearly every African country (Staniland 1991: 88). In 1986 and 1988, Moi took measures (some later removed) to limit the independence of the judiciary (removing the security of tenure of High Court judges) and civil service, and to increase police powers of detention.[34] He also limited the autonomy of private voluntary organizations (see Barkan 1991: 185–188).[35] In 1986, Moi introduced a new system of voting in the first stage of parliamentary elections: public queuing of voters behind a picture of their chosen candidate.[36] In December 1990, after months of public hearings across the country on the future of the national political party KANU (Kenya African National Union),[37] Moi announced the end of queue voting and the 70 percent rule, though at that time he still rejected a shift to a multiparty system.

A turning point came in early December 1991. After substantial international and domestic pressure to do so, President Moi and the governing council of KANU agreed to overturn the 1982 section of the constitution that legalized one-party rule. Moi made this announcement just two weeks after Western donors meeting in Paris decided to suspend $328 million in new commitments of fast-disbursing aid until Kenya adopted political and economic liberalization measures.[38] That decision received prominent international press coverage, as did stories about Kenyan "corruption" in the weeks before the meeting.[39]

The timing of the rise in international publicity given to Kenyan "corruption" is connected both to increases in its magnitude[40] and to world geopolitical changes noted above. The sudden foreign accentuation of Kenyan corruption invited local praise as well as criticism. On the one hand, for example, a wealthy rural businessman I talked with in central Kenya said that austerity measures were justified, and he drew an analogy to the steps required when an individual is financially over-extended (such as eliminating one car). On the other hand, a Kenyan white-collar employee with whom I discussed such issues in Nairobi in mid-1993 was at least as critical of the World Bank and other donors who for years had quietly tolerated such corruption, as he was of prominent Kenyans who may have misappropriated funds. Again, recognition of such international webs of complicity is absent from the overdrawn contrast between economic "miracle" and "disaster" images, and from supposed oppositions between Africa and "the West."

By mid-1992, voter registration had been completed,[41] but Moi still had not announced a date for elections, saying that choice was his "secret weapon."[42] Finally in November, Moi announced a December election date. After one postponement[43] Kenya's first multiparty elections in 26 years were held on December 29, 1992. The winner was required (by an April 1992 constitutional amendment) to receive more than 25 percent of the vote in at least five of Kenya's eight provinces (see Map 1).

In the highest voter turnout since the 1963 election, Moi was returned to office in 1992 with 36 percent of the total vote, defeating a badly fragmented opposition.[44] Opposition parties rejected the results as "rigged," while international observer teams found election day itself to be relatively fair, though they noted the preceding campaign period had been marred by a number of unfair practices. Moi's lowest vote share (2 percent) occurred in the Gikuyu-dominated Central Province. His largest shares were in Northeastern Province (78 percent) and Rift Valley (66 percent). Opposition parties won 88 parliamentary seats,[45] and the ruling party 100. An unusually small share of cabinet ministers (39 percent) and incumbents (26 percent) who sought re-election won. The opposition won majorities in 15 of the 20 principal town and municipal council elections (including Nairobi).

Months after the election, many citizens saw the ruling regime as exercising its power in ways intended to make daily life difficult for those outside the ruling party, KANU. At least one cabinet minister in July 1993 asserted publicly that opposition strongholds would be denied national resources controlled by the government, and suggested that localities showing loyalty to KANU would be materially rewarded.[46] The municipal majorities won by the opposition figured in disputes over matters such as municipal water cut-offs in mid-1993. Many Kenyans construed the water shortages as ruling-party attempts to sabotage or discredit leaders in the opposition parties.[47] Kenyans whom I spoke with in mid-1993 also asserted that political party affiliation affected decisions about which civil service employees would be dismissed under reductions mandated by World Bank structural adjustment programs. And many reports circulated in the local press about large sums of money (e.g., two million shillings, equivalent to about $12,660 in mid-1993) offered to opposition Members of Parliament (MPs) if they would defect to KANU.

The election aftermath saw continued contests over permits for public rallies, and over cancellation of public performances in the Gikuyu language of Ngugi wa Thiong'o's play *Ngahika Ndeenda* ("I Will Marry When I Choose"). This cancellation prompted an editorial cartoon in the Nairobi *Standard* newspaper[48] showing a District Officer at the scene of the banned play shouting at citizens: "Go away! This is still a single-party era of a multiparty democracy." The 1992 election did not end the new spirit of open political criticism in everyday conversation and in print (but not broadcast) media. Demands for public accountability of leaders continued as new financial scandals were exposed. Those accused of wrongdoing, however, were sometimes simply transferred to other prominent positions.[49] Opposition politicians still experienced official harassment and occasional arrest. Alternative press publications such as *Society*, *Economic Review*, and *Nairobi Law Monthly* had periodic difficulties with authorities, including the physical disabling of their printing presses.[50] Thus the practical consequences of the new culture of political accountability remained uncertain and changeable.

The country's political temperature rose markedly during the early 1990s, as the foregoing discussion suggests. The political electricity came less from revelation or novelty than from the excitement (and risk) of publicly breaking earlier silences, voicing sentiments previously expressed more covertly but widely shared in popular culture (cf. Scott 1990: ch. 8). A political euphoria and fervor caught many Kenyans in the early stages of the struggles for a return to multiparty politics, as politicians and ordinary citizens criticized the ruling regime more openly than ever before. Citizens on the streets of Nairobi in 1991 displayed the two-finger salute in support of a shift to a multiparty political system. Speakers at opposition party campaign rallies in 1992 stirred enthusiastic crowds to repeat new refrains that previously would have been unspeakable: *Kwaheri Moi! Kwaheri KANU!* ("Good-bye Moi! Good-bye KANU!" See Throup 1993b: 73).

Such periods of obvious historical flux and political conflict may be moments when cultural production "intensifies," a theme Gavin Smith (1991: 182, 202) explores:

If we advance from the notion of culture as a fixed blueprint by which people act, toward a notion of culture as something produced and reproduced through history, then ... cultural production does not occur with equal intensity from one day to the next.

One has only to talk to people about past moments of collective rebellion and resistance to discover the heightened imagery engendered at those moments of intensive cultural production.

Kenyan political culture during the early 1990s drew upon foreign and domestic symbols. These included: potent reminders of 1950s anti-colonial struggles in Kenya (see below) and neighboring Tanzania; collapsing one-party states in Eastern Europe; civil strife elsewhere in Africa; Kenya's own independence constitution; and the World Bank's language of good "governance," transparency, and accountability. These, like all symbols, are polyvalent. Both opposition politicians and those in power, for example, invoked symbols from events in Eastern Europe in 1989, whose drama was conveyed to Kenyans by the Cable News Network, the BBC, and local print media. President Moi specific-ally warned citizens against drawing parallels between Eastern Europe and Kenya, saying that Eastern Europe is "in chaos."[51] Moi also cited the "chaos" in African nations trying to establish multiparty systems, naming Liberia, Zaïre, and the Central African Republic.[52] He told Kenyan audiences that his own political opponents were out to destabilize the country, and that "women and children would suffer most in the event of chaos."[53] Advocates of a shift to multiparty politics, on the other hand, publicly drew inspiration from the changes in Eastern Europe. Some, as noted earlier, rhetorically portrayed multiparty politics as a "second liberation" – an obvious rejection of the "Moi or chaos"[54] version of political reality.

Music and theatre became important avenues through which criticisms of the ruling regime coalesced, influencing individual consciousness as the opposition grew wider and became more public by late 1991 and early 1992.[55] Some of the music built on earlier expressive forms, such as popular anti-colonial songs from the 1920s and Christian hymns sung in the 1950s whose words were altered to praise Kenyan political leaders who opposed colonial rule.[56] In 1992, Kenyan mothers of political prisoners protesting publicly at Nairobi law courts sang Gikuyu funeral songs.[57] Protest themes expressed in Kenya's contemporary music and theatre included official corruption; rapid increases in the cost of living; violent evictions from and government demolition of "shanties" in Nairobi; and government efforts to silence political opposition. Stinging contemporary political messages were embedded in expressive forms, ranging from Gilbert and Sullivan operettas (as in this chapter's epigraph) to Italian farce, popular music, and Protestant sermons.

Such expressive forms themselves create, as well as enact, political understandings and consciousness. As Barber (1987: 4) suggests, "in times of rapid social change, it seems likely that popular art forms, with their exceptional mobility (whether through technology such as the radio, record, and cassette tape, or through physical transportation from place to place by traveling performing groups) will play a crucial role in formulating new ways of looking at things." In a vigorous effort to restrict the diffusion of unofficial or oppositional political views, the Kenyan state in the early 1990s attempted repeatedly (with little success) to ban the circulation of popular cassette recordings of some sermons and songs.

"Seditious" music

"Cassettes: Ten Charged," reads a 1990 Nairobi *Daily Nation* headline. Kenyan "police made a series of raids ... arrested several people and seized saxophones, drums, dubbing machines and cassette tapes of songs," reports a British newspaper.[58] Why did "hot-selling" music attract the attention of Kenyan police and mass media?

Popular music cassettes that the government termed "seditious" circulated among a wide audience in the early 1990s. They were played, for example, in *matatu* "taxis," the crowded mini-vans and cars so central to Kenya's transport system. "Subversive" cassettes offered important alternatives to official versions of recent history (such as the 1990 Muoroto "shanty" demolition in Nairobi, discussed below). They asked "Who killed Dr. Ouko?," and chronicled Matiba's tribulations.[59] Under some historical conditions such expressive forms may be no more than a "safety-valve" that allows the political status quo to continue. Under other conditions, such as those in Kenya in the early 1990s, such forms become crucial symbolic weapons in active struggles for political transformation.

One popular "seditious" cassette connects the government's violent "shanty" demolition[60] in Muoroto in May 1990 to a notorious operation of the colonial era: the 1954 British colonial government's Operation Anvil in Nairobi. Operation Anvil included the arrest of 30,000 Gikuyu, Embu, and Meru people in one day in Nairobi (White 1990b: 193). As part of the colonial state's anti-"Mau Mau" campaign, five British Army battalions, together with Police General Service Units "'cleaned up' the city in Operation Anvil throughout April 1954."[61] One cabinet minister publicly invoked this politically-charged historical parallel as he criticized the state (and Nairobi's Luhya mayor)[62] for the 1990 "shanty" demolition, which left informal sector kiosks destroyed and thousands homeless. He was dismissed from his post and suspended for one year from KANU.[63]

The cover of the Muoroto music cassette portrays a bulldozer demolishing a shanty beside a group of slum dwellers rummaging through the rubble. Its title is "The misfortune that befell the poor villagers of Muoroto" (or *Thiina uria wakorire athini agicagi kia Muoroto*, in the Gikuyu language). The lyrics, in addition to drawing the Operation Anvil parallel, invoke the wrath of God on those who "oppress the poor," and suggest that "if there were two (political) parties we (Nairobi hawkers and their relatives) could take our complaints to the other party." Thus the Muoroto song is an explosive mixture that at once protests against the shanty demolition, highlights the plight of the poor, invokes potent anti-colonial images, and advocates multiparty democracy.

The Muoroto music tells the tale of about 2,000 poor people violently evicted in May 1990 by bulldozers and police from their shanty dwellings and businesses in Nairobi's Muoroto area. Africa Watch (1991: 252) reports that "most of the kiosks ... had actually been licensed and the owners had lost hundreds of shillings worth of property and goods as well as suffering injury and shock." Nairobi newspapers carried extensive front-page coverage and photographs of the incident, though journalists took risks in covering it. Some news reporters who covered the Muoroto story were charged in court with publishing "false and alarming reports."[64] Accounts in Nairobi's *Daily Nation*[65] told of "a bloody battle between police and residents who resisted eviction," with "tales of misery" recounted by parents "clad in muddy rags" who spent the night in the rain and cold with their hungry children, and residents "left completely destitute as their only source of livelihood and shelter had been demolished."

Officials say that the Muoroto song is "calculated to cause disaffection among Kenyans," and is a "threat to state security, peace and order."[66] Those charged with selling the cassettes could face up to ten years in prison if convicted. In 1990, Moi banned all music from *matatu* taxis, and outlawed informal street vending. Nonetheless, taxis and shops continued to blare out the "subversive" music. Some drivers silenced the music while loading passengers, only to play it at high volume once on the road. Popular music was beyond the reach of the state.

Another cassette, a sermon set to music, included the following words by the popular musician Joseph Kamaru:[67]

We pray for our president, Daniel arap Moi. President Moi cannot stop corruption in Kenya, so help him God. Moi can't even stop opposition parties from forming. So God help the president before he is thrown into the lion's den.

When Kenyan authorities called Kamaru in for questioning, he told them that his cassette is patriotic: "I tried to explain to them that I am praying to my people. I am praying to our leaders, praying for my country, so I don't see why you are trying to ban my cassette."

The linguistic ambiguity Kamaru attempted to exploit in his musical sermon (though he did not convince government authorities that his song was patriotic) can be particularly convenient for subordinate groups for whom explicit criticism of those in power is risky (see Scott 1990). During Kenya's anti-colonial struggle in the 1950s, for example, passages from the Bible that were particularly applicable to Gikuyu sufferings were read aloud, as a safe form of expressing political discontent.[68] Chinese students used a similar tactic in 1990 as they "played the official language game in reverse," using official terms to express an invented (subversive) meaning, while the original face value was a simultaneous "shield from criticism" (Link 1991). Thus, during the Tiananmen uprising students sang China's national anthem, whose words had seditious implications in that context: "The Chinese people have reached their most dangerous hour; The very last scream has been forced from each of us. Rise up! Rise up!" (Link 1991: 16).[69] Kenyan government authorities, perhaps sensitive to such double meanings, condemned the 1990 rerelease of a suddenly popular cassette recording that begins with the national anthem, and includes speeches of Kenya's first president (Jomo Kenyatta),[70] as well as 1950s anti-colonial "Mau Mau" songs.[71]

Theatre as contemporary political satire

Evading the censors becomes a fine art when state officials review plays, songs, magazines or other works to decide if they sound seditious.[72] Among those who did not evade the censors in 1991 were producers of a Swahili satire based on Orwell's *Animal Farm*. Another banned play was Dario Fo's Italian farce translated into English as *Can't Pay, Won't Pay*. The latter play concerns a group of women who cannot afford rising food prices, and who decide to rebel. They do so by stealing (or "liberating") from shops food they cannot afford to purchase. Just before its opening night in Nairobi state officials banned this play. The censors would not tell the director why they had done so, but he guesses that their reasons were as follows:[73]

It was like ... rubbing it in – that the prices have been increasing a little too fast[74] ... It is becoming increasingly difficult to survive because the cost of living is very high and because the economy has been shrinking, so to speak. We have a lot of people out there in the streets who don't have a job and we have a state of fermentation of some kind of popular, you know, discontent, which has been brewing for quite some time.

One theatre performance that did pass the censors was the Nairobi Phoenix Players' 1991 production of Gilbert and Sullivan's operetta *The Mikado*, which was sold out for six weeks.[75] *The Mikado*, written during England's Victorian age, may be taken as a masterful satire of government officials, whose viewpoints are expressed by a buffoon. In the lines quoted at the beginning of this chapter, the pompous lord high executioner lists some of the citizens whom he might like to have put to death. The Nairobi version names some of the very kinds of people blamed by President Moi and his associates in 1991 for the country's difficulties: especially journalists from the USA and Europe and domestic critics who advocate a change to a Western-style democracy.

To have a theatrical buffoon utter such words, however, is not necessarily to deny their literal meaning. If read as satire the words have contradictory targets and sympathies. Not to be ignored are the unflattering terms in which regime critics are portrayed: the "idiot" who mindlessly praises only what is foreign, the "highly paid expatriate who tells us we're all wrong," and the "expert who knows Africa but is never here for long." These themes carry their own popular resonances (upon which regime supporters capitalize).

The association of multiparty democracy with things foreign is both an advantage and a drawback. The former American ambassador's (Smith Hempstone) outspoken criticisms of one-party rule in 1990[76] prompted this headline on the front page of a Nairobi newspaper: "Shut up, Mr. Ambassador!" In November 1991, after more public criticisms from the ambassador, Kenya's Foreign Minister publicly called him a racist.[77] He also criticized the American ambassador for a "slave owner mentality to his country of accreditation." Some MPs proposed that the ambassador be recalled because of his "arrogant and contemptuous behavior toward the Kenyan head of state."[78] Moi himself suggested Kenya had no need for foreign prescriptions such as multipartyism, and he publicly claimed that "foreign masters" were behind the political protests and multiparty advocates in 1990.[79] The recent American and other foreign insistence on democratic reforms could backfire, inflaming anti-foreigner sentiments like those aroused in some quarters by the American ambassador's outspoken criticism: (as *The Mikado* song puts it, "the highly paid expatriate who tells us we're all wrong"). The political criticisms of an ambassador who is by his own admission no diplomat do not, however, annul a message many Kenyans themselves voice. The outspoken former American ambassador was a popular hero among many Kenyans.

The Mikado lines quoted above thus evoke both the strength and weakness of the state. On the one hand, to name "society offenders who might well be underground" is sometimes as effective (for the state) as placing them there: that is, such threats do help to silence critics (particularly since Kenya's post-colonial history includes a number of deaths or assassinations in which many suspect official involvement). On the other hand, to name one's enemies is to advertise one's weaknesses.

In short, theatre, music, and political rhetoric in Kenya during the early 1990s reflect a competition for moral authority in contemporary political struggles over who is to control the state, and with what accompanying political practices and ideals. Theatre, music, and speech invoke polyvalent symbols that may inspire contradictory political actions. The Muoroto cassette, for example, suggests the poor might have a more effective voice in a multiparty political system, and challenges state authorities from the ruling party who violently displaced some of Nairobi's poorest residents from their homes and businesses. The excerpt from *The Mikado* captures tensions between state officials and advocates of a shift to multiparty democracy, between politicians and journalists, and between the local and the foreign. Kenya's 1992 elections left most of these tensions and conflicts unresolved. To understand why requires a look at the economic origins of the early 1990s upheavals, at the growing ethnic tensions, and at patron–client politics.

Some economic origins of the early 1990s protests

Some of the cultural displays of political disaffection just described have rather privileged urban roots and audiences. *The Mikado* audience would be largely urban professionals, civil servants, and politicians. Hearers of Kamaru's and other "seditious" music cassettes, however, include people in both town and countryside, and large numbers of less well-off segments of the population (those who ride in *matatu* and who visit bars and shops where such music is played). Nairobi street hawkers or "informal sector" vendors, some of whom sell such cassettes (and whose numbers include recent migrants from the countryside), became a particular target of state officials. As authorities demolished informal sector kiosks and removed "hawkers" from Nairobi's streets, their actions often provoked battles between security forces and vendors that were covered in the local press. Moi believed "bad elements" were infiltrating hawkers' communities, and said that hawkers who were "only selling one or two potatoes" were simply "posing" (Africa Watch 1991: 263).

If a culture of political opposition had "infiltrated" many sections of Kenyan society, the well-publicized calls for democratic reform, as suggested earlier, initially tended to come from above (especially from former public servants such as Matiba and Rubia, and from human rights lawyers, clergy, and university intellectuals). Indeed, much of Africa's 1990 political protest emerged first in urban churches and on university campuses (Bratton and Van de Walle 1991: 49). It then drew support from citizens suffering from reductions in subsidies, services, housing allowances, educational opportunities, and jobs (especially civil servants, miners, students, and teachers). Kenyan students, for example, "attracted workers and the self-employed to join in condemning the corrosive effects of inflation on living standards" (Bratton and Van de Walle 1991: 33). Many observers interpret Africa's protests at this time as directed against declining living standards associated, at least in part, with the structural adjustment measures mandated by the International Monetary Fund (IMF) and World Bank (Nelson 1990; Sandbrook 1990; Lancaster 1992).[80] There is disagreement among Africans as well as foreign observers about what share of the blame for current difficulties should be attached to the adjustment programs themselves or to the economic crises these programs are meant to alleviate[81] (crises which themselves have complex international and national origins). Though political dissent has flourished as Africa's economies have deteriorated, scholars are just beginning to assess precisely how the two are related.

In Kenya, economic decline certainly played a part in the political upheavals in the early 1990s. The conflicts of patronage politics had intensified as state spending capacity in education, health, and other services had fallen, and as demands for such services from a rapidly growing population rose. Kenya suffered from mounting inflation and foreign debt, declining world market prices for principal export commodities such as coffee, and decreases in foreign investment and tourism revenues. By 1992 real economic growth had fallen to near zero, its lowest level since independence in 1963, according to the Kenyan government's 1993 *Economic Survey* (Kenyan government 1993: 1). Growth of real GDP was 2.3 percent in 1991 and 4.3 percent in 1990. In 1992 the agricultural sector declined by 4.2 percent, and manufacturing grew by 1.2 percent. The rate of inflation increased from 19.6 percent in 1991 to 27.5 percent in 1992, its highest rate since independence.[82] The Kenya shilling fell in value against major currencies, and foreign donors' suspension of fast-disbursing aid contributed to a foreign exchange crisis. During the last stages of the 1992 election campaign "so great was the flow of money from the Central Bank of Kenya to the president and KANU nominees that the money supply increased by an estimated 40 percent during the last quarter of 1992," as the government printed more currency (Barkan 1993: 94). And a beset ruling regime short of other patronage resources to distribute allowed land in the productive Rift Valley to become the focus of violent "ethnic" conflict (discussed below).

A careful argument about the economic origins of Kenya's 1990s moves toward "democracy," offered by Holmquist et al. (1993), is worth summarizing in some detail.[83] The authors link recent political changes to a long-term "structural tendency to fiscal crisis" and problems of deficit financing arising in part from ineffective taxing systems, increasing state expenditures, and "contradictions of economic growth" over several decades. Major sources of economic expansion, they note, included agricultural exports (a substantial share from large farms) and import substituting industrialization. Economic policies favored manufacturing characterized by capital-intensive technologies, large-scale units, and products for wealthy consumers. The health of this "modern urban sector" (as they term it) is closely tied to the fluctuating fortunes of coffee and tea export agriculture. Workers in the latter tend to be less well-organized and more poorly remunerated than those in modern urban-sector manufacturing. Most Kenyans work in a third sector (which they label the "competitive sector"), as small farmers who produce crops both for market and home consumption, and who earn significant portions of their incomes from various non-agricultural sources (especially from smallscale urban and rural enterprises and services). This smallscale competitive sector includes prosperous entrepreneurs as well as poorer farmers. It produces the largest share of the nation's marketed food, and is a vast and rapidly growing pool of mobile labor whose numbers help to keep wages down in this and other sectors. The modern urban sector, however, has a tendency to "excess productive capacity and high wages." That is, the sectors are related to one another in a way that produces "wealth and growth at one pole and poverty and stagnation at the other," a contradiction which the authors note is "fundamental to late capitalism, whether in the First or Third World" (Holmquist et al. 1993: 20).

The state itself (their fourth sector) is the largest employer in Kenya, and its patronage spending is an important source of social control. Since European settlers arrived, the article suggests, access to the state has been biased toward the ethnic cohorts at its core, which has contributed to ethnic tensions. Holmquist and his coauthors argue that mounting political strains in the 1980s are connected to state policies that contributed to increasing income inequalities and to sufficient concentration of wealth at the top to sustain a market for luxury consumer goods. Rising state expenditure on social services such as education and health contributed to political stability by providing benefits to the less well-off, but a slowing economy by the late 1970s made this more difficult, as did eventual cutbacks asssociated with structural adjustment measures. By the late 1970s inflation was eroding the buying power of Kenya's middle class, and currency devaluations made luxury imports more costly. It became increasingly expensive for the state to sustain both economic growth and political stability. To help maintain stability the state extended its coercive and repressive capacities. Repression helped to keep political contests centered not on issues of ideology or policy, but on a personal politics of patronage, factionalism, and ethnicity. Dissent was curbed and in the 1970s populist political initiatives shifted to the cities, and especially to the urban middle class. In the early 1990s a heterogeneous urban middle class suffering a declining standard of living articulated a new political agenda of electoral democracy:

Unlike the political agenda of many of the poor, middle class aspirations did not necessarily conflict with propertied interests, and therefore their demands could be cast in universal terms (e.g., meritocracy, competence, efficiency, fairness, education, honest government, and so on), appealing strongly to international constituencies. (Holmquist et al. 1993: 34)

Kenya's democratic coalition, the article continues, included large export crop farmers, and modern urban sector employees, but not working class or peasant organizations. (Trade union organizations by this time had no autonomous political life, nor were there national organizations that represented just small farmers.) The motivating forces for democratic reforms, then, were growing concerns about state unreliability and economic decline among urban middle class and wealthy individuals. These interests allied with foreign donors in calling for structural adjustment policies "mandating a shrinking of the state and the presumed liberation of market forces in its wake" (Holmquist et al. 1993: 35). The major opposition parties contesting the 1992 election had very similar economic programs favoring structural adjustment policy.

The manifesto of Kenya's largest opposition party (FORD)[84] early in 1992 argued the need to continue structural adjustment programs (including reductions in the civil service and parastatals, cost-sharing in hospitals, removal of price controls of basic commodities such as maize, wheat, and milk). FORD's manifesto states that it is "painfully aware that KANU's legacy of economic ruin and social destruction will not just disappear overnight, and that tough policy choices will have to be made."[85] FORD's public rhetoric criticizes the ruling regime for practices that made austerity measures necessary. As for the ruling regime, its willingness to hold elections was "a risky legitimizing device for a regime without fiscal options" (Holmquist et al. 1993: 35).

To the arguments of Holmquist and his colleagues might be appended the following considerations. Inflation, stagnant salaries, and cuts in social services can stir rural as well as urban political opposition, since countryside residents include salaried employees and others who depend on purchased commodities and on remittances from urban employees. Multiple ties of exchange and sociality link town and countryside, and suggest the artificiality of any presumed "boundary" between the two. Large numbers of people travel often between town and countryside, to work or to seek work, to attend school or funerals, to conduct trade and business, and to visit friends and relatives. Even farmers who seldom travel to Nairobi or smaller urban centers are likely to have significant social ties with relatives and other persons who do. One of the untold stories of the 1992 campaign concerns the role of *matatu* drivers and touts who literally and symbolically helped to mobilize support (sometimes at great personal risk) for major presidential candidates such as Matiba. They were likely to play crucial roles as political brokers between the wealthy and poor in both town and countryside. In addition to material and symbolic flows from capital city to countryside, then, there are equally significant reverse flows from the countryside to Nairobi.

Decline in the urban and national economies can strain relationships between urban employees and their rural dependants. In mid-1993, for example, one university-educated Nairobi worker described to me how she and her salaried husband are squeezed on the one hand by inflationary prices of commodities they must purchase in the city, and on the other by rising demands for assistance from rural kin who face their own mounting economic difficulties. She noted the problems her mother faces in the central Kenyan countryside because of the poor cash returns she and others now receive for the coffee they grow. As rural land, jobs, and places in primary and secondary schools and universities become more scarce, the economic insecurity and frustrated ambitions of most Kenyans can only grow, particularly in the most densely-settled and intensively-farmed zones of central and western Kenya. It is difficult for such rural areas to reabsorb returning urban migrants, and rural migrants displaced from land elsewhere (e.g., Gikuyu who left Central Province for the Rift Valley and were forced unexpectedly to return to their Central Province "home" during struggles with British colonial settlers and again during the "ethnic" clashes of the early 1990s).[86] Urban economic decline leads some migrants who had severed ties with rural dependants or clients to relocate unexpectedly to their rural homes. Such a situation may improve the bargaining position of rural dependants who had been cast off, but whose cooperation becomes newly beneficial to returning migrants. The latter are likely then to face greater and more insistent financial demands just as their capacity to respond is declining.[87]

If patrons and would-be patrons can instead translate widespread economic dissatisfaction into popular demands for electoral democracy, they may buy time among rural and other dependants and clients. That is, support for multiparty politics is a legitimizing strategy for strapped elites out of power, as well as for the ruling party. Those who succeed in capturing the state then may be better able both to (re)build their client base, and to increase their own wealth. Such a political strategy succeeds to the extent that citizens believe the regime in power has violated its contractual obligations to them, and that they would be better off under a new regime. When the outcome of political struggles (like those under-way in the early 1990s) is simply recirculation of elites, however, and longer-term structural problems and inadequate legal protections of basic rights are not addressed, the seeds have been sown for the next political "crisis."

The economic difficulties of the early 1990s are likely to fuel longer-term rural conflict along at least three axes: (a) between financially better-off patrons and their less well-off clients or dependants; (b) between family members – husbands and wives, brothers, elders and juniors – as they contest control over scarcer land, cash, and other resources;[88] and (c) among elites themselves: between would-be patrons competing both for client supporters and for access to diminishing state resources. These tensions and the structural constraints of Kenya's economy may contribute eventually to new kinds of political contests focused on competing ideologies and policies that affect rich and poor in very different ways. In the early 1990s, however, ideological differences remained submerged discourses within and between opposition parties.[89] A besieged Moi regime explicitly emphasized "vertical" divisions, especially those of region and ethnicity.

The ethnic dimension

Warriors with painted faces, wielding bows and arrows, have been on a rampage of murder, rape and pillage for some two years, but now the Kenyan government has sealed off the provinces affected. (Agence France Presse, September 22, 1993)[90]

Are these warrior images of a "natural" atavism or of an imitated, commodified tradition cleverly staged to serve powerful interests? In 1992, reports from Kenya of outbreaks of ethnic conflict, with violent deaths and burning of houses and crops, attracted international attention.[91] Some Western mass media reduced the conflict to familiar representations of "tribal warfare," an expression of stereotypical atavistic social forces supposedly endemic in Africa. Regime opponents, however, reported that state paramilitary units were arming and organizing "Kalenjin"[92] warriors with metal arrows imported from abroad,[93] creating an appearance of "traditional" warfare built on longstanding animosities. A regime whose slogan was "peace, love, and unity" faced accusations of deliberately fomenting violence in order to discredit the political opposition. By mid-1992 over 800 people may have died in the clashes, and perhaps 130,000 were left homeless (Barkan 1993: 93). A 1992 parliamentary committee that investigated the conflicts concluded that some provincial administration officers had "directly participated (in) or encouraged the clashes ... (through) public utterances" (Kenyan government 1992: 79), that slow and half-hearted responses by the provincial administration and security personnel allowed the fighting to escalate, that arrested suspects were released before being charged in court, and that youthful "warriors" were hired and "transported to clash areas from outside to reinforce the local ones" (Kenyan government 1992: 81). The committee found "root causes of the clashes" to include political motivations "fuelled by some officers in the Provincial Administration," and "the misconception that some ethnic communities could chase away other ethnic communities in order to acquire their land" (Kenyan government 1992: 82).[94]

Why might the state encourage or idly witness such civil violence? Though Moi had predicted that multipartyism would bring ethnic conflict and "chaos,"[95] his opponents in 1992 argued that such conflict did not emerge until the ruling party engineered it from above in order to undermine advocates of a shift to a multiparty system. Some suggested that Moi might use the civil unrest as a pretext to further curtail political expression and to avoid an election by declaring a state of emergency. Moi and outspoken allies in the early 1990s attempted to discredit government opponents by accusing them of "tribalism": of seeking power in order to benefit themselves and their own ethnoregional base (with the Gikuyu peoples a particular target of such criticism). Twenty-five years earlier Kenyatta described the opposition political party KPU as "tribal malcontents concerned mainly with sectional interests, who would also drag Kenya into communism" (Barkan 1987: 225). In the early 1990s official rhetoric both portrayed multiparty advocates as "tribalists," and argued that tribalism made Kenya unsuited to a multiparty political system. As the so-called "ethnic clashes" continued into late 1993 the government sealed off some affected parts of the Rift Valley, and in doing so attracted both domestic and international criticism. Opposition MPs who tried to visit the sealed-off area were charged with disturbing the peace.[96] One British MP denounced an "ethnic cleansing" program and said he would take the matter to the UN.[97] A Kenyan opposition MP who called for deployment of UN peace-keepers in Kenya was arrested.[98]

Part of the necessary background to understanding these conflicts includes a shift in Kenya's ethnoregional balance of power during Moi's first decade in office (see Throup 1987b; Barkan and Chege 1989; Bates 1989; and Hornsby and Throup 1992). (See Map 2 for distribution of official ethnic/language groups.) Whereas the Gikuyu peoples (who officially constituted about one-fifth of Kenya's population in 1979) were economically and politically dominant under Kenyatta's rule (from independence to mid-1978)[99] and during the colonial era, "Kalenjin" subgroups gained advantages under Moi's rule. (Moi himself is Tugen, a small group in the "Kalenjin" category.) During the 1980s public investment in roads and rural health, for example, increasingly favored the large Rift Valley Province (and to a lesser extent Western Province), rather than Kenyatta's Gikuyu-dominated Central Province base (Barkan and Chege 1989: 449–450). (The Rift Valley includes 40 percent of Kenya's land.) This shift was in part an intentional attempt to redress ethnoregional inequalities in development. Moi's agricultural policies also favored the interests of his own grain-growing constituency (especially largescale farmers) over wealthy central Kenyan export crop interests (Bates 1989: 137). There are wide popular perceptions that under the Moi regime, groups such as the Gikuyu and Luo (the Luo were winners under neither the Kenyatta nor Moi regime) have been losing ground to the "Kalenjin." The theme of growing neglect during the 1980s of the Gikuyu-dominated Central Province figured, for example, in 1992 political opposition rhetoric there (Throup 1993b). Popular beliefs hold that "Kalenjin" groups have privileged access to state resources and financial and legal protections, to finance capital, to public positions, land, education, and so on. On the other hand, the "Kalenjin" subgroups themselves are divided by intergroup conflicts over land and other matters,[100] and Moi has by no means built a monolithic base of political support. (So, too, Kenyatta's Gikuyu base had its own internal divisions and conflicts.) Nonetheless, ethnolinguistic or ethnoregional identities are central to current political contests, and to views of democracy from both above and below.

Ethnic competition is not a figment of Moi's imagination. Kenyan state authorities who invoke ethnic identities today play on labels and boundaries institutionalized under British colonial rule. The colonial state often confined "African" political organizations to single districts, which state officials usually conceived of as "ethnic" units. After 1900, British colonial officials envisioned "a constellation of ethnically exclusive districts that incorporated deeply rooted, isolated, and mutually antagonistic tribes" (Ambler 1988: 153). This grid of districts overlay formerly autonomous pre-colonial communities that did not fall under the authority of any indigenous state. They were not precisely bounded "societies," but rather highly mobile populations with a long history of ties of trade, intermarriage, clientage, adoption, and migration. The internal administrative boundaries institutionalized under colonial rule came to define arenas of competition for state resources. To speak of particular districts or regions today is to convey messages about ethnic categories and dominance as well.

Both opposition and ruling party politicians play on variation across Kenya's regions in the character of local ties to the colonial and post-colonial state. These differences shape reactions to current political upheavals and to rhetoric of democracy. As Hobsbawm (1990: 12) notes more generally, "'national consciousness' develops unevenly among the social groupings and regions of a country; this regional diversity and its reasons have in the past been notably neglected." Thus it is essential to keep in mind the very different experiences of, for example, peoples in Central as opposed to Western Province, or those officially classified as "Luo," "Kalenjin," "Gikuyu," "Luhya," "Maasai," and "Somali," with regard to access to state resources and perceptions of the nation. Pastoralists who occupy Kenya's sparsely-settled northern regions, for example, are likely not even to conceive of themselves as part of the nation-state in the same way as the Gikuyu peoples of Central Province do. Thus northern pastoralists who journey to Nairobi speak of traveling to "Kenya": not counting themselves as citizens of that "imagined community" even though they reside within its territorial boundaries. When Kenyan politicians rhetorically invoke local or ethnoregional identities, they can "make connections with lower classes without raising class-based issues" (Ford and Holmquist 1988: 160). A politician who emphasizes class divisions, on the other hand, may risk harassment or detention, as well as polarizing his or her ethnoregional political base (cf. Leys 1971; and Leonard 1991: 79, 101).

Underlying some of the "ethnic" violence in the early 1990s are conflicts over land. Some of these have deep historical roots, such as the threat of violence among various groups (including those labeled "Kalenjin" and "Gikuyu") over reallocation of land in the former White Highlands during the transition to independence.[101] Reports of oathing among Gikuyu resurfaced in the early 1960s and again in the early 1990s,[102] as the salience of ethnic identity increased and open conflict broke out in some areas of the Rift Valley. But land conflicts do not necessarily center on ethnicity *per se*. Some of the recent land disputes involve dispossession and violent evictions of the poor and "squatters," with accusations of land-grabbing and illegal acts against prominent public servants (see Africa Watch 1991: 237–268). In the 1960s, as in the early 1990s, the land conflicts occurred along complex lines of social cleavage: between haves and have-nots; among members of various "Kalenjin" groups; as well as between "Kalenjin" and people in other ethnic categories who had their own internal conflicts.

Contemporary political rhetoric about supposed rifts between the Kalenjin and Gikuyu includes a revival of earlier notions of regional autonomy or *majimboism*.[103] The 1991 *majimbo* proposals by Moi allies, together with anti-Gikuyu rhetoric, occurred at a time of rising tensions among Kalenjin groups themselves over land transactions and other matters.[104] In the 1960s *majimboism* set the interests of smaller ethnic groups (e.g., in the Rift Valley, Coast, and Northeastern Provinces) against those of the more numerous Gikuyu, Luo, and their allies in the densely-settled areas of central and western Kenya. In the 1992 election Moi and KANU drew strong support from the former category, the old KADU coalition (whereas the old KANU coalition supported various opposition candidates in 1992). Critics allege that the early 1990s ethnic clashes replicate the 1960s KANU/KADU ethnoregional divisions, and were a ruling party ploy to force Moi's political opponents (especially Gikuyu peoples) out of the Rift Valley before the election (Africa Watch 1993). At pre-election rallies, prominent Kalenjin and Maasai politicians in the ruling party drew a distinction between Rift Valley "natives" or "original inhabitants" such as the Kalenjin, Maasai, Samburu, and Turkana on the one hand, and the "aliens" and "foreigners" (many of them Gikuyu) who settled there since the start of colonial rule on the other. Though many of the so-called "aliens" have title deeds to land legally purchased in the Rift Valley, they have been evicted through violence and intimidation or forced to sell their land at throw-away prices (Africa Watch 1993). The Central Province "motherland" to which they are told to return is an area of very high population density that cannot easily absorb more immigrants.

The Moi regime's rhetorical characterization of rural violence in 1992 as "ethnic" conflict caused by multipartyism should be interpreted in the context of the state's fiscal and patronage crisis, structural problems in the economy, and class issues or conflicts between haves and have-nots. Land is an attractive patronage asset as other such resources disappear. To characterize the conflict this way is not to deny the force of ethnic idioms and cultural differences, but rather to call attention to the ways these interact with other lines of social conflict and cohesion, and the ways "ethnic" identities can be manipulated or accentuated from above to serve particular political interests. As Abner Cohen (1974: 93) writes, people "do not fight or kill one another simply because they are culturally different."

Nonetheless, for some members of the ruling elite to "retribalize" themselves by emphasizing some ethnoregional differences and down-playing others in their public rhetoric can only reinforce real fears among citizens. Many Kenyans I talked with in both town and countryside in mid-1993 discussed the nation's political future in explicit ethnic and regional terms, and assumed that the ethnic identity of a new president would define patterns of favoritism. Casual talk focused in particular on the pros and cons of having a Gikuyu head of state. Some believed this could only increase political instability, as it would accentuate the ethno-regional conflicts in play during both the Kenyatta and Moi regimes.

Ruling party rhetoric in the early 1990s reduced opposition maneuvers to simple ethnic arithmetic and greed. In 1990, for example, one Moi ally publicly accused the new multiparty advocates of being "people who have eaten a lot and now have rumbling stomachs," that is, those who have consumed others' wealth, and now are looking greedily for further oppor-tunities.[105] The latter criticism was easily directed against the ruling party and opponents alike. The theme resonated with popular perceptions that it was wealth and self-interest, and not multipartyism *per se*, that was at issue in the new political contests. Public cynicism grew as the opposition splintered into feuding factions (divisions within as well as between ethnic groupings). 1992 saw the splitting of the original FORD (Forum for the

Restoration of Democracy) into two separate parties, FORD-Asili (literally the original FORD) and FORD-Kenya, and further offshoots such as the Kenya National Congress, Kenya Social Congress, and Kenya National Democratic Alliance (see Throup 1993a: 390–391). FORD-Asili and the Democratic Party in particular were competitors for the Central Province (largely Gikuyu) vote. The parties attempted cross-ethnic alliances by, for example, pairing presidential and vice-presidential candidates of different ethnoregional origins.[106] But with the multiplication of opposition parties came no successful attempts to mobilize broad enough support for one party to defeat Moi.

Though this Kenyan portrait resembles a wider continental picture of a politics of clientelism, prebendalism, and ethnicity, there is nothing "natural" or inevitable about it. There are countervailing tendencies that could assume more importance in the future. These include experiments with decentralized channeling of resources to localities, redefinition of bureaucratic procedures, and reviving parties or other participatory structures (Chazan et al. 1992: 182–183). Also important are cross-ethnic informal associations (e.g., in faculty lounges, bars, offices, sports fields, schools, and neighborhoods). The social networks that link wealthier and well-educated individuals across ethnic and local boundaries are one context that can favor the emergence of political ideologies and practices that depart from a politics of prebendalism, clientelism, and ethnicity. Enduring inter-ethnic friendships are formed in schools and universities. In many secondary schools students are allowed to speak in English or Swahili, but not in their various "vernacular" languages such as Maasai, Gikuyu, or Luo. (Thus I heard Alliance High School students who were practicing basketball one Saturday in mid-1993 repeatedly call out to one another in English.) National unity and liberal democracy are among the political ideals to which the school curriculum exposes students.[107] One pre-election poster I saw hanging in an Alliance High School classroom in mid-1993 carries the slogan "many parties . . . one nation!" And today's rhetorically polarized ethnic groups, such as the Gikuyu and Maasai, have a long history of ties of intermarriage, trade, and social exchange (see Spear and Waller 1993). Again, here as elsewhere in the world, shifts in the salience of ethnic identities reflect the interests of those in power and competition for scarce economic resources, more than ancient hatreds or animosities. Though such identities become politically potent precisely when people do come to view them as "natural" or "real," "every human identity is constructed, historical" (Appiah 1992: 174–175).

In Kenya in the early 1990s it would be easy to overestimate the extent to which many citizens "believe" the rhetoric of polarized ethnic identities. They are caught nonetheless in a situation of rising political violence and uncertainty. Land, livelihoods, and life itself are at stake. Individuals violently evicted from their land may be drawn into struggles construed as "ethnic," but initially they do not kill one another over such identities *per se*. Once set in motion, however, such conflicts can be difficult to reverse. Individuals may be drawn into violent confrontations because political factions have been mobilized in fierce contests that connect the local to the struggles of national elites vying for control of the state.

The government itself, more than rival ethnic groups *per se*, easily becomes the target of popular anger, whether for instigating the violence or for failing to halt it. This was a powerful theme during the 1992 election campaign, as illustrated in a political rally David Throup attended in December 1992 in Githunguri (Kiambu District in Central Province).[108] He quotes a Gikuyu parliamentary candidate from the Democratic Party who said in her speech: "People in Central Province shouldn't vote for KANU with the example of the Molo clashes lurking in the background. What does this say about Moi's peace slogan? In Molo they victimized Kikuyus." (Throup 1993b: 83) A Democratic Party rally the previous day in the same constituency included an emotional and compelling account from a woman who had migrated from Githunguri to Burnt Forest (Uasin Gishu District) in the Rift Valley, and then just recently had been forced to flee from Burnt Forest:

The woman ... informed the crowd, which listened in angry silence, that her house and those of her neighbors had been burnt down on 13 December. Some settlers had been killed and the survivors fled to Nakuru, where they had taken refuge in the compound of the Roman Catholic Cathedral. She had only been saved by "delivering myself to the hands of God. I ran away and escaped with my life. I am very bitter although I belong to the church." She had lost her children, had escaped with nothing and was now entirely dependent on charity. It was clear, she asserted, that the violence had been planned by the Government and District Administration ... After briefly explaining how she had escaped, the woman suddenly stopped, observing, "I can't talk anymore because my tears are coming." (Throup 1993b: 75–76)

Such poignant personal accounts of the new civil strife inspired the production of more "seditious" music, building again on earlier traditions of musical protest during the struggle for independence, and at other times of political crisis, such as the 1975 assassination of J. M. Kariuki. In 1993 a group of musicians, through a local human rights organization,[109] slipped into the closed-off area of Molo (which had been hit particularly badly by the violence), interviewed victims, and made a cassette recording of songs condemning the clashes and criticizing the government and security forces.[110] The musicians' leader angered Kenyan authorities by holding an international news conference after he visited Molo. The music, which incorporates Christian tunes and Gikuyu folklore, exhorts wealthy Kenyans to assist suffering victims, and appeals to both international and local communities to help end the violence. Though the songs would be prohibited on national radio, the musicians' leader said a few copies of the cassette had been given to *matatu* private taxi drivers, and that earnings from sales of the cassette would be used to help victims.[111] In short, once again citizens found creative channels for expressing versions of current history that differed from official scripts.

Differences between rich and poor (a motif in the "seditious" music about both the Molo clashes and the earlier Muoroto "shanty" demolitions) are a common theme in everyday language about struggles over access to land, jobs, and education. For example, a man in Embu District filing a land complaint with a government officer writes:

I also would like to know whether if you have nothing or you are poor, your things would be given to people who have money? The reason of asking this is because I see as if the chief is giving my land to my opponent because they have money. Now Sir, as I am a poor man I would like you to direct me on where to go or what to do.[112]

These are politically explosive sentiments with many historical resonances, including those of central Kenya's anti-colonial "Mau Mau" rebellion (when land accumulation by both wealthy Europeans and wealthy Africans was a salient popular issue). Here again, however, official responses are likely to emphasize not class differences but "vertical" competition between localities, clans, or the constituencies of particular politicians. Thus when a speaker at a 1992 opposition rally mentioned the rich grabbing land settlement plots, she targeted the local KANU candidate and his associates as she did so (Throup 1993b: 73). Such rhetoric need not "fool" listeners in order to be effective. Rather, the rhetoric reflects the realities of a political system in which, even as differences between rich and poor grow, competition for material benefits (including state resources) is structured around elite cleavages, factions, and ethnoregional contests: that is, patron–client structures.

Patron–client politics

Contemporary patron–client structures emerged, as the foregoing discussion suggests, in part out of a colonial political system that reinforced local and ethnic identities, and discouraged broader affiliations based on class or common interest groups. Patronage ties also build on antecedent cultural assumptions about justified mutual claims, as suggested in Kenyatta's (1965: 299) Gikuyu ethnography:

Relatives help and consult one another in matters of common concern; *anyone who is in need will go to his nearest prosperous kinsman* as a matter of course, and hospitality is taken for granted. These things are a matter of good breeding and custom rather than of legal enactment, but to understand their gradations in detail would be to understand the real bonds which hold Gikuyu society together. (My emphasis.)

Elsewhere, however, Kenyatta referred to the poor as *ragai*, loosely translated as "lazy" or "useless" (Macharia 1992: 229). Patronage relations, then, are part of a cultural etiquette of social bonds that entail gradations of obligation and room for maneuver and contestation. Patronage usually is taken to be an unequal, dyadic, instrumental social tie that can be contrasted with pure coercion on the one hand, and primarily affective ties on the other (see Wolf 1966; Scott 1972).[113] Analysts differ, however, in their emphasis on the reciprocal character of such relations (Barth 1959), or their lopsidedness (Wolf 1966). In political analyses patronage relations often "focus attention on the informal means of persuasion (and coercion) built around the selective allocation of state resources" (Lemarchand 1988: 150).

Patronage politics sanction the diversion of state or public resources into private hands, and include exchanges among members of the elite, as well as appropriation of public resources by ethnoregional or sectional interests.[114] Here idioms of kinship and clanship are important, though these relationships by no means guarantee material security. To keep his (or more rarely, her) pyramid of followers intact, a patron distributes personal favors (assisting in obtaining employment, commercial loans, school admission, trade or import licenses, land, and so on). In addition, successful politicians must bring (or appear to bring) to their constituencies improvements such as roads, schools, health centers, and mains water. In Kenya they did so in part by organizing and contributing to *Harambee* or self-help development projects (see Barkan 1984, 1991; Thomas-Slayter 1985, 1991; Barkan and Holmquist 1989; Widner 1992). Competitive parliamentary elections[115] allowed voters to bring distributive pressures to bear on candidates (patrons), with clients' loyalty (and alliances between patrons) driven more by material inducement than by affective ties: as in the Swahili proverb "an empty hand is not licked" (*mkono mtupu haulambwi*), or a central Kenyan proverb "an elder does not eat stones" (*muthuuri ndariaga mahiga*). With a different moral accent, Kenyan novelist Ngugi wa Thiong'o, in *Petals of Blood*, associates the proverb "An empty hand is not licked" with post-colonial corruption, greed, self-interest, and increasing class divisions.

While leadership accountability under Kenyatta's rule came to depend upon each elected politician's ability to deliver patronage rewards to a locality, the Moi regime brought a shift in forces shaping the longevity of MPs, cabinet ministers, and party officials. During the 1980s the length of their time in office came to depend less on accountability to rural constituents and more on the personal favor of senior officials (see Leonard 1991; Widner 1992; and Barkan 1993). By the late 1980s there was a more frequent turnover in cabinet positions (with spectacles of disgrace and demotion), an associated decline in cabinet ministers' power and prestige, and the eclipse of the earlier role of cabinet ministers as long-term district bosses.[116]

Such accelerated factional realignments and conflicts between faction leaders are unlikely to challenge or to question existing power structures. By definition factions are ephemeral followings that patrons recruit through diverse social principles.[117] Faction membership, as noted, is based largely on instrumental ties involving calculations of material advantage, rather than on ideological differences. The emergence of patrons may be associated historically with consolidation of power and wealth in particular families: a process that directs attention to class dynamics. Bujra's comparative analysis of factionalism suggests that faction leaders emerge typically from similar social backgrounds, and from "within a 'dominant' category of some description, whether ... of seniority, wealth, ritual status, or numbers" (Bujra 1973: 136–137). Supporters of a particular leader are repaid not through a restructuring of the basis of power, but through distribution of patronage benefits. Where "horizontal" rather than "vertical" political divisions come into play a subordinate group may draw on external support to challenge the power structure.

Such a fundamental challenge to the power structure was not at issue in Kenya's 1992 multiparty election. Indeed, had the 1990s opposition coalition avowed a more populist or leftist agenda, it may well not have attracted the support of the urban middle class, the wealthy, and international forces who promoted democracy in the early 1990s (Holmquist et al. 1993: 37). Though opposition candidates' television advertisements emphasized the need for change (while Moi's invoked stability and progress), deep structural or ideological changes were not at issue. The principal contenders in the election were people from wealthy circles: *matajiri* (cf. Leonard 1991) or *wabenzi* in Swahili. This emergent class differs from ruling groups in many African nations in that it has a strong personal stake in agriculture, and is grounded in three strongly linked economic bases: petty-capitalist (usually export) agriculture; small trade; and clerical or government employment (Leonard 1991). This Kenyan elite, for example, now owns formerly European and other large farms, ranches, and estates (which still constitute one-third of all Kenya's agri-

cultural land).[118] Their wealth has become quite visible. In the countryside their large stone houses set them apart from most farmers' mud-
walled houses. They often drive expensive cars such as Mercedes Benzes
(hence the Swahili label *wabenzi*), and live in luxurious compounds and
prestigious neighborhoods in the city.

Political mobilization since independence has centered on competition
for access to the patronage of such wealthy individuals, rather than on
opposition to them as a class. Rural political mobilization in Kenya,
through such activities as *Harambee* or self-help projects, was oriented
toward "gaining a toehold in the system" (Thomas-Slayter 1991: 308),
rather than toward fundamentally restructuring the political and
economic systems. Thus one of the most popular types of rural *Harambee*
projects is the building of local secondary schools, since many citizens
view education as the principal means of upward mobility and make
enormous sacrifices to educate their children.

The notion that acquiring wealth may entail privately appropriating
non-private funds is a staple theme of popular culture. Individuals who
misuse official or public funds for private purposes are said to have
"eaten" the money. It is a popular stereotype that men who become
wealthy also become fat. Such plumpness can carry positive as well as
negative associations: health and well-being as well as greed or exploitation (see also Bayart 1993). As the national and international economy
deteriorated during the 1980s, however, Kenyan citizens became more
critical of wealth accumulated (sometimes through questionable means)
by individuals at the top of the political system (Throup 1987b; Thomas-
Slayter 1991). The emergent political culture of the early 1990s (with its
demands for greater transparency and leadership accountability) brought
closer scrutiny of and more critical moral judgments about the means by
which the powerful acquire great wealth.

Listen, for example, to the words of a local Democratic Party officer
addressing a political rally in Githunguri in December 1992 (from Throup
1993b: 76–77): "We ... can't pay for school or afford a kilo of meat. We
can't afford to feed our children. Yet, these other people are stealing in
broad daylight. You know these things ... Our money at the Coffee
Cooperative is being stolen but we dare not ask what is happening." He,
like other speakers, blames the ruling party for deteriorating roads, and
the general economic decline local people have suffered since 1978 in spite
of their hard work on their crops. Political candidates pointed directly to
KANU's diversion of resources to the Rift Valley rather than to Central
Province.

The growing economic pressures on Kenya's patronage machine
(which no election winner would be able to reduce easily) brought desta-

bilization of a familiar kind. When the national or global economy enters a decline, and patronage resources diminish, individual and community pressures for patronage rewards can destabilize regimes and engender conflict.[119] Ethnoregional competition may intensify, overwhelming the regime in power with demands which its reduced resources do not permit it to satisfy (Barkan 1991: 189). Such conditions augment the tension "between the ruling group's maintenance of its collective means of appropriation and the intensification of individual competition" (Watts 1989: 26–27). Some argue that when political patrons are starved of discretionary state resources "previously cohesive regimes incur elite defections" and regimes become "more vulnerable to unrest and less able to buy support and coopt opposition" (Bratton and Van de Walle 1991: 49, 47). Indeed, "consensus among rulers is more crucial than the consent of the ruled in preserving a particular pattern of power" (Lonsdale 1981: 160). Recall that as state patronage resources dried up in Kenya, the ruling party in 1992–3 tried to buy electoral support through large cash outlays made possible by inflationary expansion of the money supply, and questionable foreign exchange and credit transactions between the Central Bank and other banks.[120] By mid-1993 KANU faced the challenge of how to regularize the operations of many troubled banks and meet other IMF requirements without further destabilizing the economy and political system. Greater democracy is by no means an inevitable outcome of such circumstances, as Watts (1989: 29) suggests: "The instabilities and contradictions faced by ruling groups in *their* reproductive squeeze are as likely to amplify violence, oppression and centralization of power as revive economic growth."

Struggles at the top can ramify downward through the patron–client pyramid (which is not to deny the agency of local actors as well). During the early 1990s Kenya saw open defections from the ruling party, conflicts within and between proliferating opposition parties, and counter-defections to KANU. Under such circumstances the pyramid's constituent membership changes rapidly as rivals compete vigorously for positions of authority, and clients compete for the favor of patrons. Greater uncertainty and intensified competition for power at the top of the political hierarchy permit easy escalation of the conflict that attends everyday contests over matters such as land, bridewealth, school fees, loans, jobs, and education. In such local contests individuals who mobilize patronage ties now enter a politically charged arena of high-stakes competition for control of the state. Local organizers of a water development project, for example, must contend with notables from rival political parties whose efforts to undermine one another may sabotage the original project. Though such political contests are not new many Kenyans believe that the level of thuggery and incivility entailed by them is intensifying. In short, Kenya's growing violence in the 1990s[121] emerged from the conjunction of inflammatory rhetoric, structural constraints in the economy, unpredictable administrative practices and policies, and the more rapidly shifting sands of patronage politics.

Though the increase in violence did coincide with the re-emergence of multiparty politics, the supposedly inevitable causal connection the ruling party asserted was not necessarily convincing to many. Even so, would citizens trade democratic freedoms for assurances of physical security? That was an old bargain, familiar to those who had lived under colonial as well as post-colonial rule in Kenya and elsewhere. Would it be repeated in the 1990s?

Conclusions

The early 1990s brought more open challenges to the state's version of political reality, and a sharp rise in the country's political temperature. The charged atmosphere came less from novel revelations than from the excitement and danger of shattering earlier silences, publicly declaring open secrets.

From abroad came newly-disapproving tones that were akin to a Claude Rains/*Casablanca* style of shock at suddenly visible lapses. A negative shift in Kenya's media image accompanied the fading of pre-cold war constraints on criticizing African allies whose strategic usefulness now had lessened. Aid donors' new emphasis on political and economic liberalization measures as pre-conditions for assistance to African nations afforded new opportunities for dissident elites out of office to re-enter political competition. The 1990s thus brought a new public rhetorical emphasis on electoral democracy, calls for greater transparency in government practices, and demands for more public accountability of leaders. Agreeing to an election was a (risky) legitimizing ploy for a fiscally troubled regime in power (Holmquist et al. 1993: 35). And, in the face of national and global economic difficulties, to advocate a shift to multiparty politics became a legitimizing strategy for strapped elites out of power as they tried to recapture the state. But a crisis of accountability in the early 1990s faced Kenyan elites both in and out of office. In 1992 Kenya's first multiparty elections since the 1960s did little to resolve prior tensions and conflicts. Volatility and unpredictability, rather than stability and order, typified economic as well as political life.

Popular and scholarly accounts continued to invoke overdrawn contrasts between Kenya as either "miracle" or "disaster." Such images were misleadingly construed as a historical sequence of growing crisis that was peculiarly African, rather than a history that was jointly "Western" and African. A historical amnesia in today's mass media supports narratives that portray Africa as an inverse image of the West and that find false comfort in an imagined distance between the two.[122]

The Kenyan "corruption" that attracted much media and donor attention in the 1990s was not new, though its scale had increased. And when the Moi government attempted to ban "seditious" music it was following in the footsteps of its colonial predecessors. Kenya's ruling party had adopted parallel tactics in the 1960s and the 1990s to undermine opposition parties. But cold war ideological polarities convenient to the ruling party's marginalization of the opposition KPU in the 1960s had lost importance in the 1990s.[123] Such cold war pragmatics in earlier decades were bolstered by some American intellectuals' doubts about whether Africa was suited to liberal democracy (see Staniland 1991). Not long after independence the Kenyatta regime shrewdly invoked "tradition" and economic necessity in order to justify changes in a constitution imposed by the former colonial power. The resulting constitutional changes augmented the powers of the presidency in relation to other institutions, so returning post-independence politics to some authoritarian patterns of colonial rule. And later, under the Moi regime, Kenya's official position was that it had a "one-party democracy" that was based on traditional African culture, in which "decisions were made by consensus rather than contest."[124] Curbs on political freedoms through constitutional changes and other means again followed tough precedents set under colonial as well as post-colonial administrations. Such historical continuities and discontinuities, crucial to an understanding of the present, are seldom reflected in the opinion-shaping snapshots of Kenya offered by foreign aid donors and American and European media.

Images that accelerate the speed with which history is discounted proliferate easily in a post-modern era of intense "time-space compression," an era in which the world's spaces can be "collapse(d) ... into a series of images on a television screen" (Harvey 1989). This is a time of contradictory trends toward both global homogenization and fragmentation. On the one hand are "political–economic processes (money flows, international divisions of labour, financial markets, and the like) that are becoming ever more universalizing in their depth, intensity, reach and power over daily life" (Harvey 1989: 117). On the other, differentiated nationalisms, localisms, and an aestheticized politics of place "have become stronger precisely because of the quest for the security that place always offers in the midst of all the shifting that flexible accumulation implies" (Harvey 1989: 306). Both of these trends David Harvey (1989) connects to the accelerated mobility of capital, and the post-1973 global economic transition from a Fordist-Keynesian system to one of flexible accumulation and rapid capital mobility (with accelerated turnover times in production, exchange and consumption).

These global economic changes are associated with a volatility of politics, culture, and social life. Indeed, "learning to play the volatility right" or "masterminding" it is at least as important as any long-term planning (Harvey 1989: 286–287; see also Berry 1993). Winners respond quickly to shifts in markets, political winds, and consumer trends. Africa's political ferment in the early 1990s partly reflects such processes. But were Kenya's political upheavals at this time more than an altered flow of surface images?

This question demands a look beyond post-modernist celebrations of the ephemeral, the fragmentary, the polyphonous, and beyond an aestheticized politics.[125] The challenge here is to examine the arts of politics, to recognize the power of images and aesthetics, but not to divorce images from (contested versions of) history, or to treat the culture of politics as a domain autonomous from material political–economic processes.

The stylistics of power and the spectacle of politics bring ample material for diversion (see Mbembe 1992). Things are not necessarily what they appear to be in political life. Is a prayer meeting an illegal new political party, politics in disguise; today's defector from KANU tomorrow's counter-defector; a "traditional warrior" with bow and arrows a hired thug; a sermon, song, or hymn "seditious"? Do political activists pose as street vendors of potatoes (as Moi suggested in 1990)? Are the cheers of a crowd a cover for dissent or cynicism? These ambiguities point to more than the fears of those in power and the resourcefulness of those who would challenge them. Ruse, disguise, feint, and counter-feint are so much a part of Kenyan political life as to suggest that nothing should be taken at face value.[126] Politics turns in part on collapsed distinctions between reality and fantasy (which is not to say the distinction becomes meaningless in all contexts). Though crowds attending opposition party rallies in 1992 learned and enacted their new "scripts" with apparent enthusiasm, the zeal of *baraza* audience cheers is not necessarily an index of consent. Indeed the reverse is as likely to be true. These political arts – practiced by those in as well as out of power, by dominant as well as subordinate groups – have both entertainment value and more serious consequences.

The underside of the vigor and ferment of Kenya's opposition politics includes questions about how to resolve the economy's structural problems, as well as questions about how closely identified are the interests of opposition leaders with those of individuals already in power, and to what extent their governing practices might actually differ. In mid-1993 many

Kenyans I talked with in town and countryside were equally disillusioned with opposition and ruling party leaders. Further rifts within opposition parties after their failure to win the 1992 election, allegations against them concerning financial improprieties, and some supposedly well-rewarded defections back to KANU, all contributed to growing public cynicism about the motives of both opposition and ruling party politicians. In addition, increasing economic hardship and risks to personal safety were dominant concerns among a wide cross-section of citizens. Many spoke of the present as Kenya's most difficult moment since independence, and uneasily noted possible parallels between their situation and that of countries such as Somalia. That is, the perceptions of crisis carried in local and international media were by no means absent among ordinary citizens. At the same time, though disappointed with the 1992 election outcome, many citizens saw the recent moves toward "democracy," and the newly vigorous and open criticism of those in power as positive and not easily erased changes. Images of possible alternative worlds which circulated in Kenya during the early 1990s, constitute symbolic resources for future struggles.

Rapid global symbolic flows in the early 1990s sustained a remarkably narrow public economic policy discourse in Africa. Likely reasons include authoritarian and neo-patrimonial states, large numbers of African intellectuals living abroad, the reduced capacities of universities and research institutions, and the hectic pace and monologic (rather than dialogic) emphasis of World Bank and IMF negotiations and consulting missions in African countries (Van de Walle 1993). State patrimonialism means that there are few professional incentives for bureaucrats or others to engage in policy debates or innovations (Van de Walle 1993: 15). Public policy debate, however, is often scarce in elections in Western democracies as well, and one might ask why observers expect Africa to be any different (Young 1993: 306).

The parallels elsewhere are often overlooked, and the submergence of ideological differences and accentuation of clientelist politics too easily begins to appear inevitable or "natural" in Africa in particular. Scholars often portray Kenya and other African countries as caught between patterns in which officials either raid the state for private gain, fueling patronage politics, or build an ethic of professionalism so that the state becomes an efficient, rationalized Weberian bureaucracy, an instrument of consensual, pluralist politics. To move beyond such a view scholars might pursue comparisons across Africa of circumstances under which some leaders (such as Cameroon's Paul Biya and Ivory Coast's Houphouet-Boigny) made tentative moves toward "dismantling clientelist networks" in the 1980s (Van de Walle 1993: 10). Are newly elected leaders

more inclined to reform economies and national politics? Perhaps clientelism is simply "accorded too much explanatory sway" (Lonsdale 1992:
466), overshadowing experimental moves in other directions, and more
oblique political language and notions of accountability conveyed in
moralities asserted in "seditious" music, subverted hymns, opposition
rhetoric, and everyday conversations in bars, *matatu* taxis, schools, and
places of work. More attention could also be given to comparative
historical questions such as why in Costa Rica, but not in Kenya in the
1990s, public debate included economic policy issues, and why citizens of
Costa Rica demanded that the government make public the texts of its
agreements with the IMF and World Bank.[127] How have transnational
and domestic forces shaped differences in the mix of statist and market-
oriented policies and their associated political rhetorics in Kenya, Costa
Rica, and elsewhere? Why has Latin America, more than Africa, engaged
alternatives to the orthodox reform plans of the IMF and World Bank (cf.
Van de Walle 1993)?

One observer suggests that "when the current illusions about the 'free
market' wear off, democracy may well incline people to think again about
the distribution of and accountability for economic as well as political
power" (Young 1993: 309). There is nothing mechanical or inevitable
about the reproduction of current liberal market orthodoxy. These contemporary silences in public discourse too are susceptible to shattering.

"The profoundness of the silences generated in one sphere of power
may be proportional to the explosive speech in another sphere," writes
Scott (1990: 176). While this chapter's focus has been the "explosive
speech" of the early 1990s, the next takes up earlier silences. Such silences
are strategic rather than natural. How are they created and maintained?
To enforce them the state depends in part on instruments of physical
coercion (military, paramilitary, police, courts, prisons). Also helpful,
however, are potent symbolic means of control. In Kenya the *baraza* is the
state's principal symbolic battleground, and its central political ritual.
The next chapter considers what symbolic weapons helped the Kenyatta
and Moi regimes to survive for so long, and examines the continuities
between colonial and post-colonial moral bargains which the state has
struck with citizens. Such bargains can both contribute to state legitimacy
and define moral expectations, whose violation leads to popular outrage.

In 1978, when Moi became president, new national symbols and traditions had to be invented and diffused quickly. The urgency was to
legitimize a new regime after the death of the country's first president and
nationalist hero, the charismatic Jomo Kenyatta. Moi's own colonial
political stance had been very different from that of Kenyatta, but he
needed to create an impression of similar historical legitimacy. The

symbolic measures he took to do so during his first months in office in 1978–9 included participation in countless *baraza* across the country. *Baraza* at this moment of transition enshrine the very process of creating a national political culture, and "traditionalizing" new material (cf. S. F. Moore 1977: 7). New symbols and forms of public display were quickly routinized. Outwardly compliant citizens cheered enthusiastically, and collusively ignored open secrets. The political explosions of the early 1990s, however, illustrate the fragility of that collusion.

3   Open secrets: everyday forms of domination before 1990

> To give a government the authority necessary for it, it is not enough to feel the need for this authority; we must have recourse to the only sources from which all authority is derived. We must, namely, establish traditions, a common spirit.
>
> (Durkheim 1938: 90)

> Official language . . . sanctions and imposes what it states, tacitly laying down the dividing line between the thinkable and the unthinkable, thereby contributing towards the maintenance of the symbolic order from which it draws its authority.
>
> (Bourdieu 1977: 21)

Introduction

What is "Kenya" to women and men in Embu or any other countryside locale? A key institution that helps to anchor that abstraction in everyday life is the public assembly or *baraza*. Does a successful *baraza* help to constitute that Durkheimian "common spirit" necessary to sustain government authority? Even if answered affirmatively, this assertion provokes additional questions. As Kertzer (1988: 67) notes, "ritual can serve political organizations by producing bonds of solidarity without requiring uniformity of belief." Thus a *baraza* crowd cheering enthusiastically in outward display of compliance with the ruling regime can create "solidarity" whatever the content of its private beliefs. It is joint participation in the ritual[1] that is crucial to the polity. In precisely what sense, however, is such ritual socially integrative? To what extent do such occasions express or constitute value consensus? What models of the polity do they convey, and from what alternative conceptions do they deflect attention? Whose interests (those of which social groups) do these rituals serve?

These are questions inspired in part by Lukes' (1975) criticisms of normative functionalism, particularly the assumption "that value integration is the central aspect of the integration of a society" (Lukes 1975: 297). Instead, he suggests, individuals within a society are likely to hold "socially-patterned differences of interpretation" of values and rituals (Lukes 1975: 298). Indeed, value consensus is neither necessary nor sufficient to ensure social integration (Lukes 1975: 298). If social integration does not require value consensus, does social order depend nonetheless upon keeping open secrets out of the public domain? Many state officials in colonial and post-colonial Kenya and elsewhere would answer in the affirmative.

Keeping open secrets out of public talk requires concerted effort by the state. To preserve public silences and to marginalize critics the state deploys both coercive and symbolic weapons. In the symbolic arsenal the Kenyan *baraza* is a key institution. These state rituals were crucial to both colonial and post-colonial efforts to prevent the kinds of upheavals that occurred in the early 1990s (see chapter 2).

While the last chapter explored the "shattered silences" of 1990–3, this one takes up preceding public silences and their institutional safeguards. These "everyday forms of domination"[2] rest on paper-thin forms of collusion: between populace and state officials displaying deference to the president, and among citizens displaying deference to officials. Precisely what keeps these poses intact requires explanation. Anthropologists of late have given less attention to such "everyday forms of domination" than they have to "everyday forms of resistance" (Vincent 1990: 403–406).[3]

Baraza offer a stage on which state elites use political oratory to foster national unity, territorial identification, and loyalty to the ruling regime. Here we see the construction and diffusion of national culture: those "intentional elite products which draw on elite, folk, mass and popular forms, and use indigenous as well as cosmopolitan technologies of reproduction and dissemination" (Appadurai and Breckenridge 1988: 6). The symbolic activities of the nation-state include constructing national histories, and inventing and recycling traditions and ethnic identities (Hobsbawm and Ranger 1983, Vail 1989; Siu 1990). Such constructions or representations are the outcome of historical struggles among competing agents who press alternative political claims. Political oratory captures part of the process of such claim-staking.

In pressing alternative political claims historical agents create and sustain particular ideologies or "systems of belief that uphold sectional interests while appearing to express general ones" (Donham 1990: 49). As Kelly puts it, "it is the thrust of ideological representation both to generalize and to naturalize; to claim for specific interests a natural universality" (Kelly 1991: 423). Creating a national culture involves attempts to make arbitrary categories or boundaries appear natural and to have them taken for granted. That is, "contingent and constructed identities become rendered as attributes of a self-evident and unquestioned order of things" (Foster 1991: 237).

Who takes such a social order for granted, to what extent, and with what effects are always difficult to determine. Any oratorical assertion can "bring to consciousness evidence for the contrary position" (Murray Edelman 1988: 10). One might ask, for example, whether jovial outward shows of compliance by *baraza* audiences do not have the unintended effect of helping to constitute a solidary, though disguised, mocking of or opposition to apparently shared values (cf. Scott 1985, 1986). One effect of disguising non-belief, of course, may be to strengthen the dominant state authorities who sponsor *baraza*. Another effect, however, is the construction of symbolic resources upon which future open opposition may draw. In the early 1990s, as noted in chapter 1, opposition leaders asserted publicly that *baraza* crowds cheering and chanting official KANU slogans are "out to entertain themselves" or to "flatter their leaders" (Imanyara and Maina 1991: 17). That is, Moi's opponents drew public attention to the possibly misleading nature of customary *baraza* behavior. In doing so they converted to strategic weapons what were once open secrets politely ignored (cf. Bailey 1991).[4]

State rituals such as *baraza* have a great deal to do with what Lonsdale (1981: 160) terms the "uncertainties of rule": "the first purpose of the rituals of power is surely to give confidence to the actors, rulers." Thus *baraza* held early in the colonial era were efforts by new district officers and chiefs to convince both themselves and those they ruled of the legitimacy of a new order. The same is true of the many *baraza* Moi held across the country during his first months in office, as he grew into his new role as president.[5]

This chapter invites consideration of questions that lie at the intersection of social theory, sociolinguistics, and political anthropology. In addressing the language of politics this chapter draws attention, for example, to what Myers and Brenneis (1984: 24) in another context refer to as the "linguistic work" necessary to create and maintain any political arena.[6] It looks at the underexplored theme of how public display of linguistic affect helps to constitute relations of power or hegemony in a nation-state (see Besnier 1990: 437). To phrase the issues this way is to assume, as Gal puts it, that "language is multifunctional (and) it can be seen as denotational, indexical of social structure, and simultaneously as constitutive of it" (Gal 1989: 347). Sociolinguists (Gal 1989, 1991) are giving new attention to such questions in multicultural, largescale contexts, in ways that recognize that the boundaries of a "society" or "culture" are "different in every different context of action, and in every domain of discourse" (Feierman 1990: 35). These themes are related to larger issues of social theory concerning the balance between coercion and persuasion, between constraint and creativity, between "structure" and "agency" (see Bourdieu 1977; Giddens 1979; Abrams 1982; Ortner 1984; Karp 1986).

It is therefore helpful to consider how the *baraza* as event is related to social structure or culture. Anthropologists have taken various approaches to the relationship between structure and event. Recently scholars such as Gal (1991) and S. F. Moore (1987) have argued that social events are not best understood as simple reflections or reflexes of an already existing and presumably coherent social or cultural system. Rather, "such events are the means by which some groups make contingent claims to shore up a social order, in response to attempts by others to dismantle it" (Gal 1991: 442). Indeed rather than "an order" or "a structure," it is helpful to think in terms of "part-structures being built and torn down," "a complex mix of order, antiorder, and nonorder," and "contingencies of form" (S. F. Moore 1987: 730). Building on these theoretical points, individual orators at *baraza* can be understood to create as much as to enact political structures, or "part-structures."[7]

A *baraza* is more than a ritual with predictable consequences. Formal oratory can backfire, occasioning total challenges to the system of authority it embodies (Bloch 1975: 24–25). An audience may ridicule or refuse to accept the status of a speaker. Individuals in a *baraza* audience sometimes shout questions that refer to scandals such as misuse of local funds collected for a development project. Official speakers do refer to alternative political possibilities, even if only to criticize them and dismiss them. To mention them officially, however, is to acknowledge their importance. In short, *baraza* rhetoric offers a partly-obscured window[8] on powerful political cross-currents in Kenya.

What official oratory obscures, and how and why it does so, of course vary from one historical moment to another. The *baraza* of the early 1990s from which I quoted in the last chapter were a stunning departure from earlier practice, in that the political opposition began to speak on more public stages and eventually was allowed its own *baraza*. In earlier years regime opponents were usually offstage interlocutors at most (a common pattern in Africa's colonial and one-party states). Under the latter circumstances, which have dominated much of Kenya's colonial and post-colonial history, political contests become less public but no less vigorous.

That political energy – however channeled – makes any *baraza* an amalgam of danger and security. This chapter explores that mix in pre-1990 *baraza*. While the public assemblies from which I quoted in the last chapter were often rallies attended by thousands of people in Nairobi, those included in this chapter are rural and much smaller (100–300 people). The last chapter's oratorical quotes are from secondary sources. This chapter draws occasionally on colonial archives, but mainly on verbatim transcripts of *baraza* I attended in rural Embu District. Here I give considerable attention to gatherings held in rural Embu at a crucial turning point in Kenya's history: namely, the first months of the Moi regime, when new legitimating political symbols had to be diffused and "traditionalized" quickly. Here we see a national political culture in the making.

The chapter is organized as follows. I begin by briefly introducing Embu, the ethnographic setting of this narrative (see map 3). I then outline what occurs at *baraza* in general: who speaks and in what languages, what is said (and not said), speaking style, and rhetorical devices. Next I consider particular colonial and post-colonial *baraza* themes: notably, the ideology of "order," the tension between authoritarianism and democracy, and moral bargains the state strikes with the populace. The chapter then takes up the historic 1978 turn in Kenya's national political culture when Moi became president. The chapter's conclusions pursue theoretical issues introduced above.

Embu: a brief introduction[9]

Embu is the name of both a district and an official ethnic category (see Map 2). The district, a wedge-shaped territory in Mt. Kenya's fertile southeastern foothills, is occupied by both Embu and Mbeere peoples.[10] (Again, such ethnic labels do not represent "natural" or "primordial" units.) The Embu people, who numbered about 180,000 in 1979,[11] live in the district's agriculturally-productive highlands nearest Mt. Kenya. They are cultivators of tea, coffee, cotton, maize, beans, bananas, potatoes, and other foods, as well as herders of small stock (goats, sheep) and small numbers of cattle. The Mbeere people, who numbered about 62,000 in 1979, are farmers and herders in the lower altitude portions of the district, where rainfall is less reliable and land less fertile.

Though the people officially categorized as "Embu" represent just over 1 percent of the national population, the district has more influence in Nairobi than its relatively small population size alone might suggest (Moris 1970). The Embu population is just a fraction of the size of that of the Gikuyu, who with about one-fifth of the nation's people are Kenya's largest official ethnic category. However, the Embu and neighboring Meru peoples share with the Gikuyu strong cultural and linguistic similarities, as well as ties of exchange and political alliance. These three groups who surround Mt. Kenya were active allies in the 1950s "Mau Mau" rebellion, and later joined to form the Gikuyu Embu Meru Association (GEMA), a nationally prominent association of political and economic interests that, along with other "tribal organizations" (as they were termed in local media and official rhetoric), was disbanded by a presidential directive in 1979. Though relationships within and among these three ethnic groups include multiple lines of competition and conflict, as a bloc they form a powerful player on the national political scene.[12]

In addition to being close to the political center of power Embu is also part of a thriving regional economy that in many respects was both the colony's and the nation's economic "center." All of the groups in Mt. Kenya's fertile foothills had more privileged access to state resources and market opportunities than did people in many other parts of the country. Central Kenyan societies both suffered and benefited from their more direct exposure to colonial officers and institutions.

These aspects of Embu's position in the national political economy helped to shape local *baraza*. The particular form of the institution I describe, therefore, cannot be taken as representative of other parts of colonial or post-colonial Kenya.

Baraza

The term *baraza* may have been introduced into Swahili from Arabic or Persian or both (see Johnson 1939). Its Persian meaning is royal court. A late-nineteenth-century Swahili dictionary (Krapf 1882) defines *baraza* as follows: "a stone seat or bench table, either outside of the house or in the hall, where the master sits in public and receives his friends; hence the public audience held by the Sultan and the council then held; meeting of a council." Contemporary and later colonial meanings of the word continue to refer to a type of meeting place, to the meeting itself (council, cabinet, court of law), or to the members of a particular council or committee (Johnson 1939). One meaning the term had in colonial days, for example, refers to a shed or other structure in which a village headman or administrative officers hold public meetings. In short, the term connotes contrasting social contexts of hierarchy and relative equality: a sultan holding a public audience, a colonial administrator addressing the public, the master of a house receiving his male friends, or a council of elders meeting to adjudicate a local dispute.

My focus in this chapter is on *baraza* that are official gatherings at the level of the administrative location or division,[13] and which are organized by the provincial administration. Such gatherings usually aim at most at a pro forma popular consensus, rather than vital debate of issues. *Baraza* of this type include (but are not limited to) *Harambee* fundraising meetings, political party rallies, and multipurpose gatherings at which state officials transmit policy or program directives, or instruct people in agricultural techniques and health measures. Fundraising rallies are held for *Haram-*

bee self-help projects, such as new schools, roads, churches, and dispensaries. Organizing such development projects, as noted in chapter 2, has been one of the principal means of accountability in Kenyan electoral politics.[14] The balance of dialogue and monologue during *baraza* varies and is sometimes openly contested, but officials may permit more questions from the audience at less politically-charged, smaller meetings, such as those at which agricultural extension or veterinary officers instruct farmers on crop and livestock care. Any *baraza*, however, may provoke outbursts by individuals in the audience. For example, just as a prominent speaker at a *Harambee* fundraising rally announces his generous donation to a new secondary school, an individual in the crowd might shout out a question about a previous bounced check contributed on another such occasion by the same person.

Languages spoken

Baraza oratory is a striking linguistic *mélange*, with strategic and sociolinguistically significant shifts from one language to another both within and between speeches. For a skillful *baraza* speaker, aware of the heterogeneity of his or her audience, and of the differences in social status accorded to each linguistic code, code-switching within and between sentences is a crucial means of negotiating identity and meanings with an audience.

The principal language of the *baraza* in Kenya is Swahili (or Kiswahili, but I follow conventional use in dropping the prefix) in most urban areas and in ethnically heterogeneous rural areas. In more homogeneous rural and urban areas the first language of the dominant ethnic group is used when attending officials are of the same group. Many Kenyans are bilingual or multilingual, speaking a first language,[15] together with Swahili or English, or both (see Biersteker and Njogu 1991). English is Kenya's "official" language, Swahili its "national" language (see Whiteley 1969, 1974). Parliamentary business is conducted in both languages, and parliamentary candidates must pass exams in both languages. English is the official language of much written government business. It is also the language of instruction in universities, secondary schools, and the later years of primary school. Indeed, in some primary and secondary schools students are punished if heard speaking either Swahili or their first language.[16]

Swahili[17] is sometimes popularly known as the "language of work" (*lugha ya kazi*). It is the language of trade and markets, of many town-dwellers, of multiethnic political rallies, and of the lower ranks of the military, police, and civil service. It is not as widely spoken as it might have been had colonial divide-and-rule policies not discouraged the teaching of Swahili in Kenyan schools. In the mid-1980s Swahili became a compulsory examination subject for the Kenya Certificate of Primary Education examination.

In Kenya, as elsewhere, code-switching is a sociolinguistically significant strategy that is connected to the power asymmetries of languages, and to individual negotiation of power and status in conversation.[18] Code-switching among English, Swahili, and a first language is a mark of academic, political, and administrative elite status in Kenya. As Gal (1989: 357) remarks about code-switching in general, "code-switching and language choice ... can be interpreted as symbolic expressions of identity or relations of domination and thus as constitutive parts of political economic relations."

Language choice in a *baraza* may either reinforce or challenge the current political hierarchy, which accords higher status to English than to Swahili. For example, one of the most junior politicians at a public assembly in rural Embu that included nationally prominent individuals such as the minister of agriculture inserted a few English words and phrases into a speech in the Embu language (Kiembu: again I drop the prefix).[19] His occasional use of English words does not convey the same message to everyone in his audience. On the one hand, to the well-educated his code-switches reaffirm the gap between him and his superiors because his use of English is more forced (slower, with heavier Embu language accent) than that likely in the opening remarks of a senior official accustomed to speaking English in most of his daily work. His English words, then, are a sign of deference to his seniors and a confirmation of his subordinate relationship to them. On the other hand, his code-switching also conveys a message of superiority to the many non-educated persons in his audience, who recognize that he uses words from the country's language of power, but do not themselves perceive the differences in English fluency that are apparent to the well-educated.

The linguistic strategy might be reversed in the case of a well-educated senior politician addressing the same audience. In this instance the official may find it most important to demonstrate fluency not in English (which is taken for granted), but in the first language of his natal region: to show that he has not forgotten it after taking up life in the city or in international circles. For example, when discussing the possible political ambitions of one former cabinet minister (a Gikuyu man married to a British woman), Kenyans often mock his fine clothes and manner and speculate about whether he could address a rally in his home district in the Gikuyu language.

Finally, code-switching during *baraza* may occur with reiteration, amplification, or alteration of a point made previously in another language. For example, an Embu chief strategically repeats some key points in both Embu and Swahili, when his listeners include both a Swahili-speaking non-local district officer on the speaker's platform, and a local audience among whom many are unaccustomed to Swahili. A head of state addressing a national assembly emphasizes some points in English for his international audience, and others in Swahili or another language for various local audiences. Of course, such switches leave ample opportunity to shade meanings differently for different segments of a heterogeneous audience. And the meaning of the switch itself is open to different interpretations. That is, speakers exploit the indexical nature of code-switching, its different meanings in different contexts, and its potential to escape the audience's explicit scrutiny.

Who speaks?

Who addresses a *baraza* is a politically charged issue. This is a forum where *who* can speak is a matter regulated during the meeting by a master of ceremonies (often a government-appointed chief).[20] Before the meeting, organizing authorities (such as the chief or district officer) schedule their own meeting to discuss themes and speakers. There is always some flexibility about who will address a meeting and in what order, since it is never certain in advance who will turn up and when. The master of ceremonies and individuals on the speakers' platform make final decisions during the meeting about who speaks and in what sequence. A prominent guest of honor, such as a cabinet minister or provincial commissioner, is likely to give a keynote address late in the meeting, and may not even arrive until the event has been underway for an hour or more. It is not unusual for fifteen or more speakers to address a single gathering. The master of ceremonies invites selected speakers to "greet the people," giving them an opportunity to make a speech if they wish. Those who precede the guest of honor are expected to give much shorter addresses. The guest of honor has no time limit. Speaking time is an approximate index of social status.

What aspects of individual identity define who may speak? *Baraza* fit one of the parameters that define formal events (Irvine 1979: 778), in that they "invoke positional and public, rather than personal, identities." Which rungs of the administrative and political ladders are represented at *baraza* varies. At one end of the spectrum they may be small gatherings organized by an assistant chief for an administrative sub-location, at which he and perhaps a junior agricultural or health officer may speak. At larger assemblies organized at the level of a division or district, speakers include figures such as provincial commissioners, cabinet ministers, members of parliament, or the president himself. Since most politicians and senior bureaucrats are male it is unusual for women to address *baraza*. Nor do women in the audience often speak out publicly. Exceptions occur when, for example, health or home economics officers speak before these gatherings for pedagogical reasons.

Politicians in power in a particular locality prefer not to share a speaker's platform with political opponents or competitors who are not in office. Outside political campaign periods, then, a sitting member of parliament is unlikely to welcome as *baraza* cospeaker a rival for his elected position. Sometimes such a rival may be seated at the front of the gathering and not be invited to address it. Not inviting him or her to speak may occur by prior agreement, or it may be a surprise, and construed (by would-be speaker and attending supporters) as a slight or insult. If political antagonists are allowed to address the same gathering, then the sitting member of parliament or the administrative officer who convenes the meeting may try to set a neutral tone at the outset by stating that the focus of the gathering is "development" rather than "politics" (a contentious distinction officials often invoke in Kenya as they assert the primacy of the former over the latter). To claim "development" rather than "politics" as the meeting's focus is to attempt to discourage or undermine in advance explicitly critical or politically incendiary words a rival may utter.

The speakable and the unspeakable

By controlling who can speak at a *baraza*, the organizing officials also control to a large degree what is said. There is a moving boundary between what can and cannot be stated publicly; the president himself indirectly sets the limits of what is speakable and what invites state retribution (harassment, surveillance, detention, denial of commercial licenses). As discussed in the previous chapter, differences of ideology and class are seldom safe public themes. Indeed, scholars disagree about the extent of ideological differences in post-independence Kenyan politics. During the 1960s, in a cold war context, participants in conflicts within KANU portrayed their differences as ideological: between one party wing oriented toward the West and one sympathetic to socialism. Githu (1992: 15), however, suggests that "in reality the ideological gap was not as wide as commentators like Colin Leys have suggested." The populist rhetoric of MP J. M. Kariuki "reopen(ed) the ideological debate that had been suspended on the banning of the KPU" in 1969 (Githu 1992: 33). The ruling regime viewed this as a threat and many believed it therefore arranged Kariuki's assassination in 1975 (which itself provoked a crisis of legitimacy for those in power). In short, since independence, when various populist and leftist rhetorics have surfaced occasionally state officials have attempted quickly to marginalize or eliminate them. Denying their advocates access to the public forum such as *baraza*, as noted earlier, is one means of accomplishing this.

Although *baraza* are not a forum for open debate about official economic or political philosophies and policies, controversial matters are occasionally introduced by indirect speech, audience interjection, threats, questions, humor, and so on (as discussed below). Much of the time, however, *baraza* speakers and audiences practice what Bailey terms more generally a "strategy of keeping open secrets out of the public domain" (Bailey 1991: 52).

One hears a number of different forms of rhetoric at *baraza*, ranging from the celebratory, the hortatory, to the pedagogical. Kenyan political speech is often homiletic (cf. Firth 1975), extolling the virtues of hard work, education, and respect for those in positions of authority or leadership. Speakers urge parents to send their children to school, to dip their cattle and to plant grass for them, to spray their coffee trees, to dig pit latrines, and so on. *Baraza* also occasion local requests for various forms of government assistance, usually for social services such as schools, health centers, and improved roads. Such requests may be incorporated into special songs and dances rehearsed for the occasion by local school choirs and women's groups. Especially during political campaigns candidates addressing *baraza* compete with one another in claiming responsibility for local development projects.

A *baraza* speech usually begins with fairly formulaic greetings to a number of categories of people, as in the following two examples. (See the transcript key at the end of this chapter for an explanation of notations used in this and later excerpts from audio recordings of *baraza*.)

Chief, councillor, assistant chief, officers of the government, ladies and gentlemen.[21]

Honorable guest the Minister of Agriculture and teacher A————, Chairman of the KTDA, teacher B————, DC of Embu who is here in place of the PC Mr. C————, Mr. ————— Provincial Director of Agriculture of Eastern Province Mr. D————, Provincial Crop Officer of Eastern Province, mayor of Embu honorable guest, the head of police of this area, all chairmen of KANU, chairmen of the county councils of Kirinyagga and Embu, mayor of Embu, ... and honorable guests.[22]

Either before or after such a list, the speaker is likely to say to the entire audience "how are you," to which they reply "we are fine." The speaker might then thank the organizer of the meeting, emphasize the importance of its theme, and proceed to give a supporting address. The guest of honor and highest-ranking officials may talk for up to an hour. Others give addresses of varying length (e.g., five to twenty minutes), without explicit time limits. At the end of the body of the address and sometimes just after the opening greetings, the speaker is likely to engage the crowd in a series of formulaic repetitions of political slogans (e.g., *Harambee*! and *Nyayo*!). The end of an address is marked by a simple "thank-you," or "stay well, people of————." The master of ceremonies then introduces the next speaker, sometimes simply by giving his or her name and official title, or by adding preliminary remarks about how fine a leader the person is. When introducing a guest of honor, the chair may engage the crowd in an exchange of syncopated claps that punctuate brief phrases of personal praise and gratitude to the notable for exercising wise leadership, and so on.

The *baraza* is a forum in which both elites and subordinate groups usually conform to "the well known, if not overtly stated, ideological boundaries drawn around acceptable political discourse" (Ford and Holmquist 1988: 161). Meanings that cannot be contested openly at a public assembly are reworked in other contexts such as offstage gossip, subversive music, or underground political pamphlets. The official speeches at *baraza*, part of the state's "everyday forms of domination," both fuel and reflect political talk in offstage arenas.

The relationship between onstage and offstage political talk, or between "official" and "unofficial" language, is more complex than that suggested by an opposition between what is "real" or sincere, and what is a "cover" or hypocritical. Words spoken publicly at a *baraza* include those of officials sincerely trying to accomplish government aims they believe to have merit (see Nellis 1973; Brokensha and Nellis 1974; Parkin 1975). For a government officer to possess "a strong belief in the efficacy of administrative exhortation and control" (Brokensha and Nellis 1974: 517) is by no means unusual.

What is said at *baraza* is never entirely predictable. Indeed, in Kenya as elsewhere "it is the partial unpredictability of the oratory" that arouses interest on the part of those attending (Keenan 1975: 112). *Baraza* provide a platform for those in power to threaten rivals, opponents, and political dissidents. They capture the unexpected rise and decline of personal influence in elite political circles. Politicians speaking at *baraza* threaten to name publicly figures behind scandals, and thereby to humiliate dissenters or rivals whom they wish to eclipse. The downfall of a prominent person (such as the country's vice-president in 1989) may be orchestrated from the center of power through a series of *baraza*. Thus, such assemblies give the audience some sense of power in allowing them occasionally to see the powerful fall. Coercion as practiced among the elite is sometimes as striking as that practiced by elites on the rest of the population.

Baraza, then, afford glimpses of a wider and more secret arena of politics, and constitute a sphere of contested meanings that play into Kenya's frequent factional disputes and power struggles offstage. Words uttered onstage crucially shape public understandings of the political order, and indirectly inform listeners how to manipulate political symbols in ways acceptable to those in power.

Political oratory is a vehicle not only of official messages and ideology, but also of counter-messages, both intended and unintended. Parkin notes that "under the cover of set terms and vocabulary, the rebellious and disadvantaged (can) ... smuggle in new meanings" (Parkin 1984: 352). In addition, speakers who invoke such terms as democracy, education, or development allow "listeners to assess their existing conditions in the light of these promises." Political speech always engages opposing interlocutors: some silent, some noisy.

Finally, the backdrop of patron–client politics described in the last chapter is crucial to understanding *baraza*. These gatherings mediate the construction of new patron–client pyramids, and provide the space for leaders to appeal directly to constituents. This is an arena in which reputations collapse and blossom, as individuals negotiate positions within patron–client hierarchies. An individual in the audience who publicly challenges or antagonizes a speaker risks his or her own access to economic opportunities and resources. A politician who publicly expresses opposition to government policies or senior officials jeopardizes his or her own position, and possibly constituents' collective access to central government funds to support public goods and services (schools, roads, mains water, health centers). During Moi's first year as president, when he addressed countless *baraza* around the country, many people in Embu speculated that his reason for not visiting the district was displeasure with a senior local politician who ran against the new president's preferred candidate for the party vice-presidency. People in Embu perceived this as a financial loss for the district because presidential visits often involve large fundraising rallies for local *Harambee* self-help projects. Such material concerns help to shape *baraza* oratory and audience response.

Speaking style

Skill in oratory, or the "ability to hold a crowd," was one criterion British administrators used to select Kenyan colonial chiefs (Leonard 1991: 27). In central Kenya's pre-colonial societies oratorical skill, along with military prowess, contributed to personal reputations. Rhetorical art was displayed, for example, when councils of elders met to hear and resolve disputes.[23] So, too, *baraza* audiences today judge the rhetorical skills of those who address them. An effective speaker talks forcefully and excites listeners. The elements of success may include a histrionic style, and skillful use of humor, irony, mimicry, curses, or figures of speech.

Some pre-colonial oral skills, however, have been nearly lost. The *baraza* does not call upon the kinds of literary and oratorical skills found, for example, in pre-colonial dialogue poetry (in Gikuyu and Swahili) in central and coastal Kenya (see Njogu 1993, 1994). Dialogue poetry required individuals to compose competitively and spontaneously oral poetry that followed a specified metre and rhyme, while at the same time allowing the poets room for originality (see Pick 1973; Abdulaziz 1979; Njogu 1991). Today there are few surviving practitioners of this art. Other disappearing competitive oral genres in central Kenya include pre-colonial courtship and marriage negotiations (Kenyatta 1965; and Leakey 1977, vol. ii), and riddles (see Mwaniki 1971; Pick 1973). The use of such genres, of course, presupposes deeply shared beliefs and cultural understandings between speaker and audience. Many of today's gatherings, however, are polyglot and culturally heterogeneous. Earlier oral forms were likely to include more prominent use of ambiguous metaphors and other figurative language than is usual today. Contemporary political rhetoric nonetheless does draw on some pre-colonial cultural expressions, such as curses, proverbs, and metaphors.[24]

A Gikuyu curse (*kirumi*), for example, was one tool a cabinet minister used in May 1990 to condemn advocates of a multiparty political system: "Those out to divide us should disappear, dry up, and perish."[25] This speaker also suggested that multiparty advocates would be consumed by Kenyatta's curse: "Kenyatta died the other day and we should let him rest in peace without bringing in divisions among people, and those doing it will be haunted by his spirit ... Those who want two political parties will by haunted by Kenyatta's spirit."[26] For 1990s leaders to invoke Kenyatta in the debate about a multiparty versus a one-party political system is to appeal to Gikuyu beliefs about the dead, implying that the deceased Kenyatta left a curse on multiparty advocates. Kenyatta himself, at a large rally years earlier, had also "employed a traditional Gikuyu curse to consign the Opposition to oblivion," saying the Kenya People's Union (KPU) would be "lost in the roots of the Mikongoi tree" (Gertzel 1970: 145).[27] In a still earlier political era, before World War I, Gikuyu who converted to Christianity and received mission educations were cursed by their elders, who "even attempted to deny their rights of inheritance" (Clough 1990: 26). In short, curses rooted in notions of family morality have a long history in Kenyan political contests.

The curse has long been a potent threat in central Kenya. A father, for example, had the power to curse a son who displeased him, or who did not respect his authority. He might threaten the son with physical as well as social death, saying, for example, that the son will produce no sons of his own. Glazier offers examples of Mbeere curses: "Njiru cursed his son by throwing ashes and saying, 'may Ireri be lost like these ashes,'" and "you will perish like that soil, together with your daughters of whom you are so proud" (Glazier 1985: 153, 288).

Proverbs and figurative speech pepper *baraza* rhetoric. To quiet a grumbling and murmuring audience, for example, an Embu chief at a 1980 gathering said "let the bees enter the hive now."[28] At that meeting state officials urged farmers to apply for loans to purchase exotic breeds of cattle in order to increase local milk production. As a district commissioner advised farmers to diversify their income sources, he quoted the Gikuyu proverb: "one castor nut made the dove spend the night hungry"[29] (see chapter 5). His message was that farmers should not be like the dove that waited in vain all night for one castor nut to fall from a tree. That is, they should not rely on coffee income alone. He repeated a common theme of the time, saying that Kenya is on the run and that those who cannot keep up will be left behind.

A local cooperative society official at the same 1980 assembly compared the delicacy of exotic breeds of cattle to whites who come to Africa. He noted that whites, unlike Africans, became very concerned if they were bitten by chiggers and would do anything necessary to get rid of larvae deposited under the skin (including returning to doctors in their home countries). He used this illustration to emphasize the importance of having enough local cattle dips to keep exotic cattle healthy.

Metaphors of bridewealth and marriage are common also in political rhetoric, as indeed are idioms of kinship in much African political discourse (see Kopytoff 1987: 37–39). For example, I heard a district commissioner in 1980 draw a *baraza* discussion about the exotic cattle loan program to a close by saying, "a long controversy is only when *'uthoni'* is dying."[30] ("*Uthoni*" here refers to the marriage and bridewealth negotiations that take place between bride's and groom's families.) That is, the points of controversy (taken up later in this chapter) did not mean the actual "marriage" (here a metaphor for the loan program) was threatened. In September 1991, at a large anti-opposition rally organized by state officials in Narok, one speaker "likened FORD members to adulterers who wanted to wreck a home they had not built," and another "likened them to 'prostitutes' who went to Chester House to 'sell themselves' to foreign masters."[31] So, too, cultural idioms of generation-based authority occur in much political talk (cf. Parkin 1978). For example, to suggest solidarity among males of different lineages a man might mention their status as fathers whose eldest sons have been initiated.

Another common stylistic feature of *baraza* speeches is solicitation of audience response when posing a rhetorical question. These questions are a means of involving an audience, exerting control, inducing support or compliance, and establishing consensus.[32] When Kenyan politicians or state authorities ask rhetorical questions of an audience, the answer becomes self-evident mainly due to the authority and power of those permitted to be on the speaker's platform. Such questions are a tool of symbolic coercion by agents of the state.

Note, for example, how one Embu KANU official in 1979 solicited a show of audience support for the local MP. The official refers to Nairobi newspaper reports that local people have lost faith in their MP, an ally and supporter of the cabinet minister who is a guest of honor at this *baraza*. The KANU official then says (MAR479: A,22):

The person who does not have faith in our representative is WHO? ( ) Let him raise his hand! THOSE WHO DO HAVE FAITH IN OUR REPRESENTATIVE ( ) LET THEM RAISE THEIR HANDS. It is everyone!

In spite of the audience's outward compliance, offstage many individuals expressed dissatisfaction with the MP in question, and with his clientelist relationship with the cabinet minister. Nevertheless, the power of those on the speaker's platform is (at least momentarily) sufficient to block dissident replies, to intimidate an audience into suppressing dissenting opinions. Conventions of "politeness" and respect for authority, as well as fear of reprisals, help to preserve public silence on such occasions.

In short, the Kenyan *baraza*, a seemingly predictable state ritual, is also a risk-laden occasion for both speakers and audience. It is a crucial forum for the public expression of what Geertz terms the "symbolic dimensions of state power" (1981: 122). Here we see both the "ordering force of display" and ceremony, and the unpredictable drama of onstage perform-ances by leaders whose survival depends in part on their capacity to hold or to sway a crowd. A convincing performance requires moral force. What are the principles from which that moral force springs?

An implicit moral contract: paternalism, authoritarianism, "development"

Heir to the Enlightenment myth of progress, and building on "the myth of the civilizing mission,"[33] colonial state paternalism included promises (conveyed through its own rhetoric) of improvements in material well-being. In asserting such service to their subjects to be their aim colonial rulers laid the symbolic foundation for subsequent complaints against their rule. *Baraza* rhetoric helped to diffuse notions of a moral contract between citizens and the state. That contract inspired popular expectations that could fuel dissent as well as compliance.

In what follows I do not mean to exaggerate the institutional or ideological coherence of the colonial state. Instead I recognize, as Berman and Lonsdale (1992a: 4) put it, that "the colonial state in Kenya was only the partly intended outcome of the often contested interaction of numerous impersonal structural forces and subjective agents, both metropolitan and local." That is, historical flux more than structural rigidity, is the emphasis. In addition, there is no need to assume either that rulers' moral claims have legitimation as their purpose, or that claims to legitimacy must be phrased in idioms of morality (Kopytoff 1987: 71).

Colonial rhetoric implied that citizens could exchange their political rights for material well-being and social order. In their public rhetoric, and when they trained future Kenyan civil servants, British colonial authorities emphasized the need to preserve civil order (Leonard 1991: 53–54), rather than to institutionalize democratic processes:

It is a misrepresentation to say that the British conceptions of democratic rule, a bureaucracy oriented to service and development, and a civil service bound by strict conflict-of-interest ethics failed to take root on African soil. The truth is that the attempts to plant these ideas and the institutions to support them came very late in the colonial era and were quickly choked out by the already vigorous authoritarian conceptions that the British themselves had planted and nurtured earlier. (Leonard 1991: 285)

Colonial state authoritarianism – justified as a need to preserve order – nonetheless came into conflict with existing cultural notions of personal accountability, and with moral obligations implied by state paternalism.

An example of colonial rhetoric that conveyed to people in Embu District the paternalist bargain for material improvements is the 1925 welcoming speech of a colonial officer at the first meeting of the Embu Local Native Council (LNC).[34] The official minutes summarize his remarks as follows:[35]

Government had formed these Councils because it considered the people fit for them. Members of the Council were as elder sons who are now sufficiently responsible to be called in to advise their fathers in the management of the family's estate. *Government was the biggest father in the country and has its children everywhere.* In these days of progress the people wanted more things and more things were possible. For example, fire and light, lamps, oil, matches, etc. Children must be educated to understand these things, but that did not mean the good things of the old times should be forgotten; such as obedience to their elders and chiefs and observance of discipline. (My emphasis.)

These remarks capture themes that were to be played out over succeeding decades: the government as father and ordinary citizens as children, the benefits of progress, and the value of tradition. Of course the British did not introduce into central Kenya the notion that political authorities bore some responsibility for others' material well-being. Before colonial rule the most senior political authorities were elders whose communal obligations included various rites associated with the agricultural cycle and with rainfall (see Kenyatta 1965; Leakey 1977; Glazier 1985). The colonial state defined through its rhetoric its own arena of material responsibility for citizens.[36]

After each LNC meeting, members (chiefs[37] and elders) were to convene *baraza* in their home areas to inform people of what had been decided or accomplished. Since the LNCs were established in 1924 in part because of African demands for fuller participation in the new colonial system, *baraza* formally offered an opportunity for citizens to be heard in a state-sponsored forum. In practice, however, the LNCs "were instruments of cooptation and control," to which regime sympathizers were appointed (Leonard 1991: 31). From the start *baraza* were formally constrained by official state concerns with preserving "stability" and suppressing political activity.

Ostensibly, *baraza* afforded colonial district commissioners the opportunity to hear the complaints and requests of the ruled, as well as to announce government policies. There was, however, more lecturing than listening to complaints:

The paternalism of British administrators certainly circumscribed political expression. Until after World War I, the only opportunities for Africans to express their needs and grievances directly to the British government came at the barazas that district commissioners (DC) held irregularly in the locations, and DCs called people to these meetings more to *lecture them* on their duties and shortcomings than to provide fora for Kikuyu complainants. (Clough 1990: 36; my emphasis.)

On the surface a participatory institution, the *baraza* became instead a forum for monologues by colonial officers clad in khaki uniforms and pith helmets.

These constraints, however, did not eliminate local initiative and creative use of new political space. Individuals in the audience sometimes exercised symbolic displays of defiance.[38] Chiefs were not equally compliant colonial subjects.[39] (Nor were all farmers opposed to chiefs.)[40] Some chiefs who displeased their subjects suffered violent attacks. Embu LNC minutes in 1933, for example, refer to an attack on Chief Arthur, and officially link the assault to "a few trouble makers."[41] Within the confines of customary *baraza* behavior colonial chiefs developed subtle forms of communication in which equivocal language, affect, and gestures might undermine or soften the official messages they were to deliver (Ita 1972: 66).[42] Laughter or wide smiles from the audience might then confirm that the message had been received.

However constrained onstage behavior at *baraza* was, dissenting discourses flourished offstage. For example, people in Embu tell a story of a British district officer in that district who became quite wealthy and who was referred to locally as "Ngunja," a name derived from the verb *gukunja* "to take everything" or "to fold everything together." Citizens termed chiefs' assistants "little white men" (Mwaniki 1973b). And according to a Gikuyu proverb, "the European has (among Africans) no trustworthy man." The force of contrary opinion – and of prior norms – became apparent in the late 1950s, when a sudden shift in political circumstances broke down earlier constraints on *baraza* behavior. The rise of nationalist politics as colonial rule drew to an end brought sharp attacks on chiefs stereotyped as colonial oppressors. Suddenly citizens "could shout them down or even challenge them publicly" (Ita 1972: 60): behavior as unprecedented in the late 1950s as was the newly open political criticism of the early 1990s.

Although part of a formally coercive administrative structure, neither British colonial officers nor African chiefs were free from popular pressures of accountability to those they served. Indeed, they were subject to such pressures from both above and below. Ita (1972: 53), for example, notes that from below came complaints that chiefs exercised their power in an arbitrary and corrupt fashion to serve their own ends. From above came accusations of negligence and *ultra vires* actions. Ita (1972: 53), for example, describes an account of a colonial Mbeere chief who one day protested at a British district officer's acts of physical and verbal abuse of other chiefs as they were preparing to take a lorry on an official excursion from Siakago (in the lower altitude Mbeere division of Embu District) to the Nairobi agricultural show. Part of the Mbeere chief's outrage arose from the young district officer's violation of the cultural norms of respect and politeness that any junior owes to his elders. To protest, the chief drove to Embu town and personally complained about the district officer to his superior, the district commissioner. The latter then accompanied the chief back to Siakago and ordered the driver to take them all to Nairobi. The district officer was soon transferred to another location.

In short, while perhaps only infrequently successful in pressing claims in the new kinds of conflict that arose under colonial rule, Kenyans nonetheless did expect those in positions of authority to conform to cultural standards of appropriate behavior. Their capacity to hold them accountable was constrained, in part because the sanctions of elders' councils were weakened under the authority of chiefs and other colonial officials. Nonetheless they found ways to express dissatisfaction (sometimes in disguised forms) and on occasion to press for accountability. In this sense, "democracy" is not a Western import, but rather it builds directly on local cultural understandings (cf. Lonsdale 1986).

Both colonial and post-colonial states, however, invoked "tradition" to serve fundamentally anti-democratic purposes: that is, to shore up central state authority. In the 1960s the Kenyatta regime suggested that a search for African values justified manipulating the constitution in ways that increasingly subordinated state institutions to the presidency (Githu 1992). In 1990, under the Moi regime, KANU rhetoric suggested that African traditions were uniquely suited to one-party democracy. Traditions cited included decision-making by consensus rather than by contest.[43]

In recommending one-party rather than multiparty democracy in Kenya, the 1990 KANU Review Report discusses leaders' accountability in the context of a "mutual social responsibility (that) is an extension of the African family spirit to the nation as a whole."[44] This document also notes that "within the African traditions, leadership had to be earned through the fulfillment of certain widely recognized criteria ... political democracy in the African traditional sense militated against the exercise of disproportionate political power by economic power groups." "Members of the public ... expected leaders to work in harmony and not wash their dirty linen in public, since their public quarrels would reflect negatively on those they lead," according to the recent KANU document. The report then recommends "That all leaders in every sphere of life, particularly religious leaders, politicians, lawyers, journalists and other professionals should cease their confrontational stance and adopt a positive attitude towards issues in order to build a more peaceful and prosperous Kenya." KANU calls, not for a shift to a multiparty system, but rather for a more tolerant one-party system in which leaders, "instead of overreacting when criticized ... should be able to give proper answers to their critics instead of branding their critics disloyal."

Contrary to this ideal, both colonial and post-colonial officials often did overreact to criticism. They publicly portrayed dissent as unpatriotic, and therefore illegitimate. During colonial rule and later, officials attributed discontent to "trouble-makers," "known intransigents," or "a few disgruntled elements."[45] Embu LNC minutes in the late 1950s include several warnings of the threat to the district's prosperity that could be brought by undesirables and subversives.[46] Officials stressed then, as now, that economic development must come before politics. Instead of institutionalizing democratic processes, both the colonial and post-colonial state emphasized that politics were dangerous, and that political activity had to be curbed in order to preserve civil order. The "choice" citizens faced was the status quo or "chaos" (cf. Schatzberg 1991). As Murray Edelman (1988: 50) writes, "even in one-party states and totalitarian states where opposition is prohibited, the leader keeps constantly before the public an evocation of an alternative that has allegedly brought disaster in the past or promises to do so in the future."

Weapons of fear

Frightening rhetorical images sometimes reinforced the message that Kenyan citizens must choose between the status quo or "chaos." In the example that follows, a cabinet minister (CM) who is one of Embu District's senior politicians addresses a rural *baraza* at which he is guest of honor. The gathering occurred in September 1979, just a few months after the (April) overthrow of dictator Idi Amin in neighboring Uganda (SEP779: A,14–15).[47]

CM: Would you like this country to be like that of Amin?
CROWD :No!
CM: You wouldn't want that? ( ) In order that we stay in peace, ruling ourselves here in Kenya ( ) there is one big secret. Do you want to hear that secret? ((slowly)) It is to obey! ( ) People fear Amin's place ( ) they have guns; is that a good place?
CROWD: No!

The cabinet minister then describes how people in Uganda are pushed into a "tipper" lorry of the kind that carries sand, then put into a helicopter, transported with their hands tied, and dropped from the door of the helicopter into Lake Victoria. He asks the crowd, "Would you want leadership like that?" The crowd of course responds, "No!" He then says, "Let us obey our government".

In order to marginalize or quiet political opposition, official Kenyan rhetoric often invokes images of political disorder in neighboring nations; Uganda,[48] Somalia, Sudan, Liberia, Ethiopia, and Zaïre have all at various times provided convenient examples of the dangers of letting political conflict and dissent go too far. In 1990–1 terrifying portraits of chaos and violence figured in some authorities' exhortations to ignore multiparty advocates. When President Moi criticized those behind Kenya's violent social protests in July 1990, he invoked images of chaos and described multiparty advocates as "selfish trouble-makers" out to destabilize the country.[49] And, as noted in chapter 2, he publicly warned against drawing parallels between Eastern Europe and Kenya, saying that Eastern Europe is "in chaos," and that multiple political parties in Kenya would only encourage ethnic divisions and instability.[50] Ironically, as discussed in the last chapter, in 1992 many citizens believed the ruling party itself was instigating ethnic violence in an attempt to discredit the opposition. Also in the early 1990s some regime supporters themselves appeared to advocate violence against political dissidents, publicly urging citizens to cut off the fingers of multiparty advocates, and to arm themselves with *rungu* (knobbed sticks) and spears to crush opponents of one-party rule.[51]

Assertions about the destructive consequences of multiparty politics were not a new rhetorical theme in the early 1990s. In 1979, an election year when Kenya was still a *de facto*, but not a *de jure*, one-party state, officials had emphasized the inevitable bloodshed that must attend multiparty politics (MAR479: B,36):

The ruling party KANU has led Kenya more than sixteen years now. There are many different parties in far off nations such as Ghana, Nigeria, Egypt ... and in all, no one leads more than two, three, or four years before it collapses and by the time it collapses people wash themselves in blood. But has KANU done that?

The crowd replies "no!" The speaker, a cabinet minister addressing a KANU rally in rural Embu some months before an election, repeats the question, "Has KANU ever done that?" And again the crowd replies "no!" The cabinet minister then refers to the difficult struggle for independence, and to Kenyatta's admonition, after he was released from detention, to forgive those who did us wrong so that we can work with them. He reminds the audience also of Kenyatta's independence slogan *uhuru na kazi*, "independence and work" (MAR479: B,36–7):

CM: When we grabbed independence from Europeans, people who fought in the forest,[52] those who fought in homes here, those who cried in their hearts, those who were in detention – all were released. Even President Kenyatta was released. And the first thing he said was ((slowly)) "Let us try to say we have forgiven those who have done us wrong, so that we forget, so that we may work with them." Isn't that what he said?
CROWD: Yes! That's what he said.
CM: We used to tell you what then? After getting independence, it will be independence and what?
CROWD: And work!
CM: And work! Independence and what?
CROWD: And work!

The cabinet minister goes on to list the "fruits" (*matunda*) of independence: such as the building of many secondary schools in Embu District.

Here again, after describing the effort to bring secondary education to Embu during the 1950s, he elicits replies from the audience (MAR479: B,37–8):

CM: Today there are how many secondary schools in Embu?
CROWD: There are many!
CM: Are there many?
CROWD: Yes!
CM: They are there?
CROWD: Yes!
CM: Aren't those fruits of independence?
CROWD: They are fruits!
CM: Those who say those are not the fruits of independence during the time of KANU, put their hands up. ((pause)) Thank you!

He then attributes to the KANU government other improvements, such as tarmac roads and the sharply reduced travel time between Embu and Nairobi with the rise of the *matatu* service (here he names a particular local clan and individuals who operate such services). Here, too, he solicits crowd affirmation with the tag question, "Isn't that development (*maendeleo*)?," to which the crowd responds, "It is development!" He then praises the recently deceased Kenyatta for all he accomplished during the nation's first fourteen years of independence, and for keeping the country out of chaos. He asks the crowd, "Would you want us to spoil this country of ours after he has prepared it so?" The crowd of course replies "no!" In short, again we see an emphasis on forgetting current and past political divisions in order to avoid a descent into chaos. Instead of pursuing "politics," citizens should concentrate on development and progress. If people seek alternatives to one-party rule, they will inevitably "wash themselves in blood."

Praise for the "development" (*maendeleo*) benefits the government has brought since the struggle for independence is a standard *baraza* theme. A senior agricultural official, for example, reminds assembled farmers that under colonial rule they were not permitted to grow coffee or tea. He underlines the importance of such crops to national development and urges farmers to work hard (SEP779: A,3). A cabinet minister in the same *baraza* later picked up this theme, saying that "the colonialist didn't think the African would be able to maintain tea well, coffee well, or cattle well. He very much deceived himself" (SEP779,A: 12). He goes on to refer to the difficult days of the emergency, and asks the crowd who they have to thank for ending those colonial sufferings. He answers his own question, saying that it is our honorable government led by the late (Kenyatta), "and that is led by whom now?" The crowd replies "Moi." He then leads the crowd in a call and response sequence in which he speaks short phrases in praise of Moi, after each of which the crowd claps three times in unison. He starts by saying, "Let us clap because they have led us well that way. Three claps for those leaders of ours! One, two, three!" It is at the end of this brief interchange with the audience that he introduces the frightening images of life in Uganda under Amin.

Politics of the devil, politics of redemption

Kenyan officials variously characterize political opposition as unpatriotic, corrupt, the interest of those who travel at night, or the work of the devil or madness. For example, to discourage opposition to an incumbent MP and cabinet minister, a party official addressing an Embu KANU rally in March 1979 criticized those who practice the "politics of the devil or madness" (in mixed Swahili and Embu, *siasa cia ngoma*), the "madness of politics" (*ngoma cia siasa*), and the "politics of corruption" (*siasa cia mageendo*) (MAR479: B,18,21). He warned the audience that whenever someone slanders a leader in a private audience with his superior, word always gets back to the leader, particularly when he is as well known and respected as the incumbent MP.[53]

In another gathering the cabinet minister quoted earlier draws a distinction between "fierce politics" (*siasa kali*)[54] and "good politics" (*siasa nzuri*) (SEP779: B,8). He urges coffee farmers to abandon their conflict over subdividing the local coffee cooperative society,[55] suggesting they cultivate in peace and not trouble the police, district officer, chiefs, and local leaders.[56] He exhorts them to work hard and loyally and not to bring conflict for no reason. If they do provoke conflict, he warns, the government will be there. He then says he wants to make a few remarks about politics: not fierce politics such as that of the coffee cooperative, but the good politics of the ruling party KANU.[57]

Vigorously reinforcing the moral underpinnings of their political messages, leaders often incorporate into their rhetoric explicit Christian or other religious themes. For example, when he urged citizens in Embu to register as members of KANU in preparation for the 1979 elections, one cabinet minister constructed an extended comparison with membership in various religious denominations. He stressed the importance of possessing a new KANU registration receipt, and not an old one from earlier elections. As he did so he drew several examples of individuals who claim to belong to, say, the Catholic Church, the Anglican Church, the Salvation Army Church, or the Muslim religion, each time describing someone who is a member in name only. Thus he spoke of a person who claimed to be Muslim but who sat down to enjoy pork; of one who claimed to be Catholic but was never seen attending a service or seeing a priest; of one who claimed to belong to the Salvation Army Church but had not purchased the uniform; and of one who claimed to be Anglican but was seen in the bush and never in church.

Equating the act of registering as a KANU member with going to church to demonstrate true religious belief, he said the only way to know whether one is really a member of KANU is to see the receipt confirming registration. He referred to the volume number of KANU receipts for that portion of Embu District, and to the number assigned to each individual who registers. He suggested that the book is an important record for succeeding generations, and proceeded to compare the book of KANU registration tickets to the Book of Life, wherein are written the names of those who will ascend to heaven. And he sang a few lines of a hymn: "my name is there in the book of life." He reminded people that those who want to be members of KANU must register, and he then sang "my name is there in the book of KANU." He again asked whether we should spoil things now, implying that anyone who opposes KANU does not have the nation's well-being at heart. His religious examples and associations imply that anyone who is against KANU is against what is divinely sanctioned. Thus he merges the secular world of political party politics with the spiritual realm of Christian redemption.

The image of a peaceable, orderly citizenry whose members obey their government is emphasized in official rhetoric such as that of a district officer[58] addressing a February 1979 *baraza* organized by a chief in rural Embu (FEB2779: A,24):

And first I would like to thank the chief and assistant chief for organizing a big *baraza* like this, at which many people have arrived. And this shows your faith in the government because if not for faith in government, you would not have arrived in such numbers at this government meeting, isn't that so?

The crowd shouts "yes!," and the officer continues, "So all of you are faithful to the government?" People again reply "yes!" The district officer then says, "Alright, hands high! Fire!" (*Haya, mkono juu! Moto!*). The crowds shouts *Moto*! "fire!," a symbol of the national political party KANU, and a political catchword used also during colonial times to call attention to the fervor, seriousness, and even danger embodied in a cause or group. KANU youthwingers and stalwarts wear red shirts as a symbol of their loyalty to the party.

In the interchange just quoted we see a collusion between speaker and audience, as both endorse the myth that equates a large *baraza* turnout with support for the government, even though all know that attendance is formally "mandatory,"[59] and individuals privately grumble about the many hours lost to such meetings. The crowd heartily replies "yes!" to the district officer's rhetorical questions about being faithful to the government, and then joins him enthusiastically in an exchange of political slogans. Indeed, the success of such official speakers depends in part on the intensity of emotional display they evoke in an audience.

In short, when colonial and post-colonial state authorities addressed citizens in the countryside they struck a hazardous moral bargain. The state would protect citizens from civil disorder or "chaos": an aim, as state officials argued, that necessarily entailed restrictions on popular political activity. Law and order thus took precedence over democratic procedures. To reward citizens' compliance and obedience the state would bring the material benefits of "progress" and "development." Thus three themes in tension with one another – state authoritarianism, paternalism, and democracy – have colored colonial and post-colonial *baraza* rhetoric. The moral obligations implied by state paternalism, as well as deep cultural norms, have helped to define the terms in which citizens hold their leaders accountable. State coercion might extinguish most overt political opposition, but it could only force offstage, not eliminate, both principled objections to patterns of rule some found unacceptable, and dissatisfaction with the material rewards of compliance.

As discussed in the last chapter, in the early 1990s the Moi regime was patently unwilling to introduce the particular form of "progress" associated with multiparty democracy. At the same time a financially-strapped state was unable to deliver sufficient material benefits either to maintain elite cohesion or to sustain a semblance of popular support for those in power. These tensions contributed to national political crisis in the early 1990s. If we step back to the beginning of the Moi era, however, we find a strikingly different political and economic climate: one that allowed rapid legitimization of a new regime whose orienting symbol was "footsteps" or *nyayo*.

"Follow the footsteps": political culture under Moi

In 1978 Kenya's new president had to negotiate a particularly treacherous political passage. He could not afford to alienate, at least not immediately, the southern Gikuyu elites who had dominated the Kenyatta regime, many of whom were descendants of wealthy and powerful colonial chiefs. Nor could he, a non-Gikuyu, be a pawn of those entrenched interests. He had to demonstrate both loyalty and independence. As he energetically addressed *baraza* around the country during his first months in office he quickly acquired a populist image, and substantial popular support by appealing directly to citizens. Through *baraza*, a new national political culture was apparently "traditionalized" with remarkable rapidity. Moi, like any leader, appropriated an official version of history to serve his own purposes.

In the early months of his regime Moi "created an era of good feeling by releasing all political detainees, assembling a broad multiethnic coalition, and instituting popular new government programs" (Leonard 1991: 169). Some of Moi's earliest acts as president included mandating free milk distribution for children in primary schools; abolishing mandatory parental contributions to primary school building funds; and banning the brewing and sale of local beer. Such actions he defined in populist rhetoric as part of the *nyayo* "footsteps" philosophy of "peace, love and unity" (see Godia 1984; Moi 1986). Moi's public image in 1979 was that of a humble, ascetic Christian. His early actions, rhetoric, and demeanor received wide popular support, as he sermonized about the evils of drunkenness, tribalism, corruption, and smuggling. Although some observers had expected a succession struggle the transition proceeded smoothly.

When Moi first became president he reassured many by announcing that he would follow in Kenyatta's "footsteps" (*nyayo*). In thus associating himself with his predecessor Moi made his own legitimacy less shaky, since he assumed office with none of Kenyatta's historic claims to power:

Unlike Kenyatta Moi ... had played no direct role in the nationalist struggle leading to independence, had in fact been in opposition to the nationalist consensus as a member of KADU. Under the circumstances, his claim to leadership could at best be vicarious. Thus his rallying slogan of *Nyayo* or following the footsteps of Kenyatta.[60]

Fuata nyayo ("follow the footsteps") quickly became a national political slogan that appeared on T-shirts and in songs, records, and booklets. It was popular in everyday talk in a variety of contexts, ranging from the respectful and homiletic to the satirical. Indeed, it was popularized so quickly that some feared its significance could be demeaned, and urged early official restrictions on its commercial use. In any case, "footstep" became the widely known, unifying national political symbol of the new ruling regime.

While Moi stressed continuity with his predecessor he oversaw a gradual but decisive shift (by the mid-1980s) in the ethnic and regional balance of power, moving it away from Kenyatta's core base among the Gikuyu peoples of Central Province (as discussed in chapter 2). So, too, the meaning of the *nyayo* slogan gradually shifted from "I (President Moi) will follow Kenyatta's footsteps" to "Follow my footsteps." Later it changed again, as Moi asserted that it referred to the footsteps of Kenyans' ancestors, saying *nyayo* springs from a "universal African spirit – the spirit of the forefathers" (Moi 1986: 19; see also Katz 1985;

Abwunza 1990). With this claim Moi redefined the history of Kenyatta's rallying cry *Harambee!*, suggesting that *nyayo* is the moving spirit behind it (Abwunza 1990). Both of these slogans, he held, reflected African traditions of communal effort and sharing: a "spirit of African socialism," but one that did not interfere with individual "productivity and creativity" (Moi 1986: 19).

During the 1980s global and national economic declines meant that "Moi could no longer purchase political popularity with governmental generosity" (Leonard 1991: 178). State expenditures were cut severely at the end of the 1981–2 financial year, and there was an unsuccessful coup attempt in mid-1982. Some of Moi's initiatives that had public appeal (such as his 1988 increase in the intake of students into universities) "placed a severe budgetary strain on the Government, being inconsistent with its stated policy of reducing the proportion of public expenditures devoted to education" (Barkan and Chege 1989: 437, n.2). The long-term costs of such policies carried the risk of reduced support for the regime. When Moi first took office in 1978, however, the nation still enjoyed some lingering benefits from the 1977 coffee boom.[61]

As suggested in chapter 2 citizens view the ethnic identity of the president as a crucial influence on how state resources are distributed among regions and ethnic groups. When Moi succeeded Kenyatta as president in August 1978 many saw his non-Gikuyu ethnic origin as a strong asset. In attempting to build support for the new regime official rhetoric discreetly took up this theme. For example, a cabinet minister from Embu District addressing a KANU rally in that district in March 1979 emphasized the wisdom of God's choice of a person such as Moi to be president (MAR479: B,41):

The prayers of the song of Kipokomo[62] were heard by God; he gave us a person called Daniel Arap Moi. He doesn't come from GEMA,[63] who say we are great people. He doesn't come from Kamba who say we are great people. He doesn't come from the Luo who say they are great. God searched for the person from where? A place he found appropriate.

This is a striking invocation of God as a source of legitimacy for a new ethnoregional politics. People who lived outside the central Kenyan region that is home to the Gikuyu, Embu, and Meru peoples in 1978 looked to Moi as a welcome change in the nation's ethnoregional balance of power.[64] Those in Embu and elsewhere in central Kenya, however, apparently required some reassurance about ethnoregional politics under Moi. The speaker just quoted looks to religion for that reassurance.

How was the new *nyayo* philosophy diffused in the countryside? In part, this was accomplished during Moi's first year in office through his own extensive travels and *baraza* addresses throughout the country. His speeches and the themes of his new administration were publicized quickly through radio and print journalism, as well as through direct exposure at huge public rallies. In addition, officials in the provincial administration as well as politicians quickly adopted Moi's ideas in their own public addresses in town and countryside.

Let us listen, for example, to the words of an MP addressing a public rally I attended in 1979 in a market center in rural Embu District.[65] The audience at this gathering was mainly smallscale farmers, a few of whom also earn incomes from small businesses or salaried employment. The MP invokes the *nyayo* philosophy in warning against civil servants corruptly delaying and demanding bribes from citizens seeking their services. His remarks were primarily in the Embu language, with occasional code-switches into Swahili and (less so) English (MAR479: A,2):

And the *nyayo* government says this: to follow *nyayo* means you do your job without delaying the citizen, because he is the owner of the country. ( ) To follow the footsteps of His Excellency the President means this: (2.0) and Mr. Chairman I want this thing to be written; it is very important, it is a thing of much use. People of (2.0) Embu have been much delayed, having gone to request someone to mark a (farm) boundary, and paying money again and again. Isn't that what KANU doesn't wan – ?

The example of corruption which he cites here (which follows its mention in a question from the audience) is familiar and central to the concerns of his rural listeners. He refers to farmers who take land boundary disputes to the land registry and are then "delayed" (*agatuura acerithagirwa*) by registry officers. Such delays usually mean that officials request from farmers payments of unofficial fees before they agree to visit a farm to measure and record land boundaries for a title deed. Such practices, the speaker suggests, are exactly what the governing political party (KANU) does not want. He pauses just before the end of the phrase "doesn't want" (*haitaki*), as if to allow the audience to repeat and complete it, which at least one individual in the crowd does.

Through such examples, then, *baraza* speakers explain the *nyayo* philosophy as Moi's intention to rid the country of evils such as nepotism, drunkenness, bribery, "tribalism," and smuggling. A KANU officer at this same gathering suggested that the proper footsteps had been lost in the years since independence,[66] and that Moi will help to direct people along the correct path again. A district commissioner invoked the *nyayo* philosophy as he urged Embu farmers to take out commercial loans to purchase exotic cattle breeds. Thus it is through *baraza* that the *nyayo* philosophy is unpacked, interpreted, and reinterpreted in ways that both help to sustain the regime, and that publicize standards against which some later will judge it unfavorably.

Mass media in Kenya, as elsewhere, helped to create and sustain the "imagined community" of the nation-state (see Anderson 1991). Radio and print journalism play a crucial role in diffusing *baraza* rhetoric nationwide. The speaker just quoted draws attention to his *nyayo* statement by telling the chairman it should be written down (presumably as official minutes or by national journalists who are present). He uses the English words "very important" to emphasize his point, and then explains it in the Embu language. We shall see a salient illustration of the role of mass media in our later discussion of a beer-banning *baraza*.

In addition to illustrations of correct conduct under the *nyayo* regime, speakers "hyped" *baraza* audiences (cf. Bailey 1981: 331–332) with exchanges of political slogans. One of the patterns introduced soon after Moi took office was for the speaker to shout "*Haraambee!*," and the crowd to reply "*Nyayo!*" *Haraambee* (literally, "let's all pull together") was the national slogan of the former president, Jomo Kenyatta. Thus Moi continued the slogan, but modified the formalized crowd response. In the excerpt that follows, a cabinet minister (guest of honor) at the same KANU rally in Embu engages the audience in a loud and forceful exchange[67] (MAR479: A,22–23):

CM: *Ha : : raa : : mbee : :* !
CROWD: *Nyayo!*
CM: *HA: : RAA: : MBEE: :* !
CROWD: *NYAYO!*
CM: *RAIS MOI WAPI?* "How [literally where] is President Moi?"
CROWD: *JUU!* "Up!"
CM: *Serikali yetu wapi?* "How [literally where] is our government?"
CROWD: *Juu!* "Up!"
CM: *Chama cha KANU wapi?* "How [literally where] is KANU?"
CROWD: *Juu!* "Up!"
CM: *Asanteni! Na wananchi wa Xxxx wapi?* "Thank-you. And how [literally where] are people of Xxxx?"
CROWD: *Juu!* "Up!"
CM: *Asanteni!* "Thank-you!"

This type of exchange of slogans serves as phatic communication to establish social contact or emotional identification between speaker and audience. *Baraza* speakers often employ such exchanges at the beginning of a speech, but they also shift to them at any time during a speech as a means of crowd control: to defuse tensions or conflict; to quiet and distract a grumbling audience; to reinvigorate an inattentive or tired one. As speakers and crowds repeat formulaic phrases or slogans, implicit issues change, responses vary, and meanings can subtly alter; that is, variable meanings of set phrases are constructed through performance (see Parkin 1984: 351).

Exchanges between speaker and audience also can help to create an exaggerated impression of unity, participation, and enthusiasm in a crowd,[68] as we see in our next example.

Down with (home-brewed) beer

Beer should be banned so that people go back to their farms ... men come here [to town] leaving the wife there, being broken by firewood, being broken by cattle left at home. The husband comes home from drinking [and says] "where is the food?" "where is the food?" The husband who was where?[69]

Soon after President Moi took office he called publicly for a ban on informal brewing and sale of beer and distilled alcohol (*karubu, chang'aa, busaa, muratina*, and so on). This action was not aimed at Kenya's thriving commercial beer industry, but only at those farmers and traders who made their own alcoholic beverages (usually from sugarcane, honey, maize, sorghum, or millet). High alcohol content in the distilled beverages[70] and unsanitary brewing conditions make local brews dangerous drinks. Their consumer prices are much lower than those of bottled beer, and they find a ready market in both urban and rural areas. Though demand for bottled beer is probably very elastic, I am unaware of any evidence that Moi's move was an attempt to increase state revenue from commercial beer.

The president's prohibition efforts, part of his early populist agenda, supported his ascetic image and drew inspiration from popular stereotypes of women and families impoverished, abused, or neglected by alcoholic men. The ban, however, was by no means universally popular, since brewing and selling beer was an important income source in many rural and urban families.[71] Decisions to ban home-brewed beer were to be taken by each administrative location at a *baraza* under a chief's authority. During the months these beer-banning gatherings were held, the local press gave them prominent radio and newspaper coverage. News media portrayed each such *baraza* as yet another enthusiastic tribute to the new president.

What was the historical context of beer consumption and production in the Kenyan countryside?[72] In pre-colonial central Kenyan communities local beer (made from sugarcane, or, in drier regions, from honey or millet) was usually produced by young men, and consumed by elders on socially and ritually significant occasions. As Ambler (1991: 166) notes

No child was initiated, no marriage arranged, no planting or harvesting begun, no important case decided without the preparation, consumption, or offering of beer ... When a homestead was opened, for instance, neighbors assembled to drink and socialize, but first a gourdful of beer was hung in the house and drops sprinkled across the yard to honor ancestors. Similarly, the presentation and consumption of beer in the course of marriage negotiations sanctified the new bond between families and lineages.

Pre-colonial elders controlled drinking, normally allowing it only for men retiring from warrior service (Glazier 1985: 88–89; Ambler 1988: 166). As the Gikuyu proverb puts it, "one goes to fight holding a spear, not a container of beer."[73] Usually women were expected to drink little or not at all.

Under colonial rule beer drinking patterns changed,[74] as did the authority of elders who previously had controlled it. (The authority of elders gave way to that of appointed chiefs and district officials.) Conflicts emerged when some Christian converts refused to offer the expected beer to their prospective fathers-in-law.[75] At the November 1925 Embu LNC meeting, Chief M'Tetu attributed increased drinking to the end of warfare and raiding: "in the old days drunkenness was not rife because we were all liable to be raided by our neighbors. This fear is now absent" (Embu LNC minutes, November 29, 1925). With the spread of wage labor, young men who were once prohibited from drinking acquired the cash to purchase their own beer or the sugar to produce it.[76] Colonial officials associated youthful drinking with a breakdown in "traditional" discipline. In reality, changing habits of beer consumption were a symptom not a cause of tensions between the generations.

Fearing that rural drunkenness was increasing,[77] and that it fueled social disorder, colonial officials in the first few decades of the 1900s enacted a number of measures to attempt to regulate informal beer production, consumption, and sale among Kenyan Africans. In central Kenya, LNCs ruled on which age-sets could drink beer, prohibiting it for younger men (e.g., Embu LNC minutes, November 29, 1925). Officials also associated communal dances – an important preoccupation of young men of warrior age – with lawlessness and disorder (though not with drunkenness), and hence attempted to restrict dances as well (Ambler 1991: 173). Other regulations prescribed occasions when beer drinking was allowable, and suggested suitable quantities for consumption. Colonial rulers probably "explain(ed) away more complex phenomena with charges of alcohol abuse," and they intensified their attempts at regulation during periods of social and political unrest (Ambler 1991: 172–173). In any case, chiefs and populace often ignored the colonial regulations on informal beer brewing and drinking.

How did politicians and bureaucrats in 1979 persuade people at staged public gatherings to ban local beer? They did so by "hyping" their audiences and invoking higher political and administrative authorities.

For example, a local politician (county councillor) warmed up a February 1979 Embu *baraza* audience before the arrival of the district officer (DO) (FEB2779: A,3–4):[78]

P: The president said traditional beer will be banned. ( ) yes, because there is no person who can't speak. WHAT INFORMATION ABOUT TRADITIONAL BEER DO YOU WANT? You tell me when I am going to sit down. (2.0) IS IT TO CONTINUE OR BE BANNED?
CROWD: Let it be banned! Ban completely! Let it be banned! ((noise, talking))
P: Eeh?
CROWD: Ban it! Ban it! ((noise, talking))
P: Those who say traditional beer should be banned, raise hands!
CROWD: Ban it! Ban it! ((noise))
P: Those who want beer to continue, let them raise hands.
CROWD: ((noise and laughter)) ( )
P: ( ) All right! Those who want it banned, hands high!
CROWD: Ban it! Completely! ((applause))
P: Let's all pull together! ((national political slogan))
CROWD: Hooo!
P: It is said "Footsteps!" Let's all pull together!
CROWD: Footsteps!
P: Let's all pull together!
CROWD: Footsteps!
P: How [literally where] is our president? Up!
CROWD: Up!
P: How [literally where] is our government?
CROWD: Up!
P: How [literally where] are these people?
CROWD: Up!
P: How [literally where] is Mr. Councillor Xxx ((his own name))?
CROWD: Up! ((applause and laughter))

This politician has stirred the crowd to enthusiastic shouts of support for banning beer. He has used humor (by mentioning his own name at the end), questions to the audience that are for all practical purposes rhetorical, and political cheer-leading in the exchange of slogans. Indeed, this interchange captures formalization-in-progress. Moi's succession to office is still recent enough that the crowd must be coached gently in the appropriate response to the cue word "*Harambee!*," to which they are to reply "*Nyayo*" in a pattern that a few months later had become automatic.

Right away the speaker invokes the president's authority for the beer-banning proposition. Though public vocal opposition at such a meeting at that time and place was practically unthinkable, he says "there is no person who can't speak," and he invites those opposed to the proposition to raise their hands high: a request greeted only with noise and laughter.

Later in the meeting the district officer (DO) arrives and takes up the beer issue. As the chief introduces the district officer, he also raises the subject, saying he has left it to the district officer, who will act on behalf of the district commissioner. The DO himself is careful to invoke the authority of his superior, the district commissioner (FEB2779: B,7):[79]

Now returning to what I was sent by Mr. D. C. to do – concerning traditional beer (*karubu*). Ah, as you know, this beer has spoiled many of our people. People have ignored (literally, thrown away) their wives, have thrown away their children because of following only beer.

The DO's last phrase "to follow only beer" (Swahili: *kufuata karubu peke yake*) is a play on the national slogan, "to follow the (president's) footsteps" (Swahili: *kufuata nyayo*). He goes on to use humor in distinguishing the different interests of laborers and the sexes and generations with regard to beer:

They drink beer from morning until evening, so that even coffee farmers and tea farmers lack people to pick tea or coffee. ( ) And now we have seen that beer is bringing problems to the country. And everywhere in Kenya, they have announced they have banned it. And now Mr. D. C., ah, cannot close it without your permission because it is you who drink here. And especially old men. I know who those old men are, eh? ((crowd laughter)) Some people here, if I mention traditional beer, they start lowering their heads. ((crowd laughter)) But the women I see that they are completely happy, eh? ((crowd laughter)) Because now husbands will be home, eh? ((crowd laughter)) Children will be at home, they will be able to converse with children. And that is an important thing because we men must stay at home to converse with our wife and to converse with our child.

The DO then comments that a man who is always in bars rather than at home cannot repair or maintain his house, and does not know what problems his wife and children have. He says men can learn many things by speaking with their wives, but that women will not talk "if you make yourself a fierce hyena" (*kama wewe unajifanya fisi sana*).

The DO then shifts to an enthusiastic, sustained dialogue with the audience in order to acquire their vocal approval of banning beer. Both men and women shout hearty approval:

DO: Therefore, ah, Mr. D. C. has sent me to find out really if you people of Xxxx want this beer to continue, or you want it banned.
CROWD: Ban it completely! Ban it! ((applause, noise))
DO: Eeh?
CROWD: Ban it! ((noise))
DO: Those who want it banned, put your hands high!
CROWD: Ban it completely! Ban it! Ban it today! ((applause, laughter, noise))
DO: ( ) Bring forward the person from (the Ministry of) Information so that he

sees and then he says whether it is OK. I think people from Information see. We ban it?
CROWD: Yes! ((applause, noise))
DO: Thank-you very much! ( ) Mr. Yyyy is the person from Information, ah, he has been sent here by Mr. D. C. so that you see after meeting, ah, things will be broadcast on the radio: "People of Xxxx have refused beer."
CROWD: ((applause))
DO: (6.0) I think I want to know when you want to ban it.
CROWD: Today! Ban! Ban now! ((applause)) When leaving here, ban it!
DO: Eeh?
CROWD: Today!
DO: OK, then, thanks!

The audience's enthusiastic onstage collusion[80] with the officer and with the earlier speaker should not be mistaken for ardent universal agreement with the beer-banning proposition. Some people, of course, did support the ban for religious and other reasons. There was, however, substantial offstage opposition, since many small farmers grow sugarcane, a crop whose value obviously declines with the banning of sugarcane beer. Nor are the baraza officials unaware of the drawbacks of the ban. This recognition may contribute to their noticeable emphasis on the administrative chain of command, as several speakers (councillor, chief, and DO) have deferred to their respective higher authorities, drawing attention to the full weight of the administrative hierarchy, and of the president's personal interest in the matter. The president's association with the issue, of course, increases the risks and decreases the likelihood of vocal popular opposition.

The only possible opposition the district officer explicitly acknowledges – and this jokingly – is that of men, especially those old men who are heavy drinkers. He does this with a humorous remark about some people "lowering their heads" when he mentions traditional beer. He then emphasizes how happy wives and children will be when men stop drinking, but he never raises the financial concerns of those who produce sugarcane or beer (or both) for sale. Although this district officer does not himself consume alcohol, some of the other officials who addressed the gathering and who made similar remarks about the evils of beer, are themselves known to be heavy drinkers who frequent local bars at night. The same is true of some of the spectators cheering the ban.

In short, the collusion by speakers and audience masks financially motivated opposition to the ban, as well as contrary personal practices. More important to the participants at the moment, however, is that the public exchanges between speaker and audience convey affect-laden substantive agreement with the president's prohibition agenda. Symbolic weapons that the state deploys to effect such compliance include intimi-

dating speeches, such as that discussed earlier concerning Ugandan helicopters dropping people into Lake Victoria.

The DO emphasizes national press coverage of this *baraza*, a clear
message that the local Embu "decision" about beer brewing will be
widely known. He mentions, for example, that his superior, the DC, will
read in the newspapers about people of this location banning beer. He
remarks that the Ministry of Information is paying attention as people
agree to ban beer, and tells them that this news will be broadcast on the
radio. The coverage is important to his own status in relation to his
administrative superiors, and of course he implies that it should contribute to local pride in the action just taken, making people in the locality
feel important in the national arena. The implication he need not state is
that a local failure to ban beer would bring strong negative reactions
from higher officials, attract unfavorable national press coverage, and
cause Embu people to suffer. (Possible negative consequences include
withdrawing or reducing patronage benefits, and increasing surveillance
or police harassment.)

In short, what is at work here is not just the crowd's false deference to
authority, an "everyday form of resistance" (Scott 1985). Rather, the
baraza ritual includes a collusively "hyped" display of support for the
president by officials and populace alike. The councillor who invited
anyone opposed to the beer ban to speak knew such speech to be unlikely
and very risky, and also understood the unspoken material concerns of
opponents. Here the possibility of genuine popular participation was only
a pose, a symbolic gesture. But for a speaker even to mention it is to
remind the audience that the ideal exists. Such a reminder can inspire and
nourish opposition sentiments. For the moment, however, a collection of
people with very different stakes in national policies colluded in an
ostensibly unanimous public display. That does not mean that speakers
and audience members did not at other moments find ways to manipulate
national symbols – within acceptable limits – to advance some of their
own interests.

This meeting by no means marked the end of local beer-brewing.
Subsequent enforcement of the ban was sporadic and selective in Embu
and elsewhere. This outcome could not have been surprising to many of
those present, though the coming to power of a new regime meant that
actual enforcement was at least imaginable. In any case, for local politicians, aware of their constituents' material concerns, the apparent
brewing ban called for some public gesture of sympathy. That gesture,
however, had to be made in the context of enthusiastic displays of loyalty
for the new regime. The next example illustrates how this feat was
accomplished.

A politician sneaks in an "unofficial" message

While the disadvantages of banning local beer-brewing were not mentioned at the February 1979 *baraza* just discussed, politicians did
acknowledge them during later gatherings. During a *baraza* in the same
location just a few days later an MP made a polite request for the state to
build a local sugar mill.[81] This presumably would provide a market for
local sugarcane producers disadvantaged by the beer ban. The MP makes
the request through a polite, rhythmic hand-clapping interchange in
which he calls for the audience to clap three times in unison in punctuated
response to a series of brief phrases (MAR479: A,7–10):

MP: One, two three! ((in English))
CROWD: ((claps three times in unison))
MP: Thank-you! ((this and remainder of sequence in Embu language))
CROWD: ((claps three times in unison))
MP: Mr. Chairman!
CROWD: ((claps three times in unison))
MP: of KANU!
CROWD: ((claps three times in unison))
MP: Mr. Minister!
CROWD: ((claps three times in unison))
MP: you are here at our place
CROWD: ((claps three times in unison))
MP: We are united
CROWD: ((claps three times in unison))
MP: with the government!
CROWD: ((claps three times in unison))
MP: We shall send you
CROWD: ((claps three times in unison))
MP: to tell the President!
CROWD: ((claps three times in unison))
MP: that
CROWD: ((claps three times in unison))
MP: he should come to visit us!
CROWD: ((claps three times in unison))
MP: We follow
CROWD: ((claps three times in unison))
MP: footsteps!
CROWD: ((claps three times in unison))
MP: Back!
CROWD: ((claps three times in unison))
MP: And we cannot
CROWD: ((claps three times in unison))
MP: Go back to/follow another path
CROWD: ((claps three times in unison))
MP: We gave up alcohol/beer ((slightly drawn out))!

CROWD: ((claps three times in unison, and laughs))
MP: And we don't want it again!
CROWD: ((claps three times in unison and laughs))
MP: We left it!
CROWD: ((claps three times in unison and laughs))
MP: This question
CROWD: ((claps three times in unison and laughs))
MP: that we will ask you
CROWD: ((claps three times in unison))
MP: You bring us
CROWD: ((claps three times in unison))
MP: A mill
CROWD: ((claps three times in unison))
MP: for extracting
CROWD: ((claps three times in unison))
MP: our sugarcane!
CROWD: ((claps three times in unison, laughs, and makes sounds of surprise))
MP: (so that) we sell brown sugar/molasses
CROWD: ((claps three times in unison, and laughs))
MP: so that the farmer
CROWD: ((claps three times in unison and laughs))
MP: does not uproot his sugarcane!
CROWD: ((claps three times in unison and laughs))[82]

Two significant requests are inserted in this interchange. The first, which follows an expression of unity and loyalty to the president, is for the president to visit Embu. Presidential visits in those years were often huge *Harambee* fundraising rallies to assist local schools or for other development purposes. Since assuming office Moi had not come to such a rally in Embu (though he did address a non-fundraising Embu *baraza* in January 1979). Some Embu residents believed he intentionally slighted their district for political reasons, out of displeasure with one or two of their political representatives. The second request, for a local sugar mill, notably follows another expression of loyalty to the president: namely the recently passed local beer ban. Upon mention of the latter point the audience laughs in a good natured way. But when the MP requests the sugar mill, some members of the audience express genuine surprise and support.

Given the dangers of even appearing to question the president's wisdom, indirection[83] is a necessary strategy if the MP wishes to recognize publicly the local demand for an alternative commercial outlet for sugarcane. In audience-centered indirection, "comments are ostensibly addressed to one party, in reality the secondary audience, while one's primary target, the 'overhearer,' is also present" (Brenneis 1987: 306). The MP ostensibly addresses the president, though his primary target is voters in the audience and others who will hear about his words via gossip or the press. So the MP emphasizes the community's respect for the president, invites the head of state to visit the area, and embeds the sugar mill request in a stylized hand-clapping sequence honoring the president. Although these polite requests to senior politicians do not necessarily yield the rewards requested (this one did not), they do introduce (and soften) some offstage oppositional themes, transmit key messages from populace to leaders, and allow politicians publicly to display interest in their constituents' problems.

Such requests to the state are also inserted into songs performed by school children and women's groups at *baraza*. Like the sequence just quoted such songs praise the president and other leaders, thank them for leading the country well, confirm local loyalty to the regime, and then sometimes insert a request that addresses local needs and concerns (such as a new school, teachers, dispensary).

The MP quoted above publicly construes political reality in a subtly different way from that of the district officer. Such differences hint at and reflect the more vigorous debate that occurs offstage (e.g., complaints about losing a key income source). As the MP's remarks help to legitimize offstage talk about beer so, too, they may imply that other offstage themes will not necessarily be ignored completely.

Weber's (1946: 95) remarks on the differences between politicians and bureaucrats help to clarify the contrasting rhetorical strategies of the MP and the district officer:

To take a stand, to be passionate ... is the politician's element, and above all the element of the political *leader*. His conduct is subject to quite a different, indeed, exactly the opposite, principle of responsibility from that of the civil servant. The honor of the civil servant is vested in his ability to execute conscientiously the order of the superior authorities, exactly as if the order agreed with his own conviction. This holds even if the order apears wrong to him and if, despite the civil servant's remonstrances, the authority insists on the order. Without this moral discipline and self-denial, in the highest sense, the whole apparatus would fall to pieces. The honor of the political leader, of the leading statesman, however, lies precisely in an exclusive *personal* responsibility for what he does, a responsibility he cannot and must not reject or transfer. It is in the nature of officials of high moral standing to be poor politicians, and above all, in the political sense of the word, to be irresponsible politicians.

Kenya, as noted earlier, had experienced a blurring of the boundary between political and administrative structures. In the eyes of the public civil servants' power to dispense political patronage resources sometimes obscured the presumed distinction between bureaucrats and politicians. This blurred boundary was institutionalized under colonial rule, when "appointed African chiefs . . . were frequently asked to play representative roles that one might have expected would fall to elected delegates."[84] Colonial African civil servants also "were actively encouraged to use their positions to acquire wealth." Kenyatta, like his colonial predecessors, used civil servants to control politicians, and it was the former who made most of the daily decisions. A civil servant who was tempted to play a strong and explicit political role, however, risked losing the favor of the president, and it was from the president's personal support that a bureaucrat's power was derived. Moi did act to reduce the influence of civil servants who appeared to use their patronage resources to build independent political bases that might threaten his own power.[85] Civil servants such as the district officer quoted above, are counted on to build popular support for the government. Bureaucrats "believed that their duty to the head of state was absolute, but otherwise did not see much reason why they should subordinate their judgment to that of elected leaders" (Leonard 1991: 285).

At the beer-banning *baraza*, then, what was at stake for the district officer was his capacity to generate through his rhetoric an appearance of popular support for the president. At stake for politicians such as the county councillor and the MP were dual and sometimes conflicting loyalties to the president and provincial administration (which included the district officer) on the one hand, and to the constituents who elected them on the other. At stake for members of the audience was their continued capacity to call on patronage resources from both politicians and bureaucrats. It was therefore in the interests of all three categories (audience, politicians, bureaucrats) to stage an enthusiastic public display of support for a beer ban urged on the nation by a president who in 1979 still enjoyed considerable popular good will.

Within this framework nonetheless political struggles occur and individual speakers can smuggle "unnofficial" messages into their *baraza* rhetoric, while still deploying legitimate national symbols. Chiefs and MPs compete for popular support, though usually they must do so through outward displays of consensus. An Embu chief in 1980 described to me tensions between chiefs and MPs, noting that politicians often viewed a popular chief as a threat to their own power because a chief might stand for local political office upon retiring from the civil service. (Recall that chiefs serve in their home areas, whereas more senior administrative officers do not.) *Baraza* can thus be seen as arenas in which political rivals engage in contests of rhetorical skill and test their capacity to move a crowd. Even in a society in which most politicians were subordinate to bureaucrats, a politician could creatively use a *baraza* to lodge a public personal appeal on behalf of his constituents. Official political talk is not a simple reflex of formal constraints. Rather, public political talk entails creation as much as it does enactment (a point taken up in this chapter's conclusions).

Less pliant *baraza* audiences

It was by no means true that all *baraza* accomplished such apparently easy shows of audience consensus and compliance as did the 1979 beer-banning gathering. During the late 1970s and early 1980s in Embu coffee cooperative societies experienced intense political conflict as some of them subdivided into smaller units. Local political factions divided on the issue of whether or not the societies should split, and some participants were displeased over the provincial administration's own apparent alliances with particular factions in these disputes.[86] Recognizing the potentially explosive situation at hand state and cooperative society officials repeatedly postponed *baraza* at which farmers were to confront cooperative society managers.

At one local coffee cooperative society meeting that finally was held in rural Embu in 1980 officials allowed questions from the audience, and farmers expressed much dissatisfaction. Coffee farmers in the audience complained to one another that society officials had "eaten" farmers' money. They asked publicly why a general meeting of the society had not been called earlier, and why a commercial loan the society had taken out had apparently not helped member farmers. When a speaker mentioned the possibility of members approving another commercial loan there was much grumbling from the back, and some asked for an explicit accounting of how the previous money had been used. As an accountant reported on past budget expenditures and future plans to purchase an Isuzu lorry and coffee pumps, and to build rental housing, people continued to grumble to one another, and some shouted questions to the chair, who tried to quiet them. Among those who shouted questions, for example, was a man who said that farmers had financed a new modern cooperative union building in Embu town and had not yet received any benefit from that building. Another questioner complained that leaders hide things from farmers, never reporting to them, for example, what profits have been earned from their investments such as the new union building.

The leaders at the meeting ignored all inquiries about union profits and called them "noise." Later in the meeting, an official told farmers they should not allow anyone to deceive them that their money was being "eaten" by committee members, saying that the district cooperative officer could not allow that to happen. After a long discussion about the fate of local *Harambee* contributions to a secondary school fund[87] begun over a year earlier, one farmer in the audience spoke as follows:

We do like schools, but you people give us leaders who are untrustworthy, particularly the committee members who are learned and who speak English. They don't consider the needs of ordinary people. When choosing leaders, consider the illiterate people as well. Maybe let them know how things are operating even if they are not actually leaders; they could observe from the sidelines.

To this comment the district officer replied that the government did not force leaders on people, but rather allowed citizens the opportunity to elect councillors or committee members. He also said that if the chief or any leader were untrustworthy people should inform the district officer and he would know what to do about it. Later in the meeting the newly elected chair of the local cooperative society told farmers that if they believed any committee member had wronged anyone they should take their complaint first to the committee chair before heading to the office of the district cooperative officer. He said that if anyone felt the committee chair himself was at fault he should take that complaint to another committee member and they would convene a meeting to discuss what to do. The committee had the power to suspend a member if need be, he noted. If anyone wanted to send a delegation to the district cooperative officer, he suggested, that individual would face no problems provided he first obtained the approval of the committee chair.

The district cooperative officer then urged people to elect good leaders: individuals who send their children to school and manage their own farms and homes well. Such people he contrasted with those who make a lot of noise, who don't even take good care of their own coffee trees, and who spend time drinking in bars while leaving their wives working hard at home. He told the audience that they know the character and habits of individuals who live among them, they know very well who steals, and they should consider those habits when deciding whom to elect. Finally, he said that he will assume that any leaders elected are good, since he is not a local person and it is up to voters to make that judgment. The non-local or "stranger" status[88] of bureaucrats, such as the coffee cooperative society officer, and the district officer is intended to shield them from deep involvement in local politics. Even without local roots, however, such individuals play a key role in the outcome of local political contests.

This extended example both illustrates the deep concerns of many farmers about the honesty and accountability of their elected leaders, and hints at collusion among leaders themselves. Farmers had similar concerns about non-elected state officials, though they were less likely to express them publicly at a *baraza*. The cooperative society gathering

shows both state officials and elected cooperative society leaders down-
playing farmers' queries, and portraying a partial or misleading view of
farmers' options to protect themselves against leaders who were irresponsible or who might have "eaten" farmers' money. Such options as reporting suspected abuses by cooperative society committee members to other
committee members, or reporting a chief's misconduct to a district officer
did not acknowledge the risks to the "whistle-blower" of such reporting.
These risks were common knowledge, well understood informal rules of
the patronage game.

Officials' remarks at this meeting could only remind the audience that
foxes were guarding the hen house. Indeed, a farmer remarked to me on a
different occasion that when it comes to money, subchiefs, chiefs, and
district officers "speak with one voice," and that if you want to be the
assistant chief's enemy, you will ask him about the money collected from
farmers for previous development projects.[89] That is, he recognized the
shared interests of elected leaders and bureaucrats to whom farmers
might take complaints of misuse of funds or abuses of power. A chief, on
the other hand, commented to me that it is poor farmers from whom the
cooperative society deducts nothing who are the loudest "noise makers"
during *baraza*.

This last remark, a ploy to marginalize critics ("noise makers"), can be
an effective diversionary tactic. Given contradictory local moralities of
poverty and wealth (see chapters 4 and 5), for a chief to characterize vocal
critics as the poor is to connote social marginality, and imputed attributes
such as laziness, drunkenness, or inability to manage successfully a farm
and family. It is easier politically to marginalize poor farmers who make
"noise" during a *baraza* if poverty is portrayed as a personal failure rather
than an absence of opportunity (an alternative discourse in Kenya). And
even if most of the "noise makers" are not poor, for a public official to
portray vocal critics as socially marginal can help to discredit them. At the
same time, when the chief asserts that the cooperative society deducts
nothing from poor farmers, he indirectly affirms an ethic by which
discretionary official deductions from farmers (e.g., for *Harambee* projects) should bear some relation to their capacity to pay.

During the coffee cooperative society *baraza* farmers stretched the rules
of acceptable public talk by openly challenging some of their elected
officials. They raised questions about officials' honesty and demanded an
accounting of how the coffee income had been spent and of profits earned
from union investments. In onstage and offstage remarks farmers present
expressed resentment of a particular structure of power and material
interests. Their outspokenness, however limited in its immediate practical
effects, does confirm the existence of symbolic resources for an alternative

social order, one with more accountable leadership. To say that these farmers' immediate room for maneuver is within the confines of existing institutions is not to suggest that they are necessarily blind to wider "structural" injustices. At the moment, however, they lodge oral protests that are morally justified by officials' own rhetorical pronouncements. Officials, after all, do assert publicly that leaders should be trustworthy and that citizens should report those who are not to the appropriate officials. This was a time in Kenyan history when anti-corruption themes were prominent in official rhetoric. Indeed, subordinates' critiques of power often deploy the very symbols and morality offered by those who dominate them (cf. Scott 1976, 1985).

Conclusions

At moments of political transition, such as the start of the Moi era late in 1978, politicians and populace are likely to indulge in imaginings of a new and better social order. Political rhetoric at such times may ring less hollow, and inspire more belief in new possibilities, than would be the case later in the life of a new regime. The Moi era began with wide popular good will, though it certainly did not inspire what Geertz (1973a: 235) in a more general context terms the "near-millenial hopes of political deliverance" associated with attaining political independence from colonial rule. Nonetheless, the new *nyayo* rhetoric of the Moi era blew fresh life into *baraza*, as speakers inventively connected the "footsteps" slogan to local concerns, and relayed the president's promises of an end to corruption, tribalism, drunkenness, nepotism, and other evils. These rhetorical themes later provided symbolic ammunition to attack the very regime they were intended to legitimize. But the economy and political culture of 1979–80 were very different from those of the early 1990s. Moi's first months in office saw a new national political culture apparently "traditionalized" with remarkable rapidity.

For Moi, as for his colonial and post-colonial predecessors, the *baraza* appeared to be a crucial weapon in the state's symbolic arsenal. But is "weapon" too strong a word for this institution? *Baraza* do help to anchor in everyday realities the abstraction that is the nation-state. But how important are *baraza* to state-building if the Kenyan government, like others in Africa, "beyond their own offices and outside their own rhetoric, were practically ineffectual"?[90]

In short, why would anyone take a *baraza* seriously? First, through these gatherings the one-party state affirms itself as a symbolic presence and sets limits on tolerable behavior among citizens. Here citizens learn to deploy political symbols in ways acceptable to those in power. The costs of ignorance in this realm are serious: ranging from denial of patronage rewards to surveillance, harassment, imprisonment, and even death. Through *baraza* some individuals also draw inspiration for alternative or subversive uses of national symbols. Second, among the voices of the state heard during *baraza* addresses listeners detect clues to contending forces within the state, and to factional realignments. These public meetings offer a display of elite cohesion, but provide as well glimpses of intra-elite competition, tensions, and conflicts, and of popular discontent and resistance to elite authority. They help to reveal "shadow" patron–client networks. Individuals must factor hints of such shifts into their daily actions. *Baraza* rhetoric in part, then, constitutes (often subtly) contests between political rivals. It both shapes and reflects factional divisions and shifts (though these have not been my focus here). Third, part of the answer must be that such rituals are inspired largely by the "perplexities of the powerful" and the "uncertainties of rule," as Lonsdale (1981: 160) puts it. Rulers' *baraza* rhetoric constructs a moral armament to justify their rule. Some elites who speak at these gatherings may take their rhetorical content more seriously than do their audiences. (But when citizens do take the rhetoric seriously and find official practice falls short of the avowed ideals, acts of resistance and political change may be afoot.) Finally, *baraza* attendance is a fundamental social act that outwardly signifies membership in and ratification of a particular social order, "even if one has no interest in the issues and topics at hand" and if one wants to change that social order.[91] Not to attend is to say "one does not recognize the moral authority of those individuals whose position or office is invested with upholding that authority." Public attendance is therefore important to both state and citizens.

Baraza rhetoric is not transparent, which is not to suggest that it "fools" listeners. Rather, its interpretation requires them to read between the lines (and of course readings vary among individuals). Observers are attuned to onstage strategies for obscuring offstage matters.[92] *Baraza* participants are aware of, as well as authors of, various offstage discourses, and these both shape and reflect official rhetoric. Non-transparent political talk that incorporates rhetorical devices such as indirection, metaphor, and suppressed premises occurs everywhere, but the particular "social phenomena that must be simultaneously addressed, reshaped, and obscured from view are quite different" in varying types of social orders and at different historical moments (Gal 1991: 454).[93]

Cultural idioms such as curses, bridewealth, marriage, and patronage infuse Kenyan political rhetoric. We saw, for example, a Gikuyu state official invoke the notion of *uthoni* – marriage and bridewealth negotiations between two families – to imply that farmers and state officials were equal, reasoning partners in a dialogue and collaboration that would have a mutually beneficial outcome. Even if such a comparison leaves many in the audience skeptical, political rhetoric acquires more immediacy when it includes metaphors that incorporate the morality of relations among kin and affines. Curses, rooted in cultural obligations between juniors and elders, have for decades entered public political language. Public curses against political opponents were spoken by Moi allies in the 1990s, by Kenyatta in the 1960s, and by unconverted elders in the colonial era.

Partly through *baraza*, both the colonial and post-colonial state constructed a moral bargain with citizens, by which state authority rests in part on its capacity to deliver the benefits of "development" (*maendeleo*) in exchange for citizen compliance and obedience. As part of this bargain the state curtails independent political activity, and suppresses opposition that it argues would lead to civil disorder or "chaos."

As suggested in one of this chapter's epigraphs, official language tacitly establishes "the dividing line between the thinkable and the unthinkable" (Bourdieu 1977: 21). That imaginary dividing line helps to structure both onstage and offstage discourses, and the ways in which they engage one another directly or indirectly. Thus Moi's early anti-corruption rhetoric responded to growing popular discontent over questionable means by which political elites under Kenyatta acquired land and other wealth. Kenyatta himself was not the target of Moi's criticism. Moi's rhetoric also indirectly addressed some of the concerns raised by marginalized "radical" or populist Kenyan intellectuals who criticized a growing gap between rich and poor, and who argued the need for a ceiling on land ownership. Though Moi did not advocate any economic restructuring, his rhetoric implied that under the *nyayo* regime some earlier abuses of power would be curbed. Questions about how wealth should be distributed had historical antecedents in earlier debates about the "bargains" which Kenyatta struck with the British at independence, including the explosive question of how to allocate the vast farms colonial British settlers occupied in Kenya (see Wasserman 1976). The voices of those who believed they were unjustified losers in the independence land bargain continued to be heard in opposition rhetoric in succeeding decades. Tensions persisted between Africans on opposite sides of colonial political struggles. State-sponsored oratory often responded only indirectly to these political cross-currents.

Post-colonial state rhetoric in other respects often seemed the reincarnation of colonial authoritarianism. As Kenyan state officials in the early 1990s framed their opposition to advocates of a shift to multiparty politics, they echoed colonial assumptions that "chaos" would inevitably result from looser controls on independent political activity, or indeed from any alternative to the present regime. That theme also had offered a convenient line of attack on Kenyan nationalists during the 1950s emergency. In addition, the post-colonial state echoed colonial paternalism when it offered the material benefits of "progress" and "development" as conditional rewards for the hard work and political compliance of citizens. This bargain, as events of the early 1990s demonstrate, could be undermined by shrinking state coffers. Once the material rewards of compliance diminished citizens became more likely publicly to invoke democratic principles woven into their own cultures, or those which British colonial officials had avowed but not practiced.

Both the colonial and post-colonial state used *baraza* to control political debate. The state could, for example, simply avoid or postpone convening or licensing potentially volatile gatherings (as in the case of Embu coffee cooperatives in the early 1980s). It could, as noted in chapter 2, deny regime opponents permits to convene their own meetings, and prevent them from addressing those that were held. Official rhetoric castigated political activists and dissidents by labeling their brand of politics as the "politics of the devil or madness," or a "fierce politics" that contrasted with the "good politics" of the ruling party, KANU. In short, *baraza* represent attempts by the powerful to define political reality for their citizens.

The *baraza*, and its attendant radio and newspaper coverage, are crucial to developing among citizens an image of Kenya as a distinctive collectivity or "imagined community" (Anderson 1991). In publicly displaying the country's political and administrative hierarchy *baraza* can help to legitimize both state authority in general, and the authority of the state's individual representatives in particular. If a speaker succeeds his address confirms his authority and precludes challenges to his position or to the substance of his remarks. In one sense, the *baraza* is a ritual of power that "reproduces" the existing political hierarchy by displaying it (cf. Bloch 1975; Brenneis and Myers 1984: 4). The ritual is also, however, an arena of political struggle. Its outcome is by no means inevitable, and can include transformation as well as reproduction.

Within the formal constraints of acceptable political talk and *baraza* behavior speakers and audience members find ways to manipulate national symbols and public displays to advance some of their own interests. Thus *baraza* speakers can appear both to support fully the president's proposed ban on home-brewed beer, and draw attention to the subsistence needs of farmers who depend on sales of the sugarcane used to make beer. Through indirection, politicians can sneak "unofficial" messages into *baraza*. In so doing they use national symbols both to appeal to constituents and to demonstrate loyalty to the ruling regime. In addition, speakers use subtle affective cues to demonstrate sympathy for their audience: as in the case of colonial chiefs who might soften official messages through equivocal language, affect, and gestures (see Ita 1972: 66). That is, the constraints or unwritten "rules" about what is and is not speakable allow room for creativity as well as conformity. Both audience and speakers test and push the limits of moving boundaries between permissible and unpermissible talk, taking subtle cues from the president's rhetoric and from what others get away with saying. In politically charged coffee cooperative society meetings in the early 1980s farmers shouted questions about possible official misuse of funds. At certain historical moments (e.g., the late 1950s and early 1990s), a sudden shift in political circumstances breaks down earlier restraints on *baraza* behavior. Thus during the late 1950s citizens suddenly could challenge publicly and shout down colonial chiefs (Ita 1972: 60).

National political culture is neither an exclusively elite product nor a collective creation to be reified into a stable "text." Rather, it is a loose collection of shifting meanings that are multiply-authored and context-dependent. It is "the outcome of a constant process of cultural production" (Fox 1990: 2). Part of this culture is an officially constructed ideology that "naturalizes" a particular social order. The *nyayo* "philosophy" is in part a set of meanings spun by the president and those close to him. These meanings and symbols, however, in different hands can undermine rather than support the status quo. Dissident intellectuals, for example, give the word *nyayo* a satirical and disrespectful connotation when they use it to refer to the president.

When leaders join their audience in complicit displays of support for a presidential project such as the beer "ban," what they require in order successfully to come through a *baraza* are only outward displays of enthusiasm, compliance, and consensus by the audience. Those in the audience know that non-deferential behavior or open opposition or hostility on their part may well invite state retribution. To avoid authorities' displeasure all that is required of a *baraza* audience is that it listen politely, applaud, and when prompted provide formulaic responses with some enthusiasm. If audience affect is sometimes flat or their enthusiasm feigned as they repeat slogans or give prescribed responses, they are held publicly accountable only for the literal substance of their replies. It is always difficult to determine the extent to which *baraza* behavior means support, grudging or half-hearted compliance, or resistance.[94] As Scott (1986: 29) notes, "the kind of resistance itself may depend for its effectiveness on the *appearance* of conformity."[95]

Do *baraza* guarantee anything other than an appearance of popular support for the ruling regime? If seeing and performing are not necessarily believing the ritual display itself nonetheless is important. As S. F. Moore (1977: 170) put it in the Tanzanian context, "such meetings dramatize a political arrangement that is being constructed in part by the drama itself." Whatever undeterminable emotions and thoughts lie behind the outward display, "co-ceremonial behavior produces a multiplier effect. It hints that what is hidden in everyone's mind is as conventionally proper and uniform as what everyone is *seen* to be doing in concert" (S. F. Moore 1977: 169). *Baraza* in this sense can help to constitute a Durkheimian "common spirit" that sustains state authority.

Crucial to the political process is public display of affect-laden support for the ruling regime. As Brenneis (1990: 117) notes, "emotions are not solely "about" the world; they also help to constitute it." In Kenyan *baraza* loud and enthusiastic exchanges between orators and audiences help to constitute the political reality upon which the regime in power depends.

Countless repetitions of such gatherings across the country both dramatize and help to constitute a national political culture and its attendant political hierarchy. In one sense the *baraza* as national institution presupposes the very political culture it is trying to create.[96] Herein lies part of the analytic tension between "structure" and "agency." Cultural "production" depends in part on the linguistic acts of hundreds of individual "agents." Those agents both operate within a framework of political "rules" about acceptable and expected behavior, and at the same time creatively manipulate the rules to serve particular purposes. *Baraza* are power-laden situations in which both listeners and speakers must adopt the appropriate strategic poses, or risk serious consequences. At the same time individuals are keenly attuned to shifts in political winds, and they sometimes stretch or break the rules, in acts that may shape (usually in unintended ways) structural change.[97]

Finally, political rituals can simultaneously foster divisiveness and social solidarity (Lukes 1975). The apparent displays of consensus at *baraza* dramatize social polarities as well as national unity. These gatherings, for example, confirm the social distance and power inequalities between elites and ordinary citizens: between a baton-wielding chief or district officer clad in pressed khaki uniform and pith helmet on the one hand, and a bare-footed farmer wearing dusty, patched second-hand clothing on the other; or between a farmer and an MP or cabinet minister who arrives in his Mercedes Benz. *Baraza* draw attention to the irrelevance of state policies and rhetoric to some of the everyday realities of life, a theme illustrated in the next two chapters.

In short, as Lukes (1975) suggests more generally, political ritual does not necessarily promote or express "value integration," nor does value consensus take one very far in solving the "problem of order." Kenyan society can remain relatively orderly even if some citizens regard *baraza* as farce, or as unwelcome reminders of their own subordination to elites, and of citizens' vulnerability to the state's supporting means of physical coercion. Such political ritual, as Lukes (1975: 301) argues more generally "helps to define as authoritative certain ways of seeing society . . . it draws people's attention to certain forms of relationships and activity – and at the same time, therefore, it deflects their attention from other forms, since every way of seeing is also a way of not seeing." Thus *baraza* are significant because they convey a particular representation or paradigm of the sociopolitical order. To the extent that they convince some people of this order's inevitability, "naturalness," or justness, such assemblies may contribute to political stability.

But these gatherings also acknowledge, often indirectly, other ways of seeing the social order. For example, during the beer-banning *baraza*, the possibility of genuine popular participation in the "decision" to ban beer was only a pose, a rhetorical gesture by the councillor who said anyone could speak. Nonetheless, such reminders (in this case about the right of free speech) can nourish opposition sentiments, and become key symbolic resources upon which to draw in other contexts. Alternative conceptions of a social order, even if formally submerged, help to define political contests and the course of historical change. Thus the early 1990s saw the re-emergence of democratic themes suppressed since the colonial era. The state's capacity to preserve public silences on the subjects it chooses can never be taken for granted.

In short, *baraza* can both symbolically boost the ruling regime, and simultaneously reveal the fragility of state poses. Rulers depend upon public displays of apparent enthusiasm by crowds out to "entertain themselves." The "entertainment," as suggested in chapter 1, is a perilous mix of ostensible respect and jocular disregard.

How is the onstage collusion between citizens and leaders during *baraza* connected to other spheres of daily life? To explore this theme the next two chapters shift attention away from the spectacle of the *baraza* itself, and take a closer look at the social divisions and asymmetries that *baraza* rhetoric can silence, naturalize, or rationalize. We have seen that *baraza* afford a glimpse of interests that diverge along lines of gender and generation (as in the 1979 beer ban), along lines of literacy and class (as in the coffee cooperative society gathering discussed earlier), and along lines of ethnicity and locality (as in the 1992 political campaign (see chapter 2) and in the Embu cabinet minister's 1979 public address about God's wisdom in selecting a president with Moi's ethnic origins). And we have seen that the principal threats to social order, as construed in political rhetoric, are not differences of class, gender, or generation, but rather those of ethnicity, local identity, and uncontrolled political expression (the "politics of the devil" and the "politics of madness").

The state's capacity to convince citizens that restrictions on political expression are needed to preserve order (or to prevent "chaos") depends in part on delivering to the populace some of the material benefits of "progress" and modernity. In the early 1990s, as discussed in chapter 2, the Kenyan state faced mounting challenges in that task. The material rewards of hard work were declining for most citizens in town and countryside (a theme noted in local campaign rhetoric in 1992). Central Kenyan farmers who toiled at cultivating coffee and tea, for example, received diminishing and, in their view, unjust rewards for that work (see Throup 1993b). In addition, the state failed to protect citizens from civil disorder or "chaos" (with the "ethnic" clashes in the Rift Valley and rising levels of violence in much of the country). Such developments accentuated the tensions noted earlier between state authoritarianism, paternalism, "development," and democracy. The material rewards of political acquiescence were shrinking for many people: a situation many found less tolerable as they witnessed the vastly disproportionate material gains reaped by a small number of ruling party loyalists at the top. These conditions contrasted with an official rhetorical emphasis on individual opportunities for material advance, and with earlier local moralities of just rewards for hard work.

In chapters 4 and 5, we see why personal wealth, like political fortune, is evanescent. Here my focus shifts to a closer view of struggles for livelihood in one part of Embu District during the past century. What precisely are farmers' material concerns, and why are smallscale farmers like those in Embu portrayed as the foundation of Kenya's economic "miracle"? How do they organize the pursuit of riches, how do wealth differences arise, and what is the magnitude of such inequality? How do the unpredictabilities of domestic life, of economic pursuits, and of politics intersect? What is the relationship between accumulation and reciprocity, and what are the moral obligations of the rich toward the poor? What parallels become visible between, on the one hand, a contemporary state starved for cash and, on the other, famine crises of the late nineteenth and twentieth centuries?

Transcription key

(2.0)	length of significant pause (in seconds)
SEP779:A,20	transcript, tape side, and page number
( )	material deleted for sake of brevity or relevance
Xxxx	proper names not reported in order to protect anonymity
.	falling intonation (not necessarily at the end of a sentence)
,	continuing intonation (not necessarily between clauses)
?	rising intonation (not necessarily a question)
!	animated intonation (not necessarily an exclamation)
WORD	much louder than surrounding talk
wo : : rd	non-phonemic segment gemination
((laughter))	various characterizations of talk or context

4   Moral economy and the quest for wealth in central Kenya since the late nineteenth century

Introduction

This chapter begins with a look back to a time before Kenyans could be instructed *en masse* that theirs was a nation "on the run" toward "development," and that each individual had to move quickly to keep up with the president's rapid footsteps or *nyayo*. Whereas the previous chapter explored notions of "Kenya" conveyed to citizens through official rhetoric, this one starts with a look at life in the central highlands before radio, newspapers, cinema, and television brought Kenyans into a national and global "village." This is not an exercise in nostalgia. Rather, its purpose is to appreciate historical precedents for a public culture that valorizes collective effort as well as individual entrepreneurship and accumulation, and that projects its own Western modernity, economic growth, and political stability as counterexamples to the recent history of other African nations. It is not surprising that a state controlled by wealthy entrepreneurs would advertise the material rewards of hard work. Nor is it unusual that such a state would make a repeated show of intentions to eliminate "corruption" among public servants, without actually altering the opportunities for accumulation open to such individuals.

Who is or who deserves to be rich and who poor has probably never been a cultural zone of easy consensus. The material rewards of political leadership – whether in pre-colonial raiding expeditions or in election to parliament – are matters of discussion and argument in which everyone takes a keen interest. In a nation where it is customary for any member of parliament to acquire a Mercedes Benz, and for candidates for office to start from positions of relative wealth, Embu voters in the 1980 election found unfit for office a parliamentary candidate who publicly avowed his reliance on a bicycle for transport. Though class is not often an explicit theme of public rhetoric, when it is, official words portray prosperity as a possibility open to many, rather than as the preserve of a few. The rhetoric connects material fortune to the personal characteristics of individuals rather than to wider structural constraints. Accompanying this rhetoric, however, are continuing cultural arguments over the greed or generosity of the wealthy, as well as over the laziness or worthiness of the poor. The wealth motifs which this chapter and the next explore extend across the familiar pre-colonial/colonial/post-colonial historical markers.

What moral expectations do rich and poor have of one another? How do they justify their unequal states? These can be matters of life and death: socially as well as physically. They spark rebellion in families as well as in nations. Wealth and poverty are a fertile theme in the proverbs of central Kenya. One proverb recognizes the social inconsequence of a poor person's words: "The poor man's tongue is always thin."[1] But another notes that a rich man cannot deny a poor one natural blessings such as rain: "Whoever humiliates a poor man cannot prevent the rain from falling."[2] Kenyan proverbs attribute wealth to hard work: "He that wants to become rich must till the earth,"[3] and "A cow is never acquired by an indolent person."[4] But another recognizes the unsympathetic side of wealth: "The well-fed calls the ravenous greedy."[5] In short, riches and poverty provoke powerful and contrary emotions.

The fate of ties of moral obligation between rich and poor in agrarian societies has been a focus of much scholarly attention. Both liberal and Marxist approaches often assume an inevitable breakdown in relations of reciprocity and clientage with the growth of markets and states. It is easy, for example, to place clientage and reciprocity near a "natural economy" rather than "commodity economy" analytic pole, and to assume that such oppositional categories capture actual historical processes (in which accumulation drives out reciprocity).[6] But clientage and reciprocity, like state formation and commercialization, wax and wane and take on varied forms. Reciprocity and accumulation coexist. Most important, even if clientage and reciprocity are placed nearer a "natural economy" rather than a "commodity economy" analytic pole, their contemporary forms nonetheless are best understood as the historical product of the same forces that produced their "opposite" pole.[7] Both poles are likely to include elements of a "remade past" that figure in social constructions of the present.

These are some orienting arguments of this chapter's historical sketch of moral economy and the quest for wealth in central Kenya between about 1890 and 1980. Moral economy here concerns expectations and moral obligations between rich and poor (see also chapter 1). The chapter looks at changes in wealth: its sources, its distribution, and its accompanying cultural expectations about reciprocity and accumulation. It is not meant to be historically exhaustive, but rather suggestive of bridges to the present (a theme taken up later). For example, I propose political and cultural parallels between, on the one hand, a contemporary state starved for cash and, on the other, famine crises of the late nineteenth and twentieth centuries. In both situations patrons and dominant kin are suddenly short of material rewards to dispense, and clients and dependent kin desert their superiors to search for better opportunities, or are cast off by them. Both patrons and dependants make strategic use of cultural resources in order to press material claims and to construe social reality in advantageous ways. These cultural arguments turn, for example, on the contrast between "reciprocal duty and one-sided oppression," or between public benefactors and "anti-social swindler(s) on the make" (Lonsdale 1992: 352). In short, clientage and reciprocity remain a terrain of cultural and moral debate, as material stakes and other circumstances shift.

Ethnography sometimes characterizes as "egalitarian" the smallscale autonomous groups of the kind found in pre-colonial central Kenya. Though relations between such groups may suggest structural equality this does not imply an egalitarian ideology (Kopytoff 1987: 35). Nor do egalitarian ideologies necessarily imply equal opportunities to achieve desired ends, or equal outcomes of such pursuits (cf. Flanagan 1989: 248). And again, a presumed opposition between egalitarianism and hierarchy is misleading as a historical model. All social life includes principles of hierarchy, and these are expressed in varied structural patterns. All relations of dependence – as between juniors and elders or patrons and clients – are relations of hierarchy sanctioned by particular cultural principles. The historical question then becomes one of exploring how older social ties and cultural principles assert themselves in new ways as circumstances alter.

When contemporary scholars write about Africa's economic and political history, they often are careful not to posit a mythical "merrie Africa" as their starting point. What they wish to avoid is assuming a baseline equilibrium stage in which livelihoods were more secure, conflict less prevalent, spiritual beliefs more certain, or human populations more in harmony or balance with the natural environment.[8] The discredited narratives suggest that this earlier happy harmony was disrupted by rapid changes associated with colonial and post-colonial rule. Instead, scholars today are more likely to emphasize the dynamism and flux of life in both the past and the present.

Historical accounts nonetheless lend themselves to storytelling, to narratives with a beginning, a middle, and an end. A scholar imposes some order on the currents of history, necessarily constructing a picture of reality more coherent than the ephemeral realities of lived experience. Nor are historical narratives "socially neutral recitations that serve all equally" (Feierman 1993: 183). Narrative premises common to accounts of the past include history as a "meaningful totality," as a "series of critical moments and transitions," and as explanation based on the arrangement of events into sequences (Landau 1984: 266–267). Whether explicit attention to narrative strategies in historical or scientific accounts can help scholars to assess their validity or value is subject to debate.

The story I construct in this chapter starts with the nineteenth-century (pre-colonial) sources of economic differentiation upon which colonial and post-colonial rule built. Here I trace local and regional expressions of the familiar "grand processes" of state formation and agricultural commercialization. For pre-colonial Africa data limitations, including a thin archeological record and fragmentary written records, make constructing historical accounts a particular challenge. It is difficult to quantify agricultural production and exchange, or to reconstruct how labor was mobilized, production organized, or land distributed during pre-colonial times. These problems in defining a pre-colonial baseline from which to measure economic or agrarian change further complicate already notorious problems of assessing the magnitude and direction of rural class differentiation processes. With these caveats in mind, let us look at a few aspects of central Kenya's economic and political history. I will suggest historical continuities and discontinuities in the social order that contemporary *baraza* rhetoric helps to "naturalize."

I start with the loosely defined "region" of central Kenya, and within that wider context, I explore particularities of what is now Embu District. The wider region includes Bantu-speaking groups who surround Mt. Kenya, cultivating and raising livestock in its fertile foothills and adjacent lower altitude plains. Today these peoples are known by the official ethnic and linguistic categories: Gikuyu, Embu, Meru, Mbeere, Kamba, and Tharaka (see maps 2 and 3).[9] Any of these local "societies" can be seen partly as the historical product of wider regional processes. The mobile peoples who settled multiple African frontiers "brought with them a cultural model of the society they wished to construct," Kopytoff (1987: 35) suggests. Any particular frontier society was likely, he observes, to include groups of multiple origins who over time drew upon and resynthesized particular local expressions of wider cultural principles.

A pre-colonial snapshot: caravans, brokers, and farmers[10]

A nineteenth-century prophet in central Kenya predicted the coming of people whose skins resembled that of a certain small red frog (*kiengere*), and whose dress was like the wings of butterflies. According to various versions of the prophecy these strangers would finish off old customs, bring new forms of wealth, or steal local lands.[11] Though the arrival of

Europeans in East Africa was a momentous event, it was by no means the only significant impetus to change. Neither commercialization nor wealth differences were unknown in central Kenya during the nineteenth century.

Local identity and territorial organization

Today's official ethnic categories, as suggested in chapter 2, did not already exist in the nineteenth century as "natural" or "primordial" entities. What is now Embu District,[12] like other parts of Kenya, in pre-colonial times consisted of numerous autonomous localities and highly mobile populations. Farmers have lived in central Kenya since at least AD 1000 (Muriuki 1974; Spear 1981; Ambler 1988: 9). After about 1800 central-Kenyan cultivators dominated pastoralists, such as the Oromo groups, and hunting and gathering peoples. Though the accounts of early European travelers[13] in the region suggest that ethnic divisions were widely recognized, residents of any particular region "moved in a complex world of overlapping, layered, and shifting associations" in which ties of family, lineage, and locality were especially strong (Ambler 1988: 32). Pre-colonial territorial organization in what is now Embu was based on named, non-corporate neighborhoods whose membership and geographic extent were loosely defined and influenced but not determined by descent ties (see Moris 1970: 193–195; Saberwal 1970: 16).

In brief, nineteenth-century central Kenya was made up not of pre-cisely bounded "societies" or "ethnic" groups, but rather of peoples with a long history of relations through trade, migration, marriage, clientage, and adoption (as suggested in chapter 2). Here, as elsewhere in Africa, people moved from one locale to another for many reasons: to flee famine and drought; to acquire distance from troubled relations with kin and affines; to start a new life after unsuccessful defense against charges of witchcraft; to aquire a larger farm, and so on (cf. Kopytoff 1987). This is not to suggest that ethnic groups were mere inventions imposed from above. Rather, they reflected as well individuals pressing moral claims within communities defined from below (Lonsdale 1986: 143). But those communities had very fluid boundaries, and there was nothing foreord-ained about the ethnic units that came to be recognized under colonial rule.

Popular notions of local identity shifted situationally and over time.[14] Communities, as suggested, were accustomed to drawing in new people, including wives, captives, laborers, clients, and adoptees. There was substantial internal variation, as well as armed conflict, within what were later identified as ethnic populations. From time to time divisions arose among shifting coalitions of groups who organized raids in which live-stock, women, and occasionally men were captured. Nonetheless, par-ticular local and ethnic traditions emerged in association with oral tales of origin and migration. Elders with whom I spoke in the Kagaari area of Embu, for example, recall the legend of a man called Mwenendega who lived in the sacred grove of the same name, took a wife called Thaara, and produced a boy named Kembu and a girl named Werimba. Kembu and Werimba were driven from the grove after committing incest and pro-duced descendants who became known as the children of Kembu or Embu and settled in the district now of that name. Similar "Embu" origin myths occur in Mwaniki (1973b: 15–17), Saberwal (1970: 3), and Lambert (1950: 19). Such traditions circulated among localities that were loosely bound together through meetings of councils of elders, ceremonies trans-ferring power from one generation to another, collective military action, and bridewealth exchanges. Colonial rule later reinforced and reshaped local and "ethnic" distinctions. Indeed, here as elsewhere in Africa, colonial authorities themselves fostered antagonisms that those same authorities then construed as primordial tribal enmities (e.g., by hiring pastoralists labeled as "Maasai" as mercenaries to raid farming commu-nities).[15] And under colonial rule, "tribe became a body of defence against and demand upon the state, a formerly unimaginable role" (Lons-dale 1992: 354) which I consider below (see also chapter 2).

In late pre-colonial Embu, frequent movements of people recast social relationships within neighborhoods, which started out as small settle-ments based on patrilineages. Place names in Embu, as elsewhere in central Kenya, seldom denoted bounded territorial entities until taken over by the government to fit administratively demarcated units such as locations or sublocations (Moris 1970: 194):

Otherwise, the indigenous terms refer to geographic or situational features: to types of land form, to colours, to vegetation, to places where certain animals were once found or where certain plants blossom, and the like ... Thus we get *Mbukori*, the place where moles (sing., *mbuko*) are; *Mbubori*, where many weeds are blowing; *Gatundori*, where you find *gatundu* trees ... *Kyambogo*, where there were buffaloes, *Kyaruthi*, where there were (lions).

Indeed, the lack of territorially inclusive terms may explain the ease and rapidity of adoption of the administrative units later introduced by the British (Moris 1970: 195). In the colonial and post-colonial periods Embu neighborhoods (which today as in the past often carry more than one name) acquired more consistent boundaries as they became important informal subdivisions (referred to as *ituura* or ridge) of the least inclusive official administrative units, which are now termed "sublocations" and are headed by assistant chiefs. In pre-colonial Embu society, however, individual conceptions of the neighborhoods making up the society's wider territory were idiosyncratic and inconsistent:

Looking beyond his neighborhood, the Embu man appears to have perceived not sharply delimited territorial units but rather long stretches of ridges and streams wherein the importance of membership in particular neighborhoods was diluted by such cross-cutting ties as those of descent, age-set, and elderhood. (Saberwal 1970: 16)

Within the small territory that later became Embu Division of Embu District, residents today note variations in accent and dialect as clues to an individual's particular local origins. The boundaries of colonial and post-colonial administrative units there tended to follow rivers and streams that in the past to some extent would have restricted interactions among the residents of different localities.

Of more widely recognized importance than neighborhoods in the late pre-colonial period were the special ceremonial sacred groves, warriors' dancing grounds, and particular outdoor sites used for litigation and other public purposes. These were the locus of activities whose organization cross-cut ties of kinship and neighborhood. The territorial, descent, and residence units from which groups of elders were convened to hear disputes at such sites, for example, varied and were determined in an *ad hoc* fashion in accordance with circumstances and personalities involved in a particular dispute. Geographic locations constituted loosely defined sacrificial units whose members practiced joint ceremonies to bring rain, to bless seeds before planting, to bless crops in the field, to give thanks for a good crop just before harvest, and to ward off illness or epidemics.

Today some of the sacred groves have been set off as County Council forest reserves, one of which is the Mwenendega grove in Kagaari Location, which is still associated with legends mentioned above concerning the origins of the Embu people. Also of continuing spiritual importance are the forests of Mt. Kenya (or Kerenyaya, "mountain of brightness"), one of the favorite earthly resting spots of the supreme deity (MweneNjeru, MweneNyaga, or Ngai).[16] Other resting places of the high deity include sacred groves such as Kirimiri in Embu (Kagaari). Nineteenth-century spiritual life in central Kenya included the worship of a high deity, as well as communion with ancestors and various sacrificial rites (see Kenyatta 1965).

Finally, claims to land (see below and chapter 5) depended in part on who arrived first and began to cultivate it.[17] These "original" claims might be expressed in terms of group and lineage identities. As noted, however, kin groups were territorially dispersed, so that in any particular neighborhood one would find a mix of lineages. If descent was a corporate ideal, it was one activated in variable ways and according to situational contingencies: to deal, for example, with particular local issues such as marriage negotiations or dispute settlement. Glazier (1985: 29) argues that among Mbeere peoples, "descent groups were historically shallow and only minimally corporate." They became more corporate, he shows, during the scramble for land stimulated by the state's ambitious tenure reform program. These later conflicts had their roots in processes of agrarian change already underway at the end of the last century.

Commercialization and regional ecology: "vertical" strategies

By the late 1800s, there was a well-developed regional trade system linking central Kenya's uplands and lowlands.[18] Products such as yams and bananas were traded downhill, and animal fats and beans uphill. Much trade in such commodities "moved through networks that linked neighboring areas rather than along the longer distance routes."[19] Ties would have been strong, for example, between the Embu highlands and the Mbeere lowlands, constituting a dense network of exchange relationships. Even within a less productive area such as Mbeere, significant crop variation (e.g., in bean cultivars) probably encouraged local trade. Exchanges between Embu and Mbeere did not constitute an encapsulated system, but rather an open one with extensive commercial ties as well to other communities around Mt. Kenya. Though ecological complementarities were part of the context of ties of commercial exchange among communities in Mt. Kenya's foothills, this is not to suggest that historical processes can be reduced to an inevitable ecological "logic."

As part of the exchange networks that linked localities around Mt. Kenya Embu was rather close to what became the center of the colony's emerging capitalist economy. (The capital, Nairobi, was not far south of Embu.) The primary Embu settlement zone late in the nineteenth century was choice agricultural land[20] lying approximately between the 6,000 and 4,500 feet (1,830 and 1,370 metres) altitude contours (Mwaniki 1973a,b; Ambler 1988: 21). The upper limit was the Mt. Kenya forest, whose boundary since then has receded to higher elevations as agriculture expanded during the last century. In the late 1800s, the wedge-shaped settled area narrowed at the forest and widened to a base about twenty miles (or 32 kilometres) across at lower elevations. In this small territory "several tens of thousands of people" lived by the late 1800s.[21] Settlements extended from the forest edge down about ten miles (16 kilometres): a distance that spanned a 1,500 feet (nearly 460 metre) drop in elevation. Administrative boundaries defined later followed rivers flowing from the mountain.[22]

Farmers exploited resources across this altitude gradient: from the forest to mid-elevation crop land and grazing in the plains.[23] The natural vegetation of the uplands is moist-to-dry forests of camphor and hardwoods, while that of the Embu lowlands is dry forest and moist woodland. Upland topography is steep ridges and valleys associated with a dense network of rivers and streams that flow radially from Mt. Kenya. With declining altitude the terrain becomes less steep, with more widely scattered ridges and valleys. The uplands on average are cooler and wetter, and have longer growing periods than the lowlands.[24] The rainfall pattern is bimodal and defines two principal cropping seasons per year (with a third crop season and rainfall peak in some higher altitude areas). The heaviest rainfall concentration occurs during the long rains of March, April, and May and the second heaviest during the short rains of October, November, and December.

In a pattern that continues today (albeit in altered forms), farmers cultivated dispersed plots in order to spread risks and labor, and to exploit different micro-environments. They grew a wide array of crops, including bananas, grains, pulses, and root crops. One nineteenth-century traveler passing through central Kenya describes the plentiful food supplies traded with passing caravans and travelers: "The camp was soon crowded with men, women, and children bringing food and tobacco for sale, the food including sugar-cane, maize, beans, cassava, millet and eleusine" (von Hohnel 1968: 297). And, "in the light grey volcanic soil of Kikuyuland grow nearly all the cereals native to East Africa, and it is, in fact, the granary of a very extended district. Several kinds of bananas are grown as well as beans, sugar-cane, maize, potatoes, yams, eleusine, dhurra, millet (*Panicum italicum*), mawale (*Pennisetum spicatum*), gourds, colocasia, and tobacco" (von Hohnel 1968: 352; see also MacDonald 1897: 109.) While most cultivation was on the sides and tops of ridges and hills, many farmers also took advantage of the darker soils and greater water availability in valley bottoms, using this lower land for crops such as sugarcane, arrowroot, and vegetables in a seasonal cycle different from that of hill crops.

In short these conditions contributed to a nineteenth-century pattern whereby during any season, many farmers at some time purchased and sold foodstuffs and other goods. Such exchanges helped to alleviate periodic production shortfalls, to diversify diets, and to meet social obligations. Trade was associated with production differences arising from pronounced micro-environmental variation (in rainfall, pests, crop diseases, soil quality, topography, elevation). Production also varied over time; in any particular location, rainfall amounts and hence crop output differed substantially from one season and year to the next. And household production levels fluctuated, in association with vagaries of health, weather, and personal relationships. How were these patterns connected to wealth differences?

Pre-colonial wealth differences

In addition to production differences among communities, within any locality families also had varied capacities to produce sufficient food to meet their own needs. Labor was a crucial resource in this regard. Indeed, security, prosperity, and power depended largely on access to and control over labor: *andu ni indo* "people are wealth" (Ambler 1988: 25). Labor was mobilized through ties of kinship and patronage, as well as through hire. Though oral records suggest no land scarcity in the late nineteenth century, dense populations were building up in both highlands and lowlands.[25] Frontiers and buffer zones absorbed migrants who left their home areas in search of more land to cultivate. One of these buffer zones was a sparsely settled area between the Embu and Mbeere peoples, which in the 1980s was absorbing growing numbers of migrants from the Embu uplands (see chapter 5).

Differential access to labor, however, did not necessarily create large wealth differences. Curbs on accumulation included social and ceremonial obligations to redistribute property to kin and neighbors. These included divisions of the spoils of raiding parties. A well-off individual who attempted to sever these social ties risked losing collective military protection, and might be poisoned, cursed, or accused of witchcraft. Accumulation was also limited by crop storage technology, since crop surpluses could not be stored for more than a few months.

In spite of curbs on accumulation, however, a few individuals did acquire more wealth and influence than others:

The richest men were ... those who could command the resources of labor necessary to open new fields for cultivation, watch over large herds, protect their settlements, and engage in trading, hunting and raids. (Ambler 1988: 25)

Such individuals could acquire many wives, clients, and other dependants. That less well-off neighbors might look to the wealthy for assistance or protection is acknowledged in the proverb, "you cannot afford to boycott a rich man" (*Gitonga gitiumbagua*). A young man who could not pay even a part of his bridewealth might start his married life as an adoptee in the home of his wife's father. After working hard a few years and acquiring some property, he would pay some bridewealth and the couple would leave the father's compound to establish their own.[26] Not all poor young men had such opportunities, of course.

A cultural morality defined the terms in which wealth was socially useful and "deserved." A number of proverbs suggest that wealth is the just reward of hard work and that poverty is the result of laziness. "Idlers" who begged from others rather than growing their own food might be refused assistance and were likely to be socially ostracized.[27] So said Chief M'Tetu at a 1926 meeting of the Embu Local Native Council. Chief M'Tetu spoke of longstanding social sanctions against "idlers" and suggested they be prosecuted (Embu LNC minutes, November 1, 1926). For the hard-working poor, on the other hand, clientage and individual energy could be avenues to upward mobility. As a proverb suggested, a poor person did not necessarily expect to be poor all of his or her life: "Poverty has no roots."[28]

Some Embu elders, war councillors, and medicine men undoubtedly acquired greater wealth and influence than their fellows. Among the qualities that contributed to individual reputations were skills in oratory, healing, dispute settlement, and military operations. Elders known beyond their local councils as skilled arbiters might attract local and immigrant tenants who became attached to their land and homesteads.[29] The "wealth in people" (cf. Miers and Kopytoff 1977; Bledsoe 1980) represented in such accumulated followings, based as they were upon shifting tides of influence, would be likely to dissipate, however, with the death of the elder.

During the late 1800s, some Embu farmers produced food surpluses that fed the long-distance caravan trade, to which I now turn. Expansion of trade may have strained ties of moral obligation between rich and poor. While the caravan traffic stimulated increases in production of food crops and livestock,[30] it also diverted some surpluses away from poorer individuals and from communities that often depended on food imports to supplement poor local harvests.

Caravans and commercialization

Contrary to some popular stereotypes commercial agriculture did not appear suddenly as a result of colonial and post-colonial interests and "development" projects. As Tosh (1980: 90) argues more generally, in both pre-colonial and colonial times "African cultivators were planning regular food surpluses in the light of market demands." During the late 1800s central Kenya became an important supply zone for the growing long-distance caravan trade between the East African coast and the Lake Victoria region. Central Kenya offered Swahili, and later European, caravans plentiful food and livestock supplies, as well as ivory, which local peoples exchanged for goods such as cloth, beads, and copper wire. Though it is difficult to quantify their impact, increasing demand for food from caravans passing through central Kenya in the late 1800s stimulated agricultural expansion, with local producers offering both livestock and foodstuffs for sale.[31]

The caravan trade created new opportunities for local brokers to amass wealth and power: "caravans, interested mainly in ivory exports, reinforced the position of accumulating notables in the agrarian economies, extending their markets and range of allies" (Lonsdale and Berman 1979: 495). Such notables later became key players in early contacts with agents of British colonial rule.

By the late 1800s Embu people were less involved in the caravan trade than their Kamba-speaking neighbors in Kitui, some of whom were developing more commercial links to world markets and new patterns of long-distance trade, displacing men from the coastal hinterlands who in the late 1700s established trade routes between their home areas and the southern parts of the central Kenya region (Ambler 1988: 46–47, 8, 68). Both declining elephant herds (which drove hunters and traders to the north by the mid-1800s)[32] and (perhaps less plausibly, but as reported to Ambler), Embu elders' active discouragement of outside contacts may have contributed to their diminished role in long-distance trade. The largest regional trade centers emerged just outside of Embu in neighboring localities populated by Gikuyu and Kamba speakers. Thus as the late nineteenth century saw a widening of the scale of influence, trade, and interaction in some parts of central Kenya, the local impact of these processes was quite variable.

In addition to threats to ties of moral obligation between rich and poor posed by fluctuating trade opportunities, challenges came through repeated crises of famine and food shortage. For the analyst, such "revelatory crises" can offer a window on social structure (Firth 1959: 77–105; Sahlins 1972: 127–130).

Famine and moral economy crises

Famines (*mayura*)[33] strained existing norms of reciprocity, as is suggested by the very names local people gave them. The 1917–18 famine was known as *yura ria kithioro*, a derivation of the verb *kuthiora* "to twist" or "to trick." That is, people in Embu recall it as a time when individuals deceived one another in order to obtain food, and prevented friends from finding food.[34] One Embu elder attributed the *kithioro* famine in part to a scarcity of agricultural labor caused by the war (Mwaniki 1974: 12).

People also associate this famine with building the winding, twisting mountain road from Embu to Chuka. Many worked on the road to earn payment in maize meal from the government. Many also died of hunger and beatings suffered as they built the road. The name of an earlier famine – *kavovo* – derives from the verb *kuvova* "to hate without reason" (Mwaniki 1974: 13). And another – *gatanthoni* – meant "destroyer of shame," suggesting that people ceased to care about morals or honesty, including those norms most closely associated with relations between juniors and elders and between affines. In times of famine moral ideals are strained, both because nearly everyone has fewer resources to redistribute, and because there are greater opportunities for big gains by a fortunate few.

Embu has long absorbed famine migrants as temporary laborers, wives, and adopted kin.[35] Inadequate rains and poor yields in the lowlands sent migrants to the uplands in search of food, which they acquired in exchange for work in the fields or for livestock and other products. In comparison to their lowland neighbors in Mbeere Embu farmers did not suffer as seriously or as frequently from drought and famine. Nor did their oral traditions include the vivid accounts of hunger found among the tales of neighboring lowland peoples (Ambler 1988: 44). Nonetheless, in Embu there were at least three major locally named famines between about 1890 and 1920. Rainfall uncertainty is a significant constraint for farmers in the Embu uplands as well as in the Mbeere lowlands.[36]

The quest for food under conditions of rainfall uncertainty in the pre-colonial past helped to shape relations within and between households and communities in ways that remain important today. Colonial regulations, however, sometimes disrupted the temporary and longer-term migrations from lowlands to uplands, and exchange relations across zones that had for decades helped to ease the consequences of variable food crop output. Though the colonial state sometimes attempted to reduce such migrations and exchanges,[37] they persist today. During the 1980 drought and famine, for example, I saw large numbers of Kamba and Mbeere migrants trudging up to the Embu highlands in search of food and work. Many were taken in temporarily by local families, and some of them reactivated older ties of kinship and clientage that had endured several generations.

In the context of famine what was the moral economy of obligations toward the less well-off? Embu families took in famine immigrants for a number of reasons, including fear of poisoning and sorcery if needy Mbeere and Kamba peoples were turned away, and fear of future non-reciprocity if Embu farmers suffered a famine (see below). Some Embu farmers welcomed immigrants as a source of labor. Aid to lowland immigrants was not necessarily ungrudging, and not without expectations of repayment and claims of moral superiority.

Old Embu songs, for example, mock Mbeere dependence on food from Embu during times of drought. One such song includes the following lines: "In Mbeere from Kamarandi to Evurori, I hear from *njumo* [a traditional dance song] that the sorghum has been infected with smut. Let it be infected again and again, for they must pay back the grain we gave them during the famine of *kithioro*. Woe unto you Mbeere people; I will mock you again and again, even if you do not give me water. If you don't dance at home, how will you dance in a foreign land?"

Talk about food is often talk about politics. Whether food is scarce or plentiful is a matter connected to the nuances of power between sexes and generations within households,[38] as well as between localities, and between state and locality.[39] As Cohen and Atieno-Odhiambo (1989: 131) write of Siaya in western Kenya, "food is, pre-eminently, about power; and discussions among the folk of Siaya about scarcity, about the quality of soil, about diet and taste and food colour ... about prices, and about women's control of household economies, are in a very fundamental sense about the distribution of power and rights in the wider society."

In short, a failure of rains and crops can precipitate crises of political accountability at many levels of social agency: from state officials to elders in a kin group. Sometimes political crisis is provoked because citizens believe their rulers lack the spiritual powers necessary to sustain material well-being.[40] In any case, during times of hardship some wealthy patrons pick up new clients, while the political status of others suffers as it becomes difficult for them to support clients. Some they shed intentionally and others voluntarily depart in search of better opportunities. When better times return some of these relations are rebuilt.

Rural livelihoods have always been unstable, subject to the vicissitudes of rainfall, crop pests and diseases, personal and political relationships, and family illnesses and deaths. To cope with this uncertainty Kenyan people rely on relations of exchange, clientage, and kinship (see also chapter 5). The framework within which they do so changed considerably under colonial rule: the topic to which I turn now. That era did not necessarily make rural livelihoods more precarious, but it at least altered the risks and rules of the game. It both increased exposure to market risks and opportunities and vastly expanded the political hierarchy. Though individual survival might still depend largely on negotiated relations of dependence on kin group elders, the largest material gains were to be had by manipulating the new networks that came to link elders, appointed chiefs, and more senior officials.

Colonial wealth differences and patronage

Chiefs and European takeover

Initially attracted to Embu by prospects for possible European settlement (which did not occur) and exploitation of the forest and people's livestock wealth (which did occur), the British established effective political control over Embu peoples in 1906. In that year, unlike most central Kenyans, Embu communities organized collective military resistance to colonial rule.[41] British conquest followed visits to the district by a few European-led trading expeditions and at least two locally resisted punitive parties from the colonial administrative center that had been established in 1901 at Fort Hall, forty miles (sixty-four kilometres) southwest of the present Embu town.[42] Richard Meinertzhagen's diary includes an account of a military expedition in 1904 to "Embo" (1983: 147–152). In March 1904 he writes: "The people of Embo are showing a considerable amount of fight and in two cases have charged right up to our bayonets. They must have lost heavily" (1983: 148–149). The next day Meinertzhagen writes, "They [Embu] tried to concentrate for a fight against one of my patrols, but we were too quick for them, and I threw my small reserve, which I personally commanded, into the fight, and we picked up 47 of the enemy in no time. We lost 7 levies killed and 8 wounded, while one of my men got killed and I had 3 slightly wounded by arrows, including my colour sergeant. We also captured 410 head of cattle and over 1,000 sheep and goats. It was a grand day." And the following day he notes (1983: 151): "We have so much captured stock with us that I am not too anxious to have another fight for the present."

The early twentieth-century British takeover[43] began with the imposition of local chiefs on communities that formerly knew no such political authorities. The introduction of chiefs altered the position of the councils of elders who previously were the most senior of local political and judicial authorities. Elders' councils were coopted into new roles under colonial political control (see Moris 1970; Glazier 1985). Pre-colonial authority patterns were contravened by actions such as the colonial administration's attempt to give the new colonial chiefs and their assistants formal responsibility for controlling and regulating drinking among younger sets of elders.[44]

Some of those whom the British appointed as local chiefs were notables associated with the rise of particular centers of long-distance trade.[45] (Some collection and distribution points where caravans obtained provisions became colonial administrative centers.) Here, as elsewhere, chiefs "often vied for power with local merchants, modernizing capitalist

farmers, and mission-educated elite for control over the countryside"
(Isaacman 1990: 43). Once each Kenyan locality had a chief these individuals could use their positions to eliminate competing trade centers and
brokers, monopolizing power and augmenting their own wealth. Under
the new and perhaps less fluid colonial order, a clear hierarchy of regional
centers emerged, with small shops in local trading centers acting as
branches of larger enterprises in district headquarters (Ambler 1988).

Among historians of Gikuyu-speaking areas many emphasize that the
British chose as chiefs "opportunistic upstarts" who had no traditional
authority.[46] Others note that the newly invented colonial position of chief
offered important novel opportunities to ambitious men with and without
significant prior standing in their own communities. Such individuals
could attempt to become allies of powerful and wealthy outsiders, and
thereby defeat local rivals, increase their popularity, and secure both
material and social advantages within their own societies. Central
Kenya's many local frontiers offered ambitious individuals great scope to
pursue unconventional avenues of personal advancement. Lonsdale and
Berman (1979: 497) remark that some early chiefs and headmen had been
"African military auxiliaries and camp-followers of conquest, perhaps
marginal men in their own communities." They suggest, however, that
such individuals were soon replaced as chiefs by men who had already
attained some local wealth and prominence.

In addition to the introduced division between chiefs and subjects the
early decades of colonial rule saw the emergence of the social category
"mission children" (*ciana cia miceni*): those who first became literate by
attending schools run by European missionaries. In Embu the Christian
missions that soon followed the British takeover[47] established a number
of primary schools throughout the district. In the Kagaari region of upper
Embu the first groups of "mission children" went on to become locally
prominent, and included an elected county councillor, an assistant chief,
an agricultural officer, a forestry officer, a teacher, and a pastor. Literacy
itself (however acquired) became a defining characteristic of privilege,
and of an important social category: the "readers" or *athomi*. With
education an individual who became a government clerk, for example,
could acquire rare material advantages such as better housing, clothing,
and furniture. In addition, educated individuals in official positions
acquired increasingly important patronage resources.

Though wealth differences pre-dated colonialism, the colonial state
provided a new and crucial framework within which such differences
could grow. Under colonial rule clientage flourished. New patrons
appeared (chiefs, clerks, teachers, traders), and individuals' claims on
patrons carried very different stakes as wealth differences grew during the

twentieth century. Successful accumulation did not necessarily entail severing earlier relations of reciprocity and dependency among kin, neighbors, and clients (though it might involve their redefinition). Some individuals bought their way out of dependent relationships by converting to Christianity and attending mission schools, or by becoming wage laborers. Such moves altered relations between juniors and elders, with the former, for example, no longer as dependent on the latter for bride-wealth livestock. Education allowed some persons of marginal social standing to improve their status and material prospects.[48] Accumulation came to depend largely on access to state resources and on "straddling" a variety of economic pursuits, including farming, trade, state employment, and small businesses (see chapter 5).

Political leaders who became rich (often as brokers with the state) and who wished to preserve their moral standing in the eyes of neighbors had to justify themselves in altered circumstances using "whatever symbolic language best combined their own literacy and the understanding of the local population" (Lonsdale 1986: 143). Among the strategic symbols they deployed in a changing moral economy were ethnicity and locality.

Ethnic and local competition

Ethnic and local boundaries institutionalized under colonial rule defined new arenas of competition for state resources. By the time of independence growing ethnic conflicts had come to be seen as the direct product of ancient tribal animosities, and "precolonial history became the record of the migration and resettlement of coherent tribes" (Ambler 1988: 155). Yet official rhetoric itself encouraged people to think in "tribal" categories. Those in Embu were urged to adopt new livestock development programs, for example, in order to keep up with or to surpass Gikuyu-speaking peoples in neighboring districts. "If you can convince the Embu that they can surpass the Kikuyu it will mean a big boost to morale," wrote one colonial officer to his successor in 1956, as he discussed prospects for livestock improvement in Embu District.[49] Under colonial rule people in each district were encouraged to see their own fates as separate from those of people in other districts, and as matters to be negotiated with state officials.

In Embu, for example, colonial officers invoked the threat of European alienation of local land as a possible consequence of non-compliant political behavior, thus setting the interests of the district apart from those of its neighbors whose land had already been alienated.[50] In 1925, at the Embu Local Native Council's first meeting, Chief Runyenje brought up the question of possible land alienation in Embu, and was told the matter was under consideration (Embu LNC minutes, July 12, 1925). At a 1926 meeting a district official warned that "if the natives wish to retain their present land they must show themselves worthy of it" (Embu LNC minutes, November 1, 1926). The official made the remark as he emphasized that local people must demonstrate their willingness to work, and to answer administration calls for labor recruitment.

People of Embu District also consciously competed with neighboring Gikuyu-speaking peoples in matters such as access to education. At a 1948 meeting, Embu LNC members complained that most secondary schools were concentrated around Kiambu in the southern Gikuyu-speaking area, and requested that a senior secondary school be built in their own district (Embu LNC minutes, May 20–21, 1948). After Kangaru School was built in Embu council members complained that students from other districts outnumbered those from their own (Embu ADC[51] minutes, November 8–9, 1956). This complaint apparently was acted upon, so that while in 1956 just 13 of 62 pupils at Embu's Kangaru School were from the district, by 1959 33 out of 60 were from Embu (Embu ADC minutes, August, 19–21, 1959).

The latter arguments about education are just one example of a situation in which Embu people (like others in the region) made strategic use of an emergent language of ethnic and regional competition. So too "Asian" (that is Indian) applications for permits to build mills were declined at Embu Council meetings in 1927–8 in order to allow local people the opportunity to do so instead (Embu LNC minutes, October 10, 1927 and May 10, 1928). A January 1941 Council meeting included complaints that African and Indian traders could not operate on equal terms, and were not allowed to purchase produce and engage in trade on the same premises. Participants in another 1941 Council meeting voted against allowing Africans from other districts to hold plots in Embu markets, at a time when Gikuyu immigrants were perceived as the immediate threat (Embu LNC minutes, January 23, 1941). Gikuyu-speaking peoples were often a focus of such talk among Embu speakers, since the former were familiar neighbors who, under colonial rule, had achieved a head start in education and formal sector employment.[52]

Relations between ethnic groups were affected also by colonial efforts to redirect regional exchange, including longstanding patterns of exchange that contributed to survival in times of famine.

Wandering strangers and regional exchange

Colonial rule helped to restructure exchange relationships among regions and localities.[53] The colonial state redirected existing regional trade networks, shifting the flow of labor and commodities in a way that emphasized each district's ties to Nairobi and to European-owned agricultural estates (Ambler 1988: 154). These state efforts did not suddenly or completely overturn longstanding patterns of regional exchange of livestock, food, and labor among communities in the highlands and plains. Inter-district food exchanges did not cease, and droughts continued to send migrants from lowlands to uplands in search of food in exchange for labor or products such as pottery. But eventually new patterns of commerce displaced earlier ones, as the state restricted trade and as wage labor and cash crop opportunities spread.

As these changes occurred Embu leaders and colonial officials debated controlling the movements of peoples and products that had long helped to even out access to food across localities. In 1928–9, for example, large numbers of Tharaka and Kamba peoples were coming to Embu to purchase food.[54] The colonial administration "did not like so many strangers wandering about the villages,"[55] and in May 1930 an agricultural officer recommended closing all food markets to outsiders (particularly those of Mbeere to the neighboring Kamba peoples). Council members who expressed doubts about such a measure noted both the practical difficulty of enforcing the ban, and the negative effect it would have on tax collection.[56] A 1934 Embu Council meeting voted in favor of famine relief funds for Mbeere, noting the total failure of the long-rains crop and poor output from the short-rains crop. Chief Kombo spoke in favor of having Embu absorb as many Mbeere families as possible, so that the latter could work on Embu fields in exchange for food[57] (that is, continuing pre-colonial exchange patterns noted earlier). And in 1943 two chiefs (M'Tetu and Naaman) disagreed about whether Embu should be closed to Kamba peoples suffering drought in Machakos and Kitui, in order to feed migrants from Mbeere.[58] Chief Naaman suggested the Kamba should not be excluded, because to do so would reflect badly on the district's reputation as a good neighbor and might bring negative repercussions were the situation to be reversed in the future. In short, the terms of debate included strategic considerations that were part of earlier moral economies, as well as appeals to contemporary administrative concerns, such as tax collection.

Chiefs and the reach of the state in rural life

The attempted reach of the state into rural life went far beyond the regional exchanges just noted. The British took the new structure of chiefs and their assistants as the foundation for attempting an unprecedented range of control over rural economic, social, and political life. Examples of duties of the new chiefs include: issuing permits to allow people to carry a maximum of two chickens per month to friends or relatives in Nairobi; ordering the digging of pit latrines in all villages; supervising and organizing soil conservation measures,[59] such as digging bench terraces and planting rows of grass; distributing government issues of quinine to treat malaria; giving women permits to travel outside the district; inspecting individual farms to ensure that government agricultural directives were being carried out; selecting the "best" farmers in their areas to distribute improved seed varieties issued by the government; and issuing permits for beer-brewing on special occasions.[60] In addition the chiefs collected taxes and recruited men for military service and for wage and unpaid labor (the latter for public works projects such as digging roads and clearing land). This list of responsibilities, while by no means enforceable, captures the remarkable breadth of penetration into rural life intended by the new colonial administration, and suggests the wide patronage powers available to the new chiefs. As suggested earlier many of these tasks provoked among chiefs' subjects various kinds of resistance, ranging from gossip and footdragging to acts of physical violence. But collaboration with chiefs could bring material rewards.

Colonial officers, for example, depended heavily on chiefs to filter information about candidates for local and overseas education;[61] for business or trade licenses; or for agricultural improvements such as a plow or improved seed or permission to plant coffee. For example, distributing improved seed varieties among farmers was the responsibility of exemplary cultivators whose names chiefs were to submit to the Local Native Council, a move adopted in the early 1930s following previous wider distribution of improved seed which colonial officers believed had been wasted. As the December 1933 Embu LNC minutes record it, the government "hoped the body of the population would learn the value of such (seed) issues when they saw them withheld." In short, access to many new economic opportunities depended largely on an individual's personal relationship with his or her chief.

Under colonial rule opportunities for enrichment quickly came to depend significantly on access to state resources. Chiefs were among the first local people to earn salaries, but these were small and not in themselves crucial to wealth differences. Rather, chiefs "grew wealthy through accumulation of livestock, land, and unofficial gratuities exacted from individuals seeking some favor" (Glazier 1985: 89).[62] That is, official positions such as that of chief afforded opportunities for personal enrichment beyond those of salary itself.

For ordinary citizens subsistence security came to depend in part on chiefs as channels of access to state resources. Patronage relationships that pre-dated colonial rule were redefined. As Berman and Lonsdale (1992a: 2) put it, "chiefs and their clients divided the benefits of colonialism for themselves and transferred its costs – principally the coerced export of labour – on to those with weaker claims on their patronage." In doing so they reworked "local histories of allegiance and custom," inclusion and exclusion (see also Glazier 1985).

Family labor was one of the first productive resources to be affected by the colonial administration in Embu, as male labor for domestic agricultural production was made to compete directly with that demanded by the colonial state for public works, government agricultural schemes, and European settler estates in neighboring districts.[63] Some young men voluntarily became hired laborers for a few months or years in order to acquire livestock for bridewealth. Others were forced by chiefs to become migrant laborers on settler farms. Still others became tenants or squatters on European farms in the Rift Valley in the early years of this century, only to lose rights to cultivate and raise livestock in later years (see, for example, Kanogo 1987).

Many Embu men worked in other districts on European farms, or as domestic servants in Europeans' homes in Nairobi or rural administrative centers. All of ten Embu men born in the 1930s or earlier whom I interviewed about their younger years had spent some months or years as wage laborers outside their natal district. Most worked on European farms or estates and as domestic servants and gardeners. Several had worked for the same employers, particularly for a British farmer to whom they referred as Bwana Chege, who lived near Ruiru. These individuals all settled eventually on their own farms in Embu.

Colonial officers preached repeatedly against "idleness in the reserves," instructed chiefs to stress the necessity of every adult male performing some kind of work in order to pay taxes,[64] and, as noted, warned Africans that they must show themselves worthy of retaining their land.[65] British officers instructed chiefs to keep lists of "idlers" in their locations and to call them first for communal work. One council member at a 1946 meeting noted the abuses of power open to chiefs in such a blacklist system, to which the council president replied that citizens could appeal to the district commissioner in such cases. That reply ignores the reliance of a largely illiterate population upon chiefs themselves for information about such avenues of recourse. And the remark echoes those of officials at the 1980 coffee cooperative society *baraza* discussed in chapter 3. In both cases, of course, citizens would encounter considerable difficulties and risks if they attempted to lodge official complaints about abuses of power.

The European estate agriculture for which African laborers were recruited had uneven effects on African farming. These consequences were mediated by local relations of lineage and clientage (see Lonsdale and Berman 1979; Berman and Lonsdale 1992b). The economic significance of circulating labor migration in Africa is subject to wide debate, with Africanist scholars divided on "whether these peasant migrants have impoverished rural households and communities by depriving them of labor or have provided new opportunities for capital accumulation through technology, thereby compensating the households for the loss of their labor" (Isaacman 1990: 62, n.27). Scholars disagree on whether "oscillating" workers who straddle the boundary between town and countryside represent a partial peasantry, and contribute to the social reproduction of rural households (Kitching 1980), or whether they are proletarianized workers whose rural footholds are simply "patches of land" (Murray 1981; Njonjo 1981).

Early colonial labor policy in Kenya did not necessarily "strangle" peasant production in order to export labor to European estates (Berman and Lonsdale 1992c: 92).[66] Expanded African commodity production increased differentiation, and this also facilitated the growth of capitalist settler agriculture. Higher taxes on African producers stimulated domestic production as well as wage employment, though individuals were not equally well-placed to increase their domestic production. For example, "chiefs in particular could displace the costs of experimentation onto the labour of others" (Berman and Lonsdale 1992c: 92). The needs of estate production contributed to African differentiation processes in which some prospered as producers, others were drawn into the labor market, and still others were pushed into it. The colonial state's interests in these processes were by no means uniform. It was not a monolithic agent of European settlers, or of "indigenous" or "transnational" capital. Rather, the state dealt with the conflicting interests of settler capitalism and rural Africans, and attempted in various ways to stimulate production in both smallscale African and largescale European agriculture.

In addition to external labor demands that took adult men away from agricultural and other work at home, the colonial administration through the chiefs attempted increasing regulation of production within the domestic unit. The state advised people what crops to grow,[67] and attempted to restrict where they could be grown, and to regulate sale of output. Embu chiefs were instructed to urge people to grow such crops as black wattle, wheat, groundnuts, buckwheat, cotton, peas, simsim, and European beans: most of which generated little local interest. Not only did the food crops advocated have no place in the existing diet or farming system, but the proposed cash crops had no guaranteed market. The state nonetheless exhorted people to grow them, saying that if production were sufficient buyers would come, but offering no security to early planters who bore the risks of innovation.[68] In later years Embu farmers frequently complained that the district's sales quota of black wattle was too low given the supply produced, and that permits were inequitably distributed.[69]

Cultivation of coffee, an export cash crop in which there was considerable African interest, was initially prohibited and then allowed under severe restrictions (see Van Zwanenberg and King 1975). At least as early as 1926 Embu chiefs requested the government to allow Embu people to grow coffee.[70] Officials responded that general agricultural standards must be improved first, that people should concentrate on increasing food production, and that poor husbandry standards then practiced would produce diseased coffee of poor quality. While officials continued to cite such justifications as they prevented Africans in other districts from growing coffee, Embu was among the first districts (together with Meru and Kisii) to be permitted to grow coffee on a very limited and restricted basis as early as the 1930s.[71] Some African coffee production was permitted in Embu sooner than in other non-European areas in part because the Embu population and area were small, particularly in comparison to potential Gikuyu coffee-growing areas. In addition, the Embu labor contribution to the settler farming sector was much less significant than that of the more numerous and land-poor Gikuyu peoples. Indeed, these factors, together with the high agrarian potential (fertile volcanic soils and good rainfall) of the present tea and coffee zones helped make highland Embu one of the first African areas to receive a number of colonial programs to improve smallholder agriculture (see Moris 1970). Chiefs, prominent government loyalists, and Christian converts (overlapping categories) were among the first to be allowed to grow coffee, with village headmen, chiefs' assistants, political allies, and relatives of such individuals following. In the Kagaari area of Embu, for example, among the first to grow coffee were a colonial chief and a local preacher in the Anglican church.

In sum, I have suggested a number of ways in which the colonial state began to reach into rural life, particularly through the agency of colonial chiefs. An individual's best channel of access to new economic opportunities (coffee, education, loans, licenses) was often his or her local chief. As the colonial years advanced chiefs of course had growing numbers of educated competitors for power in broker roles. These included teachers, clerks, church leaders, traders, politicians, and public servants. Chiefs, however, were central starting players in the patron–client networks that proliferated under the colonial and post-colonial state.

To illustrate how the processes described above are expressed in the lives of particular individuals, I offer two biographical sketches of colonial headmen in Embu.

Biographical sketches of two colonial headmen[72]

Mr. S was born during the 1890s and he died in the late 1970s. He was a wealthy man who had four wives, large livestock herds, and a shop. Mr. S recalls how when the Europeans first arrived in Embu in the early 1900s they captured some of his family's cattle and took them to their post. A few years later Mr. S was one of a group of young men of dancing age who were captured by their colonial headman and sent off to work on a European sisal estate in Ukambani during the early 1900s. Mr. S became a farm foreman or *munyapara*. After about two years he returned home to Embu, and used part of his earnings for bridewealth for his first wife. He was appointed headman and acquired a shop. A few years later he went to work as a gardener in Nairobi for a European he had known in Ukambani, and stayed there about four years. He describes his responsibilities as weeding flowers, washing the vehicle, and cooking for the dogs. That period included the famine of *kithioro* (c. 1918), during which he says he recalls bringing flour home to his family in Embu. While working in Ukambani and Nairobi he learned to read the Bible in the Gikuyu language at a mission school. He comments that when he returned to Embu and began preaching local people strongly opposed his conversion to Christianity. He stayed with it, however, and had his ears cut and stitched to remove the large holes left from a traditional piercing, a change, he said, which symbolized his renunciation of dancing.

During the land adjudication in the 1950s[73] Mr. S was an influential clan elder who was among those responsible for deciding ownership and boundary disputes, demarcating clan land boundaries, and consolidating each family's fragments within the clan holdings so that the state could later issue individual title deeds. He was able to claim for himself and his clan unusually large parcels of land. For example, according to Land Registry records, Mr. S, his brother, and at least two of his sons all acquired in the present cotton zone parcels of 50 to 100 acres (20–40 hectares): five to ten times the mean size for that zone. They acquired, in addition, farms larger than the mean size in the adjacent coffee zone.

Mr. S's son, Mr. P, was an assistant chief from 1953 to 1972. He was born in the mid-1920s, and his mother was his father's first wife. Mr. P was a wealthy man who had two wives, large land holdings and livestock herds, and, at various times in his life, a bar, a butchery, and *matatu* taxis. By 1979 his first wife had eleven surviving children, and his second wife had eight children. His eight years of formal education gave him unusual advantages in his generation. He attended an independent school for four years, and then a Catholic mission school for four years. After that he spent one year making shoes in his father's shop, then married his first wife, and a year later (1949) was employed by the Ministry of Agriculture. That position included work on the district's first coffee blocks, and he began to grow his own coffee in 1951. He notes how, in the years when Africans were first permitted to grow coffee, the district agricultural officer would request the chief to select these men. As an assistant chief during the 1950s land adjudication Mr. P was able to acquire substantial land holdings for himself and his children in both coffee and cotton zones. In 1972 Mr. P was succeeded as assistant chief by a man of his own patri-clan.[74] In the late 1970s and early 1980s I saw Mr. P on many occasions seated with other local notables on benches or chairs at the front of local *baraza*. They were not necessarily there to speak, but the seating arrangement was a sign of their status in the community.

A number of historical patterns noted earlier are expressed in the lives of these two individuals[75]: the shocks of early European rule (e.g., confiscation of cattle and forceful labor recruitment); migratory wage labor to earn bridewealth; and accumulation via economic "straddling," literacy, and access to state resources. Mr. P, as an employee of the colonial Ministry of Agriculture, was among the first people in his locality to be permitted to grow coffee, and in the 1980s his neighbors still regarded him as a particularly innovative and successful farmer. Moreover, under colonial rule, more privileged individuals such as he and the chief had the power to select others who would be allowed to grow their own coffee. Colonial processes of rural economic differentiation thus depended very much on sociopolitical relations: particularly on kinship and patronage ties to Africans such as Mr. P who were employed by the state. Mr. P's neighbors spoke with mixed admiration and envy about how well-connected individuals such as he had managed to obtain land even for infant children, and for daughters as well as sons, and how such persons were also able to finance formal education of both sons and daughters. In short, there were a number of material advantages which such well-placed individuals were able to pass on to their children. Out of such beginnings eventually grew the *matajiri* or *wabenzi* elites who had become so visible by the 1970s and 1980s. Mr. P himself does not fall into this category, but to the extent that the offspring of such men are more likely than many of their neighbors to acquire advanced education and favorable employment opportunities, the foundation is laid for increasing class differentiation.

Patronage and personhood

In the early 1980s, as discussed in chapter 5, large landowners such as Mr. P seldom attempted largescale, heavily capitalized farming. Instead, they usually lent out portions of their land to others, allowing them various rights of cultivation, grazing, and firewood collection. Thus the material security of the less well-off often depended on their "vertical" ties to individuals such as Mr. P. That is, they reconstituted earlier forms of land clientage, within the new, sometimes less secure, framework of private title deeds issued by the state. These cliental ties persisted (in varying strength and form in different parts of Kenya), owing partly to wider demographic and economic circumstances that encouraged large land-owners to diversify and pursue non-agricultural investments (see chapter 5). As the Kenyan land frontier contracted during this century, however, "patrons moved out of providing land and into the mediation of state power," invoking myths of equal opportunity, as they searched for new ways of proving wealth's virtue (Lonsdale 1992: 354). In their domestic and neighborhood circles wealthy men were still bound by local norms of generosity and sociability.

A small rural locality defined by face-to-face interactions among neighbors and kin remains for most Kenyans (whether Nairobi bureaucrat, politician, businessman, or farmer) a crucial point of reference in individual competition for rank, acceptance, and security. The texture of life in the countryside, where four-fifths of Kenya's people dwell, crucially underwrites national politics (which is not to say that the state is a simple "reflection" of local processes). The patronage networks upon which the ruling regime depends, as noted earlier, have *rural* roots. The relative leverage or bargaining power that rural clients can exercise with national patrons (politicians and bureaucrats) of course varies locally and historically. Moral economy is always a domain of conflict and contestation, rather than a mechanical reproduction of "traditions" of sharing. As in the Malaysian village Scott studied (1985: 192), so too in central Kenya the rich help the poor "less from a spirit of liberality than as a response to the palpable pressures their neighbors and kin brought to bear upon them." Even when the material rewards are small the achievement of any redistribution from rich to poor may help to keep cultural notions of mutual obligation alive. During times of hardship, such as famine, the cultural debate may become more explicit and vigorous, even if (or especially when) the material levels of redistribution diminish. A subsistence ethos and its material consequences wax and wane historically, rather than appearing and disappearing in a preordained evolutionary fashion.

As opportunities to accumulate wealth grew in central Kenya, so too did the stakes for individual displays of "generosity" as opposed to "selfishness." New opportunities for accumulation bring new cultural arguments over the appropriate distribution of wealth, and norms of sociality. One elderly Embu man commented on how divided people are today, and specifically suggested that enmities have arisen due to wealth. Several people spoke of the narrowing range of kin among whom one shares goats on ceremonial occasions, such as those associated with marriage and childbirth. In addition, livestock or cash received as bride-wealth are now more likely to go to the father alone. And an Embu man explained his decision not to open his own small shop, saying that such businesses often failed within one year, that customers asked for credit and called the owner "proud" if he or she refused to extend the credit, and that sorcery against the owner might follow. Less well-off individuals also termed "proud" wealthy individuals whom they believed did not assist others enough in finding jobs or places in secondary schools.

As the last examples suggest arguments over wealth are fundamentally arguments over cultural notions of good and bad persons. People in Embu, for example, have strong norms of food-sharing, hospitality, and sociability: norms that become strained in times of crisis, as the famine names noted earlier confirm. Treating visitors well includes preparing food for them rather than hoarding it for one's own family.[76] Selfishness and social isolation, in contrast, may carry associations of witchcraft and sorcery, and at the very least invite negative gossip. Longstanding norms of sociality and patronage include the expectation that the less well-off will seek assistance from the wealthy, and that the latter indeed will respond with good will to such requests.

Conclusions

A cultural theme that persists in Africa's history, Kopytoff (1987: 39) remarks, concerns the interpenetration of domains of sentiment and those of economic relations and material exchange: "on the frontier, new relations could thus be initiated within any one of the three realms – of kinship, of politics, and of material relations – and later redefined into one or both of the others." Thus there was "a repertoire of ways of expanding one's group, of acquiring people whose diverse statuses merged, often imperceptibly, into one another – relatives, quasi-relatives, adoptees, dependants, adherents, retainers, and clients" (1987: 46). The processes he describes on the land frontier occur also on today's political "frontiers," as individuals maneuver for access to and control over state resources. New relations among political actors in state arenas build on older cultural principles such as those just noted. In Kenya illustrations of this pattern include the material exchanges that underwrite both past and present relations of clientage. Cliental relations themselves occur in inter-penetrating domains of kinship and politics.

The material flows in Kenya's patron–client pyramids reproduce in part familiar cultural patterns in which a few individuals become prosperous and maintain material exchanges with subordinates. The terms of those exchanges were and are negotiable, albeit by individuals in unequally advantaged positions. Subject to historical change (and local variation) was the precise balance of coercion and seduction in attracting clients, and the openness or camouflaging of unequal status in everyday life. Nonetheless there was no question that subordinates' allegiances to superiors hinged on material rewards. In the late nineteenth century such rewards often included access to livestock, or to land to cultivate. In the twentieth century they include access to land and livestock, as well as to education, salaried employment, commercial loans, and so on. Under colonial rule chiefs and their assistants became crucial links between farmers and the state. The economic rewards of political compliance grew, both in relations between chiefs and officials in higher levels of the colonial administration, and in those between chiefs and their subjects.

In short, one thread that ties pre-colonial, colonial, and post-colonial rural economies together is that the material security of cultivators depends on both "vertical" ties to better-off patrons and on "horizontal" ties among farmers of less unequal status. How much material security these ties offer and to whom, however, varies from one locale and historical moment to another. They should not be idealized or romanticized as guarantees of egalitarianism or material security. As Scott (1976: 6) notes:

Where they worked, and they did not always work, they were not so much a product of altruism as of necessity. Where land was abundant and labor scarce, subsistence insurance was virtually the only way to attach a labor force; where the means of coercion at the disposal of elites and the state was sharply limited, it was prudent to show some respect for the needs of the subordinate population.

Although the general course of European and Asian agrarian history has seen a shift from a more personal and protective landlord relationship to a more purely contractual one, these are not inevitable or irreversible processes. A paternalistic morality of obligations to buffer subsistence crises might wax and wane in response to wider market and state forces. From below, the importance of building ties to wealthy and powerful patrons increases when land is scarce, though that scarcity itself is likely to decrease tenants' bargaining power with landlords. And from above, the importance of building a loyal local clientele varies, for example, with the state's capacity to enforce formal property rights, or to guarantee tenure security. Nor is the fate of horizontal ties of mutual aid a foregone conclusion. There is a middle range of alternatives between mutual aid among rural villagers who "share poverty" on the one hand, and "mutual hostility" or "amoral familism"[77] among villagers undergoing economic differentiation on the other.

Kenya, and not Kenya alone, remains a land where "The poor man's tongue is always thin."[78] But it is also a land where poor and rich alike confront the uncertainty and unpredictability of personal fortunes. "The person who first acquires wealth will not necessarily be the one to end with it."[79] And, "Poverty has no roots."[80] Livelihood is precarious for reasons that range from the flux of national politics, economy, and institutions to the vagaries of weather, health, and interpersonal relationships. This uncertainty itself contributes to the persistence of reciprocity and clientage, in coexistence with accumulation.

Counterpoised to the evanescence of wealth and political fortune are the "mock certainty" and assertiveness[81] of *baraza* rhetoric. Rhetorical ingenuities help to safeguard the *baraza* as political entertainment and a didactic forum rather than as a spectacle that provokes overt outrage. For both the colonial and post-colonial state repeatedly staging orderly *baraza* offered an appearance of successful statecraft. The appearance is sustained in part by the simple fact of public attendance, which, as noted in chapter 3, signals membership in a social order and symbolically creates the very social order *baraza* rhetoric presupposes. The edifice rests in part on a fragile phatic connection, or "the aspect of interaction that keeps all parties engaged with each other during the duration of communication" (Beeman 1993: 386): hence the importance, for example, of speakers' energetic rhetorical exchanges (of greetings, political slogans, responses to rhetorical questions) with audiences (see chapter 3). As the colonial and post-colonial state continually reconstituted itself, partly through the public ritual of *baraza*, chiefs – whether hated or respected – appeared on a public stage as the most locally familiar face of a state attempting to extend its reach into rural life in the ways noted in this chapter. At the same time local understandings, such as moral economies of famine relief, influenced state practices: as when colonial chiefs at meetings of the Embu LNC invoked notions of pre-colonial reciprocity in times of need to justify colonial famine relief for people from neighboring districts.

Famine once again seized the political stage in late 1993 and 1994. Kenya faced a serious food shortfall, due both to poor rainfall in some areas and to civil conflict in the productive Rift Valley which had displaced thousands of people from their farms (see chapter 2). In a remarkable invocation of moral economy notions in early 1994 Moi publicly urged the wealthy to assist those facing famine. He asked them to donate food, transport, and storage facilities to their poor countrymen, and said he wanted to be informed directly of such offers of assistance.[82] In a February 1994 public address on the drought Moi assured citizens that the government would assist all, "regardless of their political persuasion," and he appealed to the international community, as well as to wealthy Kenyans, for help:

> The costs of drought relief must be borne first and foremost by those Kenyans that are fortunate enough not to have been affected by the drought. . . . the government will introduce a temporary drought levy on high-income individuals and corporations . . . I appeal to all Kenyans and to the international community to contribute to the drought relief effort so that we can overcome the challenge posed by the drought.[83]

Meanwhile, his political opponents criticized the government for delay in dealing with famine, noting that just a few weeks earlier the Minister for Agriculture had assured citizens that Kenya had enough food to feed the nation.[84] The government asserted that no one had died from the drought and officials, such as district officers and assistant chiefs, were quoted as saying they were not allowed to give out information about deaths related to the drought.[85]

Moi's populist rhetoric about the famine in the early 1990s attempts to capture some of the same moral territory occupied by his opponents. Recall, for example (see chapter 2), that dissident music about the 1990s "ethnic" clashes in the Rift Valley called upon the wealthy to help refugees who had been displaced from their farms. Both of these contemporary instances reintroduce older moralities whereby the well-off have some obligation to assist the poor in time of crisis. Today, as in the past, such obligations are a source of social tensions and contestation over who should assist whom, and how much. Famines, as noted, make the positions of some political patrons, as well as their clients, more precarious. At such moments of crisis rhetorical contests and moral claims intensify on both sides (as well as along other lines of social cleavage, such as gender, age, locality, and ethnicity). By 1993, when Moi's own political position was more precarious than it was a decade earlier, his call for the rich to contribute famine relief could easily remind listeners of the vulnerability of both ruling party and opposition politicians to charges of ill-gotten gains (particularly given the new public salience of questions of leadership accountability, see chapter 2). Indeed, the calls for public accountability in the early 1990s may well have intensified because growing numbers of citizens simultaneously faced material or economic shocks associated with the state's fiscal crisis, structural adjustment measures, food crop shortfalls, and possible famine.

Though current economic stringencies, like famines of the past century, trigger or intensify moral economy debates, these discourses are not conceived in the same way today as they were a century ago. Earlier this century it was wealthy neighbors, kin, or patrons in one's locality whose assistance the less well-off might seek in times of need. People at greater distances who spoke variant dialects might be aided more grudgingly or at higher cost: as in exchanges of Mbeere labor for Embu food (see above).

Moi's 1994 call for the wealthy to assist poor victims of drought accords with a local, personal morality of mutual economic obligation, rather than, for example, invoking obligations of the state *per se*. Indeed, the state is bypassed in the sense that Moi's next level of moral appeal for food aid is to the international donor community. In both cases he can claim some personal credit for any resulting material assistance to the less well-off (hence, as noted, he asks to be informed directly of offers of assistance from wealthy Kenyans). At the same time he avoids placing the burden of material obligation on the state itself (though he does propose a temporary tax on the rich). By the 1990s, then, the scale of moral economic obligation to which people in Kenya can lay claim has expanded considerably beyond that of the late nineteenth century, now extending well into the domain of international aid and the politics of nation-states: arenas that help to constitute local economic moralities. That Moi's rhetoric does not suggest a state moral economy, however, is significant. Though he may intend to deflect such claims on a fiscally-strained state, that poverty of government resources itself opened his regime to opposition party accusations of economic mismanagement and other shortcomings (see chapter 2).

In sum, this chapter's historical sketch has suggested some bridges between past and present crises of political accountability and material subsistence. I have briefly noted a few points of political convergence and divergence between contemporary economic stringency and famine crises during the past century (a theme to which I return in the book's conclusions). And I have sketched some of the wider processes within which *baraza* are situated, including the historical origins of rural wealth differences in central Kenya, the colonial emergence of the vertical political ties on display during *baraza*, and the growing reach of the state in the countryside.

The next chapter takes a closer look at the vicissitudes of daily life, by exploring more recent struggles for livelihood among Embu farmers with whom I have worked since the late 1970s. That field of vision brings into focus local and individual expressions of wider tensions and conflicts that *baraza* rhetoric silences and naturalizes.

5 The dove and the castor nut: Embu household economy in the 1980s

Introduction

This chapter is the final step of an analysis that has taken us from the "seditious" music and social protest of Nairobi's political culture in the early 1990s, to strategic public silences preserved in earlier years, and to daily struggles for livelihood in the countryside during the past century. Now let us take a close look at the lives of small farmers in Embu in the late 1970s and 1980s. This narrative highlights the local uncertainties, contests, and social asymmetries that both reflect and fuel the "high politics" of the state. Again one recognizes cultural and conceptual continuities between smallscale and largescale organization: from kin group elder, to chief, cabinet minister, and head of state (cf. Kopytoff 1987: 52). Hence the frequent inclusion in Kenyan political rhetoric of metaphors of bridewealth, marriage, and fatherhood: allusions to a moral universe to which many people do have deep attachments. To suggest that an official has betrayed citizens' trust in the manner of a father who squanders a son's bridewealth savings is to strike a resonant chord. (An elder publicly made such an assertion about local coffee cooperative society officials during a 1980 *baraza* in rural Embu.) To speak of "state–local" interactions and "above–below" dichotomies can suggest misleadingly discrete categories of social interaction and moral imperatives.

Presumed boundaries between town and countryside, like those between state and locality, are fuzzy at best. Urban Kenyans – including those who attend National Theatre performances such as *The Mikado* (see chapter 2) – are engaged in life in the countryside in quite diverse ways. Four-fifths of the nation's population is rural, and many of the rest have rural origins and kin ties and spend part of their lives in the countryside. And many of those who live in the countryside spend time in the city: working, trading, visiting friends and relatives, seeking employment, or attending school. An emerging generation of elite urban offspring (few in numbers but likely to be great in social influence) have more remote ties to rural areas. Some barely speak their parents' first languages, and find it an unusual hardship to spend a few vacation days with rural grandparents whose homes lack mains water or electricity. The vast majority of Kenyans who have more direct experience of rural life, however, and who recognize the uncertainty of the nation's economy and political order, foster rather than sever urban–rural ties. Any urban job or residence may prove temporary, as may physical safety or political stability. Thus urban workers attempt to maintain rights in rural land, which often entails material and social exchanges with rural kin and acquaintances. Rural land rights, even if one possesses a title deed, often are no more secure or predictable than urban resources. Hence it is advantageous to spread one's risks by cultivating access to a range of people, resources, and income-earning opportunities. Most urban Kenyans' images of rural society, therefore, are likely to be less removed from the realities of life in the countryside than were those rural images enjoyed under the classical European processes of urbanization explored by Raymond Williams (1973).[1]

The interpenetration of town and countryside, state and locality is expressed in rural *baraza*, and in the patron–client ties that pervade Kenyan society and politics. The "rural" realities explored in this chapter provide clues about why the struggles in the early 1990s among factions competing to capture the state so quickly escalated into rural violence. The volatility of life in both town and countryside is in part a legacy of colonial and post-colonial authoritarianism and repression, of the incapacity of the state to guarantee secure rights in land, of a shrinking economy, and of a patronage machine that is periodically short of cash (a shortage reaching "crisis" proportions in the early 1990s).

The small farmers whose lives I explore in this chapter are in part historical products of larger-scale processes of commercialization, state formation, population expansion, and increasing land scarcity as mentioned in the previous chapter. A closer look at the lives of individuals in such households allows us to trace more particular expressions of those "large processes" and "big structures" (Tilly's 1984 phrases), as they are played out locally and individually in highly varied ways. Individual lives and localities, however, are more than a simple reflection of larger structures and processes, and more than variations on an inevitable global historical theme. Particular locales are also the site of processes that historical actors themselves shape and create. That is, "real individuals and groups act in situations conditioned by their relationships with other individuals and groups, their jobs or their access to wealth and property, the power of the state, and their ideas – and the ideas of their fellows – about those relationships" (Roseberry 1989: 54). Processes that unfold locally are influenced also by what has gone before, both locally and globally. As Tilly (1984: 14) puts it, "*when* things happen within a sequence affects *how* they happen ... (and) every structure or process constitutes a series of choice points. Outcomes at a given point in time constrain possible outcomes at later points in time." This chapter, therefore, aims at capturing some of the nuances of individual lives and local processes, without losing sight of the larger circumstances that over time shape and are in turn shaped by those individuals.

The particular themes explored here center on processes of rural economic differentiation. As noted, regime survival depends in part on how successfully it incorporates rural clients into wider patronage networks fed by state resources. This chapter asks: Who are these rural clients and what are their material concerns? How do they cope with the precariousness of rural livelihoods? What are the sources and magnitude of wealth differences among them? How are wealth differences among households connected to their exchanges of land, labor and food? What material circumstances are associated with interpersonal conflict within households, and with the instability of household membership? To what extent are wealth differences attributable to "random oscillations" (Shanin 1982), to household demographic cycles (Chayanov 1966), or to long-term polarization into classes of rich farmers and landless laborers (Lenin 1964)? How are both intra- and inter-household dynamics (e.g., interpersonal conflict, and exchanges of food, cash, and land) related to random and non-random patterns of household mobility? What is the significance of the striking pace of change which I observed as I revisited Embu households during the 1980s?

Structural regularities which an analyst discerns at a distance may appear to dissolve into "chaos," indeterminacy, or unpredictability upon close inspection. In this chapter, unlike many related studies, I wish both to bring into view the daily contests, conflicts, and instability of rural Kenyan life and also to step back from these features in order to appraise possible structural regularities.

Upward and downward mobility

What structural regularities may be discerned in the mobility of farm households? Summarizing Shanin (1982), the analytical possibilities include: (a) centripetal mobility in which poorer households ascend toward the median wealth and richer ones descend; (b) centrifugal mobility in which wealthy households rise away from the median and poor ones descend further below the median; (c) cyclical mobility in which any given household ascends and declines according to regular stages of a family life cycle; and (d) multidirectional mobility in which opposing movements of individual households cancel one another out. Each of these patterns entails processes with different social characteristics or dynamics. In central Kenya, for example, levelling mechanisms that might contribute to centripetal mobility include partible inheritance and subdivision of land among sons, and household fissioning or partitioning as offspring marry and move elsewhere. Random influences on household wealth include fluctuations in the natural environment (especially in weather that affects crop output). In central Kenya, as shown below, rainfall variation across seasons contributes to sharp fluctuations in crop production. Forces that might contribute to centrifugal mobility include individual accumulation associated with state-building, patronage politics, and diversion of public resources into private use.

As social scientists search for the cumulative effects of such diverse influences on household mobility, they often emphasize structural changes, or linear trends, rather than non-structural or non-linear issues (Shanin 1982: 239). Shanin, however, draws attention as well to "random oscillation"[2] and unpredictable influences on peasant households that take the form of multidirectional mobility[3]:

A successful contract, a hard-working son, a useful merger, or, conversely, the illness or death of a working member, a fire, the death of a horse, the obligation to provide a dowry, or even a family quarrel culminating in partitioning, could lead to a complete change in the socio-economic position of a household (Shanin 1982: 238).

Unpredictable influences on mobility of individual households, as well as on the overall welfare of farmers, include fluctuations in weather, in the terms of trade between urban and rural sectors, and in state policies toward agriculture (Shanin 1982: 236–237). Peasants are keenly aware of the effects of such vicissitudes on their well-being. For example, a local survey reports: "The middle peasants say 'Today I am a middle peasant, tomorrow I become a poor peasant. If the horse dies, I'll have to hire myself out.'" (Shanin 1982: 238) Central Kenyan farmers also are acutely aware of this type of unpredictability in their lives, as is apparent in their proverbs: "Riches have wings" or "Riches are a shadow"; "The person who first acquires riches will not necessarily be the one to end with them"; and "Poverty has no roots."

For people to perceive wealth as fleeting or transitory of course does not mean that household mobility necessarily is random. Before exploring these themes let us consider an example of how Kenyan officials portray household mobility when they address small farmers.

The dove and the castor nut

"A single castor nut made the dove spend the night hungry." (Gikuyu proverb)[4]. This proverb – about a dove that waited all night in vain for a castor nut to be blown down from a tree – was a singularly unnecessary bit of advice which a district commissioner (DC) offered to a rural *baraza* in Embu in 1980. The words of such *athomi* (literate or educated persons), were sometimes uttered with more force and conviction than their content merited. The DC, a young Gikuyu man with a university education, spoke words of the ancestors. But the assembled farmers to whom he held up the importance of diversification were people who already cultivated on each farm some dozen or more different crops destined for market and home consumption, and who in addition were likely to raise chickens, goats, sheep, and cattle, and to earn incomes from supplemental activities such as making baskets or sisal ropes, tailoring, carpentry, charcoal production, beer-brewing, rental of plows or ox carts, and casual agricultural labor for their neighbors. In addition, a minority operated their own small businesses or earned regular salaries from formal wage employment.[5] Diversification, they already knew well, conferred a flexibility that could reduce subsistence risks and enable accumulation.

Why then did the DC speak of the dove and the castor nut? He did so as he encouraged farmers in Embu to take advantage of a new "development" project through which they could apply for commercial loans that would allow them to purchase exotic breeds of cattle. That is, he urged farmers to go into debt to adopt exotic cattle in order to increase milk production to help meet the requirements of Moi's new primary school milk program. (As noted in chapter 3, soon after he became president Moi announced a new program that would distribute free milk to children in primary schools.) The DC's message was that farmers should not rely on coffee income alone, and that if they adopted exotic cattle they would have income from milk sales when coffee income was unreliable. (Other ironies of this advice are discussed below.)

The DC further suggested that anyone unwilling to adopt hybrid cattle was ignorant and tradition-bound, and would not prosper. He noted, for example, that when the new provincial commissioner (the DC's administrative superior) had toured Embu, he was disappointed to find a lot of native cattle grazing by roadsides. This image contrasts with agricultural textbook notions of stall-fed exotic cattle on well-managed small farms: tradition versus progress and modernity. He invoked the familiar metaphor of a nation "on the run," reminding the assembled farmers that the *nyayo* philosophy (see chapter 3) means that Kenya is moving fast, and anyone who cannot keep up will be left behind. Other speakers suggested that the cattle loan program was one of the fruits of independence, and that only those who did not want to increase their wealth would turn down an opportunity for such a loan. One compared the cattle loan opportunity to a Christian hymn about a train headed for heaven, and said that the loan was a train headed for development led by the provincial commissioner (PC) and DC, asking his listeners, "if you don't take this train, which one will you take?" In short, religion, enlightened self-interest, nationalism, and political loyalty were all part of an attempt to persuade the audience that an application for a loan was an opportunity that was not to be missed. The official bearers of this message were among those who, as Lonsdale (1986: 153) writes in a different context, "appropriated the new civilising mission of 'development.' They accepted, still more fervently than whites, that it needed a moral release from the shackles of tradition as much as economic planning." The arrogance that tinged some official expressions of this conviction was not lost on farmers.[6]

Farmers who listened to these exhortations knew well that exotic hybrid cattle were more susceptible to local diseases than were crossbred and "local" cattle. They also knew that veterinary services were inadequate, and that a market for increased milk production was by no means guaranteed. In addition, it was not easy to carve pasture space out of the small and intensively-cultivated farms many occupied. Nor was it easy to meet the additional labor requirements of exotic cattle, especially the need to fetch water for them from nearby streams. The latter task was most often done by women who carried the water on their backs up and down steep slopes, and who were already hard-pressed to fetch enough water to meet their families' requirements. In short, to follow the DC's advice to adopt exotic dairy cattle would be to add yet another unpredictable element to a diversified production system in which domestic labor was already heavily burdened. The addition might or might not prove profitable, but no farmer needed to be told that producing milk for market would help her or him to survive the times when coffee income was unreliable.

Among the ironies contained in the DC's advice not to rely solely on coffee is the state's own incapacity to make coffee cooperative societies' payments to farmers more reliable. Such payments were often delayed for months. As discussed in chapter 3 farmers questioned the honesty of cooperative society officials, and were dissatisfied with the "non-transparency" of their managerial decisions and practices. They avoided dependence on coffee precisely because local payouts were unreliable, and prices were subject to international market fluctuations. Farmers spoke, for example, of the effects of both local cooperative society management and of frost in Brazil on their own coffee incomes. Returns from this export cash crop were no more predictable than were yields from any of their principal food staples.

In short, once again, farmers heard state officials speak of and from a world removed from the everyday realities of their lives. Even when officials were not unaware of these realities they were driven nonetheless by bureaucratic pressures to make the cattle loan program a "success" by recruiting impressive numbers of farmers to participate, and thereby appearing to promote "development." Contrary to the DC's implication, however, the cattle loan program and other such agrarian innovations had relatively little to do with becoming wealthy. This is not to say that they had no effect at all on wealth, but rather that they were seldom the deciding factor that allowed a farm household to make the "structural leap" (Shanin 1982) to a higher wealth category. How people do become wealthy, and how they cope with the precariousness of rural livelihoods are this chapter's principal themes.

Patron–client pyramids

Even though farmers knew exotic cattle were a risky avenue to accumulation, they also knew that their access to better opportunities than the cattle loan program depended very much on retaining the good will of their chiefs, their elected politicians, and bureaucrats. Opportunities for rural peoples to accumulate wealth were structured in part by their "vertical" ties to influential patrons. Once again, therefore, polite listening during a *baraza* was the safe strategy for farmers. Politeness, of course, is a cultural convention, and not an exclusively "strategic" consideration. (The instrumental/expressive dichotomy is one best avoided.) Among people in Embu customary *baraza* behavior involves displays of the valued personal qualities of being even-tempered, peaceable, polite, and friendly, although the imperatives of political competition allow as well for forceful speech and direct and indirect attacks on rivals. A polite pose by farmers at this *baraza* at least would not reduce their chances of pressing their own interests in other contexts. The language in which they could do so, and the moral imperatives they invoked, built in part on notions of just reward for work that were conveyed in colonial and post-colonial rhetoric, as well as in local cultural understandings. As Lonsdale (1992: 355) puts it, "At bottom, Kikuyu argued with each other and complained to the British about the loss of calculable relation between obedient labour, civic virtue and rights in land and power."

For rural families to survive and prosper requires not just strategic economic actions, but political skill as well: whether it is to defend the boundary of one's farm against a litigious neighbor (land disputes being very common in the region); to call one's neighbors to a work party; to borrow land; or to obtain pesticides for the coffee crop, fertilizer for the maize, veterinary treatment for a diseased cow, health certification to allow sale of a slaughtered animal, or permission to brew beer for a daughter's wedding. The success or failure of such endeavors, and the current distribution of wealth depend, therefore, not just on the strategic economic and political actions of individuals, but on a wider arena of patron–client and other structures. The latter are both shaped by the actions of individuals, and channel access to economic resources in ways that are beyond an individual farmer's range of manipulation. These structures include, as noted earlier (see chapter 2), a pyramid of patron–client ties that link farmers in the countryside to cabinet ministers and the head of state (with intermediate links including assistant chiefs, chiefs, councillors, district officers, coffee cooperative society officials, school headmasters, and members of parliament, among others). As suggested earlier, the patron–client structure of Kenyan society resembles the "inflationary democracy" (Scott 1972) characteristic of other poor nations, and by the early 1990s mounting fiscal pressures threatened Kenya's political order. Shrinking national resources meant patrons had less capacity to deliver benefits to clients. Just as farmers' material well-being depends in part on ties to patrons who have access to state resources, so too the fortunes of these patrons rise and fall with the vicissitudes of national politics and factional realignments. That is, patrons are dependent brokers[7] who draw their power and wealth from state patronage. Cabinet reshuffles, corruption scandals, and other shake-ups at the top therefore quickly ramify downward.

These are the larger realities of farmers' lives. They are structures and processes that are captured in part through public assemblies or *baraza*, which offer one public window on the patron–client pyramids that every farmer must manipulate daily if she or he is to survive or prosper. The *baraza*, as a symbolic display of state influence, captures one of the most important divisions in Kenyan society: that between those individuals who have profitable ties to the state and those who do not. For most citizens the most familiar local face of the state remained the chief and assistant chief. For the more influential minority, the state wore other faces: cabinet minister, district and provincial commissioners, and others whom the majority might observe onstage at *baraza*, but were unlikely to meet personally.

What changed in the transition from pre-state to state moral economies in central Kenya is suggested by Lonsdale (1992: 400):

In stateless, fee-paying, forest-clearing society, the reciprocity between service and protection was personal, public, calculable. Successful patrons deserved to eat well; who herded goats ate meat. But under the state, direct, personal rewards were in the gift of its chiefs alone.

Whereas earlier in history, "wealth earned power; fertile power fed clients," with the coming of chiefs and the colonial state "competition risked being called subversion, the new sorcery; hidden bribe could ruin open investment; cash was not people. Office bought wealth; police could make good a lack of supporters. *But the state's power made its favour vital to all*" (Lonsdale 1992: 363, my emphasis). Wealthy individuals continued to engage the less well-off in relations of material exchange couched in a language of paternalism and of wealth as virtuous reward for hard work. The putative virtue of wealth was a convenient weapon to justify or naturalize economic inequality, to guard one's privileges by limiting numbers of or assistance to dependants. While this would have been true earlier in history as well the material stakes were now higher.

Struggles over access to state coffers and patronage fuel both diversification and accumulation. Institutional and economic uncertainties often encourage diversification and proliferation of personal networks (see Berry 1985, 1993). Let us examine these processes of diversification and differentiation in one part of rural Embu District.

Rich and poor in Embu

In Embu, as elsewhere in Kenya and in Africa, the most pronounced wealth differences occur between literate and non-literate, between town and countryside, and (again) between those with privileged access to state resources and those without (Hart 1982: 139). One might, for example, contrast children of state elites who live in Nairobi and attend first-rate schools, with offspring of small farmers who attend poorly-equipped and inadequately staffed rural schools. (Some rural offspring of course attend elite urban schools.) Elite city children are likely to live in comfortable and spacious stone houses with electricity and indoor plumbing, while their poorer rural cousins dwell in mud houses with roofs of thatch or iron sheets, and neither electricity nor piped water nearby. Within rural Embu itself one finds occasional stone houses, a few of which have electricity and mains water. Most people, however, live in mud houses without electricity, and fetch water by walking up and down steep slopes to the streams that flow through the highlands from Mt. Kenya.[8]

The particular locale upon which I focus here (shown on map 3), is neither the poorest nor the wealthiest in the Embu uplands. It is situated in the northwestern portion of the district where the people officially categorized as "Embu" are concentrated,[9] and which administratively was known as Embu Division[10] before 1969, and Runyenje's Division thereafter. (Divisional boundaries and those of some administrative locations and sublocations were redefined again in the late 1980s.) In the early 1980s each of Runyenje's Division's four administrative locations was a wedge-shaped unit extending from a narrow apex at the Mt. Kenya forest in the northwest across tea and coffee zones to a broad base in the lower lands of the upper cotton zone (or, in the case of Ngandori Location, the lower coffee zone) bordering the territory of the Mbeere peoples. Within Runyenje's Division the area of most concentrated study included two sublocations of Kagaari Location. (Kagaari Location recently split into two locations: Kagaari North and Kagaari South.)

The two study sublocations span coffee and cotton zones. The coffee zone sublocation borders the divisional headquarters and market of Runyenje's, which holds thrice-weekly market days, and lies 14 miles (22 kilometres) by paved road from the town of Embu (administrative center of Embu District and of Eastern Province). Embu town in turn is 75 miles (120 kilometres) by paved road from Nairobi. Assistant chiefs' *baraza* help to constitute a sense of identity at the sublocation level. Each sublocation includes a number of loosely defined, named neighborhoods, but sublocation boundaries do not necessarily coincide with any indigenous territorial units (see chapter 4). The two study sublocations include a number of different churches (Catholic, Independent, Anglican, Pentecostal, Salvation Army, Seventh Day Adventist) and primary schools, and in the late 1980s the first secondary school opened in the coffee zone sublocation. Each sublocation includes a small commercial center of some dozen modest enterprises such as retail shops, bars, butcheries and tea "hotels." These carry names such as "New London Enterprises" and "California Butchery."

At least three partly overlapping crop zones may be defined as one moves southeastward from Mt. Kenya across the Embu uplands: (1) an upper zone where tea is an important export crop (approximately 5,300–7,000 feet, or 1,615–2,135 metres in altitude); (2) a middle zone where coffee is the dominant export crop (4,500–6,500 feet, or 1,370–1,980 metres); and (3) a lower zone where cotton is grown (3,800–4,500 feet, or 1,160–1,370 metres), but less widely than tea and cotton in the two upper zones. As one moves down this altitude gradient rainfall declines, as do agricultural potential, population density, market development, and the availability of social and administrative services. In 1979 about four times as much land was available per capita in the Embu cotton zone as in the coffee zone (Kenyan government 1979). As noted in chapter 4, residents often use land in multiple zones, thereby diversifying their production, reducing the risk of crop loss, and distributing labor requirements more evenly over the annual cycle.

This study's focal research area, which ranges from the middle coffee zone to the upper cotton zone, covers a decline from 5,000 to 3,800 feet (1,525 to 1,160 metres) in altitude across a distance of less than five miles (eight kilometres). The lower portion of this range, which merges into what was formerly a buffer zone between Embu and Mbeere peoples, is more recently settled than the upper part, and still includes large uncultivated areas used for quasi-collective cattle pasture (see Haugerud 1989a). Recent immigrants come from upper Embu as well as from neighboring districts that are dominated by Gikuyu-speakers. Land purchases are more common in this lower zone than in the uplands.

Most people in Embu live in dispersed homesteads (sing., *mucii*[11]) on farm parcels averaging three or four acres (1.2–1.6 hectares) in the coffee zone and about twice that in the cotton zone. An Embu homestead is often a scattered arrangement of mud-walled buildings set in a clearing bounded, at least on its more public sides, by hedges. With the exception of the granary, and sometimes the kitchen, most houses today are rectangular, with roofs of thatch or corrugated iron sheets; formerly they were round with conical thatched roofs. Each building usually has two or three rooms; walls of mixed earth, ash, and dung (with cement for the well-off); a wooden door; no ceiling beneath the roof; and a few windows with wood shutters but no glass. Most have floors of bare, swept earth, while a few better-off homes have floors and lower walls of cement. Families who can afford an iron sheet roof on at least one building in their compound often attach to the roof a gutter to collect rainwater run-off which drains into an oil drum next to the building. During the rainy season such containers greatly reduce time-consuming trips to the river to fetch water. Granaries, kitchens, sleeping quarters, and visiting areas may all be separate buildings or they may adjoin one another in varying combinations. A compound's largest building, rarely more than two or three rooms, is usually the main family living quarters. Most compounds contain as well at least one granary: a round structure constructed of wood poles and thatched roof, and supported about three feet above the ground by wooden poles. It is used to store maize, beans, and other crops, and may also sometimes serve as sleeping quarters for unmarried circumcised sons (cf. Mwaniki 1973b: 116). In many compounds the kitchen is also a separate building, with thatch roof and a single room, where cooking pots and dishes are kept and where food is cooked over a three-stone fire, or in some homes over charcoal burners or (rarely) kerosene burners. Kitchens were larger in the past and served as both the male household head's sleeping quarters before he built his own house and also as a courting house in which unmarried daughters entertained suitors (see Mwaniki 1973b: 114). In the past a husband often had a separate house, but today he is likely to share the main family living quarters. In polygynous households each wife has her own house, usually her own kitchen, and often her own granary. In such households the husband is also likely to have separate sleeping quarters or a separate house, as are post-adolescent sons, and sometimes today, daughters. A resident grandmother or grandfather usually has her or his own house in the compound, and a grandmother may sleep in her kitchen. Small stock may sleep in a portion of the kitchen or living quarters, while larger animals sleep in a small wooden enclosure or shed near home.

Household visitors are received and served food in a sitting room, which is usually the only public room and is often part of the structure that contains family sleeping quarters. Furniture in this public room ranges from a few simple wooden stools or folding chairs in less well-off homes, to sturdier wood chairs, tables, wood storage cabinets, and cushioned plastic sofas in better-off homes. Tables, chairs, and sofas are covered with hand-embroidered cloths of bright red, green, pink, blue, or yellow. On the earth walls are family photographs, calendars, newspapers, and colorful advertisements for products such as cigarettes, soap, and detergent. Framed photographs of family members, weddings, graduations, and local committees and boards to which a household head or spouse belongs are signs of prestige and sometimes wealth. In the homes of chiefs, councillors, school headmasters, and other prominent persons, half a dozen colorful calendars given them by local merchants, as well as group photographs of committees and boards on which they have served, and numerous family photographs may cover the walls. In homes of less wealthy and prominent individuals, walls may be nearly bare of photographs and decorations. This, then, is the physical setting of the domestic units whose composition, interpersonal relations and conflicts, and economic pursuits are considered in this chapter.

My particular focus is on 82 farm households[12] in the Embu coffee and cotton zones among whom I did field research from mid-1978 to mid-1981 (while living in Runyenje's), and whom I have revisited a number of times during shorter stays since then. The sex and age structure of this research sample (739 individuals in 82 households in 1980, or 714 persons in 1979) is almost identical to that of the district population.[13] Sample households (drawn from two contiguous sublocations) were selected publicly in the manner of a lottery,[14] at a *baraza* chaired by the two assistant chiefs of the study sublocations. Many of these individuals know one another quite well as kin, neighbors, and friends.

Differences in their material circumstances are reflected in livestock,

Table 1   *Wealth ranks of Embu survey households*

Household wealth rank[a]	Range of wealth index scores	Mean wealth score	Coffee zone residents[b]		Cotton zone residents[b]		Total	
			N	%	N	%	N	%
Wealthy	3,600 – 50,605	11,102	10	26	7	16	17	21
Upper middle	2,000 – 3,599	2,858	12	31	11	26	23	28
Lower middle	500 – 1,999	1,049	9	23	10	23	19	23
Poor	0 – 499	79	8	20	15	35	23	28

Note: [a] The wealth index is an additive scale based on possession of 15 items weighted according to their approximate cash value when new. The items and their weights are as follows: automobile (30,000); motorcycle (14,000); gas cooker (4,500); ox cart (2,000); sofa set (1,500); sewing machine (1,500); plow (1,000); bicycle (800); radio (500); pressure lamp (180); paraffin stove (60); hurricane lamp (40); charcoal stove (30); and wood chairs (25). The median score for the total sample is 1,803.
[b] The difference in mean wealth scores between coffee and cotton zones is not statistically significant.

land, homestead construction, clothing, foods consumed, household furnishings, agricultural implements, and other material assets. To quantify such differences I have constructed a wealth index that consists of an additive scale of 15 material possessions weighted in proportion to their cash cost when new. The items so counted, which include some productive assets as well as consumer goods, are easily verified and are important in local perceptions of economic differences among households. (In addition to wealth differences among households there are important differences in material well-being within households, which I consider below.) The wealth index and categories defined in the study, together with the distribution of scores in coffee and cotton zones, are given in Table 1. Table 2 gives the frequency of ownership of the individual items that make up the score, as well as some additional assets excluded from it. The contrast between rich and poor is illustrated by noting that the three wealthiest households own motor vehicles, as well as paraffin-burning lanterns, radios, and sofas, while the poorest not only own none of these items but also have no bicycles, ox carts, or folding wooden chairs. They do all of their cooking over traditional three-stone fires, and have only candles as lighting.

The principal avenues to wealth accumulation lie in diversification into activities other than crop production. Education, salaries, and businesses are the means for accumulating wealth in land, cash, and material possessions. As Table 3 shows wealthier households are significantly more likely

Table 2   *Assets inventory of Embu survey households by agroeconomic zone*

	Coffee zone		Cotton zone		Total	
				Number and percentage of households owning item		
Automobile	(1)	3%	(2)	5%	(3)	4%
Motorcycle	(1)	3%		0	(1)	1%
Bicycle	(18)	46%	(13)	30%	(31)	38%
Oxcart	(20)	51%	(9)	21%	(29)	35%
Wheelbarrow	(12)	31%	(7)	16%	(19)	23%
Plow	(7)	18%	(9)	21%	(16)	20%
Shovel	(24)	62%	(6)	14%	(30)	37%
Jembe (hoe)	(29)	74%	(39)	91%	(68)	83%
Forked *jembe*	(36)	92%	(42)	98%	(78)	95%
Panga (machete)	(39)	100%	(43)	100%	(82)	100%
Saw	(23)	59%	(17)	40%	(40)	49%
Hammer	(29)	74%	(29)	67%	(58)	71%
Spanner	(13)	33%	(16)	37%	(29)	35%
Diesel water pump		0	(1)	2%	(1)	1%
Maize grinder	(3)	8%	(1)	2%	(4)	5%
Weeding machine	(1)	3%		0	(1)	1%
Sugarcane grinder		0	(1)	2%	(1)	1%
Iron (non-electric)	(18)	46%	(17)	40%	(35)	43%
Radio (non-electric)	(24)	62%	(17)	40%	(41)	50%
Sewing machine (non-electric)	(3)	8%	(3)	7%	(6)	7%
Phonograph (non-electric)	(3)	8%	(4)	9%	(7)	9%
Wristwatch	(18)	46%	(18)	42%	(36)	44%
Thermos	(19)	49%	(14)	33%	(33)	40%
Umbrella	(32)	82%	(32)	74%	(64)	78%
Gas cooker	(1)	3%	(1)	2%	(2)	2%
Paraffin stove	(16)	41%	(8)	19%	(24)	29%
Charcoal stove	(24)	62%	(20)	47%	(44)	54%
Pressure lamp	(2)	5%		0	(2)	2%
Hurricane lamp	(24)	62%	(17)	40%	(41)	50%
Flashlight	(33)	85%	(37)	86%	(70)	85%
Sofa	(6)	15%	(6)	14%	(12)	15%
Stuffed chair	(6)	15%	(6)	14%	(12)	15%
Wood chair	(35)	90%	(33)	77%	(68)	83%
Wood stool	(27)	69%	(13)	30%	(40)	49%
Water tank	(27)	69%	(22)	51%	(49)	60%
Total number of households	(39)		(43)		(82)	

Table 3 *Relationship of wealth to purchased and borrowed land, employment, education, committee membership, agricultural improvements and food surplus production for Embu survey households*

	Wealthy (N = 17)	Upper middle (N = 23)	Lower middle (N = 19)	Poor (N = 23)	Gamma correlation	Chi-square	P
Own purchased land	8	2	2	1	0.66	15.98	0.001
Borrow land	5	12	7	10	−0.05		N.S.
Salaried employee	7	6	5	5	0.22		N.S.
Small business	2	5	0	0	0.63	9.28	0.03
Casual labor	6	9	6	16	−0.34	7.95	0.05
Children attend secondary school	5	7	4	0	0.53	8.41	0.04
Non-resident children who completed secondary school or university	6	5	3	1	0.52	6.54	0.08
Committee member	9	7	7	4	0.35	5.79	0.12
Own improved cattle	9	9	5	4	0.43	6.37	0.09
Planted hybrid maize in 1979 or 1980	11	12	12	8	0.27	4.78	0.19
Used chemical fertilizer in 1980 long rains	9	15	13	4	0.39	15.32	0.002
Produce consistent food surpluses	5	6	0	1			

than poorer ones to have purchased some land,[15] to include someone who operates a small business, to have children attending secondary school,[16] to produce consistently more food than that required to meet domestic consumption needs, and to use chemical fertilizers on their crops. Members of wealthy households are less likely than those in poorer households to engage in casual or daily wage labor. Salaried employees, however, are not significantly more frequent in wealthy households. Wage employment is both the primary agent and product of rural differentiation. At one end of the wealth scale it is part of a cycle of rural impoverishment that removes crucial adult labor from the farm without producing sufficient cash income to compensate for the loss; while at the opposite end it permits accumulation of land and other forms of wealth.[17] As discussed below, wealthy households are not heavily-capitalized large farmers. The wealthiest households do, however, own significantly more land,[18] coffee trees,[19] and cattle,[20] and they spend more on hired farm labor than do poorer households (see Table 4). If land, rather than the index defined above (which excludes land and livestock), is taken as the

Table 4   *Relationship of wealth to land, coffee, cattle, and hired labor for Embu survey households*

	Wealthy (N = 17)	Upper middle (N = 23)	Lower middle (N = 19)	Poor (N = 23)	F Significance level
Mean land acreage owned	26.94	12.00	9.80	6.85	0.005
Mean mature coffee trees	390.00	305.00	162.00	143.00	0.003
Mean cattle [a]	6.29	4.35	4.05	2.17	0.007
Mean hired labor expenditure in long rains 1980 (in shillings)[b]	201.00	121.00	62.00	35.00	0.02

Note: [a]   Local and improved breeds of cattle, excluding animals less than a year old.
[b]   The official exchange rate averaged 7.4 Kenya shillings per US dollar in the second and third quarters of 1980 (IMF 1981).

indicator of wealth, then similar patterns hold (see Table 5). Larger land-owners are more likely to have purchased some land, to operate a small business, to have children attending secondary school,[21] and to own a plow.

These, then, are the bare statistical outlines of material differences in the Embu countryside in the early 1980s.[22] What are the associated social dynamics? One indicator of community social standing – membership on local committees of schools, churches, cattle dips, and so on – drops off markedly only for households who are most economically and socially marginalized, namely those in the poorest category and the smallest land-owners (Tables 3 and 4). Such committee positions both enable and reflect accumulation of wealth and patronage resources. By serving on a local primary school or cattle dip committee, for example, an individual may cultivate further patronage relations with his or her assistant chief, school headmaster, or veterinary officers who serve on the same committee.

To explore the social dynamics of patterns of household mobility outlined earlier, I consider below the instability of household mem-bership, and relations within households and families. I then step back from these micro-dynamics to examine exchanges of land, labor, and food among households, and possible structural regularities in patterns of economic differentiation. I begin by discussing the vagaries of agri-cultural production, and how people cope with them.

Diversification and the uncertainty of agricultural output

A quarter of a century ago Allan (1965) pointed out that the precarious existence of African cultivators requires production at levels that yield a

Table 5 *Relationship of land holdings to purchased and borrowed land, employment, education, committee membership, and agricultural improvements for Embu survey households*

	16+ acres (N=17)	10–15.99 acres (N=20)	5–9.99 acres (N=30)	Less than 5 acres (N=15)	Gamma correlation	Chi-square	P
Own purchased land	8	4	1	0	0.83	19.02	0.0003
Borrow land	5	10	12	7	−0.08		N.S.
Salaried employee	6	5	8	4	0.09		N.S.
Small business	4	1	1	1	0.48	6.32	0.10
Casual labor	6	10	13	8	−0.12		N.S.
Children attend secondary school	7	5	2	2	0.50	8.98	0.03
Committee member	9	8	7	3	0.41	5.92	0.12
Own improved cattle	7	7	9	4	0.17		N.S.
Planted hybrid maize in 1979 or 1980	10	9	17	7	0.05		N.S.
Used chemical fertilizer in 1980 long rains	8	11	13	9	−.04		N.S.
Own ox cart	9	8	8	4	0.32	3.98	.26
Own plough	7	1	5	3	0.21	7.92	0.05

"surplus"[23] in years of average weather. The size of the "surplus" fluctuates with weather variations from one cropping season to the next, but it helps to guarantee that consumption needs are met in years of poor rainfall or other environmental hazards. Thus the "surplus" is greatest in years of abundant rainfall and least or non-existent in years of poor rainfall or drought. The unreliable nature of this "surplus" became a growing problem as demand for it rose with increasing population and urbanization. Today the problem has become a crisis whose magnitude, origins, and potential solutions are widely debated (e.g., Heyer, Roberts, and Williams 1981; World Bank 1981, 1989; Berry 1983; Cohen 1989; Watts 1989). As Berry (1983: 3–9) points out, widely quoted aggregate figures purporting to demonstrate declining growth in the volume of African agricultural production in the 1970s are "limited to officially sanctioned activities," while an increasing volume of agricultural output has been driven out of official marketing channels. The available statistical data simply do not permit accurate assessment of the magnitude of production increases or decreases since they overlook alternative output channels, such as illegal markets or higher standards of consumption for producer households. In short, we do not know what becomes of the "normal surplus" (Allan 1965) of subsistence agriculture when producers must adjust not only to the vagaries of weather but also to those of government price, marketing, and credit policies.

For most Embu farmers crop production (most of which is carried out by hand with hoe and machete) is both a means of acquiring food to meet family consumption needs, and an important source of cash income. Though many farmers grow export cash crops such as coffee and cotton, few, if any, substitute such non-edible crops for food production entirely. Diversification, rather than specialization, is farmers' response to the vagaries of weather, of international prices of export crops, and of national and local prices of food crops. Within this framework, however, small farmers are quick to respond to market opportunities and to adjust their production strategies to them.[24]

In the study area, four crops – arabica coffee, beans, maize, and cotton – dominate in terms of cultivated area, but at least fifteen other crops are grown by more than half of the sample households. These additional crops include: cowpeas; potatoes; sweet potatoes; cassava; arrowroot; bananas; pawpaws; mangoes; oranges; lemons; passion fruit; peppers; pumpkins; onions; and Napier grass. In addition, between one-quarter and one-half of the sample households grow some sorghum, sugarcane, castor, and tomatoes. Smaller numbers grow millet, limes, carrots, cabbage, kale, and sunflower. There is great diversity of cultivars, as well as crops. For example, at least nine different varieties of bananas are grown to suit varying tastes and end uses, such as fodder and raw and cooked food for human consumption. A number of different beans (*Phaseolus vulgaris*) are cultivated, including haricot beans, kidney beans, pinto beans, and navy beans (known by local names such as *runi, gatune, muviru, mbiraru, eru,* and *gaceru*). They are usually grown as genetic mixtures (landraces) rather than pure lines. Quite popular for home consumption is Rose Coco, a landrace of fairly uniform appearance: a speckled red and purple bean locally called *kithiga*. Mexican 142 beans, an early-maturing small white bean (*gaceru*), is the only annual food crop most farmers produce primarily for sale rather than for home consumption. Unlike other bean varieties grown here Mexican 142 is quite small and colorless and not appreciated in local staple dishes such as *githere* and *nyenyi*.

Among the many Embu farmers who grow coffee most devote about 10 to 20 percent (about one-half to one acre, or 0.2–0.4 hectare) of their coffee zone land to that crop. Among the 50 percent or so of cotton zone residents who cultivate cotton, most devote about 5 to 15 percent of their cotton zone land to the crop.[25] Most households grow in addition at least one or two acres (0.4–1.0 hectare) of maize and beans. The remaining area is devoted to other crops named above and, especially in the cotton zone, to grazing and fallow.

If we look at harvests of the two principal staples – maize and beans – in four consecutive crop seasons,[26] we find substantial seasonal fluctuations in both output and in the proportion of households whose output is sufficient to satisfy their consumption requirements.[27] This instability arises in part from variation in the onset, distribution, and amount of rainfall. The highest mean harvests for maize (7.28 bags) and beans (2.87 bags) were recorded for the 1978 short rains season, when rainfall was heavy. The poorest mean harvests occurred in the 1979 short rains (maize: 1.25 bags, and beans: 0.56 bag), and moderate harvests were produced in the long rains of 1979 and 1980.

Comparing the same four seasons, a larger percentage of households in the favorable 1978 short rains than in any other season produced maize and beans harvests in excess of consumption needs (74 percent for maize and 48 percent for beans), while in the poor 1979 short rains season a larger percentage produced deficits than in any other season (84 percent for maize and 83 percent for beans). (From the worst harvest, that of the 1979 short rains, only eight households sold maize and eleven sold beans.) Production shortfalls of maize and beans are made up through substitution of other less desirable foods, and through purchases, gifts, and in-kind payments for labor.

Given this expected seasonal variation, to what extent are farm households' food production levels within any given season related to their consumption requirements? That is, to what extent do subsistence needs determine production levels? In most of the crop seasons monitored the relationship between food crop harvest and number of consumers per household is positive and statistically significant (see Haugerud 1988: 173). Most of the correlation coefficients are lower than 0.3, however, suggesting that there are important additional influences on production decisions and output.

It might be expected that the ratio of consumers to workers in a household (dependency ratio) would contribute to differences in food crop output per worker. That is, in households with higher ratios of consumers to workers, each worker would produce more food than would be the case in households with fewer consumers per worker. Such a relationship between agricultural production and household developmental cycle stage is implied, for example, by the Russian economist Chayanov's (1966) theory of peasant household economy, in which differences in household production are related to their demographic characteristics (especially the ratio of consumers to workers).

The Embu data do not show that household structure as reflected in dependency ratio has a significant effect on food production. The household ratio of consumers to workers is not strongly correlated with output of maize and beans per producer; the correlation is not statistically significant in most of the crop seasons monitored (see Haugerud 1988: 173). The relationship is strongest, however, in those seasons when rainfall conditions are most favorable for each crop. In other, less favorable, seasons the capacity to mobilize labor from outside the household becomes a crucial determinant of food production levels. The seasonal differences in the strength of the relationship are related to differential access to hired and cooperative labor, which is especially important in dealing with uncertain weather conditions, such as early, late, or interrupted onset of the rains.

Labor availability crucially affects household capacity to adjust to rainfall uncertainty at key points in the agricultural cycle. Under any circumstances, with two cropping seasons per year, land preparation and planting are often periods of serious labor shortage. In addition households must be able to respond quickly to circumstances such as unusual rains in January and February (normally relatively dry months, but very wet in 1979). Rain in those months delays harvesting of the previous season's crop, and therefore delays land preparation for the long rains crop. For example, households who obtained smaller bean harvests in the 1979 long rains than in the previous season (1978 short rains) most frequently attributed the difference to late planting or late or inadequate land preparation. Those who cannot mobilize sufficient labor quickly under such circumstances suffer reduced planting and harvests. Households that have unfavorably high dependency ratios (few workers per consumer) and that cannot readily recruit hired and cooperative labor are most disadvantaged in seasons when rainfall conditions delay land preparation and planting, and when weather conditions shorten the period of time in which these tasks must be accomplished.

Among many influences on household capacity to mobilize timely domestic labor are illness and interpersonal conflicts within households. (Other influences are considered later.) One household head's wife, for example, during the 1979 short rains season was unavailable at planting time because she had left the home for some weeks following a quarrel with her husband. In another household the only adult female was ill at planting time. Coping strategies include greater reliance on casual labor by other family members, in order to earn cash to purchase food; or recruiting extra-household labor through hiring or kin ties. In short, a second kind of instability which has crucial material consequences is that of interpersonal conflict and fluctuations in household composition.

The instability of households

Although it is no surprise that relations within a household change as members move in and out, quarrel, go away to school, separate from a spouse, remarry, die, or take a job in the city, it is difficult to capture the consequences and implications of these changes in analytical models based on a unitary conception of the farm household. While it is helpful for some analytical purposes to assume households to be unified production and consumption units whose internal relationships are taken as given, for other purposes it is useful to open the lid of this black box that represents the farm household. That is what I do here. I start by quantifying instability arising from interpersonal conflict. These figures demonstrate a fluidity in household structure that is seldom made explicit in economic models of household behavior. I then discuss why domestic conflict arises and how it affects material well-being and economic pursuits. Domestic conflicts and exchanges merge into wider patron–client networks. An individual's circle of kin and affines is the core from which he or she mobilizes wider cliental ties of material exchange and social commitment.

Interpersonal conflict leads to frequent changes in household composition. About one-quarter (27 percent) of the Embu sample households experienced substantial change in membership due to interpersonal conflict during the twenty months when I kept such records (June 1979 until February 1981). Fourteen households lost one or more members for periods ranging from weeks to months, while eight households gained one or more members as a result of domestic conflict. Among those that lost members, in four households a wife of the senior male left the household due to quarrels with her husband or co-wives; in eight households a son's wife left to return to her parents; and in one household the senior male and his young second wife left following quarrels between this woman and her husband's sons by a previous wife. Among households that gained members as a result of conflict, in five a married daughter rejoined her natal homestead following quarrels with her husband; in two a sister of the senior male joined the home following disputes with her husband; and in one the senior male's father quarrelled with and left his own wife to join his son's household.

Some households experienced multiple disruptions from interpersonal conflict during the twenty month monitoring period. In household 17, for example, there were repeated changes that involved the return of both wives of one son to their natal homes at different times. In household 32 two daughters rejoined their natal home following disputes with their husbands. Household 45, the most striking case, is headed by a man with an erratic personality who is on occasion affable and outgoing, and at other times drinks to excess and quarrels with and beats his wives. His first wife had already left him when the research began. His second wife left a few months after the surveys began, and she took with her her younger children and left the older ones under the care of their father and paternal grandfather. About four months later the second wife left and was replaced by a third. A few months after that the third wife left and the second returned. During the months of the economic surveys the number of children in this household varied from zero to eight and the number of adults from one to three. Computing a Chayanovian consumer/worker ratio for such a household produces an obviously problematic figure. Such household membership changes that arise from interpersonal conflict, taken together with those associated with developmental processes of birth, death, marriage, and migratory employment, demonstrate a striking fluidity in household composition.

Changes in household composition occur within a framework I will describe briefly here. Embu households often consist of a husband, his wife or wives,[28] the unmarried children of each wife, possibly a married son and his wife and children, and the husband's mother or father or both.[29] Married brothers seldom share a residence and do not necessarily even live near each other or near their father. In only two of the sample households (52 and 65) are married brothers co-residents in a compound, and in both of these cases one or both of the brothers is a part-time resident employed outside the district. In a third household two married brothers whose father is dead share a farm and live in separate compounds a few yards apart. A son's decision as to where to reside upon marriage depends on the availability of land at his natal homestead and elsewhere, and on interpersonal relations within his parents' homestead.

Each farm in Embu is registered under the name of a household head (usually male) under an official system of freehold tenure. In principle, each registered farm is managed by a single family who lives on that farm. Actual access to land, however, is much more complex than this. Different individuals within a household frequently enter into separate transactions of borrowing or renting land from members of other households. Individuals often have overlapping access to the same parcels of rural land. Disputes over "customary" use rights and titled land ownership are common.

An example illustrates how households organize access to multiple parcels of land. Household A occupies a four-acre (1.6 hectare) farm in the Embu coffee zone. That farm is registered in the name of the household head's father, who lives a couple of miles away on a farm which the son purchased in the adjacent cotton zone. The son and his wife and children cultivate portions of three land parcels: (1) his coffee zone residence, where he grows coffee and food crops; (2) an unoccupied coffee zone parcel which he also owns, where he grows additional food crops; and (3) the cotton zone parcel where his father lives and which is used for cultivation of cotton, food crops, and livestock production. In addition, the son owns another piece of land in the cotton zone, and he lends a portion of it to a clan-mate who lives in the coffee zone. Such access to dispersed parcels is by no means unusual. What is uncommon is a family farm that is actually owned and cultivated only by a nuclear family who live on it.

A woman at marriage usually leaves her natal homestead to join her husband either at his original home or at a new location chosen by him. An unmarried woman with children often remains in her natal home and her children become members of their maternal grandfather's patrilineage until or unless their mother later marries their father or another man. If she marries someone other than her children's father she may well leave at home with her own mother the children she has borne by another man; these children are then sometimes adopted into her father's lineage. Divorced or separated women usually return to their natal homes with some or all of their children;[30] the number of children accompanying such a woman and consequently adopted by her father's lineage depends, for example, on the children's ages (young children being more likely to accompany their mother), the duration of the marriage, and the payment or return of bridewealth installments associated with rights in children. Today, as in the past (Saberwal 1970: 10), "in such situations the future affiliation of the children was somewhat indeterminate, giving them the option to assess the relative advantages and to choose."[31] A widow is inherited by the eldest of her husband's brothers (though this practice is dying out in the younger generation), and can move to the residence of the deceased husband's brother or live separately.[32] In either case the husband's brother becomes stepfather to her children and represents her husband in transactions (such as bridewealth) that require a father's authority, and in any legal proceedings or disputes over property. A widower can entrust the care of his children to a brother's wife or to his own mother if he does not remarry. In addition to these kin, households occasionally include a less wealthy relative's child (e.g., household 36) or a salaried farm laborer (e.g., household 54).

Given the variable composition and organization of households one may well ask whether this unit of analysis should not be abandoned altogether. Though it is an unstable structure in which rights and responsibilities are continually renegotiated, the household nonetheless is one arena within which individuals interact, maneuver, mobilize resources, and cope with the vicissitudes of crop yields, interpersonal conflict, and income. In assessing economic differentiation processes the household should not necessarily be the exclusive focus of analysis (see below), but it is a useful starting point. Also important are the ways individuals maneuver in multiple social networks and pursue various affiliations beyond the household (see Shipton and Goheen 1992; Berry 1993).

Here I wish to take up a theme that is often underemphasized in studies of peasant differentiation processes: namely intra-household dynamics, and especially the ways in which individual economic options are shaped by interpersonal conflict within the household. What are the common sources of domestic conflict, and how are they connected to access to and use of economic resources?

Interpersonal conflict and relations within households and families

Certain sources of tension and conflict that have long existed in Embu communities have become more pronounced following changes in the nature, availability, and value of economic resources. Saberwal (1970: 93) writes that in pre-colonial Embu, "hatred was especially likely to exist between close agnates, brothers with their eyes fixed on the same herd for inheritance and patrilateral cousins who might owe each other livestock." Today conflict is particularly likely to arise among agnates competing for land. Conflicts arise from a number of other sources as well, and those that result in a change in household membership are no more frequent among wealthier than among poorer households.[33] Below I consider conflict between juniors and elders, between co-wives, and between wives and husbands. In addition, conflict between brothers, though not addressed separately here, is repeatedly associated with competition over land.

Interpersonal conflict in Embu is often associated with economic inequalities within the household and family. A widowed mother-in-law on poor terms with her sons may receive only minimal material assistance from them. A son on bad terms with his father may inherit none or less of his wealth than does a brother. Children of different co-wives sometimes receive from their father vastly different levels of material support (clothing, food, school fees: as in household 7). Wives and children may be less well off than a husband who seldom works and who controls household income to his own rather than to his family's advantage.

Personal relations within households and families affect material inequalities between, as well as within, households. Households that include more than a husband and wife as fully cooperating adult members often have an important labor advantage over households with fewer productive adults who can cooperate with one another. A resident grand-mother, for example, may help with child care and cooking while the mother does other tasks such as cultivating or fetching water and fire-wood. When resident relatives are unavailable, however, non-resident kin or neighbors must occasionally be called upon to assist with child care, as in the case of the co-wife in household 5. This woman needs help with child care when she cultivates her plot away from home, but must seek it outside the home because she is on poor terms with her husband's resident mother and lives in a compound separate from that of the rest of the household on the same farm. Seeking such labor assistance from a neighbor rather than a household resident in turn entails reciprocal obligations that further reduce hours available for work at home.

Cooperation in agricultural and other economic activities between co-wives, between husband and wife, and between parents and children expands production possibilities, while domestic conflict often reduces them. In the absence of divisiveness some households can expand the area of land under cultivation, increase livestock holdings, and diversify income-earning activities (e.g., devote more time to marketing crops and livestock, open a shop, hire out a plow) which is more difficult if they are beset by quarrels and subterfuge. Household 1, for example, manages to cultivate several separate parcels of land in two ecological zones by using a resident grandmother (husband's mother) for child care and cooking, keeping some of its livestock with the husband's father on its additional cotton zone farm (where more grazing land is available than on its smaller coffee zone parcels), and sharing crop production tasks on all the parcels. The grandfather sells milk for them daily and the husband and wife from time to time spend several days at the grandfather's cotton zone residence in order to cultivate their lower zone land, while they and their children maintain a permanent homestead in the coffee zone.

In short, cooperation among extended kin is an advantage where farm plots and grazing lands are dispersed across uplands and lowlands, and where farmers practice other forms of diversification. The variations in domestic labor organization mentioned here intersect with other crucial influences on household prosperity, namely, access to salaries, education, and state resources. As suggested in the last chapter the rise of *athomi* or literate people created new social divisions noticeable particularly in relations between juniors and elders. I discuss this theme next.

Relations between juniors and elders

In the Kenya of today, unlike in the past, girls are educated and when they marry they forget their own parents and instead help their husband's parents. This is too bad; you young girls cannot even remember the one who tethered you like a small calf. Young girls today should become educated with the intention of helping their own parents in the future.

The elder wife (in household 5) just quoted refers to the increased frequency of education of girls and to their subsequent obligations to their parents, a theme that also applies to sons and is a common source of tension between generations. Education and salaries, quite rare in the generation born before the late 1950s, decidedly set later generations apart from their elders and place new financial burdens on employed juniors expected to share the new-found wealth with their parents and a host of other relatives. Parents who sell off much of their land and livestock in order to finance their children's education do so in the expectation that once (or if) those children are employed, benefits will flow in the opposite direction. For school and health care fees, land purchases, and a number of other expenses, parents and other family members often turn to a relative with a regular cash income. In order to maintain friendly relations with parents and other relatives whose support he or she may one day require, the young primary school teacher or government clerk regularly sends some portion of even a small salary to parents, and where possible, assists with siblings' and cousins' school fees. In addition to the long-term benefits of such investment in kin relations, over the short term the urban worker is likely to receive return gifts of home-produced food such as maize, beans, potatoes, and bananas from rural relatives. Flows of food and cash between town and country-side are an important element of circular labor migration here as else-where in Africa.[34] Mature sons and daughters in rural Embu are expected to provide occasional labor as well as financial assistance, not only when their parents become too old to perform such tasks themselves, but throughout life. A married daughter is expected occasionally to help her mother with planting, weeding, and harvesting, while a son, even if living away from home, should help his father with such tasks as clearing land or building a fence, house, or cattle enclosure.

Maintaining good relations with parents and other kin is an important hedge against future uncertainties that affect individuals and the wider economy. Urban migrants thus retain a foothold in rural areas; as Leys (1971: 316) put it, "the whole social and political focus of the greater part of the wage labour force remains in the rural areas, in which in any case most workers' families are resident." On weekends, holidays, and in times of possible national political crisis, such as the August 1978 death of President Kenyatta, workers in Nairobi leave the city in large numbers to return to their rural homes.

Access to rural land is one means by which rural residents, as well as seasonal and longer-term migrants, maintain local and descent group affiliations. Land is a symbol of kin ties across generations; an "owner" is a trustee for others both living and unborn (Kenyatta 1965: 299). Even if securely employed in the civil service, a man does not consider himself well-established until he has agricultural land of his own. In densely-settled areas such as the central Kenyan highlands the nearly universal desire for land leads to intense competition between and within families for access to this resource. Given a father's power to decide how his land is to be divided among his sons after his death, the competition for land places a particularly severe strain on relations between brothers and between fathers and sons.

Acquiring land was so important to one young man in household 14, for example, that a dispute with his father led him to sacrifice his father's support of his secondary education for a secure hold on some of his land. The conflicting interests within this household led to fission and a change of residence by the father and his young second wife. This case study is described below.

A dispute between father and son over land

In this household, Njagi (a fictive name) is the oldest of two sons of his father's deceased first wife. The title deed for the four acres (1.6 hectares) of coffee zone land the family occupies is registered in the name of the deceased first wife's oldest son, while that of another four acres of unoccupied and uncultivated land in the adjacent cotton zone is in the father's name. Njagi and his brother cultivated a portion of the coffee zone farm used by their father and stepmother. His father's remarriage after his first wife's death did not please Njagi because sons produced by the second wife could threaten his and his brother's claims to both pieces of land. Tension in the home between Njagi and his father and his new wife led Njagi to stay with some neighbors during his boarding school holidays rather than staying at home. Another source of tension in this home was the young wife's complaints that her husband was giving financial priority to school fees for his first wife's sons and ignoring the needs of her own young children for nursery school fees and clothing. Njagi's father was paying for his son's secondary education and had sold some of his land and livestock in order to do so.

When Njagi's father requested that he exchange land parcels with him, Njagi refused. His father also spoke of selling still more of his land; some of the income from such a sale would have gone not only toward Njagi's education, but also toward the bridewealth for his father's second wife. The father complained that he wanted Njagi to share some of his land with his younger brother, and argued that some of the younger brother's land had already been sold to finance Njagi's education. One day Njagi and his brother beat their father's new wife. Njagi's father and stepmother then moved to the unoccupied land his father owns in the cotton zone. Njagi's father refused to continue to pay his son's school fees and Njagi discontinued his education. He began working on his farm with his younger brother.

This case illustrates several lines of intra-household conflict: between a father and son over land and over the father's remarriage; between a son and his father's second wife; and between the second wife and her husband over financial provisions for her own children. Later on when the two brothers wish to marry and establish their own households, new conflict is likely to emerge between the two brothers, as well as between the younger brother and his father over the lower zone land for which he and sons of the second wife will compete.

Such conflict arising from a father's second or third marriage is not uncommon. In household 31, for example, the father complained that when he married again after his first wife's death his sons were so annoyed that they departed from his compound and refused to continue to help him with his hundreds of coffee trees. In such situations sons may also attempt to drive a wedge between the father and his young wife before more sons are born with whom sons of the first wife may have to share the father's wealth.

Sons and daughters in open conflict with their fathers or mothers are likely to lose not only their material support, but also to diminish their parents' willingness to lend the support of their authority in disputes and conflicts with others. A son whose wife has left him to return to her parents, for example, is likely to need the support of his own parents to help negotiate her return. Moreover, when a wife leaves because of her husband's misbehavior or ill-treatment, her parents are likely to require some material payment such as a goat or sheep from the husband to effect her return, and a young man may need his father's assistance in making such a payment. Similarly, a daughter separated from her husband often needs to be able to return to her natal home and also may require help from her parents or other relatives to negotiate her return to her husband.

The parents in household 7 complained that their son Kariuki seldom helped with work at home after his wife returned to her parents' home in a neighboring district. When Kariuki's wife wrote a letter saying she was willing to return Kariuki went to get her, only to be told by her father to return to his home and report back with his own father and mother. Kariuki's stepmother commented that he then began to improve his behavior by doing more work at home because he knew that otherwise his father would refuse to accompany him to his estranged wife's home to negotiate her return. In this case, where neither the father nor the son has wage income, the dynamics of control of elders over the labor of juniors through marriage transactions leaves the balance of power tipped in favor of the elder.

Relations between co-wives

An Embu proverb says that "two wives are two pots of poison."[35] Polygyny is both a sign of status and prestige for the husband and a possible source of conflict, or even an invitation to poverty. Co-wives and their children compete for the husband's affection and attention; for shares of cash he controls to cover school fees, food, clothing, and other material goods; and for portions of his heritable wealth.[36] A perception of neglect or unfair treatment on the part of one co-wife can initiate a cycle of ill-feeling or feuding that can lead to poisoning or sorcery. Thus the father of the head of household 36 briefly moved into his son's homestead because he believed his third wife was trying to poison him. He then nearly caused his son's wife to return to her parents' home because he continually suspected the food she prepared for him had been poisoned. His son's wife herself believed her father-in-law's mind had been affected by sorcery or poisoning directed at him by his abandoned second wife.

Even when a husband professes and attempts equal treatment of his wives, the elder wife may be jealous of the younger and feel neglected. A second wife in some sense displaces the first, particularly when the second marriage follows the first wife's failure to produce any sons (as in household 16, where the husband married a second wife with the consent of the first). A wife's failure to produce sons almost compels an Embu man to take another wife in order to produce sons to inherit his property. Let us look briefly at contrasting patterns of relations within two polygynous households.

The two co-wives in household 7 share the same compound but have little to do with one another and receive markedly different attention and material support from their husband, Njeru. Wanja, the middle-aged first wife, produced two sons and several daughters. Her oldest son recently married and shares the compound, though his young wife has already twice left him to return to her natal home following quarrels. Before home-brewed beer was banned in 1979 the first wife is said by neighbors to have drunk heavily and to have neglected her work at home through frequent absences. The first wife shares a compound with Muthoni, the young fourth wife, who has already produced several sons, the eldest of whom is in nursery school. Njeru had divorced a second wife, several of whose children live in the homestead, while their mother lives a mile or so

away in the same division of the district. This divorced wife is also said to
have been a heavy consumer of alcohol. When she left Njeru she took
with her her youngest son, whom Njeru says is still his and he will one day
reclaim. A third wife Njeru inherited from his deceased brother left him to
stay on a separate farm, which is registered in the name of Njeru's
deceased father and is Njeru's legal responsibility now that his father and
brother are dead.

There are visually striking differences between the two co-resident
wives (one and four), their houses, and their children. While the youngest
wife wears bright new dresses and has a well-maintained new house with
an iron sheet roof, the first wife and her children have poorer clothing and
a smaller house in worse condition in the same compound. When I
photographed them one day some of the resident children of the divorced
second wife cried and argued when their father told them to be photographed with the first wife rather than the fourth. They complained
because they thought their father himself would appear only with the
youngest wife and they wished to be pictured with him.

Though they share a compound the two co-wives, Wanja and Muthoni,
cook in separate kitchens (which is not always the case among co-wives)
and cultivate separate portions of the farm (which is the norm for
co-wives). When their husband buys food he divides it between the wives
according to the size of their household segments. This household produces little food surplus and receives most of its cash income from coffee
(800 trees) and a plow (both controlled by the husband) and from
occasional agricultural labor. Its internal relations are not happy.

Household 35, on the other hand, includes three co-wives, among
whom two cooperate well, work together, and cook in one kitchen. The
third wife has little to do with the other two, and after her husband's
death built her own compound apart from them in a separate portion of
the same farm that belonged to her husband. A fourth wife left the
household before the husband died because (according to neighbors) of
disagreements with the other wives. The husband was with her when he
died. The second wife complains that the first wife hates her, that she
disputes the property she inherited from her husband, and that she visited
a medicine man (*murogi*) to arrange to poison the second wife or her
young son, or both. When her husband married his third wife the new
wife and the first wife became allies against the second and for a time
turned their husband against the second wife as well. At that time the
second wife left her husband and returned to her parents' home for some
months. The first wife also had problems with the husband; he is said to
have beaten her and to have knocked out her front teeth.

One day during her separation, the second wife went back to her husband's farm to harvest sorghum. She left her three-year-old son, who was said to be very bright and envied by others, sleeping under a tree. That night when she returned home, her son fell ill and died. She is still very bitter about this and believes he was poisoned. After some negotiations between her clan and that of her husband, she did eventually return to her husband's homestead, but her relations with the other two wives living there did not improve, and the home continues as two separate compounds whose residents cultivate separate portions of the deceased husband's land.

Tensions within a household can arise also when one wife shares a residence with the children of another wife who has separated from or divorced her husband. In household 17, for example, the son's second wife refuses to care for the children of the separated first wife. When the latter left she took with her only her youngest child and left the others in her husband's home. These young children are now cared for by their paternal grandmother. The son is building a new house in the compound for his separated first wife in the hope that she will return to live there again. The son's marriage with his second wife is also unstable; she too has returned to her natal home, taking with her two children and leaving one behind. This leaves two elderly grandparents (the son's mother and father) charged with the care of five small children. Their son was imprisoned briefly for theft and is said to waste on beer and prostitutes the income he earns assisting local shopkeepers in the market a mile or so away. Though its four acres of land (under an acre at the homestead residence and another parcel in a nearby neighborhood) should be sufficient to meet subsistence needs, there is a serious labor shortage in this home, with two elderly people required to produce food for five grandchildren, and with only erratic assistance from their son and daughters-in-law. Difficult interpersonal relations thus underly this household's poor material conditions.

Relations between husbands and wives

As we have already seen some conflict between spouses arises from the circumstances of polygyny, and from remarriage after divorce or separation. In addition, conflict arises in the negotiation of male and female control of resources such as land and cash. Women's access to cash varies from one household to another, and is related to personality characteristics of the wife and husband, to wealth levels, and to a household's mix of income sources. The cultural norm is that husbands provide cash to meet household needs, whether that involves making purchases themselves or giving wives money to do so. Wives in turn must keep husbands well-informed of domestic needs, be able to demonstrate specific needs in order to obtain cash from the husband, and show that she has used money wisely. When husband and wife quarrel, and intra-household cooperation breaks down, the husband is likely to withhold cash, while the wife may refuse to prepare food for the husband, to fetch water for him, or to wash his clothes. In so doing she may run the risk of being beaten.

One type of quarrel that occurs frequently between husbands and wives is that over money intended to be spent for food, clothing, or other necessities and instead spent by the husband on beer or roasted meat in town. In some households (such as 21 and 33) where the husbands regularly consume nearly all of the households' meager cash resources on drink and hide money from their wives, the compounds themselves reflect material poverty associated with the husbands' neglect. Households 21 and 33, for example, each consist of only one very small and poorly maintained thatched-roof house with only a few wooden stools for seating. In both homes husband and wife quarrel frequently and the wives openly scorn their husbands in front of visitors. Neighbors say that in household 21, the wife, in spite of her husband's bad behavior, depends too much on him for support instead of trying to find alternative ways of meeting household needs and solving problems. The wife complains bitterly that although they never receive less than about 700 shillings (US $94 in 1980 prices) from their coffee, her husband refuses to provide even primary education support for her children's school uniforms and building fund fees. She openly blames the husband for their lack of furniture and poor house with its leaking thatch roof for which the husband will not buy iron sheets. She says that although her husband's own clothes are torn, instead of using his money to repair or replace them he simply buys beer. The wife said her husband even demands to know what she does with the money she earns from selling her bananas (no more than a dollar or so per week) and she tells him that that small amount is her own to do with as she wishes because he uses his money for drinking. One day, for example, they quarrelled when the husband demanded a few shillings that the wife earned selling bananas and a bottle of milk, and she refused to give him the money.

In some homes a husband secretly "steals" food from his wife, sells it, and uses the money himself even when the family has too little food to be able to afford to sell it. In household 33, quite a poor home in which the husband has a reputation as a drunkard, the wife must firmly hold onto her own income from occasionally selling bananas or hiring herself out as an agricultural laborer for neighbors. Though this household owns less than an acre of land it borrows from a member of the husband's patri-clan sufficient additional land to meet its subsistence requirements. It still has difficulty meeting its needs, however, because the husband's labor is seldom available, the extra land is a couple of miles from home, and any cash earned tends to be squandered by the husband. The husband does occasional casual wage labor. The wife frequently does casual labor to help support herself and her children. Both the husband and wife in this home have been previously married and divorced. The wife is from a neighboring Gikuyu district and was at one time the second wife of a man whom she said she left because he drank a great deal and frequently beat her with a stick. Her present (second) marriage to an Embu man whom she met while he was working on a settler's farm in a nearby Gikuyu district has also been difficult. She and her present husband have twice separated for six and seven month periods.

One day when one of my female research assistants[37] visited this household for one of many biweekly interviews on economic activities, the wife (to whom I will refer by the pseudonym Wangari) had earlier walked very rapidly up the road to find her husband, who had taken a chicken from their home to sell in the local market at Runyenje's. After some time the two walked back home, Wangari sat down opposite her husband, leaned against the mud wall of their small house, and the two began to quarrel loudly. My assistant and a neighbor from the adjacent farm who was on good terms with the family and whom my assistant had just interviewed went to ask what was wrong. Wangari explained how her husband had stolen her chicken from home to sell it just when he knew she was away. She had gone to do her required day of communal work in the local coffee cooperative factory to which they belonged, and on her way met a woman who told her that she had just seen her husband near the market carrying a chicken. Wangari then guessed that the chicken must have been from home; she went back home to confirm this, did not find the chicken, and then went back to the Runyenje's market to find her husband. By the time she met him there, he had already sold the chicken for 25 shillings (about US $3.34 in 1980). She asked him for the money but he refused to give it to her.

Wangari said that although that morning her husband had asked her to sell the chicken to obtain money to take their children to the hospital, she had told him to get the money from another source. She said her husband had earlier done some casual labor but used the cash earned to buy beer without considering his family's needs. Wangari then began loudly cursing her husband as he weakly defended himself. She called him a thief and said he had on another occasion secretly taken some of their dry coffee berries (*buni*), sold them, and used the money to buy beer. When she asked for the money, he gave her just five shillings (US $0.67 in 1980) and told her to buy sugar with it. Wangari also told my research assistant and her neighbor how the previous week her husband had brought some meat home and told her he had paid for it, but that, later in the day when walking down the road toward another market (Ugweri), Wangari met the butcher from whom her husband had purchased the meat, he asked her to pay for it, and she did so.

By this time,Wangari was speaking very loudly and holding a *panga* (machete) as she argued; the noise attracted another neighbor woman. When this woman asked the husband to explain what was wrong the latter said that he had received a message from his children's primary school telling him to take his children to the hospital the following day to be treated for a disease spreading among children in the school. Because he did not have the money for that he said he decided to take the chicken and sell it while his wife was away because he knew that when she came home he would not be able to do so. His wife then interrupted him to ask whether if she had been the sick one he would have sacrificed his beer money to take her to the hospital, and he told her to keep quiet about that. The neighbor woman who had come last then suggested the husband produce the money just received and divide it with his wife; he refused. The neighbor then asked in a light and teasing manner whether he was sure he had no intention of using that money for beer. He said he could not do that. They then calculated the cost of the journey to the hospital in Embu town and realized that in any case the money was insufficient.

The husband angrily asked his wife why she had followed him to the market, said he had never been followed in such a way by a woman before, and that if he had not thought twice he would have beaten her in public. Wangari then asked why he did not do so and he threatened to do it then and there. The neighbor calmed him and said it would be a shame to do so while they had a visitor. Wangari then shouted that after her husband went to the hospital she would destroy the house and return to her parents' home in Central Province. Her husband told her she could do as she liked.

My research assistant began the interview after the discussion grew calmer, and when the husband began talking of the maize and beans they had planted his wife shouted that he should not talk about any of her activities since it was she who had done the work of planting. The interviewer then obtained separate responses from each about what work he or she had done. Wangari's anger subsided during the interview and when her children came home from school she gave them lunch but pointedly did not give food to her husband. My research assistant completed the interview and left after wishing them a peaceful resolution to their problems.

The details of the quarrel in household 33 are not unusual and the case illustrates the crucial connection between interpersonal relations within households and access to and use of economic resources. Domestic conflict over use of material resources is by no means confined to poorer households. For example, one day the wife and husband in household 8, a fairly prosperous home, were arguing over 300 shillings (US $40 in 1980) which the husband was to have used to purchase beans but which he instead consumed on beer. The frequency of conflict that produces changes in household membership is as great in the top two as in the lower two wealth categories defined earlier.

Men and women dispute the allocation of household labor as well as cash. In household 7, for instance, the husband and his first wife argued because she wanted to earn some cash by spending the day planting beans for a neighbor. Her husband, on the other hand, ordered her instead to remove manure from the cattle enclosure and apply it to his coffee trees. This the wife did, in part because the presence of a younger co-wife in the compound reduces her leverage over her husband. The first wife, however, does sometimes sneak away to do casual labor without first informing her husband, in order to acquire some cash of her own.

As these examples suggest material inequalities within households are as important as those (discussed below) between households. Differentiation processes within households are associated with struggles over cash, labor, and land. In this highland region of rising population densities on productive agricultural land, domestic disputes over land sales have particularly serious economic consequences. It is to this theme that I turn now.

Family disputes over land sales

Land, as noted, is a symbol of kin ties across generations. Spiritual and social ties across generations are part of the cultural understandings that shape central Kenyan peoples' views of past and present. Elder children are named for their grandparents, and represent the rebirth of that alternate generation. The behavior of the living may please or displease one's deceased ancestors (Kenyatta 1965: 253–258; Glazier 1984). To sustain good relations between the living and spirits of the dead in the past (and to some today) requires various ceremonial offerings of food and drink to the ancestors. Kenyatta (1965) invokes this moral imperative in a political context, as he dedicated his Gikuyu ethnography: "To Moigoi and Wamboi and all the dispossessed youth of Africa: for perpetuation of communion with ancestral spirits through the fight for African Freedom, and in the firm faith that the dead, the living, and the unborn will unite to rebuild the destroyed shrines."[38] These spiritual beliefs are part of the symbolic content of rights in land.

Under early twentieth-century (pre-reform) land tenure in Embu, individuals who acquired land through first cultivation (or *runo* rights; cf. *kuuna* "to clear the land for the first time") or through purchase controlled both use and transfer rights to that property.[39] Individuals usually were free to cultivate new land in any locality so long as someone else was not using it, and had not claimed it as *runo* land. Under *runo* rights an individual placed an initial claim on a parcel of land by placing stones or planting trees along its boundaries and having it blessed with honey in a ceremony overseen by clan elders. The claimant was then required to put the land into immediate use to validate his claim. He and his patrilineal descendants ideally were entitled to cultivate portions (sing., *mugunda*) of the original parcel (*kithaka*), though long-term co-residence of a father and all his married sons was not usual. Although land in pre-colonial Embu was inherited by one or more of a man's sons, customary residence practices and the relative abundance of land meant that sons did not necessarily depend upon inheritance to acquire it. Sons left their natal homesteads at marriage or some time afterwards to establish new homesteads and acquired rights in land through first clearing or purchase.

When the founder or first claimant to a piece of land died his descendants did not exercise the autonomous use and transfer rights of the founder. Once an individual acquired use rights to a piece of land through inheritance he was free to plant whatever crops he chose and his lineage exercised no rights in the harvest. Should the individual wish to transfer use rights to another person through tenancy or sale, however, he first had to obtain approval from other members of his lineage.[40]

For some decades before the state began to issue individual land title deeds, rising population densities, commercialization, and other changes were associated with indigenous moves toward land privatization in Embu and elsewhere in Kenya.[41] As early as the 1920s some African political leaders in Embu and elsewhere had requested that people be allowed title deeds for their land (Moris 1970: 124). As land grew scarcer in Embu purchases increased, as did conflict over corporate land rights activated by individuals who claimed to represent particular lineages or clans (see Embu LNC minutes, May 21–22, 1941). During the 1930s the Embu LNC received increasing reports of secret or "illegal" land sales: that is, sales transacted by individuals without prior approval of other lineage members or witnessing by elders. Early government proposals to alleviate the problem by registering sales were declined, however, by local chiefs on the Embu Council (Glazier 1985: 202). Under some circumstances, although the evidence is historically contradictory, purchases were redeemable; that is, land could be "refunded" to the seller if the latter returned the total amount of livestock or cash originally paid (see Kenyatta 1965; Sorrenson 1967; Glazier 1985: 200).

When the Kenyan state demarcated land and issued individual titles in central Kenya during the late 1950s and early 1960s,[42] most parcels were listed under male names and it is therefore men who usually have the legal right to sell land. Though many land sales, subdivisions, and successions are not recorded in the register, the state formally requires that any sales, leases or mortgages first be approved by local land control boards. Members of these boards tend to be relatively well-educated individuals who command significant farm and off-farm incomes (see Coldham 1978a). Divisional land control boards frequently deal with cases in which wives or sons file complaints to prevent a man from selling land essential to a family's subsistence, or land promised for sons to inherit. Just as in the case of the man who secretly sold his wife's chicken, the income from land sales is often used for drink, bridewealth for additional wives, or other purposes not agreed upon by some of a man's kin. Family members who discover in time a man's intent to sell their land can try to have the sale blocked by the land control board on the grounds that it will negatively affect family subsistence and welfare. Here are two letters[43] that attempt to block such sales.

I have learnt that my husband————, the proprietor of the above land is subdividing the same to another person. I would like to inform you that if this consent will be given, it will mean selling of the whole parcel and we shall be left landless while we have got children who don't know where to send them. We have no other land to reside and I would kindly request you not allow consent no matter whether he comes with a forged wife or not.

Yours faithfully,

————

Dear Sir,
    Re: Objection to sale of land parcel no.————
    Registered in the name of————
I am the legally and lawfully married (certificate with me) wife of Mr.————
and I understand from reliable sources he is intending to sell the above piece of land which is approximately 3 (three) acres. The grounds for my appeal/objection are as follows: 1. My husband and I have nine (9) children of whom four (4) are boys. 2. We haven't got any other piece of land to live in because even the 1/8 acre point we had was sold by him. 3. The three acres land we have has coffee (about 300 stems) in two ———— Farmer Cooperative Society Ltd. shares – one belonging to my husband and the other belonging to our first born son ———— son of ————. 4. The sales of this coffee help our children's school fees, clothing, and other necessities of life. The money we get helps me to bring up children, and buy food as the land is not very good for maize and beans. 5. If

therefore the land is sold or any part thereof, we shall not only miss children's education and our daily bread but we shall live like homeless birds in the air. 6. Since my husband has an illegal wife, he may think of selling the land secretly without my knowledge. It is for these reasons that our children and I object to the sale very strongly.

Yours faithfully,————
wife of ————

These letters, like the splitting of household 14 described earlier, illustrate the seriousness of land disputes that pit family member against family member.[44] Where land is at stake interpersonal conflict can disrupt the agricultural cycle and threaten family subsistence. Increasing land scarcity means that among the Embu, as among the Chagga of Kilimanjaro,

> individuals are placed in structurally loaded positions of mutual competition from which there is virtually no egress. Any tipping of the balance that favors one competitor or brings misfortune to the other is likely to burst into an episode of hostile action or accusations of witchcraft. (S. F. Moore 1975: 128)

Domestic conflict arising from tensions inherent in a particular social structure thus can be aggravated and the economic consequences altered by changes in the nature and availability of economic resources such as land.

As the foregoing discussion suggests assumptions about farm households' unitary qualities pose analytic problems. Farm households represent simultaneously units of production, consumption, kinship, and co-residence. Household structure and composition are very fluid, however, so that just what kinds of "units" they are must be qualified. A household model can mask variable relationships that define access to resources both within and between households. Individuals within households sometimes pool their resources amicably and relatively equally, but they also may contest them or refuse to pool them. A focus on internal relationships draws attention to variable forms of domestic organization, and to the negotiability and manipulability of relationships within households (see Guyer 1981). A household model in addition can hide relationships between domestic groups of unequal wealth, power, and control over economic resources. It is to these that I turn next.

Relations between rich and poor

Rich and poor exchange labor, food, and land in patterns I shall describe briefly here. First, as suggested earlier, households differ in their capacities to produce enough food to meet their own consumption requirements.[45] Deviations from "subsistence" levels are not necessarily random, and are not independent of one another. A minority of households fairly consistently produce more than they need to feed the family, while others usually underproduce. Household failures and successes constitute an interrelated "social system of production" (Sahlins 1972: 114–115). The survival of households who usually underproduce is linked to the existence of a set of households who consistently produce beyond their consumption requirements. Social relationships among households help to define access to any surplus product, whether the producers make that product available to others as a purchasable commodity, as a gift, or as in-kind payment for labor.

The distinctive characteristics of the minority of Embu households who usually produce more food than required for domestic consumption are summarized in Table 6.[46] In brief, they are wealthier, hire more labor, and recruit more reciprocal labor[47] than do other households. They own nearly twice as much land[48] and more than twice as many mature coffee trees, and their wealth score (as defined earlier) is significantly higher than the mean for other households. They spent significantly more cash to hire farm labor. They *received* reciprocal non-wage labor more often and in greater quantity than the rest, and they *provided* such labor to other households less often than other households.[49] Heavy users of hired labor are also heavy users of cooperative labor.[50] The contribution of cooperative labor to growth and accumulation should not be overemphasized, however, in part because of the organizational and other costs associated with such work parties (cf. Saul 1983: 91). In addition, people in Embu note that the work performed by cooperative and hired labor often is of poorer quality than that done by household members. Nonetheless, as noted earlier, timely access to crop labor crucially affects output. It is clear that the consistent food surplus producers do enjoy better access than other households to labor when they need it. The role of extra-household labor is crucial, as suggested by the absence of a statistical relationship between household dependency ratio and consistency of "surplus" production. (The mean dependency ratio is exactly 1.5 for both the 12 most consistent "surplus" producers and for the remaining 70 households.) In addition to their superior access to labor, the wealthy "surplus" producers also are better able than the majority to afford cash outlays to purchase seed, including the extra seed required for a second planting when late rains prevent germination of the first planting.

Who are the largest users of cooperative labor? One is a household headed by an important local notable (an elder appointed as assistant to the subchief). That household used five times the mean quantity of cooperative labor (47 days of cooperative labor between August 1979 and

Table 6A *Characteristics of Embu survey households that usually produce food surpluses and those that do not*

	Household Surplus production		Mean of total sample (N = 82) (Range)
	Usual[a] (N = 12)	Not Usual[b] (N = 70)	
Mean dependency ratio (C/P)[c]	1.5	1.5	1.5 (1.0–2.3)
Mean wealth score[d]	7,564	2,648	3,368 (0–50, 605)
Mean number of mature coffee trees	423	211	242 (0–1, 200)
Mean number of acres of land owned	22	12	12 (0–151)
Mean cash expenditure on hired labor in 1980 long rains (in Kenya shillings)	337	61	99 (0–898)
Mean number of occasions exchange labor *given* during 10 months of 1979/80	2.5	3.7	3.6 (0–13.0)
Mean number of occasions exchange labor *received* during 10 months in 1979/80	5.2	3.1	3.4 (0–14.0)
Mean number of person days exchange labor *received* during 10 months in 1979/80	17.5	7.8	9.2 (0–47.0)

Note:
[a]   This category includes households that produced maize/beans in excess of consumption requirements in at least six of the eight crop seasons monitored (counting four rainfall seasons × two crops each season).
[b]   Households that do not usually produce food surpluses are those that produced maize/beans in excess of consumption requirements in fewer than six of the eight crop seasons monitored.
[c]   Dependency ratio is the ratio of consumers to producers in a household, using the following age weights:

Consumer coefficients		Producer coefficients	
61 + years of age	= 0.50	61 + years of age	= 0.50
16–60 years	= 1.00	16–60 years	= 1.00
11–15 years	= 0.75	11–15 years	= 0.50
11 years	= 0.50	11 years	= 0.00

[d]   The wealth score is an additive scale of 14 assets (automobile, motorcycle, bicycle, ox cart, plow, gas cooker, sewing machine, sofa set, radio, pressure lamp, kerosene stove, hurricane lamp, charcoal stove, wood chairs) weighted according to their cash value when new. The median wealth score for the 82 sample households is 1,803.

Table 6B   *Kendall correlation coefficients[e] for table 6A*

	Surplus production[f]
Dependency ratio	0.02
Wealth score	0.23**
Mature coffee trees	0.21**
Land ownership	0.09
Hired labor expenditure	0.21**
Occasions exchange labor *given*	−0.03
Occasions exchange labor *received*	−0.15*
Person days exchange labor *received*	0.20**

Note:
**   Significant at 0.01 level (one-tailed test).
*   Significant at 0.05 level (one-tailed test).   (N = 82 households)
[e]   Kendall's tau is a non-parametric rank–order correlation coefficient that varies from
      + 1.0 to − 1.0, and whose absolute value tends to be less than that of Pearson's r. This
      table shows correlations between the dependent variable (surplus production) and each
      of eight independent variables. A correlation matrix of all of the independent variables
      is given in Table 7.
[f]   Surplus production of each household is here coded as one of three ranked classes: *3* =
      usually produce maize/beans surplus (did so in at least six of the eight crop seasons
      monitored); *2* = occasionally produce maize/beans surplus (did so in at least one and
      fewer than six of the eight crop seasons monitored); *1* = never or seldom produce food
      surpluses (did not do so in any of the eight crop seasons monitored). Twelve households
      fall in class *3*, 56 in class *2*, and 14 in class *1*.
Sources: Tables 6A and 6B are from "Food Surplus Production, Wealth, and Farmers'
Strategies in Kenya," by Angelique Haugerud in *Satisfying Africa's Food Needs: Food
Production and Commercialization in African Agriculture*, ed. Ronald Cohen. Copyright ©
1988 by Lynne Rienner Publishers, Inc., and from "Food Production and Rural Differentiation in the Kenya Highlands," by Angelique Haugerud in *Food and Farm: Current Debates
and Policies*, ed. Christina H. Gladwin. Copyright © 1989 by University Press of America
and Society for Economic Anthropology. They are reproduced here with permission of the
publishers.

March 1980), while the sample mean is 9.2 person days. Another heavy
user of cooperative labor is a household of high local standing whose
head is a retired civil servant and whose wife is a primary school teacher.
Such families are called upon to assist with food or cash needs in poor
seasons; with dealings with bureaucrats to secure land title deeds, agricultural inputs, and credit; with school headmasters to gain secondary
school admission for children; or with potential employers of those
children once they leave school.

   The consistent food "surplus" producers include several households
with offspring well-employed in civil service positions (e.g., households 3,
4, 8, and 36). Among those fourteen households who produced no food

Table 7   *Matrix of Spearman*[a] *correlation coefficients for 8 independent variables, Embu survey households*

	(2)	(3)	(4)	(5)	(6)	(7)	(8)
(1) Wealth score	0.06	0.39**	0.39**	0.36**	−0.18*	0.09	0.13
(2) Dependency ratio		−0.21*	0	−0.18	0.04	0.02	0.02
(3) Mature coffee trees			0.22*	0.30**	0.02	0.12	0.14
(4) Land owned				0.16	0.15	0.20*	0.25**
(5) Hired labor expenditure					−0.24*	0.20*	0.23*
(6) Number occasions exchange labor *given*						0.45**	0.30**
(7) Number occasions exchange labor *received*							0.91**
(8) Number person-days exchange labor *received*							

Notes: **   Significant at 0.01 level (one-tailed) test.
*   Significant at 0.05 level (one-tailed) test.   (N = 82 households)
[a]   Spearman's rho is a non-parametric rank–order correlation coefficient that varies
from + 10.0 to − 10.00.
Source: Table 7 is from "Food Surplus Production, Wealth, and Farmers' Strategies in Kenya," by Angelique Haugerud in *Satisfying Africa's Food Needs: Food Production and Commercialization in African Agriculture*, ed. Ronald Cohen. Copyright © 1988 by Lynne Rienner Publishers, Inc. It is reproduced here with permission of the publisher.

"surpluses" in four seasons, on the other hand, are included a poor widow who lives alone (which is unusual) and who receives little material support from her children, as well as some of those households discussed earlier that experienced multiple disruptions in membership due to interpersonal conflict (e.g., households 7, 17, 32, and 14).

Farmers who consistently produce food "surpluses" use them to earn cash, as well as to build and maintain political support through clientage. They use some of the extra food they produce as payments in kind for agricultural labor and as "gifts" to kin and others. These well-off individuals are likely to take in famine refugees in times of hardship. And as noted in chapter 4, the rural wealthy are judged locally by (contested) cultural norms of generosity, hospitality, and sociability in networks of everyday interaction. They are criticized for "proud" behavior by those who find them remote or unwilling to assist others in their economic struggles. Food "surplus" producers can better feed their visitors, which enhances their prestige. And most of the "surplus" producers who fall in the top quartile of land ownership lend out some land to others, so investing in the local social system and not just in expanded production.

Such redistribution of food and land through informal social relations, however, does not necessarily level class differences. Though the less well-off may negotiate tenancy arrangements, for example, these leave a privileged minority with more secure access to larger land acreages.

In short, the wealthy Embu farmers who consistently produce more food than they require for home consumption are not specialized farmers who have cut themselves off from rural sociopolitical relationships and obligations. Rather, they owe their positions in part to successful nego-tiation of these relationships. Wealthy "surplus" producers tend to be better placed than the majority in the wider patronage networks that channel access to education, jobs, and improved agricultural inputs such as hybrid seed and fertilizers. These "vertical" social ties, however, do not necessarily guarantee material security to either the poor or the wealthy, and their persistence does not signal the dominance of collective over individual needs. Indeed, redistribution of food "surpluses" here reinforces economic inequalities by converting wealth into prestige, which in turn can be converted into authority.[51] How that authority is used defines the terms of incorporation of the local economy into wider political and economic arenas (Wolf 1986: 327).

Such incorporation, as noted, takes the form of cliental relations that build in part on material exchanges among kin and affines, and that invoke a language of paternalism. The family morality explored above is part of the cultural framework within which relations between rich and poor are negotiated, and upon which patronage relations beyond the family are built. Thus Kenyan public rhetoric, as noted earlier, includes metaphors of bridewealth, marriage, and fatherhood[52]: allusions to a moral universe to which people do have deep attachments (albeit on contested terms).

There is only a fuzzy boundary between relations built on ties of affect and those based on material incentives: a customary academic distinction between non-patronage and patronage relations. As the case material on domestic relations suggests ties between kin are often more lopsided than reciprocal. And the lopsided/reciprocal distinction itself is one about which analysts of patronage disagree (cf. Barth 1959; Wolf 1966). As noted in chapter 2, Kenyatta (1965: 299) wrote of "traditional" Gikuyu society that "anyone who is in need will go to his nearest prosperous kinsman as a matter of course, and hospitality is taken for granted." What "hospitality" entails, of course, is negotiable and subject to his-torical change. Today cultural assumptions about obligations between kin or between rich and poor are stretched sometimes to breaking point, as land grows more scarce, and as an individual who earns a salary faces multiple demands on the income from a wide array of kin and others.

Nonetheless, kinship, politics, and material relations are intersecting realms. Through merging statuses (as kin, quasi-kin, clients, dependants), individuals cope with the uncertainties of daily life: with the unpredictability of crop output, household composition, interpersonal relations, markets, and rights in land.

How are the patterns and processes outlined here connected to possible long-term structural regularities? That is, what cumulative effects are discernible if we step back from the flux or unpredictability of micro-level relationships? In particular, what is the probable fate of small farmers?

Disappearing small farmers? Debating agrarian change

What is the long-term fate of small farmers in Embu and elsewhere in Kenya? Scholars of Kenya have produced a lively and contentious literature on the class dynamics of agrarian change. As elsewhere, such debates turn on differences of ideology, politics, theory, and method (including what to quantify and how to count it). Debates in Kenya about these issues have well-known parallels in other times and places: late nineteenth- and early twentieth-century Russia (Lenin 1964; Chayanov 1966); Mexico (Hewitt de Alcantara 1984); early modern England (see reassessment in Roseberry 1991); and Indonesia (Geertz 1963, 1984). At issue is whether small- and medium-scale farmers endure, or are polarized into rich farmers and landless laborers; that is, whether or not they undergo long-term structural changes captured by labels such as "proletarianization" or "(re)peasantization." Does agricultural commercialization, for example, stimulate class polarization along classic Leninist lines (a small agrarian bourgeoisie; a large class of agricultural laborers who may or may not have access to land; and a disappearing "middle" peasantry)? Or do peasants, though not necessarily a homogeneous lot, survive, in part because they are more efficient producers than largescale farmers (see Johnston and Kilby 1975)? Here some scholars argue that differentiation is likely to arise from demographically-determined cyclical processes, rather than from long-term class polarization (Chayanov 1966). Others assume secular differentiation may occur, but nonetheless "peasants" survive and retain significant control over their own land and labor (Shanin 1982).[53] These debates occur in the context of three generally recognized paths of agrarian transformation: (1) the development of largescale capitalist farming, or of (2) largescale state farms or collectives, or (3) the capitalization of small farms.[54] These alternatives have both descriptive and prescriptive or normative content; that is, they entail debate over what does occur as well as over what should occur or what policy should encourage.

Scholarly disagreements about patterns of structural change in agriculture arise in part from the contradictory and fluid social situations they
attempt to characterize (see Roseberry 1991: 31). Farm households that
earn supplemental non-agricultural incomes, for example, include those
who have diversified for multiple reasons: to survive, to avoid full proletarianization; or to acquire cash to invest in improving their farms
(Roseberry 1989: 191). Some of them are on the way to forced dependence
on wage labor, others to agrarian accumulation.[55] In addition, rights in
land are often ambiguous, fiercely contested, and inconsistently resolved
in courts, making it difficult even to quantify farm size or land holdings.
This is as true of fifteenth-century rural England (see Roseberry 1989: 31),
as it is of mid to late twentieth-century rural Kenya. Estimates of landless-
ness or near-landlessness, for example, are shaky, given the multiple
claims on any particular piece of land, variability in the security and terms
of "tenancy" arrangements, and the unpredictable outcomes of contested
claims. Often one finds the same individuals simultaneously working as
wage laborers, renting land in or out or both, cultivating their own land,
and both cultivating as tenants on others' land and taking in tenants on
their own land. The same individual may be simultaneously farmer,
trader, and civil servant. And one finds within a single household tenants,
casual wage workers, smallholders, and salaried government clerks. In
short, agrarian life does not lend itself to easy definition of unambiguous,
non-overlapping economic categories ("tenant," "owner," "laborer").
Nor does agrarian social change always produce unambiguous winners
and losers. This complexity and diversity work against collective action or
collective opinion.[56]

Quantification itself produces little consensus about processes of social
change. Geertz (1984: 522), for example, notes:

The percentage of the "destitute" in rural Java (i.e., those consuming less than 180
kg of rice-equivalent a year) is claimed on the one hand to have markedly risen in
recent years ... and on the other to have, about as markedly, fallen.

In assessing the effects of the Green Revolution, scholars of Indonesia
have variously argued that it has increased the income gap between large
and small farmers, that most farmers have benefited (albeit unequally)
from recent economic growth, that income distribution has remained
relatively egalitarian since 1965, and that the poor have moved ahead
more quickly than the rich (Geertz 1984: 522–523). Such stark contradictions in analyses of the same quantitative data are by no means
unusual. The indeterminacy of such quantitative studies, Geertz (1984)
argues, is associated with a tendency to "externalize" or set aside cultural
factors. To reduce the imprecision, economic processes must be recontex-

tualized "within Javanese and Indonesian life as concretely enacted" (1984: 523). That is, social change cannot be understood without attention to "the passions and imaginings that provoke and inform it," or "the moral substance of a sort of existence" (1984: 523, 524).

In short, what is at stake is not simply to find better ways of counting or collecting figures on farm size, livestock holdings, labor, income, and crop output: what Geertz (1984) terms "runaway quantophrenia," or the "'what you count is what you get' sort of analysis." That is, there is "no safety in numbers."[57] While such data can be helpful in assessing differences in wealth or economic resources, they leave important questions unanswered. Some of these center on the consciousness or subjective experiences of individuals, and on the cultural understandings that mediate relations of class, gender, ethnicity, neighborhood, faction, patronage and so on. Political motivations and actions, for example, cannot be deduced directly from class identity, which is itself often difficult to define. And "peasant classes are not equivalent to landholding size categories" (Harriss 1992: 211). Categories such as "tenant" or "smallholder" often carry strong local social or cultural evaluations that are quite independent of actual differences in income. A community's norms of social hierarchy, for example, may assign higher status to marginal smallholders who are poorer than to tenants who can rent large plots (Scott 1976: 35). Scott argues that the "social sticking-power" of such a hierarchy arises from the sharp drop in subsistence security implied in each level (1976: 36).[58] Thus in central Kenya, as novelist Ngugi wa Thiong'o (1964: 19) writes, "Any man who had land was considered rich. If a man had plenty of money, many motor cars, but no land, he could never be counted as rich. A man who went with tattered clothes but had at least an acre of red earth was better off than the man with money."

Given these complexities, what can be said of structural change in Kenyan agriculture? In the Kenyan agrarian debates the available evidence does not suggest anything "inevitable" about pauperization, proletarianization, or increased differentiation as consequences of "capitalist penetration of peasant agriculture" (Kitching 1985: 140). It is not my intention to review the large Kenya literature here,[59] but rather to note schematically some of the significant divisions of opinion. Very briefly, Njonjo (1981) emphasizes the proletarianization of a Kenyan peasantry who offer the "illusion of a property owning class ... with relations to patches of land." Leys (1971, 1975), who later modified his position (Leys 1978), argues the resilience of a relatively undifferentiated peasant society and associated clientelist political structures. Cowen (1981) suggests that smallholder differentiation processes in central Kenya that had begun early this century slowed in the last several decades as small farmers expanded production of marketed crops.[60] He suggests that smallholder viability subsidized the low wages of partly-proletarianized laborers in agriculture, commerce, and manufacturing (cf. Wolpe 1972). In brief, scholars working in different parts of Kenya, and from varying theoretical perspectives, have drawn contradictory conclusions about rural class differentiation processes.[61]

Among the lessons of this work, like that Harriss reviews on India, are that "it is no longer enough, if it ever was to attempt to study rural differentiation by examining agricultural production and landholding in isolation from other activities" (Harriss 1992: 197). Also crucial are patterns of diversification in rural economic activities, changes in off-farm economic opportunities, and the implications of these processes for economic growth. Second, "fallacies of aggregation" may be entailed in generalizations from micro-studies to the national level. Third, there has been some neglect of politics and of historical analysis rather than "purely structural conceptions of causality" (Harris 1992: 190, 223).

As the work of the scholars noted above and my earlier discussion of Embu suggest, a number of analytically distinct processes are underway in the Kenyan countryside. There is evidence of cyclical, centripetal, and centrifugal mobility. Though assessing their cumulative effect is difficult some trends are discernible.

It would be inappropriate to draw longitudinal inferences from the cross-sectional comparisons of Embu household wealth presented above. Nonetheless, there are larger-scale processes that at least constrain the possibilities, though they do not define the outcome. First, there are familiar demographic facts. Kenya's population is growing at one of the highest rates in the world, and is heavily concentrated on the small proportion of the nation's land that is agriculturally productive. Over four-fifths of Kenya's people live on less than 20 percent of the land. Population densities in some farming communities exceed 1,200 persons per square mile (over 460 persons per square kilometre). In Embu District's uplands (Runyenje's Division), population density increased substantially between 1969 and 1979: from an average of 570 to 860 persons per square mile, or from 218 to 330 persons per square kilometre (Kenyan government 1969, 1979).[62] Second, although the growth of small scale agriculture in Kenya has been praised widely,[63] many observers now recognize that the success was built on "soft" development options whose potential had nearly been exhausted by the mid-1970s.[64] These measures included: removal of colonial restrictions on African dairy production and on cultivation of export cash crops such as coffee, tea, and pyrethrum; widespread adoption of hybrid maize (Gerhart 1975); and expansion of cultivated land in fertile regions, where some of the former largescale farms were transferred to small farmers (see World Bank 1982; Cox 1984; Lofchie 1986).[65] Third, projected industrial growth is far from sufficient to absorb growing numbers of school leavers, or landless or near-landless people. And finally, land is unequally distributed nationally,[66] and substantial redistribution is politically unlikely (though an occasional "radical" politician proposed it during the first several decades after independence).

These "facts" begin to suggest why commercialization of Kenya's agrarian economy has preserved rather than stripped away many of the props that allow small farmers a measure of self-sufficiency.[67] Maintaining smallholder viability accords with the Kenyan state's interest in preserving social order. As long as small farmers have access to even marginal opportunities to stabilize subsistence to meet short-term needs, they are less likely to resort to "more direct and violent solutions," as Scott (1976: 204) notes in a more general context. Against smallholder interests the colonial and post-colonial Kenyan state has had to balance the interests of largescale agrarian capitalist enterprises.[68] But smallscale farming remains central to most individuals' material well-being and to regime stability. For the poor access to a patch of land to cultivate is a buffer against starvation and must be supplemented by other pursuits such as casual wage labor. For the wealthy cultivating food crops is a hedge against inflation, and against personal loss of political influence that might undercut other income sources such as public salaries or businesses.

This is the wider context in which the local dynamics of Embu households must be understood. The study locale is one of hundreds with rising human densities on scarce but productive agricultural land. In Embu in the 1980s it appeared that differentiation coexisted with at least some brakes on dispossession.[69] A land frontier, formerly a buffer zone between Embu and Mbeere peoples, absorbed migrants from the crowded uplands (obviously a short-term safety valve). Various tenancy arrangements allowed the poor and landless to acquire cultivation rights on others' land. Should agricultural capitalization or specialization become more profitable, however, it is likely that larger landowners would allow fewer poor people cultivation and grazing rights on their land.

Moreover, rights in land even for holders of title deeds remain uncertain. As discussed earlier members of the same families fiercely contest such rights, which are subject to renegotiation both informally and through the courts. And ownership of title deeds itself is disputed. Land control board files include numerous reports of theft and forgery of title deeds, many of them between fathers and sons, and between brothers. This tenure uncertainty contributes to unstable gains and losses in individual landholdings. Such instability arises as well from other sources already noted, so that today's largest landholders are not necessarily an enduring privileged group. In any case, as suggested earlier, rural differentiation owes more to access to education and to off-farm incomes from salaries and businesses than it does to agrarian investment and land accumulation *per se*.

Wealth differences observable today arise in part from differentiation processes that began in pre-colonial times as local notables accumulated land and other wealth, and that continued in the colonial era with the emergence of *athomi* whose privileged access to state resources allowed accumulation. Current inequalities of landholdings in central Kenya, for example, emerged in two different ways: (1) from use of political influence to acquire holdings of larger than average size at the time of adjudication and first registration in the early 1960s; and (2) through subsequent purchase of additional land (especially by those farmers who have access to significant off-farm incomes).[70] Some individuals acquired little or no land at the time of first registration because colonial officials confined them to political detention camps, or they were absent as freedom fighters in the forest. Others did not fare well during land adjudication because they did not contribute to clan adjudication costs and did not secure places in lineage genealogies (cf. Glazier 1985).

In short, some wealthy individuals in the 1980s owe their positions in part to their own or their parents' colonial advantages of early access to education, salaries, and large landholdings acquired through strategic manipulations of land adjudication proceedings during the tenure reform. Such advantages, however, by no means guarantee prosperity in this or succeeding generations. In Embu, for example, by the late 1980s, some large landowners who belong to clans of influential colonial chiefs and elders had subdivided their holdings among many sons.

Differentiation into a landless proletariat on the one hand, and prosperous "yeoman" farmers on the other, was the aim of the state's land tenure reform (see Sorrenson 1967). The unexpected consequences of this reform include: (1) a widening gap between the land registry and actual patterns of land use and access on the ground (see Haugerud 1983); (2) increased conflict over land within and among families; (3) increased litigation and tenure insecurity; and (4) continued subdivision (formal and informal) of small plots below the sizes that the Swynnerton Plan defined as "viable" holdings.[71] Individuals who accumulate land through purchase acquire fragmented holdings, rather than the large consolidated holdings that were the aim of the Swynnerton Plan.[72] Moreover, contrary to official intent, farmers accumulate land for speculative purposes, for the future subsistence security of sons, and for the increased commercial borrowing power that each additional title deed confers. With land title deeds as security commercial loans that range in size from a few hundred shillings to several hundred thousand shillings are available from commercial banks, and various agricultural lending institutions. In 1979, about 15 percent (225 out of 1,545) of title deeds from the central research area in Embu had loan charges appplied to them. Agricultural loans are not necessarily used for farm investments, but may go instead to school fees, home improvements, rental properties, and small businesses. Wealthy land accumulators are not necessarily agrarian innovators or heavily-capitalized farmers.

Though rising population densities on Kenya's best agricultural land in this century contribute to multiplication of micro-holdings (especially with partible inheritance), it is not precisely clear at whose expense this process occurs. It may, for example, follow a pattern similar to that Ladurie describes for Languedoc between the fifteenth and seventeenth centuries, in which the largest landowners survived, the smallest proliferated, and the medium-sized holdings "bore the brunt of the process of atomization" (Ladurie 1976: 22). Conditions that might contribute to a shift in such tendencies include a decline in the viability of the smallest properties, a drop in population, or changes in off-farm employment opportunities. Though no reliable statistics are available anecdotal evidence in Kenya suggests that accumulation continues among very large elite landowners, especially those who are well-connected to the state. In the Embu study sample those who had purchased land by the early 1980s were disproportionately represented among households in the top quintile of both wealth and land ownership,[73] and who have children attending secondary school (a major expense).

When I returned to Embu in mid-1986 I found both changes in household membership of the kind described earlier in this chapter, and changes in material fortune, some of which people there described as life-cycle effects. Changes in household composition, for example, included household 31, where the second wife had left and the head had married a third, who also left. In household 5 one son and his wife and children moved to another farm which they had been in the process of purchasing five years earlier. A younger son and his wife were now living in the parental homestead. Life-cycle effects were highlighted when neighbors said that one family was less well-off because the father had subdivided his large landholdings among a number of sons (household 27). Another family was said to be improving its wealth as sons planted coffee (household 9). A family that had been in the lower middle wealth category had become poorer after selling off most of its livestock in order to pay hospital fees for the elderly household head (household 59). The poorest family in the coffee zone sample (household 33) had, with the help of a lineage member, acquired cultivation rights in a larger farm in the adjacent cotton zone, and shifted their residence there. Neighbors expected their wealth to improve as they developed the new farm, though they were still poor (with just 100 coffee trees, very little land, and only one native cow that produced little milk).

Sample households who sold land between 1981 and 1986 are not concentrated in any particular wealth category; they included two wealthy, two upper middle, four lower middle, and one poor.[74] Farmers sell land in order to meet expenses such as school tuition, medical care fees, and bridewealth. There is little evidence at present that land purchasers acquire land in pronounced disproportion from the poorest people. Although some wealthier farmers are accumulating land through purchase, descent-group sanctions and the powers of local land control boards afford some protection against sales that would leave families either landless or with insufficient acreage to meet subsistence needs. As rapid population growth continues, however, without national redistribution the landless can only increase in number. Acquiring cultivation rights on others' plots at present helps some of those with little or no land to meet their subsistence needs. Such informal land exchanges are based on cultivation rights which the courts are under no obligation to recognize.

These instances of change over the short term of five years do not permit specification of long-term processes. The cumulative effect of patterns described above will depend largely on developments in the non-agricultural sectors of the economy, and on the relationship between farm and non-farm sectors.[75] By one estimate, "twenty percent of the wage bill of the urban formal sector is remitted to rural areas" (Greene 1983: xiv). Any expansion of urban public and private sector employment contributes to individual rural investments in education, land purchases, trade, small business, and (less so) farming. By contrast, shrinking or stagnant public and private sector employment, particularly with an increasingly youthful population, narrows opportunities for accumulation, fuels political discontent, and strains economic and social ties between town and countryside.

How, then, might we connect the unpredictable micro-dynamics of household mobility to possible longer-term structural regularities in differentiation processes? To define secular trends in household differentiation is problematic, in part precisely because the household itself, as noted, is not a structure that defines stable, predictable rights, responsibilities, or membership. But the household is one crucial arena within which individuals continually renegotiate certain types of rights and responsibilities (e.g., over land, food, cash, labor). Other such arenas include the *baraza*, the sublocation, the church, the parliamentary constituency, and so on. Given the fluidity of entities such as households, in order to "measure" rural differentiation one would need to document shifts over time in peoples' capacities successfully to negotiate and maneuver in a rather wide variety of flexible, mutable, "structural" entities or arenas.[76]

Even though rural social differentiation cannot be "measured" through conventional single variables, there is evidence of accumulating advantages among a minority of households. Though land purchases and sales suggest no clear linear trends in the 1980s there are other signs of differentiation. For example, recall that the subset of households who consistently produce food crop surpluses are wealthier than others, command more hired and reciprocal labor, and own more land and mature coffee trees. They are better positioned than the majority to convert off-farm employment opportunities into capital accumulation, improved skills, and vital political connections. There are long-term rewards from such advantages that are not necessarily visible in standard measures such as farm size or even salaried income.

Berry's (1993) comparative analysis suggests that in central Kenya, with less use of hired labor than in Ghana's or southern Nigeria's cocoa economies, differentiation among rural households has been more pronounced, and social mobility less so than in West Africa's cocoa economies. She suggests that expansion of commercial food crop production in Kenya did not produce wide demand for hired labor (unlike the expansion of cocoa production in West Africa), partly because fluctuating output and incomes from food crops kept farmers from hiring labor on a regular basis.[77] At the same time it has become more difficult, Berry argues, for farmers to mobilize labor through relations of dependency. This has occurred not because social networks disintegrate with commercialization, but rather "because members of rural households and communities have become involved in a growing number of income-seeking activities and social networks" (Berry 1993: 145). Again, at both ends of the wealth scale these networks include relationships in which there often are indistinct boundaries between individual statuses of kin, quasi-kin, dependant, client, or friend.

Conclusions

I noted in chapter 1 that a starting point of this analysis is the image of Kenya as a showpiece of political stability and of an economic prosperity that rests in part on "progressive" small farmers. This chapter illustrates the fragmented, diversified, and precarious nature of that presumed small farmer bulwark. Paradoxically, to the extent that small farmers do become wealthy, they are unlikely to do so by adopting exotic cattle and other strictly agrarian innovations advocated by officials speaking from Western textbook images of "progress." Contrary to what some official rhetoric implies, wealth differences among rural families have more to do with access to state resources, non-agricultural income, and education than with agricultural commercialization or innovation *per se*. Small farmers in Embu and elsewhere in Africa are masters of economic diversification. For many the best opportunities for material security and advance lie not in agrarian specialization, but in diversification outside of agriculture. Those farmers who become prosperous do so by cultivating not only the soil, but also multiple social ties and non-farm economic activities. Security is elusive, but for both wealthy and poor it is improved by practicing new and old forms of reciprocity and redistribution, as well as market exchange. These patterns run counter to evolutionary assumptions about the inevitable demise of relations of reciprocity and clientage with the growth of markets and states.

Uncertainty and flux are the striking features of daily life in the countryside: for example, the unpredictability of crop output, markets, domestic relations, and rights in land. To stay afloat in an uncertain world means that individuals must successfully negotiate and maneuver in a rather wide variety of arenas, constructing and actively maintaining multiple social networks. In daily struggles for livelihood the material stakes are high. One may starve, lose one's land, become a millionaire, live peacefully, or become a victim of violence. Violence may arise from a quarrel between brothers of modest means who compete for the same piece of land, from official moves to auction the land of a wealthy loan defaulter, or between factions of rival candidates for political office. Such sources of conflict ramify and become more volatile as political uncertainties and competition at the top intensify: (as has happened during Kenya's recent contradictory moves toward "democracy" and repression).

Amidst the uncertainty rural households face, one of the striking continuities is the repeated staging of *baraza*. Indeed, the "mock certainty" of *baraza* rhetoric may grow in proportion to the strains and unpredictabilities of daily life.[78] It is precisely when citizens are most besieged and the state most vulnerable that the state needs the repeated display of orderly hierarchy staged during *baraza*: the bemused, ostensibly loyal crowds who watch and listen to a parade of dapper men in dark suits, along with chiefs and district commissioners wielding batons and attired in khaki uniforms and pith helmets.

6   Conclusions: the showpiece of an hour

> States have little purchase on society except, literally, what they can
> purchase.
>
> (Lonsdale 1986: 145)

> Probably it is a good working rule to be suspicious about political and
> intellectual leaders who talk mainly about moral virtues; many poor
> devils are liable to be badly hurt.
>
> (Barrington Moore 1966: 492)

"Rain we must and will have" were words Gikuyu speakers shouted again
and again during that late nineteenth-century gathering with which I
opened this work.[1] The European "caravan people" present during these
speeches repeatedly heard pleas for rain during the weeks they traveled
through Gikuyu country, negotiating permission from local notables to
traverse their territory. At one stopping point, for example, von Hohnel
(1968 [1894]: 298) gives the following account:

> The chief then went on to impress upon the Count (Teleki) that it would be very
> foolish of us to attempt to travel in Kikuyuland accompanied only by inexper-
> ienced men, but that, as he had heard a good report of us and understood that *we*
> *would give rain to the land*, he would take upon himself the heavy responsibility of
> seeing us safely through our enterprise. (My emphasis.)

Material well-being (rain, crops, food) are crucial to political accountability. Those nineteenth-century shouts that the Gikuyu needed rain are
matched by early 1990s demands for food, jobs, schools, and land. A
ruling regime short of funds is as politically vulnerable as were earlier
central Kenyan notables short of food. During famine crises rural clients
left patrons, voluntarily or otherwise, in search of better opportunities.
During the Moi regime's early 1990s crisis citizens left his ruling political
party for the same reason. The regime no longer had "rain."[2]

This book's starting point was the image of Kenya as a showcase of
political stability and of an economic prosperity assumed to rest in part
on "progressive" small farmers. But the wealth of nations, like that of
individuals, can be evanescent: "Riches are a shadow." "Riches have
wings."[3] "Bubble millionaires"[4] appear overnight, thanks partly to the
right political connections. Kenya's coffee earnings are subject to the
caprices of frost and fair weather in Brazil, its oil import costs tied to
fickle international markets, its tourist dollars vulnerable to domestic
political upheavals. This is not to suggest that the state's fiscal health is

beyond its control, but rather to note the instability of state revenues. Individual riches are fleeting, also subject to vagaries of markets, politics, weather, health, and interpersonal relations. This is not to de-emphasize accumulation (see chapters 4 and 5), but rather to point to the uncertainty of Africa's institutions, economies, and politics. Indeed, "no condition is permanent," as Berry (1993) puts it in the title of her comparative study of agrarian and social change in Africa. Uncertain economies, institutions, and politics place a premium on flexibility, and encourage people to multiply social relationships and networks in order, for example, to acquire and safeguard access to markets, creditors, and laborers. Individuals constantly must renegotiate and protect social identities and rights in property such as land (see also Berry 1985, 1988). This impermanence, and the associated patterns of smallholder diversification and differentiation, may be contrasted with the image of a Kenyan prosperity assumed to rest largely on smallscale farming itself.

One of the intended props of small farmer prosperity was the Kenyan government's ambitious land tenure reform. Exercises such as registration of land titles and population censuses are common forms of state-building. Creating a land registry in order to categorize people as owners and non-owners, as owners of holdings of varying size and so on was but one of many state efforts at documentation and certification. These attempts to reorder rural life and categorize citizens are means by which, as Foster (1991: 246) puts it more generally, "the state asserts its presence and power as a natural condition of daily affairs." It is easy, however, to overprivilege "the state" as a unified, monolithic entity that can effect change.

Rather than successfully channeling daily practices to conform to state categories and rules, Kenya's land tenure reform, like the political ritual of *baraza*, opened new spaces for maneuver and contestation (cf. Berry 1993; Comaroff and Comaroff 1991). *Baraza* allow individual speakers room for creativity as well as conformity, and these gatherings are a mix of the predictable and the volatile. The land registry diverges markedly from actual patterns of land use and access on the ground.[5] While the discrepancies may not immediately affect a regime's capacity to rule they reveal nonetheless exploitable cracks or flaws in the facade of state power. Individuals use this room for maneuver to shape their own histories. They informally subdivide land and exchange it with one another, and petition the state to block sales to which some members of a family object. People create patterns of overlapping access and complex rights to land that reveal state codes to be little more than simplifying fictions.

Though programs like Kenya's tenure reform might be expected to enhance state legitimacy, they simultaneously gave citizens "an inexhaustible resource of (mis)information to manipulate – either to protect themselves from or to gain a purchase on the intervention of the state" (Lonsdale 1981: 161). Individuals in different structural positions had unequal capacities to manipulate such (mis)information to their own advantage. It was often the powerful and wealthy, literate insiders for example, who used their advantages to gain most in official tenure reform procedures. We saw in chapter 4 that some colonial chiefs and their assistants were able to use their official positions to acquire large land holdings. Tenure uncertainties have led to forced dispossession of the poor, "squatters," and relatives of deceased individuals in whose names titles were registered. In the late 1980s and early 1990s there were growing numbers of violent evictions of "squatters" from, for example, the western forested slopes of Mt. Kenya, and from formerly European farming areas such as Trans-Nzoia.[6] These events are a reminder that limits on the reach of the state create opportunities not only for resistance or "exit," but for new forms of subordination and oppression as well.

This study has developed during years when representations of Kenya in the West changed profoundly. As Kenya's burnished image was shattered in the early 1990s some tried to replace it with its opposite. This reversal simply perpetuates the misleading premises of the original image. To explore why this is so I have looked at historical continuities and discontinuities, since the late 1800s, in the nature of political accountability, crises of livelihood, and material inequalities. I suggested parallels between a cash-starved state in the 1990s and food famines decades earlier, between past and present struggles for wealth, power, and survival at multiple levels of social agency (from individual to household to state). These are some of the realities behind the pre-1990 image in which Kenya became the "showpiece of an hour."[7]

Just as important as Western constructions of Kenya as either "miracle" or "fallen star" are the wider historical processes out of which such images develop. Once African nations ceased to be superpower battlegrounds the West tried to avert its gaze from the unleashing of destructive forces to which its own prior interventions had contributed. Somalia in 1992, for example, was portrayed as a domain of irrationally feuding "warlords,"[8] with press accounts seldom exploring heavy prior US military aid to the regime overthrown. The end of the cold war brought new Western support for moves toward "democracy" in Africa, and conferred new authority on African dissidents whose voices their own governments as well as those of foreign powers once ignored or suppressed. The apparent burgeoning of "democracy" in some parts of Africa then became another momentary showpiece in Western circles.

The early 1990s were not the first time in Kenya's history that opposition political parties attempted to form, or that attention was called to the plight of the poor, to "corruption," or to abuses of power. Global changes, however, helped to confer new authority on previously marginalized and submerged political discourses in Kenya and elsewhere in Africa. These changes included global economic decline, political upheavals in Eastern Europe, the end of the cold war, and new donor attention to "governance." As previously marginalized discourses briefly seized center stage in Kenya during the early 1990s, they carried forward earlier social tensions and conflicts over land, wealth, and colonial state actions such as the slum clearances which violently evicted Nairobi's urban poor from their homes and businesses. The public silences that dissidents shattered in the early 1990s concerned possibly ill-gotten wealth of officials close to the president, state complicity in political assassinations, violent and coercive tactics against Nairobi's poor, and unlawful detention of political dissidents. Discontent over rapid increases in the cost of living and declining living standards also fueled anti-regime sentiments. The public war of words, "seditious" music, and banned theatre performances reflected contests over who had the moral authority to rule.

Both burnished and tarnished images of Kenya themselves can become targets of contention in "the ideological construction of the present."[9] As noted in chapter 2, the image of Kenya as a paragon of political stability and economic prosperity in a troubled continent itself enters into contemporary political rhetoric within the country: supporters of the Moi regime attribute criticisms of Kenya to "jealousy" of the nation's success, and to deliberate attempts to undermine it. Moi's portrayals of a nation "on the move" or "on the run" toward rapid development accorded well with Western images of Kenya as a "miraculous" exception to continental patterns. Regime defenders depict opponents as being out to destroy the nation's peace and prosperity because they are "disgruntled," frustrated, and greedy for power and wealth. Each side attributes to the other a willingness to destroy the nation in order to grab power or to hold on to power.

Kenya's political communities were in a state of rapid flux in the early 1990s. Such communities "are not formed around images of 'the state' itself" (Roseberry 1989: 226) but around shifting local, ethnic, regional, and religious identities that are sometimes manipulated from above. State rhetoric helps to define the terms in which such communities may mobilize. For example, in Kenya some officials in the early 1990s accented ethnoregional divisions in ways that may have helped to spark rural violence. Such violence can grow in part out of the kinds of daily struggles over land, labor, and cash noted in chapter 5. Official rhetoric in the early 1990s also encourages political communities to form around such notions as the putative "African-ness" of one-party as opposed to multiparty rule.

The supposed opposition between what is "traditionally" African and what is foreign, especially "European," is a crucial one in Kenyan political culture. This disputed distinction, multiparty advocates say, is used to defend a single-party status quo that is not necessarily any more "African" than the proposed alternative.

A national political culture is institutionally elaborated and expressed in particular through *baraza*,[10] which mediate representations of the Kenyan state in the countryside. Roseberry (1989: 227) expresses the more general point: "it is through control of the state that imagined communities can be given material form . . . The political community that begins as a regionalist, religious, populist, or anticolonial project, turns to a struggle for the state, and maintains itself through control of the state." Thus the *baraza* itself became a battleground in the early 1990s, as factions competing to capture the state fought as well over access to this crucial public forum. In 1992 access to *baraza* permits was fiercely contested as the state made contradictory moves, sometimes apparently complying with the demands of political pluralism by issuing *baraza* permits to regime opponents, and at other times defying those demands by denying permits. The *baraza* as a symbolic display of state influence captures one of the most important divisions in Kenyan society: that between those with and without privileged access to state resources.

Baraza rhetoric transposes into moral themes the daily material concerns of citizens as they struggle to survive or prosper. Officials often place responsibility for economic success or failure on individuals' internal states (see Karp 1992), moral character, or self-control (for example, by implying a crucial distinction between those who do and do not drink home-brewed beer, but ignoring the profitable commercial beer industry in which elites have substantial financial interests). *Baraza* rhetoric, when it alludes to wealth differences at all, implies that they arise from the moral character or personal qualities of individuals. As we saw in chapters 3 and 5 state officers suggest wealth originates in individual willingness to abandon home-brewed beer or unproductive "traditions" such as raising native cattle and grazing them by roadsides.

Contemporary official rhetoric follows a pattern which Karp (1992) defines in colonial and post-colonial "development" ideology. All imply that development "works for some *kinds* of people, and that, by implication, only personal transformations will make development work" (Karp 1992: 10). This belief implies a "theory of culture and personhood . . . that . . . see(s) the person as either material to be developed or as trapped in a system that prevents development" (Karp 1992: 13). The emphasis is on particular categories of persons and cultures rather than on economic and political structures. Thus politicians and bureaucrats perpetuate colonial ideas about the need to change tradition-bound farmers, and offer impracticable programs inspired more by Western agronomy textbooks than by the realities of farmers' lives. They imply that farmers foolishly resist change if they do not eagerly go into debt in order to adopt innovations such as exotic cattle. Official rhetoric suggests that there are opportunities for all to get ahead: Kenya is a nation "on the run" toward rapid "development," and the unmotivated will be left behind.

Late 1970s political rhetoric, as we have seen, called not only for individual changes such as renunciation of home-brewed beer, but also for a moral regeneration of officials of the state itself, an end to "corruption" and bribery. *Baraza* rhetoric promoted the ideal of a state that serves citizens equally according to mandated formal obligations, rather than the reality of a state which citizens often must approach through complex forms of bargaining, manipulation, and payments of unofficial fees. But publicizing an ideal can have the unintended effect of promoting dissatisfaction with the reality. When a state official asserts that *nyayo* means the end of home-brewed beer or of bribery at the land office, his words simultaneously evoke alternative possibilities.[11] These might include memories of similar previous official pronouncements that did not lead to changes in practice. Even if discontent remains suppressed the state's own rhetoric has provided symbolic resources that nonetheless remain available for possible future resistance and opposition. Indeed, the political culture invented to legitimize the Moi regime provided symbolic ammunition for later attacks upon it. As the Kenyan state attempts to define political reality for citizens through *baraza*, it also unintentionally reminds citizens of alternative possibilities, and of past unfulfilled promises. That is, "dominant meanings rationalize existing social inequalities, but always in ways that subvert those values and premises as well" (Murray Edelman 1988: 119).

One of the primary symbols around which recent political opposition mobilized, for example, was the nation's own constitution: its original provisions for an independent judiciary, for multiple political parties, for protections against unreasonable arrest and detention, and for free elections. During the early 1990s opposition rhetoric called for restoring eroded democratic freedoms guaranteed in Kenya's original constitution. That is, these were political struggles inspired in part by the post-colonial state's own symbols of legitimacy.

A state fiscal crisis, such as that Kenya faces in the early 1990s, reduces its capacity to dispense patronage. Such patronage, in Kenya as elsewhere, is an alternative to structural change, that is, to addressing more fundamental reforms and distributional issues. When state coffers are not empty state patronage "can often neutralize incipient class demands" (Scott 1976: 216). But unless the state addresses underlying structural problems, patronage is a short-term solution to the problems of political order and regime legitimacy. Scott's (1976: 217–218) remarks on Southeast Asia apply as well to Kenya: "so long as the structural issues remain unresolved, so long as population growth creates new demographic pressures, and so long as the urban sector absorbs only a small fraction of the rural displaced, the volume of subsistence problems is likely to outstrip the financial capacity of the state." The political costs of structural changes such as land reform in turn make increasing repression a likely alternative (Scott 1976: 219). That too has happened in Kenya over the last decade, replaying a "bargain" which the colonial state struck with its subjects decades earlier. Voices of both the colonial and post-colonial state argue that "chaos" is the inevitable alternative to the political status quo (a common ploy in Africa's one-party states). Warding off "chaos" in turn requires, they imply, curbs on political freedoms. In addition, many of Kenya's post-independence leaders genuinely believed that both the constitution and cultural and social "traditions" were obstacles to economic "development."[12]

The Kenyan state cannot indefinitely both protect the interests of large landowners and of a small farm majority.[13] Official agricultural policy in Kenya continues to leave unresolved critical issues of land distribution, tenure, and use. Rapid population growth and very limited arable land mean that rural land accumulation (whether for agricultural or non-agricultural purposes) already contributes to proletarianization. If policy measures were to stimulate the wealthy to invest more heavily in agriculture rather than to continue accumulating land primarily for purposes of speculation, loan security, and their sons' future inheritance, then proletarianization most likely would accelerate. The future of the landless and land-poor would be determined in part by the larger farmers' decisions (affected by macro-economic policies) concerning wage rates and labor-versus-capital-intensive methods of agricultural intensification.

For a number of decades in Kenya, political and bureaucratic patrons built careers in part by helping rural people meet their rising material aspirations (demands for education, jobs, land, and loans). Protection of a rising subsistence standard was the "moral economy" for which citizens held the state accountable. By the early 1990s, however, it had become extremely difficult to meet even a fraction of the material demands of an increasingly youthful population. And as the national and international economy deteriorated during the 1980s, Kenyan citizens became more critical of wealth accumulated (sometimes through questionable means) by individuals at the top of the political system (Throup 1987b; Thomas-

Slayter 1991). Some of those at the top had also become discontented. Kenya's early 1990s political crisis arose in part from a common African pattern by which, as Lonsdale (1986: 155) puts it, ruling regimes "have strangled the ambition of independent capitalists who might become their rivals."[14] In the early 1990s, when some of Kenya's disaffected elites became advocates of "democracy," and acquired international support in a post-cold war era, some citizens saw their advocacy as opportunism rather than democratic idealism. And that is how the ruling regime depicted its enemies.

The struggle for control of the state in the early 1990s was not a battle over any proposed fundamental restructuring of the economy. Indeed the rhetorics of "democracy", like the late 1970s themes of anti-corruption and bans on home-brewed beer, might be categorized as what Barrington Moore (1966: 492) in a more general context terms "a great deal of talk about the need for a thoroughgoing moral regeneration, talk that covers the absence of a realistic analysis of prevailing social conditions which would threaten the vested interests behind (it)." Land redistribution, for example, is a possibility rarely mentioned by politicians competing to capture the state in the early 1990s.[15] When political opposition groups in the 1990s discuss economic policy they generally embrace market liberalization and the structural adjustment measures that the World Bank advocates. If they compare Kenya's prospects to those of Asian "success stories" such as South Korea and Taiwan, they do not discuss the land reforms or industrial policies on which the Asian "successes" built.[16]

Kenyan rhetoric about moral regeneration – such as calls for a ban on home-brewed beer, an end to corruption, or attributions of greed to regime opponents – diverts attention from issues that the state does not wish to address. Such diversionary tactics, peculiar neither to Kenya nor to Africa, are masterfully described in the fiction of Nigerian writer Chinua Achebe. A character in *Anthills of the Savannah*, for example, speaks as follows:

All right, you tell me one thing we ... this government ... any of us did in the last three years ... or for that matter in the previous nine years of civilian administration that wasn't altogether diversionary ... This letter here and all this new theatre of the absurd that Sam is directing to get rid of me and to intimidate Chris, what's it in aid of? *Diversion pure and simple.* Even the danger I see looming ahead when the play gets out of hand, what has any of this to do with the life and the concerns and the reality of ninety-nine percent of the people of Kangan? Nothing whatsoever. (Achebe 1987: 135, my emphasis.)

The diversions in question in this "theatre of the absurd" include day-to-day factional struggles, personal rivalries, and differences of opinion among individuals in the president's inner circle that are played out through grand accusations of "treason," "sedition," and "tribalism." They include as well public battles between the president and journalists whose criticisms of government practices earn them the label of "traitor" and may cost them their jobs or their lives. These daily dramas of state politics invite artistic satire, as in Achebe's fiction, and in the Nairobi Players' version of *The Mikado*. The state as political theatre conveys more tragic outcomes as well: lives lost, rights denied, poverty perpetuated.

Such theatrical metaphors – whether comic or tragic – in no sense connote political essences "natural" to Africa or to any other part of the globe. Rather, it is their history, their contingent quality, that must be understood. Why does a politics of spectacle, fantasy, and image-making dominate this "post-modern" era? In the United States, as in Kenya, the energy of the spectacle may accelerate in proportion to the severity of problems ignored. The United States is host to a thriving politics of diversion (on full display, for example, during the 1988 presidential election campaign's spotlight on rival candidates' staged recitations of the pledge of allegiance to the American flag). Meanwhile offstage, the US government was cutting emergency aid to the homeless, personal indebtedness continued to rise, and a "plague of homelessness, disempowerment, and impoverishment ... engulfed many of the central cities" (Harvey 1989: 332). An aestheticized politics depicts as passive "otherness" poverty in America, the threat of fascism in the former Soviet Union, and political instability in Africa, Eastern Europe, and elsewhere. African politics easily becomes foil to America's or Western Europe's definition of itself. Whatever these political fantasies, any imagined gulf between Africa and the rest of the world, between their history and ours, is not only a false comfort but a dangerous one.

Notes

1 INTRODUCTION: STAGING POLITICS IN KENYA

1 I thank Jessica Kuper at Cambridge University Press for this title.

2 Hohnel 1968 (1894): 310, recounting an encounter in 1887 during Count Teleki's travels in East Africa.

3 The lines quoted are from a political party rally I attended in rural Embu District just six months after the death of the country's first president, Jomo Kenyatta, and a few months before national elections were held. The speaker just quoted is the ruling political party (KANU or Kenya African National Union) treasurer for the district. (MAR479:B,3: see transcript key at the end of chapter 3 for an explanation of this reference notation for my transcripts of *baraza* I attended and audio-taped.)

4 The widely-used Swahili term for "development" is *maendeleo*, derived from *enda*, which includes "a wide range of meanings under the general idea of motion," such as moving forward, progressing, continuing, or advancing (Johnson 1939).

5 He said, "to the person who makes you lose the path of [the president's] footsteps, you should say: 'sit aside, my friend.' Because even Moi said: 'he who will be defeated by those rapid footsteps, let him give way in a ditch; the thing moves ahead.' Isn't that what he said?" The crowd then shouts "It is!" (MAR479:B,11).

6 (MAR479:A,2).

7 This study assumes, as Fox (1990: 4) puts it, that a national culture emerges out of struggles between competing nationalist ideologies, that is, out of competing forms of "consciousness or perception of what the nation is or should be, which then may gain public meaning and be put into action." Furthermore, "national culture does not consist of rigid institutional and cognitive pieces properly fitted together into a stable and immobile structure ... national culture is malleable and mobile. It is the outcome of a constant process of cultural production ... A national culture is always 'temporary' because, whether antique or recent, its character and puissance are matters of historical practice; they are plastic constructions, not cultural givens." (Fox 1990: 2, 4)

8 Cf. Fox's (1990: 7) comments on Anderson.

9 The new president and other leaders did not blame Kenyatta himself for problems such as corruption. Instead the implication was that during the last years of his rule, some influential individuals had "taken advantage of Kenyat-

ta's failing health to gain wealth, particularly land, through irregular means" (see "Moi's First 100 Days as President," *Weekly Review* (Nairobi), December 8, 1978: 4).

10 This assertion has multiple theoretical implications. Among many pertinent threads is the growing contemporary attention given to "language and political economy" (reviewed by Gal 1989), "culture and political economy" (see, for example, Schneider 1976, and Roseberry 1988, 1989), and "political language" (reviewed by Parkin 1984). Historical antecedents include figures associated with the Frankfurt School.

11 As discussed in chapter 2, the requirement that *baraza* be licensed means that authorities can deny permits to regime opponents. Such a permit denial, for example, figured in Kenya's social protests in July 1990.

12 See Vincent's (1968: 249–253) ethnographic account of elite corporateness expressed in a tax meeting in Teso, Uganda.

13 They are sometimes inappropriately opposed (cf. Ortner 1984: 157). S. F. Moore (1975: 109), for example, suggests that to place "dispute in opposition to an ideology of community harmony, [means] treating them as antithetical when in fact, not being of the same analytic order, they are not contradictory. An ideology is a set of ideas, disputation is a complex of events; consequently they are not always as directly opposed as they might first seem." She shows how a Chagga community "deals with internal quarreling and seeks to reconcile its actions with its ideology of community harmony in the midst of ubiquitous dispute."

14 See, for example, several articles by Jane Perlez in the *New York Times*: "Attacks in Kenya Drain Hard Money," March 1, 1992; "Aid Donors Insist on Kenya Reforms," November 27, 1991; "Aid for Kenya Cut as Donors Cite Corruption," October 21, 1991.

15 Some of Kenya's foreign aid was suspended (initially for six months) by the World Bank and other donors at the Paris Club conference in late November 1991. In November 1993 much of the suspended aid was restored, with donors asserting that its continuation still would require progress with economic and political reforms. In 1990 Kenya received more aid from the USA than any other nation in sub-Saharan Africa (Africa Watch 1991: 372, "Kenya: Taking Liberties"). Between 1990 and 1992, however, US aid to Kenya was cut nearly in half.

16 In skeletal form, the usual facts called upon to support the "economic miracle" narratives are as follows. During its first decade of independence Kenya enjoyed high rates of economic growth (averaging 6.4 percent per year, with inflation below 4 percent). Agriculture, especially export crops such as coffee and tea produced by both large- and small-scale farmers, was the backbone of this growth. Increases in marketed production by smallholders were especially striking, with large farms' share of total marketed agricultural output declining from 81 percent in 1958 to just 45 percent in 1975. The impressive growth in small-scale agricultural production which Kenya enjoyed during its first fifteen or so years of independence came primarily from area expansion into less densely-settled zones, an option now largely exhausted. Increases have also come from shifts into commodities with higher cash returns (once colonial restrictions on African cultivation of export crops such

as coffee and tea were lifted), and (least important) from yield increases. Many observers (such as Lofchie 1990: 209) also praised Kenya's political system for being more stable, competitive, and open than those of many other African nations. Some observers found Kenya's press to be relatively free "within unstated but well-understood limits" (Lofchie 1990: 209; see also Barkan 1991: 180, 191, n.14).

17 Other scholarly accounts stressed the social costs of economic growth, growing inequalities in access to crucial resources such as land (Hunt 1984), and dependency and underdevelopment (Brett 1973; Leys 1975). Kenyan novelist Ngugi wa Thiong'o portrayed through powerful fiction a vision of growing political repression that was downplayed or absent from many scholarly accounts.

18 That is, overtly political activity was increasingly channeled through and controlled by bureaucratic state institutions. Such post-colonial restrictions have striking colonial counterparts (see, for example, Leys 1976 and Crowder 1987). On state expansion see Hart 1982.

19 In the 1960s some critics labeled as "ethnocentric" those Western liberals who argued that democracy was essential to economic development in Africa's newly independent nations (see Staniland 1986, 1991). See Staniland (1991) on disagreements among Western liberals about the prospects for and definition of democracy in independent Africa. He notes, for example, that some argued that "the new African one-party states had, in their own ways, provided for [democratic] ... processes and functions" (1991: 83). Other Western observers "were often prepared to provide active support and earnest justification for authoritarian measures, so long as they were taken in the name of modernization" (1991: 81–82). Among scholars taking a new look at human rights issues in Africa are Cohen (1991) and An-Na'im and Deng (1990).

20 Kelly (1991) addresses this theme in the anthropology of contemporary Japan.

21 Parkin (1990) offers a stimulating discussion of these issues in an East African context. He considers, for example, the influence of colonial research institutes in demarcating ethnographic areas, the overprivileging of the segmentary lineage framework, and underprivileging of East African age-set and generation-set cycles.

22 Contemporary understandings of "the state" have moved beyond earlier liberal and Marxist paradigms. For a discussion of state theory in the Kenya context see Berman and Lonsdale (1992a and 1992b) and Leonard (1991). For an African overview see Bayart (1993). For a general review of theories of the state see Krasner (1984), Lentner's (1984) response, and Evans, Rueschemeyer, and Skocpol (1985).

23 Parkin (1990) makes these remarks as part of a critique of contrasts between East Africa and West Africa, and between Asia and Africa that invoke the presence or absence of "Great Traditions." He suggests that there is no need to resort to the criterion of scriptural texts as the basis of a Great Tradition, and calls for attention to a "contrast paradigmatically expressed as that between over-arching concepts and local, vernacular ones" (1990: 195).

24 Appadurai (1991: 196, 198–199) remarks, "the task of ethnography now becomes the unraveling of a conundrum: what is the nature of locality, as a

lived experience, in a globalized, deterritorialized world? ... ethnographers can no longer simply be content with the 'thickness' they bring to the local and the particular, nor can they assume that as they approach the local, they approach something more elementary, more contingent, and thus more 'real' than life seen in larger-scale perspectives."

25 (See also Abrams 1982; Giddens 1979; Karp 1986; Ortner 1984.) Small farmers, for example, are best characterized neither as simply rational, autonomous entrepreneurs on the one hand, nor as hapless victims of structures of neocolonial dependency on the other. Rather, they are active agents who shape historical processes, though they do not do so under circumstances of their own choosing. (The latter point of course is the oft-quoted statement by Marx: "Men make their own history but they do not make it just as they please; they do not make it under circumstances chosen by themselves, but under circumstances directly encountered, given and transmitted from the past." [Marx 1990 (1869): 15].)

26 See Roseberry (1988) on the disadvantages of "layer cake metaphors" in such analyses.

27 As Scott (1976) uses the term, the "moral economy" of peasants is "their notion of economic justice and their working definition of exploitation – their view of which claims on their product were tolerable and which intolerable" (1976: 3). The concept is central to his analysis of the "normative roots of peasant politics," and to explanations of resistance and rebellion. See also Thompson (1966, 1971) on popular protests that reflect violation of a "moral economy of the poor" or a "moral economy of provision."

28 Minutes, Embu Local Native Council (LNC), July 12, 1925.

29 Scott (1976: 195, n.3) does note that rebellions may occur when subordinates perceive threats to improved levels of welfare "that have come to be taken as the subsistence norm." His reading of the Southeast Asian literature, however, suggests that such improvements in welfare levels were rare. I do not suggest that in Kenya the politically important question among subordinates became "what are my chances of making it into the elite?," but rather it remained, "is the elite doing its duty?" See Scott's (1976: 185–188) discussion of these two questions, and their very different origins and political implications. Compare also Chayanov (1966: 105), who notes that "a certain similarity to an immobile consumption standard occurs only in those areas and periods when, because of the productivity of peasant labor, incomes obtained barely meet the physiological minimum for existence."

30 Vincent 1990: 403–406.

31 I do not assume that households are monolithic or unified production and consumption units, but rather I consider the variability of domestic organization, and the negotiability and manipulability of relationships within and among households (see Guyer 1981 and chapter 5 below).

32 Cf. D. W. Cohen's (1983) exploration of this theme in the Lakes Plateau region during the nineteenth century.

33 These two phrases are from Tilly (1984). Large processes considered in chapter 4 include state formation, commercialization, population expansion, and increasing land scarcity.

2 SHATTERED SILENCES: POLITICAL CULTURE AND "DEMOCRACY"

1 Author's transcription of Daniel Zwerdling's National Public Radio report from Nairobi in May 1991.

2 Hereafter I shall avoid placing "democracy" and "liberal democracy" in quotation marks, but I do so in this instance to signal recognition of definitional problems (see Keller 1991; Lentner 1984, Young 1993 and Williams 1993). On problems of defining "liberalism," see Staniland (1991: 4–8). Liberal democracy, according to Keller (1991: 53), is an ideal type found nowhere in its purest form, and "refers to a political system where the state's intrusion into the lives of citizens is minimal, and its activities are circumscribed by the rule of law. In addition, individual liberty is paramount and basic human and political rights are constitutionally protected. All citizens are equal and have the same potential to influence politics and public policy." Other elements include "popular participation in electoral politics ... the accountability of elected public officials according to the rule of law ... and civilian control of the military."

Lentner (1984: 370) contrasts liberalism with Marxism, noting that "liberalism emphasizes the private sphere of the individual that belongs only to the person and stresses the mechanisms of public choice that are designed to protect both civil liberties and governmental responsiveness to the electorate." Marxism, in contrast, "emphasizes the historical and economic foundations of social and political arrangements as well as the divisions of interests among classes, clarifying especially the conditions of workers in a capitalist economy."

3 My use of the term "political culture" is closer to that which Robinson (1994) defines as the "culture of politics" than to earlier political science definitions of political culture: "the notion of a culture of politics ... is de-centered, historicized and contextualized, it accomodates contested meanings, acknowledges asymmetrical power relations, and encompasses marginal as well as modal political practices" (Robinson 1994: 2).

This chapter draws heavily on secondary sources (mass media and scholarly accounts), and my interpretations are shaped by my own experiences in Kenya (including a one-month revisit in mid-1993, as well as earlier visits in 1989, 1986, 1985, 1984, and 1978–81).

4 "Record crowd at epic FORD rally," *Daily Nation* (Nairobi), January 19, 1992: 1+.

5 *Daily Nation* (Nairobi), January 19, 1992: 4,1+.

6 *Daily Nation* (Nairobi), January 19, 1992: 3.

7 See also Mueller's (1984) discussion of measures to sideline the opposition during the 1960s.

8 The opposition between "state" and "civil society" is a problematic notion for reasons recently well-discussed by (among others) Bayart 1992, Fatton 1992, and Gupta 1993. Here, again, I drop the quotation marks henceforth.

9 At one funeral in Nakuru in 1991, for example, a clergyman's public address advised those attending not to follow the footsteps of any person, but rather to

follow the path of God alone. One implication of these words is that the president, whose slogan is "follow my footsteps," is not above the law, and is not infallible (Biersteker, personal communication).

10 Across the border Feierman (1990: 23–24) notes that during the 1950s Tanzanian peasant intellectuals debated the nature of *demokrasi*: "Was it rule by a council of elders? Was it a system in which only the best-educated held jobs? Would all power be given to the lineages of nonroyals? Would a peasant king sit on the throne? Should each man and woman be given a vote in formal elections?" (See also Feierman 1990: 44–45.)

11 Indeed, one opposition party parliamentary candidate, for example, assured a 1993 campaign rally in Central Province: "I am not a radical," prefacing her remark with, "I know you are willing to listen to me but are scared of voting for me" (Throup 1993b: 117).

12 See, for example, Hyden (1991a: 3–4) and other chapters in Hyden and Bratton (1991). On structural, diffusionist, and historically contingent explanations of Africa's new political currents see Bratton and Van de Walle (1991).

13 Some suggested, for example, that the 1991 Zambian election "should hasten Africa's 'second independence' – the end of the post-colonial autocrats who rule their countries as personal kingdoms" (Jane Perlez, "Zambia's Democratic Shock to Africa," *New York Times*, November 5, 1991: A14). (With the "first liberation" of the 1960s many believed Africa's newly independent nations were embarked on a progressive path toward both democracy and sustained economic growth.)

14 In Kenya the early 1990s opposition pressure group FORD (Forum for the Restoration of Democracy) was "inspired by the Civic Forum in East Germany and Czechoslovakia" (Throup 1993a: 390).

15 See "Africa: Democracy is not enough," *Africa Confidential*, 33(1): 1, 1992.

16 Williams (1993: 421) notes, however, that "it is clear from other World Bank sources that political issues which have a direct effect on 'economy and efficiency' can be taken into account."

17 Of course the existence of contradictory opinions within these aid institutions should be recognized. In 1987, for example, a senior IMF official resigned in protest against the Reagan administration's "pressure on the Fund to loosen the lending conditions for Zaire" (Schatzberg 1991: 72).

18 See, for example, "The DP's Constitution," *Weekly Review* (Nairobi), January 10, 1992: 8. See also the 1992 campaign speech of a Democratic Party parliamentary candidate addressing a Kiambu constituency, quoted in Throup (1993b: 117): "And the man from England has come to report on you guys to the world. The world is willing to help if they can be shown that aid is really reaching the poor and not being stolen."

19 See "Violence Mars Kenyan Rally for Political Pluralism," *Washington Post*, July 8, 1990; "Kenya Riots Spread," *Manchester Guardian Weekly*, July 15, 1990; "Nairobi Tense as Violent Opposition to Moi Increases," *Independent* (London), July 9, 1990; "Death Toll in Kenya Rises to 28," *Independent* (London), July 12, 1990; "Democracy Rally Routed in Kenya," *New York Times*, July 8, 1990.

20 "Moi: It's the work of hooligans, drug addicts," *Daily Nation* (Nairobi), July

11, 1990; and "Drug addicts are bent on breaking law – President," *Standard* (Nairobi), July 11, 1990.

21 Rubia was one of the early members of a new Gikuyu business class emerging by the early 1960s. As Gertzel (1970: 157) describes him, he "had been a Nairobi City Councillor in the 1950s and then a nominated member of the Legislative Council between 1958 and 1960. He had become the first African Mayor of Nairobi in 1962. A leading Kikuyu businessman, he also held a large number of company directorships." Rubia joined Moi's Cabinet in 1979 and was dismissed from it in 1983 (Throup 1993a: 386).

22 Matiba resigned from Moi's Cabinet in 1989, after "he was 'rigged' out of the KANU branch chairmanship in Murang'a and was immediately expelled from the party and Parliament" (Throup 1993a: 386). Throup (1993a: 384) terms Matiba "the most outspoken defender of Kikuyu interests within the Cabinet."

23 Although the Constitution guarantees freedom of assembly, the Public Order Act (CAP 56, part III, para. 5(10)(d)) states that "Any person who prints, publishes, displays, distributes or circulates a notice of, or in any other manner advertises or publicizes, a public meeting or public procession which has not been licensed under this section, shall be guilty of an offense" (quoted in Nowrojee 1992: 28)

24 Kenya had been a *de facto* one-party state during most of the years since independence. An opposition party, the Kenya People's Union (KPU), emerged under the leadership of Oginga Odinga in the mid-1960s and was banned in 1969.

25 For example, a headline in Nairobi's *Daily Nation* announced: "Churches, LSK team up for special prayers" (June 13, 1991: 1 +). (LSK is the Law Society of Kenya.)

26 "Church–LSK call off prayer crusade," *Daily Nation* (Nairobi), June 17, 1991: 1 +. See also "Moi tells clergy not to misuse Church" on the front page of the same day's newspaper.

27 *Daily Nation* (Nairobi), June 15, 1991: 22.

28 In April 1991 Oginga Odinga attempted unsuccessfully to register the National Democratic Party, and challenged in court the government's refusal to allow registration of political parties other than KANU.

29 These included Paul Muite, Gibson Kamau Kuria, Kiraitu Murungi, G. B. M. Kariuki, and Japheth Shamalla, among others. See *Weekly Review* (Nairobi) April 17, 1992: 7; Africa Watch 1991: chapter 11: "Lawyers: Challenging Legitimacy"; and issues of *Nairobi Law Monthly*.

30 Clergy who became outspoken advocates of multiparty politics include Anglican Archbishop Manasses Kuria, Bishop Henry Okullu, Bishop David Gitari, Rev. Peter Njenga, and Rev. Timothy Njoya. Many, however, avoided any public identification with FORD or other opposition parties, claiming instead non-partisan advocacy of democratic and human rights reforms. (*Weekly Review* (Nairobi), April 17, 1992: 10.) See Africa Watch 1991: chapter 13: "Church and State."

31 *Weekly Review* (Nairobi), April 17, 1992: 5.

32 See "A Strike for Freedom," *Weekly Review* (Nairobi), 6 March 1992: 3–6; and front page coverage in *Daily Nation* (Nairobi) March 5, and March 6, 1992.

33 The first years of independence saw Kenya's Provincial Administration reclaim

wide powers that its colonial predecessors had held (Gertzel 1970: 167). See Gertzel's (1970) discussion of the 1960s conflict between the bureaucracy and the political party over who should control the state. See also Leonard 1991; Widner 1992.

34 "Under the Preservation of Public Security Act, CAP 57 (see part VIII, para. 23, 1987) of the Laws of Kenya, a person may be detained and held without trial at the discretion of the Minister of Internal Security" (Nowrojee 1992: 12, n.16).

35 These included ethnic welfare associations such as the Gikuyu–Embu–Meru Association (GEMA), *Harambee* or self-help organizations, the women's organization *Maendeleo ya Wanawake*, the Central Organization of Trades Unions (COTU), Kenya Farmers' Association (KFA), the National Council of Churches of Kenya (NCCK), and the Green Belt Movement led by Wangari Maathai.

36 The new 1986 rules also specified that a candidate who received at least 70 percent of the votes cast during the queuing procedure would be elected unopposed. Barkan (1991: 182) notes that "Although queuing was only to be used at the first stage of elections for the National Assembly to determine the three finalists for whom secret ballots would then be cast, the fear and intimidation that accompanied the procedure reduced turnout to a historic low."

37 The KANU Review Report was published in *Daily Nation* (Nairobi), December 4, 1990.

38 Two years later (in November 1993), at another Paris meeting, the Consultative Group on Kenya restored much of the suspended aid, and again stated that new disbursements would depend on progress in implementing reforms. This news was prominently covered on Kenyan radio and in print media. Kenyan radio reported that Moi thanked donors for resumption of aid, and that he assured them he would "personally supervise and monitor closely all development projects funded by donors to see that the money is properly utilized" (KBC radio, November 27, 1993, LEXIS, Nexis Library). (See also "International Donors Resume Aid to Kenya," *Christian Science Monitor*, November 26, 1993.)

39 See, for example, "Aid for Kenya Cut as Donors Cite Corruption," *New York Times*, October 21, 1991: A1 +; and "Aid Donors Insist on Kenya Reforms," *New York Times*, November 27, 1993: A1 +. In November 1991, the Kenyan government impounded issues of *Newsweek*, the *International Herald Tribune*, and *Der Spiegel* because they carried unwelcome analyses of Kenyan politics (including corruption and political opposition groups such as FORD). Local distributors such as Nairobi's *Daily Nation* suffered financial losses as a result, since they still had to pay air freight charges at the European departure points (see *Daily Nation* [Nairobi], November 26, 1991).

40 Funds misappropriated in 1992 alone were "reliably estimated to be in the range of $300 to $500 million," amounts which, some economists estimate, "would add up to two percentage points to the country's annual rate of real economic growth" (Barkan 1993: 90).

41 The opposition criticized the Electoral Commission "for refusing to register an estimated 1.2 million young voters who had not been issued identity cards

upon reaching 18 years of age" (Barkan 1993: 93). Observers dispute the actual numbers and the probable effects on the election outcome.

42 Agence France Press, November 16, 1992; LEXIS, Nexis Library.

43 Presidential and parliamentary elections first scheduled for December 7 were postponed after the Kenyan High Court upheld a petition from opposition politicians, who argued they had been given too little time to nominate their candidates and present the names to the electoral commission.

44 Figures in this paragraph are taken from Barkan 1993: 94–97 and Table 1. See also Throup and Hornsby (forthcoming), and the 1992 reports by the International Republican Institute's Kenya Election Observation Mission, and the 1992 National Election Monitoring Unit (NEMU). Throup (1993a: 392) reports that Moi obtained 38 percent of the vote. His vote totals are 1.9 million for Moi, 1.4 million for Matiba, 1.0 million for Kibaki, and 904,000 for Odinga (Throup 1993a: 392–393). For ethnic breakdowns of election results see Throup (1993a: 393–394) and Throup and Hornsby (forthcoming).

45 Throup (1993a: 392) reports that FORD-Asili and FORD-Kenya each won thirty-one seats, and the Democratic Party secured twenty-three. The Kenya National Congress, the Kenya Social Congress, and an independent each took one seat.

46 *Daily Nation* (Nairobi), July 26, 1993.

47 See, for example, *Standard* (Nairobi), July 19, 1993: "DP leaders in Embu District led by MPs Norman Nyagah and Njeru Ndwiga have ... alleged political sabotage in the current water shortage within Embu municipality." The Embu council is dominated by the opposition Democratic Party, and local leaders claimed the water problems were orchestrated to discredit the council's work. (The quoted statement is from a subsection titled "Sabotage" in an article whose headline is "DP Faces Mass Exodus in Meru.")

48 *Standard* (Nairobi), July 28, 1993: 8.

49 *Economic Review* (Nairobi), July 26, 1993: 2–8.

50 *Economic Review* (Nairobi), July 26, 1993: 26.

51 Official rhetoric defines the differences between one-party politics in Kenya and Eastern Europe as follows. The 1990 KANU Review Report states: "Inappropriate comparison has been made between KANU and single political parties which operated in Eastern Europe and the Soviet Union. KANU, unlike the ideological vanguard parties of those countries, is a mass party, a mobilizing force and a democratic instrument of social change and economic development." The KANU report is reproduced in *Daily Nation* (Nairobi), December 4, 1990.

52 "Multi-party: Moi says no to Matiba meeting," *Daily Nation* (Nairobi), June 10, 1990.

53 See "Multi-Party System Not For Africa – Moi," *Daily Nation* (Nairobi), March 24, 1990; and "Tough Talking: President Moi Hits Out at Critics of KANU," *Weekly Review* (Nairobi), May 18, 1990.

54 Cf. Schatzberg (1991).

55 As Isaacman (1990: 56) notes, "There is no consensus on whether the act of constructing an oppositional culture constitutes resistance *per se* ... or whether it merely represents the creation of a context for subsequent acts of insurgency."

56 For an example of the latter see Maina 1977: 15–16.
57 "Chained mothers march to courts," *Daily Nation* (Nairobi), March 11, 1992: 1+.
58 "Moi stands firm against rising tide of democracy," *Independent* (London), July 5, 1990.
59 *Daily Nation* (Nairobi), July 6, 1990 and *Independent* (London), July 3, 1990. The cassettes included "*Mucemanio wa nyamu*" ("Meeting of the animals"), "Matiba saga (or tribulations)," "Patriotic contributions," "Who killed Dr. Ouko?" and "*Thiina wa Muoroto*" ("The Troubles of Muoroto").
60 After the demolition the Minister for Local Government warned against "living under the illusion that unplanned kiosks will be allowed ... Nairobi will be turned into a carton city and this has very many things at stake as they could pose health hazards, security risks and could scare away tourists" (quoted in Africa Watch 1991: 256). See Africa Watch (1991: 260–268) on subsequent shanty demolitions in Nairobi. In October 1990 a reconstructed Muoroto was once again bulldozed, this time with a leaked advance warning, without resistance, and with a heavy police and paramilitary presence (Africa Watch 1991: 261).
61 White (1990b: 211). In addition, "every night for two years following Operation Anvil military control of the city was reasserted with a vengeance," and residents of some neighborhoods "were rousted from their rooms at gunpoint ... while their rooms were searched" (White 1990b: 211). See White 1990b for discussion of other violent official acts against Nairobi squatter communities. A few of the many fine works on the 1950s "Mau Mau" anti-colonial struggle include Cooper 1988; Furedi 1989; Kanogo 1987; Lonsdale 1990, and Throup 1987a.
62 Macharia 1992: 231. As Macharia (1992) notes many Muoroto residents perceived Gikuyu peoples from Murang'a District as a particular target in the slum clearance; the public rhetoric of the president had also singled out that district as a site of opposition politics.
63 See Macharia (1992) and *Weekly Review* (Nairobi), June 15, 1990. Criticism of the Muoroto incident came from a number of politicians and churchmen, including one whose parish included part of Muoroto – the Provost of All Saints Cathedral in Nairobi (Africa Watch 1991: 253–254).
64 Africa Watch (1991: 252) reports that the local press did not report the incident until two days later, and "the press had apparently received instructions not to cover the incident." See also Africa Watch 1991: chapter 12; "The Media and Self-Censorship."
65 "The pain of Muoroto people," *Daily Nation* (Nairobi), May 25, 1990.
66 See "Music cassettes: 19 on sedition charge," Nairobi, *Daily Nation* (Nairobi), July 6, 1990; and "'Subversives' strike wrong note in Kenya," *Independent* (London), July 3, 1990.
67 The words quoted from the cassette, and the account that follows are from the author's transcription of a National Public Radio report from Nairobi by Daniel Zwerdling in May 1991.
68 Maina (1977: 16) makes this point and cites as an example a passage from the Book of the Lamentations of the Prophet Jeremiah.
69 Page number references to Link (1991) refer to a pre-publication manuscript version of his work.

70 A "pirated" cassette recording of Kenyatta's speeches (released as an LP in 1978 by the Ministry of Information and Broadcasting), which enjoyed a sudden new popularity in 1990, includes his well-known press conference during his 1961 detention in Maralal, as well as speeches he made later as prime minister and as president, including his first Kenyatta Day Address (1963) and 1964 Jamhuri Day speech, and a 1963 speech to white settlers in Nakuru. See "Brisk Business in Cassettes," *Weekly Review* (Nairobi), June 22, 1990.

71 The latter, for example, praise the nationalist hero Dedan Kimathi, and call for British settlers to return land to Kenyans. Such themes may evoke unfulfilled expectations about the fruits of independence. Gakaara wa Wanjau's (1988) "Mau Mau" detention diary includes examples of anti-colonial songs, as do works by Paul Maina (1977) and Maina wa Kinyatti (1980). See Maina (1977: 9) for an example of a colonial government ban on a popular anti-colonial song in the Gikuyu language during the 1920s.

72 Kenya's Constitution guarantees freedom of speech, but laws forbid anything that is seditious and threatens state security.

73 The lines quoted and the prior summary of the play's theme are from the author's transcription of Daniel Zwerdling's National Public Radio report from Nairobi in May 1991.

74 Food prices in Kenya had nearly doubled between 1986 and 1991.

75 This paragraph is based on the author's transcript of Daniel Zwerdling's National Public Radio report from Nairobi in May 1991.

76 In May 1990 Ambassador Hempstone gave a speech to Kenyan businessmen in which he stated that foreign aid in the future would be given to nations that "nourish democratic institutions, defend human rights and practice multiparty politics" (Jane Perlez, "US Envoy Steps Into Political Firestorm in Kenya," *New York Times*, May 6, 1990. See Africa Watch (1991: chapter 21) on changing State Department policies toward Kenya.

77 See Jane Perlez, "Stormy Relations for US and Kenya," *New York Times*, November 21, 1991; and *Daily Nation* (Nairobi), November 19, 1991.

78 *Daily Nation* (Nairobi), November 20, 1991. Both "Moi ... and Mugabe of Zimbabwe were vociferous in rejecting efforts by Western governments to promote multiparty competition as interference in the sovereign rights of African states" (Bratton and Van de Walle 1991: 35).

79 See "Multi-party system not for Africa – Moi," *Daily Nation* (Nairobi), March 24, 1990; and "Tough Talking: President Moi hits out at critics of KANU," *Weekly Review* (Nairobi), May 18, 1990.

80 The effects of structural adjustment measures of course are widely debated (for one overview concerning effects on women, see Gladwin 1991). Watts (1989: 2), for example, writes that "the major economic crisis of the 1980s and the assaults by international regulatory institutions such as the International Monetary Fund (IMF) on state-funded health, education and social services in the name of 'adjustment' and 'stabilization', have manufactured new sorts of consumption insecurity for millions of Africa's rural and urban poor."

81 See Van de Walle 1993. In addition, actual compliance with World Bank/IMF conditions attached to structural adjustment lending often is modest (Van de Walle 1993: 6).

82 All of the above figures are from Kenyan Government (1993: 1–3).
83 With the authors' permission, these arguments are summarized in this and the subsequent two paragraphs. Page numbers refer to their pre-publication manuscript.
84 Later in 1992 (as noted below) FORD split into two parties: FORD-Asili (with a Central Kenyan stronghold) and FORD-Kenya (with strong support in Western Kenya).
85 *Weekly Review* (Nairobi), April 17, 1992: 10.
86 On the recent "ethnic" clashes see the 1992 Parliamentary report, the 1993 NEMU report, Africa Watch 1993, and discussion below.
87 Ferguson (1990b, 1992) describes such changes in Zambia, and connects them to recent tensions between earlier images of an idealized, idyllic countryside, and the rural realities returning urban migrants are forced to confront (1992). He remarks that some urban migrants forced by a failing economy to relocate to their "homes" in the countryside find the latter a place of impossible demands, treachery, witchcraft, and selfishness. As urban images of rural life become less rosy, the failings of the urban economy, he suggests, then "come to appear as attributable not to any external force, but to the internal moral faults of the Zambian character" (Ferguson 1992: 90).
88 See chapter 5.
89 See Throup and Hornsby (forthcoming) for a discussion of subtle differences in the appeal of various opposition parties to particular class interests.
90 LEXIS, Nexis Library, Wires File.
91 See, for example, the lengthy article, with photo, "Kenya, a Land That Thrived, is Now Caught Up in Fear of Ethnic Civil War," *New York Times*, May 3, 1992: A3.
92 The "Kalenjin" category includes a number of subgroups such as the Tugen (Moi's group), Nandi, Elgeyo, Marakwet, Kipsigis, and Pokot. I use terms such as "Gikuyu" and "Kalenjin" to denote official "ethnic" categories and not natural or primordial entities.
93 The parliamentary investigation (1992: 76) found no evidence of imported arrows.
94 See also the reports by NEMU (1993) and Africa Watch (1993).
95 Equating multi-party politics with civil disorder was a theme Kenya's vice-president (Saitoti) also voiced. In October 1991 he blamed civil unrest in Zaire on the emergence of multiple political parties, and suggested that if violence were to occur in Kenya, it would arise from the divisions caused by multi-party advocates (*Weekly Review* (Nairobi), October 4, 1991: 9).
96 Agence France Presse, September 23, 1993; LEXIS, Nexis Library, Wires File.
97 Agence France Presse, September 22, 1993; LEXIS, Nexis Library, Wires File.
98 Agence France Presse, September 12, 1993; LEXIS, Nexis Library, Wires File.
99 Today the Gikuyu peoples have the highest rates of secondary school completion (form IV) in the country (Thomas-Slayter 1991: 309). Also salient, however, are broader class differences. For example, Leonard (1991: 35) cites surveys of university students in East Africa that show that "the children of schoolteachers are overrepresented by twenty times their proportion in the population."

100 See, for example, *Weekly Review* (Nairobi), September 13, 1991: 12–13.
101 See, for example, Bates (1989: 52–57), Gertzel (1970), Wasserman (1976).
102 See Bates (1989:60) on oathing in the early 1960s, and on how a potential civil war was avoided during the transition to independence. On recent oathing see "22 held on oathing charge," *Daily Nation* (Nairobi), July 24, 1993.
103 The 1963 federal or *Majimbo* constitution would have made "Regional Assemblies responsible for wide areas of policy such as housing, local government, social services, education and the police, leaving the National Assembly in Nairobi with responsibility for defence, foreign affairs and central finances" (Throup 1993a: 372). In 1991 some MPs spoke publicly of a plan to present to Parliament a draft of a "*Majimbo*" constitution of semi-autonomous regions, under which "outsiders" in the Rift Valley would be required to return to their central Kenyan "motherland" (Kenyan Government 1992: 9). One MP said that he would introduce such a draft document if multi-party advocates continued their crusade. See also *Weekly Review* (Nairobi), September 13, 1991.
104 On why it was convenient to unite Kalenjin peoples around a supposed Gikuyu threat see, for example, *Weekly Review* (Nairobi), September 13, 1991: 12.
105 *Daily Nation* (Nairobi), May 13, 1990.
106 FORD-Kenya was headed by Oginga Odinga (Luo from Siaya District), FORD-Asili by Kenneth Matiba (Gikuyu from Murang'a District), and the Democratic Party by Mwai Kibaki (Gikuyu from Nyeri District). Cross-ethnic alliances were present in the original FORD and in its replacement parties. For example, Paul Muite (Gikuyu) was FORD-Kenya's vice-presidential candidate, and Martin Shikuku (Luhya) was FORD-Asili's vice-presidential candidate. Additional smaller parties included Kenya Social Congress (George Anyona), Kenya National Congress (Chibule wa Tsuma), Kenya National Democratic Alliance (David Mukaru-Ng'ang'a), and PICK (John Harun).
107 Kenya's standard secondary school syllabus includes under the study of history and government the topic of participation in democratic processes such as elections and public meetings, and the growth of representative government in Kenya. Attention is given as well to symbols of national unity, patriotism, national integration, and problems in achieving national unity.
108 I am grateful to David Throup for allowing me to quote from his manuscript (1993b) the material that follows.
109 The National Democratic and Human Rights Organization, or NDEHURIO (*gutehura* "to tear apart" in Gikuyu). See the Executive Director's (Koigi wa Wamwere) founding statement in the Nairobi publication *Monthly News*, July 1993.
110 The account given here is from Inter Press Service, September 21, 1993; LEXIS, Nexis Library, Wires File.
111 An October 1993 Nairobi newspaper reports a large police raid on a Nairobi shop associated with the production and sale of the cassettes: "Armed police raid music store," *Daily Nation* (Nairobi), October 24, 1993.
112 Embu North Land Control Board file, letter dated December 29, 1978.
113 See the fine edited collection by Schmidt, Guasti, Landé, and Scott (1977) for

theoretical and ethnographic discussions of clientelism and factionalism by anthropologists, political scientists, historians, and sociologists. See Lemarchand (1988) for a useful overview of African states and patronage systems, and for discussion of analytical problems with the concept of patronage itself. See also Weber's (1947: 62, 346–354) discussion of patrimonialism and prebends.

114 As Watts (1989: 25) notes, "the issue is less one of the existence or scale of corruption than the use of a privatized public purse ... how is privatized state capital actually invested, what are the positions and capacities of ruling classes, what is the social structure of local accumulation?"

115 See Barkan 1987, and Barkan and Chege 1989. Until the 1988 elections (in which there was widespread rigging), about 50 percent of Kenya's members of parliament were routinely defeated in national elections held every five years (see Barkan 1991: 190, n.5). In 1992, as noted earlier, an unusually small share of incumbent MPs who sought re-election won.

116 Hornsby and Throup (1992: 189–190). They note, for example, that fourteen cabinet ministers were sacked between 1982 and 1991. See also Throup (1993a: 385–386).

117 The general discussion of factions in this paragraph draws in particular on the work of Vincent 1978 and Bujra 1973.

118 Leonard 1991: 93–94. See his book for a wider discussion of elite business and agricultural interests, and for detailed biographies of four prominent public servants, including their own diversified economic interests.

119 See Lemarchand 1988, 1972; and Scott 1972 on the "inflationary democracy" associated with patron–client politics in many industrializing and poorer nations.

120 See, for example, *Economic Review* (Nairobi), July 26, 1993.

121 Both local and international media carried reports of growing violence, including (in addition to the "ethnic" clashes) mob beatings of suspected thieves and executions of suspected "witches". See, for example, "A World Unhinged Gropes for New Rules" (with photo of passersby beating a supected thief in Nairobi), *New York Times*, December 26, 1993: E5; "Campus mob beats student to death," *Nation* (Nairobi), July 24, 1993; "Commentary: Explaining the violence that stalks Kenya today," *Nation* (Nairobi), March 22, 1992; and "Mob beats up theft suspect," *Standard* (Nairobi), July 28, 1993.

122 As civil wars in countries such as Somalia, Burundi, or Rwanda are reduced to supposed "traditions" of clan or tribal warfare, little account is taken, for example, of years of American military and other support to the dictator Siad Barre. Instead Somalia as imagined in the mass media becomes another foil in America's own definition of self: part of the process "by which the West has constructed and controlled non-Western identities, seeking in Africa answers to Western preoccupations" (Miller 1993: 218).

123 In the 1960s KANU had pro-Western sympathies and KPU was identified with the Eastern bloc.

124 "The KANU Review Report," *Daily Nation* (Nairobi), December 4, 1990.

125 Harvey (1989) explores the dangers of "aestheticizing politics."

126 This feature of politics is by no means confined to Africa of course. To note

just one example, officials in the USA often speak "off the record" in the hope that their comments will become "on record."

127 Edelman (1993) explores these issues in the Costa Rican context.

3 OPEN SECRETS: EVERYDAY FORMS OF DOMINATION

1 "Ritual" and "political ritual" are notoriously difficult to define. For discussions of definitional problems see Kertzer 1988; Lukes 1975; and Moore and Myerhoff 1977. For present purposes, I adopt Lukes' (1975: 291) condensed definition: "rule-governed activity of a symbolic character which draws the attention of its participants to objects of thought and feeling which they hold to be of special significance."

2 The phrase "everyday forms of domination," inspired by Scott's (1985) "everyday forms of resistance," comes from Vincent (1990: 404–405). This chapter draws in part on Haugerud and Njogu 1991.

3 Little pursued, Vincent (1990: 404) notes, was Scott's (1986: 28–29) idea that "the forms of peasant resistance are not just a product of the social ecology of the peasantry. The parameters of resistance are also set, in part, by the institutions of repression." (See also Abu-Lughod 1990 and Rebel 1989.)

4 Moreover, there is no reason to assume that the cheering crowds being coached in new slogans at *baraza* organized by opposition parties in 1992 were any less likely to construct new alternative discourses offstage that challenge both the new opposition groups and the besieged ruling regime. After all, those who address opposition rallies themselves fall into the category of "the powerful," and hence provoke countervailing discourses among the less powerful.

5 On the structural and historical conditions that allowed him to do so see Throup 1987b, Leonard 1991, and Widner 1992.

6 Oratory has been the subject of a number of outstanding ethnographic works. These include intriguing accounts of Ilongot "crooked language" and "straight speech" (Rosaldo 1973), Malagasy *kabary* (Keenan 1975), Tikopia *fono* (Firth 1975), and many others. See, for example, edited volumes by Bloch (1975), Bailey (1981), Brenneis and Myers (1984), O'Barr and O'Barr (1976), Paine (1981), Richards and Kuper (1971), and Watson-Gegeo and White (1990); and recent overview articles by Brenneis (1988), Gal (1989), and Parkin (1984). Today, of course, as Parkin (1984: 352) notes, attention to political language joins growing interest in figurative speech (Sapir and Crocker 1977) and in society as discourse (Foucault 1980; Dreyfus and Rabinow 1982).

7 Within political anthropology, an emphasis on individual room for maneuver within situational constraints is connected to the concerns of action theory; see the fine review by Vincent (1978). See also Murray Edelman (1988) on how political observers and what they observe "construct one another."

8 What observers or listeners perceive to be obscured and how they interpret oratory vary along many dimensions (some of them quite ephemeral), including those of social and economic status.

9 I take up the wider regional and historical contexts of Embu district and the Embu people in the next chapter.

10 See Middleton and Kershaw 1965. Ethnographic works on Embu peoples

include Moris 1970, Mwaniki 1973a, 1973b and Saberwal 1970. Works on Mbeere peoples include Brokensha and Glazier 1973; Brokensha and Riley 1980, 1988; Glazier 1984, 1985; Hunt 1984; Mwaniki 1973a, 1973b, 1974.

11 According to the 1979 Kenya population census, 8.8 percent of the Embu people lived outside of Embu District, most of them in Nairobi, Central Province, and the Rift Valley Province. Seven percent of the Mbeere people lived outside of Embu District in 1979.

12 In February 1992, for example, a politically-charged controversy arose when the ruling party newspaper (*The Kenya Times*) quoted Paul Muite as having called upon the GEMA ethnic groups – the Gikuyu, Embu and Meru – to join forces to overthrow the Moi regime. Muite himself a month later published a transcript of his speech, "indicating that he had urged the GEMA tribes not to be selfish but to join hands with other tribes in the task of removing KANU from power" (see *Weekly Review* (Nairobi), April 17, 1992: 5). Whatever the intention behind Muite's original remarks, delivered at an opposition rally in Murang'a (a predominantly Gikuyu district in Central Province), the media attention they received underscores the point that many would assume the Embu and Meru peoples to be allies in, and joint beneficiaries of, any successful Gikuyu effort to regain control of the state.

13 Kenya's administrative units, in descending order of inclusiveness are province, district, division, location, and sublocation. Provinces, of which there are eight, are headed by provincial commissioners. Districts, of which there were forty in the early 1980s, are headed by district commissioners. Divisions are headed by district officers, locations by chiefs, and sublocations by assistant chiefs. Only chiefs and assistant chiefs serve in their natal areas; other officers are frequently transferred from one place to another.

14 For discussion of changes in such accountability mechanisms under Moi, see Barkan 1991; Barkan and Chege 1989; Barkan and Holmquist 1989; Thomas-Slayter 1985; and Widner 1992.

15 Kenyans speak over 40 different first languages, with no more than 20 percent of the population speaking the same one. Those spoken by the largest shares of the population include Gikuyu (c. 20 percent), Luo (14 percent), Luhya dialects (13 percent), and Kamba (11 percent) (Leonard 1991: 78).

16 Several of these first languages (especially Gikuyu, Dholuo, Kamba, and some of the Luhya languages) are kept alive not just through daily conversation, but also in popular music and in published religious, academic, and popular works. The writer Ngugi wa Thiong'o, for example, in the early 1980s reversed his earlier practice of publishing in English, and began to publish his novels first in the Gikuyu language and later in English translation.

17 This lingua franca is Bantu in its phonology, morphology, and syntax. Most of its lexicon is also Bantu, but in addition includes borrowings from Arabic, English, Portuguese, Hindi, and other languages with which it has had contact. Since the 1920s there have been efforts to standardize Swahili orthography, vocabulary, and grammar (see Whiteley 1974).

18 On code-switching, see the 1992 special issue of the *Journal of Multilingual and Multicultural Development*, edited by Carol Eastman. See also Gumperz 1982, Myers-Scotton 1983, and Heller 1988; on Kenya see Whitely 1974 and Njogu 1990.

19 See Haugerud and Njogu (1991: 10–11) for an excerpt of his speech.
20 Location chiefs are appointed by the government to serve in their natal areas. Officials at higher ranks of the central administration (district officers, district commissioners, provincial commissioners), on the other hand, do not serve in their natal areas, and are frequently transferred from one location to another.

In addition to calling a *baraza*, a chief may appear at and address various other kinds of gatherings, such as burial ceremonies, family gatherings, and weddings; all of these require speakers to obtain permits from a chief. Not only the chief but a host of other notables sometimes arouse participants' displeasure when they use occasions such as funerals to make "self-serving" political speeches: the subject of an editorial page essay in *Daily Nation* (Nairobi), July 15, 1991.
21 These are the opening words of a district officer's speech at a chief's *baraza* (FEB2779:A,21); the district officer is the guest of honor and speaks for a half hour or so near the end of the meeting.
22 These are the words of a member of the board of the KTDA (Kenya Tea Development Authority) addressing a KTDA "field day" *baraza* held to celebrate successful tea development in the region (SEP779:A,4).
23 On elders' councils among Mbeere peoples see Glazier (1985); among Embu peoples see Saberwal (1970) and Mwaniki (1973a and 1973b); among Gikuyu-speakers see Kenyatta (1965), Leakey (1977), and Middleton and Kershaw (1965).
24 Many younger individuals, though, do not comprehend the richly figurative language and proverbs spoken in their own first language by their elders. See Barra 1939, Mbaabu 1978, Mwaniki 1986, Njururi 1983, Wanjiku 1983 and Wanjiku and Mutahi 1988, on central Kenyan proverbs, idioms, songs, and poetry.
25 In Gikuyu, *Acio maraatugayania maroora, marooma, maroitika.* "Multi-party: Leaders invoke Mzee's spirit," *Daily Nation* (Nairobi), May 13, 1990.
26 Literally, the Gikuyu words said that those who want two political parties will be "eaten" by Kenyatta's curse. "Multi-party: Leaders invoke Mzee's spirit," *Daily Nation* (Nairobi), May 13, 1990.
27 Gertzel (1970: 145), citing Rosberg and Nottingham (1966: 275) quotes the curse as "*kura na miiri ya mikongoi.*"
28 At this point in the meeting people were reacting to a public question from a farmer in the audience about how reliable a market existed for milk produced by the exotic cattle that officials were urging farmers to incur debts to purchase. Some thought the question irrelevant and others agreed that marketing was a problem.
29 In Gikuyu, *kaariki kamwe ni karaarariirie ndutura.*
30 *Ciira mwingi ni wa uthoni ugikua,* in Gikuyu.
31 "A Show of Solidarity," *Weekly Review* (Nairobi), October 4, 1991: 10.
32 On the strategic use of questions see Brown and Levinson 1978 and Goody (1978).
33 This phrase and the theme of the next sentence are from Lonsdale (1981: 160). See also Scott (1976: 185–186).
34 The Local Native Councils "had the power to levy taxes and to make bylaws concerning agriculture and education, but they were only advisory to the

English district commissioners" (Leonard 1991: 31). In 1951 Local Native Councils became African District Councils, and later County Councils (elected bodies). The 1925 minutes quoted above record two dozen "native" or African members of the Embu council, whose meetings were led by a British district commissioner. The latter appointed other members, who included chiefs and elders representing the various parts of the district. Among African members, chiefs predominated, and their disproportionate membership was the cause of some popular discontent (Glazier 1985: 88).

35 Minutes, Embu Local Native Council, July 12, 1925.
36 Precisely how local cosmology contextualized colonial state claims merits attention. For a fine account of colonial changes in the expression of such cosmological understandings about the relationship between rulers and rain in Shambaai (Tanzania), see Feierman (1990).
37 Among many works that discuss the contradictory roles of Africa's colonial chiefs are Fallers 1955 and 1956, Fortes and Evans-Pritchard 1940, Gluckman 1940, Richards 1939, Turner 1957. Lonsdale (1981: 201) remarks, "there is a new interest in colonial chiefs as elements of a continually changing ruling class, rather than the distracted bearers of intercalary roles and values that they were once seen to be." See, for example, Tignor 1971 and Vincent 1977.
38 For a vivid post-colonial example, see Nellis' (1973) account of a 1971 Pokot *baraza* he attended, at which spear-carrying Turkana men symbolically threatened a district officer by raising their weapons in a hostile posture at close range.
39 See Beinart and Bundy (1987: 27–29) on conceptual problems with the category "collaborator." In addition, as Tignor (1976) discusses, colonial chiefs played a much more central role in Gikuyu society than they did among the neighboring Maasai or Kamba peoples.
40 See Isaacman 1990: 42.
41 Embu LNC minutes, November 22, 1933.
42 Silas Ita was a post-independence chief in Mbere (1964 to 1969) who wrote a BA thesis (Ita 1972) on the changing role of colonial chiefs for the Department of Government at the University of Nairobi. I am grateful to David Leonard for bringing Ita's work to my attention.
43 1990 KANU Review Report, in *Daily Nation* (Nairobi), December 14, 1992. In 1990, after KANU's annual delegates conference resolved that he do so, President Moi appointed a KANU review committee, which in July and August then heard hours of public testimony from citizens in Nairobi, Nakuru, Eldoret, Kisumu, Kakamega, Nyeri, Embu, Mombasa, and Garissa. In the committee's interpretation of its terms of reference, it was to "examine the nomination, electoral and disciplinary procedures of the Party and the nomination procedures for the Parliamentary and civic elections, with view to making them more democratic and revising them so as to make them fulfill better the purpose for which they were intended." The hearings produced testimony on a wide range of social, economic and political concerns of citizens.
44 Here the KANU Review Report quotes Sessional Paper no. 10 on *African Socialism and its Application to Planning in Kenya. Daily Nation* (Nairobi), December 4, 1992.

45 See, for example, Embu LNC minutes, November 22, 1933 and March 22, 1935.
46 Embu LNC minutes, November 8, 1958; April 26, 1958; May 25–26, 1961.
47 During this speech the cabinet minister often switches between Embu and Swahili languages. His audience includes local farmers more fluent in the Embu language than in Swahili, and many visiting dignitaries who speak Swahili but not Embu. This occasion, sponsored by the Kenya Tea Development Authority (KTDA), is a field day for smallscale tea farmers, and includes visits to demonstration plots, as well as speeches, music (drumming and singing), and dance performances. The *baraza* is held near the Kianjokoma tea factory in the Embu highlands. The cabinet minister's quoted words occur about fifteen minutes into a speech of about forty-five minutes. These remarks immediately follow a formulaic interchange with the audience in which the cabinet minister praises President Moi in short phrases, each punctuated by three synchronized hand claps from the audience.
48 In the early 1990s, on the other hand, with more civil disorder apparent in Kenya than in Uganda, Ugandans were citing Kenya as an example of the type of politics to be avoided.
49 "Tough Talking: President Moi Hits Out at Critics of KANU," *Weekly Review* (Nairobi), May 18, 1990.
50 See "Multi-party System Not for Africa – Moi," *Daily Nation* (Nairobi), March 24, 1990; and "Tough Talking: President Moi Hits Out at Critics of KANU," *Weekly Review* (Nairobi), May 18, 1990. Moi's recent arguments in favor of a one-party state echo those Kenyatta made in the 1960s (see Kenyatta 1968: 226–231).
51 See October 1991 issue of *Nairobi Law Monthly*, and 1992 Parliamentary report on the ethnic clashes.
52 This is a reference to "Mau Mau" freedom fighters based in the forests during the anti-colonial struggles of the 1950s.
53 The cabinet minister here speaks from personal experience. Some years earlier, people in Embu say, a delegation of citizens from his district called on President Kenyatta to complain about him, only to be surprised that the target of their complaints had been tipped off about the meeting and showed up himself. Members of the delegation, who were well-educated and occupied prominent positions, were later demoted in various ways.
54 The adjective *kali*, for example, is found on the "fierce dog" (*mbwa (m)kali*) signs that are so common on the gates of Nairobi residential compounds.
55 Coffee cooperative societies in Embu District, as elsewhere, are beset by conflicts over delayed payments to farmers and over management accountability, honesty, and efficiency. At the time of this *baraza* there was intense political conflict over the wish of some Embu coffee farmers to subdivide their coffee cooperative geographically.
56 At a 1979 coffee cooperative society meeting a district cooperative society officer told his audience of farmers that coffee cooperatives should not be mixed up in politics, because then things are spoiled.
57 Here he proceeds to mention elections and candidacy eligibility. He notes that candidates must be literate in both English and Swahili, and says that anyone is free to notify the appropriate party official in writing that he or she wishes to

contest a local council seat. He repeats this and criticizes the "clever" ones who say otherwise and who wish to create trouble.

58 This speech is entirely in Swahili, as the district officer is from the Kenya coast and does not speak the Embu language. The language he uses on such occasions differs considerably from Swahili dialects spoken on the coast in Mombasa or Malindi (Biersteker, personal communication). Rather than use the dialect of his own natal region (where Swahili is most widely spoken), the district officer has adjusted his language to his rural, central Kenyan audience.

59 The attendance requirement is enforced loosely. Informal bargaining some-times occurs between a chief and individuals who wish their absence excused. Ita, for example, notes that colonial Mbeere chiefs relieved some timely tax-payers from the obligation to attend locational *baraza*. He refers to a subtle process of private bargaining and negotiation that chiefs used to "make people feel obligated to pay their taxes" (Ita 1972: 67).

60 Ooko Ombaka (1982), quoted in Githu (1992: 34).

61 The surge in world coffee prices that resulted from heavy frost in Brazil that year translated into solid foreign exchange earnings at the national level, to the making of many fortunes, and to an infusion (albeit uneven) of cash into rural coffee-producing areas.

62 The tune of Kenya's national anthem is said to come from a song of the Pokomo people of eastern Kenya (Biersteker, personal communication): hence "Kipokomo song" in the passage quoted above, which follows the cabinet minister's recitation of a few lines from the national anthem.

63 GEMA is the Gikuyu Embu Meru Association, which, along with other "tribal" organizations, was disbanded by presidential decree in 1979.

64 An earlier attempt by some prominent Gikuyu to change the constitution to prevent Moi from succeeding Kenyatta had failed (see Karimi and Ochieng 1980).

65 This meeting was a political party (KANU) rally, held on March 4, 1979. Speakers included the local MP, a cabinet minister, and many other politicians and bureaucrats. One of the meeting's purposes was to encourage voter registration, in preparation for national elections later that year.

66 His words are quoted in the first paragraph of chapter 1 above.

67 After this interchange the cabinet minister made some brief remarks to the gathering. A number of other local notables then continued to take turns greeting the crowd, most of them engaging in similar exchanges of slogans with the audience, and making short speeches. Later in the meeting the cabinet minister gave the longer keynote address.

68 Compare, for example, contrapuntal or antiphonal patterns in African–American sermons and other oratory (see Asante 1987: 47, 53, 68, 92; Davis 1985: 109–110).

69 These are the words of a local politician addressing a KANU rally in rural Embu in March 1979 (MAR479:B,11).

70 Alcohol content in the distilled beverages was perhaps 80 percent, and in the home-brewed beers perhaps 3 to 5 percent (Michael Dietler, personal commu-nication).

71 On female beer brewers in Nairobi, see Nelson 1978. In the early colonial era as well, sugarcane and beer were crucial to rural trade: "all across central

Kenya it was the sale of sugar and the introduction of cane mills that propelled the expansion of trade during the early colonial years" (Ambler 1991: 168).

72 See Karp (1980) on the social contexts of beer drinking among the Iteso of western Kenya. Karp argues that "beer is a symbol of diffuse solidarity and unencumbered sociability which expresses the ideal form of relations among men that Iteso would like to achieve. The association of beer drinking with sorcery and poisoning, however, points to the inability of Iteso to achieve desired forms of relations among men" (1980: 84). For a West African case study on beer see Netting 1964.

73 Quoted in Ambler 1991: 166.

74 Constraints of seasonal availability eased, and production became easier and moved beyond the control of elders as mechanical cane crushers and then refined sugar became more available (eliminating the labor-intensive task of hand crushing sugarcane) (Ambler 1991: 168).

75 Ambler 1991: 176, 179, n.4.

76 Officials assumed that restrictions on rural beer consumption would both reduce social disorder and make it less difficult to recruit young men to meet the growing demand for labor in public works and settler agriculture. At the same time, "employers often used the availability of alcohol as a lure to attract workers" in Kenya and in southern Africa (Ambler 1991: 174).

77 Ambler (1991: 169) says that oral records suggest that "drunkenness was actually far less pervasive than colonial reports suggest."

78 The politician's interchange with the audience quoted below includes a number of code-switches from the Embu language into Swahili. When the crowd shouts for traditional beer to be banned, it sometimes uses Swahili (*funga kabisa*), and sometimes Embu (*kathire!*). The politician himself switches into Swahili when leading the crowd in routinized national cheers for the president and the government.

79 The district officer does so more than once in his speech; later, for example, he says "I don't have the power to ban beer and I don't have the power to open (allow) it. The one to ban and open is Mr. D. C."

80 Besnier (1989: 337, n.) suggests that "collusion can be described as the achievement of congruent points of view about or evaluations of a particular situation." See also Goffman 1974, 1981.

81 The county council chairman, who spoke immediately after the MP, also publicly requested a sugarcane processing machine (*macini ya kuthia igwa*), MAR479:A,16.

82 The MP goes on to praise the president's new program of distributing free milk to children in primary schools, and then requests a dairy for the area, and soon thereafter stops and calls the next speaker to the stand (a local party chairman, who immediately engages the crowd in an exchange of political slogans).

83 Indirection, as Brenneis (1987: 504) notes, not only allows but compels listeners to draw their own conclusions beyond what the text literally says.

84 Leonard (1991: 285) is the source of points made in this paragraph and of the phrases directly quoted in this sentence and the one that follows it.

85 See, for example, Leonard's (1991) analysis of Simeon Nyachae's official downfall in the late 1980s.

86 The coffee cooperatives in one Embu location refused state supervision as they

went through the subdivision process, because they assumed officials would favor one local faction over another. The cooperative society in a neighboring location, on the other hand, did agree to state supervision of elections held after subdivision of the local cooperative society.

87 The school fund contributions were deducted from farmers' coffee earnings, after separate local committees proved unable to collect them directly from farmers.

88 See, for example, Simmel 1950: 402–408.

89 When I asked a chief about some past self-help project collections, he said the sums collected were far too little to accomplish the intended goals, and that citizens did not understand this.

90 The phrase comes from a more general discussion of Africa in Staniland (1991: 91).

91 The phrase quoted here is from Ben Blount, to whom I am grateful for the theme developed in this sentence and the two that follow it.

92 See Murphy (1990) for a fine analysis of Mende strategies for creating an appearance of consensus in political discourse, and for concealing "divergent, unsanctioned ideas and practices ... to the 'backstage' domains of social life."

93 As Gal remarks, "the question is not what kinds of rhetorical devices are used in public discourse, but rather what social groups have control of them and how exclusive that control is" (1991: 454).

94 Difficult epistemological problems attend analysis of the subjective, psychological, or unconscious consequences of ritual. As S. F. Moore (1977: 13) puts it, these "consequences may or may not occur at all, may occur in every shade of intensity from an image in the mind, to a slight murmur of the heart, to a profound ecstasis. They may occur in only one or a few participants, may be simulated for myriad reasons, particularly by those specialists responsible for staging and conducting of the ritual."

95 Scott (1986: 30) reserves the term "resistance" for "only those survival strategies which deny or mitigate claims from appropriating classes."

96 Joe Errington phrased the point this way.

97 As Ortner (1984: 157) notes, "major social change does not for the most part come about as an *intended* consequence of action." An analytic framework that effectively links practice or agency to structure must encompass a long-term span of two or three generations (1984: 156). See also Donham's (1990: 52, n.5) distinction between "historical agency" and "epochal agency." The former "involves struggles between groups of various kinds ... that put into question the continuance of inequalities," while "epochal agency" explains how structures are reproduced.

4 MORAL ECONOMY AND WEALTH IN CENTRAL KENYA

1 Barra (1960), proverb number 811.
2 Njururi (1983), proverb number 306.
3 Barra (1960), proverb number 628.
4 Njururi (1983), proverb number 429.
5 Njururi (1983), proverb number 169.

6 See Roseberry (1989: 197–232) on natural economy and oppositional historical models.

7 This point is one Roseberry (1989) makes about oppositional histories in general: "instead of an oppositional model that sees a movement from folk to urban, natural economy to commodity economy, or peasant to proletarian, both poles would be seen as the contradictory products of the creation of the modern world" (1989: 216).

8 Landau (1984: 264) notes that scientific accounts of the story of human evolution "often begin in a state of equilibrium ... where we find the hero leading a relatively safe and untroubled existence, usually in the trees."

9 Again, where I use such labels, I refer to these officially constructed categories, and do not imply "natural," primordial, or monolithic units.

10 My discussion of pre-colonial central Kenya draws substantially on Charles Ambler's (1988) fine oral historical research in the region. His work focused on the nineteenth-century central Kenyan societies now known by the ethnic labels Gikuyu, Embu, Mbeere, Meru, and Kamba.

11 Versions of the story are told in a number of central Kenyan communities. It was, for example, mentioned by Embu people with whom I spoke in Kagaari. See Kenyatta's Gikuyu ethnography (1965: 41–44); Muriuki's history (1974: 137–138); Leakey's ethnography, vol. 3 (1977: 1151); and Ngugi wa Thiong'o's novel *Weep Not, Child* (1964: 25). See also Ambler (1992) for a wider discussion of prophecy in colonial central Kenya.

12 The East African Protectorate became "Kenya" in 1920. Embu District was opened in 1906, and was part of Kenia Province from 1908 to 1920, when boundaries were redefined and the name changed to Kikuyu Province. In 1933, Kikuyu Province (consisting of five African districts (Kiambu, Fort Hall, South Nyeri, Embu, and Meru) and two districts of European settlers (Nairobi and North Nyeri) was merged with Ukamba to form Central Province (see Gregory, Maxon, and Spencer 1969: 9–10). Central Province included territory occupied by the Embu, Mbeere, Meru, Kamba, Ndia, Gikuyu and Gicugu peoples. At the close of the colonial period the district's boundaries were redefined so that the Ndia and Gicugu territory in the west became a separate district (Kirinyagga) that became part of the now primarily Gikuyu Central Province. The redefined Embu District then comprised only the Embu and Mbeere areas, and became part of the ethnically heterogeneous Eastern Province (which includes in addition to the Embu and Mbeere, the homelands of the Kamba, Meru, Chuka, Tharaka, Boran, Rendille, and Gabbra peoples). The Ndia and Gicugu, unlike the Embu and Mbeere, are now usually identified as Gikuyu.

13 See, for example, von Hohnel (1968: 351–361) and Meinertzhagen (1983: 147–152).

14 See the "Introduction" in Vail (1989) on changing explanations of ethnicity and its relationship to nationalism in African studies. See also Ekeh (1990), Kopytoff's "Introduction" to his 1987 edited volume, and the volume edited by Spear and Waller (1993).

15 Ambler (1988: 111–114).

16 See Mwaniki 1974: 149 and Kenyatta 1965: 222–258.

17 Intensified contests over land during the twentieth century enormously com-

plicate historical interpretations of pre-colonial tenure. The "principle of firstcomer authority" is common in African political culture (Kopytoff 1987: 148). See, for example, Murphy and Bledsoe (1987) on semantic and social ambiguities in "firstcomer" and "latecomer" roles in a Kpelle chiefdom in Liberia.

18 This paragraph draws especially on Ambler (1988: 57–65).

19 Ambler (1988: 57). See his work for maps of local and long-distance trade routes through central Kenya.

20 The Kenya Soil Survey (see Braun 1980) classifies this area as "volcanic foot ridges on the dissected lower slopes of major older volcanoes and mountains, with soils developed on Tertiary basic, igneous rocks." Soils in what is now the Embu coffee zone are described as "well drained, extremely deep, dusky red to dark reddish brown, friable clay, with acid humic topsoils," while those in the adjacent lower-altitude cotton zone are also "well drained, extremely deep, dusky red to dark reddish brown, friable clay," but have "inclusions of well-drained, moderately deep, dark red to dark reddish brown, friable clay over rock, piso-ferric or petro-ferric material" (Braun 1980).

21 Ambler (1988: 44). By 1930 there were at least 38,000 people, and by the mid-1960s over 101,000 (1988: 44, n.39).

22 The Rupingazi and Kiye Rivers separate Embu peoples from Ndia and Gicugu groups (now classified as Gikuyu), in what is now Kirinyagga District to the west; the Thuci River separates Embu from the Chuka peoples (a Meru subgroup) to the northeast in what is now Meru District; and the Ena and several other rivers define the boundary between peoples classified as Embu and Mbeere, with the former occupying a separate administrative division of Embu District.

23 On similar "vertical strategies" in mountainous environments elsewhere in the world, see Netting (1976, 1977) on the Swiss Alps, and, on the Andes, see Brush (1977), Guillet (1981), Murra (1970), and Orlove (1977).

24 Mean annual temperatures in what is now the coffee zone in the uplands are 68–72°F (with a mean minimum of 46–52°F); the rainfall-evaporation ratio is 65–80 percent (Braun 1980); and annual rainfall averages 35–50 inches. In what is now the cotton zone in the Embu lowlands mean annual temperatures are 72–75°F (with a mean minimum of more than 57°F); the rainfall-evaporation ratio is 50–65 percent (Braun 1980); and annual rainfall averages 30–40 inches. The length of the growing season for annual plants is 135–154 days in the main coffee zone; 115–134 days in the lower coffee zone; and 85–114 days in the cotton zone (Jaetzold 1982).

25 Ambler (1988: 44, n.42, 118).

26 See, for example, oral text in Mwaniki 1974: 111.

27 See Kenyatta 1965 and Mwaniki 1973a and 1973b.

28 Njururi (1983), proverb number 510.

29 It is not clear whether or under what circumstances the weight given within councils to any single elder's opinions might be influenced by his seniority within a lineage or his status as a tenant, but this was likely to have varied with the matter under discussion (see Middleton and Kershaw 1965: 31–32). In any case, however widespread their fame, as council members, elders operated as one voice among many.

30 Ambler (1988: 116) suggests that households increased production through labor intensification, and that the heaviest burden fell on women. Some scholars believe that both male and female labor was under-utilized at the time (see Kitching 1980: 14–16). Tosh argues against the vent-for-surplus theory as applied to Africa (except in some forest zones). This model assumed that "the slack in the traditional economy means that producers using indigenous technology can grow for the export market while still maintaining domestic production at its accustomed level" (Tosh 1980: 81). Tosh questions the theory's central assumption "that on the eve of the cash-crop revolution the indigenous economies possessed substantial surpluses of both land and labour," and he calls for more attention to labor variations across environments and cropping systems (1980: 91).

31 (Ambler 1988: 101, 115–116). The data limitations Ambler (1988: 115) mentions in this context appear to preclude any immediate answers to a problem upon which McCann (1991: 507–508) remarks: "For East Africa the arrival of hungry Swahili caravans in the mid-nineteenth century or the first European settlement a half century later, despite a lack of empirical research on the volume and demand on local agricultural goods, has been a conventional compass point from which to begin analysis of economic, political, and agricultural change." Ambler (1988: 115) notes that "the development of the (caravan) supply trade beyond the British spheres of influence is not well documented ... Even for the areas immediately surrounding the British stations, it is impossible to estimate the scale of food sales for the external market and difficult to assess their impact on domestic economies."

32 In 1926 and later, some elephants continued to threaten crops in the northeastern portion of upper Embu (Embu Local Native Council minutes, August 25, 1926).

33 Less serious famines were termed *tuwathima*, "the measurer of toughness" (Mwaniki 1974: 101).

34 These examples of famine names and meanings occur in a number of oral history texts collected by Mwaniki (1974: 7, 12–13, 65, 101–102).

35 On such immigration during the colonial era, see, for example, minutes of 1928–9, 1934, and 1943 meetings of the Embu Local Native Council. On earlier times, see Ambler 1988 and Mwaniki 1973a and 1973b.

36 In the Embu uplands, at the 4,900 feet altitude contour, rainfall statistics from 1964 to 1978 suggest that crop failures occur about one year in ten, while very poor yields occur about three years in ten. Rainfall ranged from a fifteen-year low of 29.6 inches in 1975 to a high of 89.4 inches in 1968 in Runyenje's (altitude 4,900 feet). In that location, with a mean rainfall of 52.5 inches between 1964 and 1978, annual totals fell below 40 inches in half of those years, and below 30 inches in two of those years (Ministry of Agriculture, monthly divisional reports and annual district reports, 1964–79).

37 See, for example, Embu Local Native Council minutes of July 20, 1928; January 3, 1929; May 29, 1930; and April 16–17, 1934.

38 On such relations in pre-colonial Gikuyu society, see Clark 1980.

39 Food also acquires a broader metaphorical meaning in politics, as various groups compete for their share of the "national cake" (see, for example, Achebe 1966: 136), or for the "fruits of independence" (*matunda ya Uhuru*).

(See, for example, Ngugi's [1977] scathing critique of the unequal distribution of these "fruits" in post-colonial Kenya.) Post-colonial state legitimacy hinges in part on such matters as the color of maize imported during a national shortage (as well as on the timing and source of the imports). During Kenya's 1980 drought, for example, there was wide popular grumbling about the yellow maize imported from the USA. Many Kenyans, accustomed to eating white maize, saw the yellow maize as an insulting gift from Americans who presumably fed yellow maize only to their livestock.

40 Cf. Feierman's (1990) study of the Shambaa kingdom.

41 See Ambler 1988: 46 and Mwaniki 1973b: 41–49. On internal debates (e.g., between Embu elders and juniors) over whether they should resist the British militarily, see Ambler (1992: 16–18).

42 The Imperial British East Africa Company, given a royal charter in 1888, built a caravan station at Dagoretti in a southern Gikuyu area in 1890, which was destroyed in 1891 (see MacDonald 1897: 111–113). Government stations were established at Fort Smith (now called Kabete, and located in the southern part of central Kenya's Gikuyu area) in 1891, at Meru town (in the district of that name north of Embu) in 1908, and at Chuka (in the southern portion of what became Meru District) in 1913 (see Mungeam 1966). See MacDonald's (1897: 111–126) personal account of early conflicts between Europeans and Gikuyu over Dagoretti and Fort Smith stations.

43 The famine and ecological crisis that struck central Kenya in the 1890s (see Ambler 1988) had political consequences. As Berman and Lonsdale (1992a: 86) note, "collaborative access to British resources was the more attractive for coinciding with the ecological crisis of the 1890s, when cattle plagues, small-pox and drought wiped out up to a quarter of the human population of some areas of central Kenya and set the survivors squabbling over the means of subsistence."

44 In pre-colonial Embu, as noted in chapter 3, elders controlled drinking, and restricted it to men retired from warrior service. See Glazier 1985: 88–89 and Ambler 1991.

45 One of these centers was Gutu's in Ndia (Ambler 1988: 103), a few kilometres from the western boundary of what is now Embu District.

46 This paragraph draws largely on Clough's (1990: 13–15) discussion of his-torians' assessments of the various kinds of individuals the British appointed as chiefs in Kenya and other colonies.

47 In 1910 the Church Missionary Society built a mission at Kigari in what later became Ngandori Location. A Consolata Catholic mission was built in 1923 in Kyeni in eastern Embu, and in 1944 at Kevote in central Embu. Additional Christian sects that arrived later include the Salvation Army, Seventh Day Adventists, African Brotherhood Church, and several Pentecostal churches.

48 See Achebe's (1958) powerful fictional portrayal of these social processes in West Africa: "None of his converts was a man whose word was heeded in the assembly of the people. None of them was a man of title. They were mostly the kind of people that were called *efulefu*, worthless, empty men ... Chielo, the priestess of Agbala, called the converts the excrement of the clan, and the new faith was a mad dog that had come to eat it up" (1958: 101).

49 Embu District Handing Over Report (R. H. Symes-Thompson, H. C. F. Wilks), November 17, 1956: 8. A quarter-century later, I heard a district officer addressing a *baraza* repeat this theme of Embu competition with Central Province as he encouraged people in upper Embu to apply for loans to purchase exotic breeds of cattle.

50 The neighboring Gikuyu peoples lost about 6 percent of their land, much of it pasture, to European settlers (Lonsdale 1992: 355).

51 By the early 1950s African District Councils (ADCs) had replaced Local Native Councils. The former eventually were succeeded by county and municipal councils.

52 Lonsdale (1992: 348) remarks that "the history of their opposition, the resistance to pan-Kikuyu ethnicity among Embu and Meru, has yet to be told."

53 Local trade within and between districts was controlled and government revenues collected through such measures as licensing traders, charging fees of any individual selling in local council markets, prohibiting any trade within a three-mile radius of established council markets (see Embu LNC minutes, December 1953), licensing ox-carts, and fixing rates of ox-cart hire. (In 1945, this was –/29 per mile when leaving the point of origin fully loaded and –/25 per mile returning home empty.) Food exports from a district were particularly carefully controlled (see, for example, 1942 Embu LNC minutes), and in times of drought or famine prohibited entirely. Enforcement of bans on inter-district food exchanges was by no means certain.

54 Embu LNC minutes, July 20, 1928 and January 3, 1929.

55 Embu LNC minutes, July 20, 1928.

56 Embu LNC minutes, May 29, 1930.

57 Embu LNC minutes, April 16–17, 1934.

58 Embu LNC minutes, November 3, 1943.

59 The colonial soil conservation measures were politically disastrous. Until the administration's soil conservation campaigns late in the 1940s destroyed chiefs' legitimacy, Embu politics had been largely loyalist, at least on the surface (Moris 1970: 56–57). Before then, the threat of losing some of their own land to European settlers, as their Gikuyu neighbors had done, must have encouraged loyalist politics in Embu. See Feierman (1990: 181–203) on the intersection of national and local politics during Tanzania's colonial soil conservation campaign.

60 Embu Local Native Council minutes include numerous references to this range of responsibilities.

61 Overseas education bursaries were granted by the Local Native Council and later the African District Council (see, for example, Embu ADC minutes, July 9, 1957).

62 See also Vincent 1982 on colonial chiefs' emergent class interests in Teso, Uganda.

63 Embu LNC minutes contain references to a failure to meet military labor service quotas (October 1941) and to a need for more laborers to pick coffee in the district as output on state-operated farms increased (May, October, 1941). At the November 1, 1926 LNC meeting Chief Kathendu complained that mandatory communal work took up too much time, to which the council

president responded that six days per quarter was a very small proportion of the total year. The British officer termed such labor a necessary evil, saying people were not yet rich enough to pay for all the amenities desired.

64 The February 1926 meeting passed a hut tax of 20 shillings per adult male.

65 Embu LNC minutes, November 1, 1926.

66 This paragraph summarizes arguments made by Berman and Lonsdale (1992c) and Lonsdale and Berman (1979).

67 For example, colonial regulations concerning food crop production included a requirement that each family grow a fraction of an acre of cassava or sweet potatoes as a famine reserve, and that due to erosion problems, only arrow-roots and sweet potatoes but not sugarcane (a popular riverbank crop) be planted next to streams or rivers (Embu LNC minutes, August 1947). As Paul Richards (1982: 60) notes, a number of colonial regimes encouraged planting of famine reserve crops during the 1930s depression: advice local populations often resented and sometimes resisted. In central Kenya during the 1940s the government encouraged farmers to cultivate sweet peppers and European beans to feed soldiers during the Second World War. Officials urged local cultivation of Canadian Wonder and Boston beans as cash crops to supply a vegetable factory in what is now Kirinyagga District (at that time called Ndia and Gicugu) (Embu LNC minutes, May 1942). Such enterprises tended to be abandoned when demand dropped after the war.

68 See Embu LNC minutes of February 1926 and May 1928.

69 See Embu LNC minutes of February 1945, February 1947, and August 1948.

70 See, for example, Embu LNC minutes of November 1, 1926; February 22, 1926; December 19, 1932.

71 The first coffee block in Embu was established at Kithungururu in 1934.

72 These sketches are drawn from two sources: my interviews with Mr. P and others in Embu, and Charles Ambler's interview with Mr. S, who died in 1979. I am grateful to Ambler for sharing notes on his interview with Mr. S.

73 See chapter 5 and references therein.

74 The two assistant chiefs who preceded Mr. P were men from two other clans. (His father had been headman in a different locale.) Assistant chiefs are selected through written examinations and interviews by a panel of govern-ment officers and local politicians. As noted earlier assistant chiefs and chiefs, unlike more senior public servants, must serve in their home areas.

75 Such biographies of course are not a "neutral, transparent window into history" (Comaroff and Comaroff 1992: 26).

76 It is women who are responsible for carrying out the domestic tasks required to conform to these ideals and their capacity to refuse to do so is politically important.

77 Scott (1976: 213), for example, writes of "mutual hostility" and Banfield's "amoral familism" as probable consequences of increasing labor migration, which introduces important external financial links that help to weaken "the nexus of local social pressures and economic imperatives that held the sub-sistence-oriented village together."

78 Barra (1960), proverb no. 811.

79 Njururi (1983), proverb no. 375.

80 Njururi (1983), proverb no. 510.

81 I thank one of the manuscript's anonymous reviewers for suggesting this phrase and theme.
82 Reuters Library Report, February 9, 1994; Agence France Presse, February 11, 1994; and The *Independent*, February 11, 1994; LEXIS, Nexis Library.
83 BBC, February 19, 1994, text of Moi's drought statement on February 17, 1994; LEXIS, Nexis Library.
84 Inter Press Service, February 9, 1994; LEXIS, Nexis Library.
85 Inter Press Service, February 23, 1994; LEXIS, Nexis Library.

5 THE DOVE AND THE CASTOR NUT

1 This is a theme Ferguson (1992) explores in Zambian images of town and countryside.
2 Cf. Sahlins (1972: 74) on random deviations from "subsistence" production levels that arise in part because the family labor force is normally small, and variation in the size and composition of households itself leaves some susceptible to "disastrous mischance."
3 He calls for analysis of such random oscillations together with other patterns of mobility such as cumulation of economic advantages and disadvantages, cyclical mobility associated with the family life cycle, and levelling mechanisms.
4 *Kaariki kamwe ni karaarariirie ndutura.*
5 Nine percent of this study's 82 sample households (see below) in the early 1980s operated small businesses such as butcheries, tea "hotels," and retail shops. Over 25 percent of the households included at least one full-time salaried employee. Most of those who were employed within the district (fourteen individuals) were in the services sector; nine of these were teachers. Among fourteen individuals working outside Embu District were one teacher, two military or paramilitary employees, one preacher, one policeman, one administrative policeman, one cook, one automobile mechanic, one hospital worker, one dock-worker, two hotel workers, and two coffee factory workers.
6 Cf. Scott (1985: 197): among villagers, "what is demanded, ironically, is patronage that is not patronizing."
7 Cf. Scott 1985: 132–137.
8 By the early 1990s more rural people in upper Embu could walk a kilometre or so to recently-installed piped water.
9 The number of people classified as "Embu" more than tripled from 1918 to the late 1970s. In 1918 the Embu District Commissioner (R. G. Stone) estimated the Embu population at 53,000 and the Mbeere at 31,550 (Mwaniki 1973a: 2, 7). The 1962 national census puts the Embu population at 95,647 (with 6.6 percent of those enumerated outside of Embu District), and that of the Mbeere at 38,172 (with 3.4 percent outside the district). By 1979 the Embu numbered 180,400 (with 8.8 percent outside the district), and the Mbeere 61,725 (with 7.0 percent outside the district) (Kenyan government 1979).
10 Recall that Kenya's administrative hierarchy (from most to least inclusive) is province, district, division, location, and sublocation.
11 Saberwal (1970: 4–5) summarizes Embu terms to designate residential and descent groups as follows: "*Mucii* (pl. *micii*) referred to a house or homestead

including its patrilineal core ... *Nyomba* (sing. and pl.) had a much wider range of meanings. It referred to a woman's hut within the homestead. It also indicated one wife's sons and their descendants as against another wife's; but when fission came to a homestead, it was individual sons who founded new homesteads and not a group of full brothers ... The term (*nyomba*) also denoted a still larger group, a maximal lineage or a sub-clan depending on one informant's ability to show his link with his apical ancestor ... *Muviriga* (pl. *miviriga*) means a door or entrance to a homestead. It also refers to a descent group of any size, with members living in more than one homestead: the people who come out of the door of one homestead. Next, it denotes a group of elders assembled in a moot ... *muviriga* may mean a moiety, a clan, a sub-clan, or an elders' council gathered to hear a family dispute."

12 The household here includes those individuals who occupy and manage a given farm parcel and who share production and consumption activities associated with that and sometimes additional parcels. Fluctuations in household membership were tracked over twenty months (from June 1979 until February 1981). I discuss these below. To take this instability into account, figures on household composition used in statistical analyses represent the membership structure that prevailed during most of the fifteen months between June 1979 and September 1980, when the bulk of the economic survey research was carried out. (A follow-up survey was done in 1986, and informal interviews in the mid- and late-1980s and early 1990s.) In the case of a death of a household member, for example, the deceased individual is counted as a member unless he or she died before January 1980, the approximate mid-point of the surveys monitoring economic activities.

The mean number of full-time adult residents per sample household is 3.6; part-time adult residents 1.1; full-time child residents (15 years of age and younger) 4.1; and part-time child residents 0.2. Part-time child residents include, for example, boarding school students or children who stay with a relative one-quarter of the year or more. Part-time adult residents include household heads employed outside the district or within the district but beyond commuting distance of the homestead; boarding school students who spend three months of the year at home during the three school holiday periods; and temporarily employed sons or daughters with some housing in town who spend weekends at home. Not included among part-time residents are employed sons or daughters who come home infrequently (usually less than two weeks annually) and who do not have a spouse resident in the sample household.

13 In age structure, for example, 19.3 percent of the district population and 19.7 percent of the study population are 0 to 4 years of age in 1979. For other age categories, the district and study population figures respectively are: 17 percent and 15.1 percent (5–9 years); 14.4 percent and 12.0 percent (10–14 years); 11.6 and 12.6 percent (15–19 years); 22.5 percent and 23.2 percent (20–39 years); and 15.3 percent and 17.2 percent (40+ years). District figures are from the 1979 Kenya Population Census.

The 1979 sex ratio is 96.8 in the study sample, 96.8 in the two sample sublocations, 94.5 in Runyenje's Division, and 94.5 in Embu District. Once the sample is broken down into coffee and cotton zones, the discrepancy between sample sex ratios and those of the population increases. The sex ratio for the coffee zone sample is 84.0, while that of the entire sublocation (coffee zone) is 91.3. The comparable figures for the cotton zone are 111.4 for the study sample, and 102.2 in the sublocation population. Non-sample figures again are computed from the 1979 Kenya Population Census.

14 The sampling frame was title deeds listed in the land registry. See previous footnote on sample representativeness.

15 Individuals who cannot afford to purchase land sometimes acquire it through inheritance, or they may acquire temporary use rights from others.

16 The educational profile of adults in the sample of 82 households is as follows. Among the 286 individuals who had completed their education, only 2 individuals (both male) had a university education in 1980. The next best-educated are 21 individuals (13 males and 8 females) who had finished four years of secondary school (form four). Those who had completed seven or eight years of primary school included 29 males and 15 females. Adults with no formal education included 27 males and 76 females.

17 The difference between agricultural and non-agricultural incomes is substantial. In the study sample the average annual salary of employed individuals (most of whom work in the services sector as clerks, teachers, etc.) is five times the average coffee income earned from 350 mature trees, which is the sample mean.

18 Among sample households, land holdings range from less than one acre to 150 acres (or 0.5 hectare to 61 hectares). The distribution is skewed, with a mean of 13 acres (5 hectares) and a median of eight acres (3 hectares). Just one household owns over 100 acres of land, and two others own between 50 and 100 acres (20–40 hectares). In the study sample, there is neither a linear nor a non-linear relationship between land acreage and household size. Pearson's *rho* is 0.03 and is not statistically significant. A test of linearity indicates no non-linear relationship between the two variables either.

In addition, there is no statistically significant relationship between wealth (a score that excludes land) and household size, or between wealth and dependency ratio (ratio of consumers to producers in a household).

19 Coffee zone households sampled own a mean of 356 mature trees (minimum = 30 and maximum = 1,200; standard deviation = 240). Cotton zone residents own a mean of 137 mature trees (range = 0 to 800; standard deviation = 201).

20 The mean number of "native" cattle over one year old owned by sample households is 3.5 (range = 0 to 21). In addition, a few households own exotic cattle breeds such as Jerseys or Guernseys, or crossbreeds.

21 For sample education profile, see note 16 above.

22 Problems with the reliability of such statistics are taken up below.

23 On the well-known difficulties of determining minimum subsistence requirements, see Orans 1966 and Pearson 1957.

24 For example, in the 1979 short rains season, many Embu farmers who increased the area allotted to beans specifically mentioned favorable prices (11 households), particularly in comparison to maize (4 households), as their reason for doing so. At that time, the producer price of beans had risen to 200 shillings per bag, coffee payouts were unreliable, and cultivation of beans was

a good way to earn a fairly quick cash return. Official maize prices were then about one-half to one-third the price obtainable for beans.

25 As a group, sample cotton zone residents devote less than 4 percent of their total acreage in that zone to cotton. Here as elsewhere in Africa, cotton is a labor-intensive crop with poor cash returns: "The statistical correlation between cotton growing and poverty is startling" (Zimmerman 1972: 326, quoted in Vincent 1982: 189).

26 The seasons covered range from abundant rainfall (1978 short rains), to somewhat below-normal rainfall (1979 long rains), to drought (1979 short rains), to moderate rainfall (1980 long rains). The year 1978 was one of record-high rainfall, averaging 70.8 inches at the 4,900 feet altitude contour (or 1,798 millimetres at an altitude of 1490 metres) in the study area, as compared to a sixteen-year average of 52.5 inches (1,334 millimetres) (Embu District Annual Reports).

27 This analysis is based on sample households' own stated consumption requirements, which are not standardized to the same level across all households. Mean preferred per capita consumption levels of maize and beans calculated from Embu households' stated consumption requirements yield figures of approximately 265 pounds (or 120 kilograms) of maize and 132 pounds (or 60 kilograms) of beans per consumer equivalent per year. These are nutritionally reasonable figures for such a population (see Latham 1981). Deviations from mean consumption levels, of course, occur as poorer households that produce food deficits substitute other foods such as bananas, sweet potatoes, and cassava for maize and beans; and wealthy households consume more wheat, meat, and rice as purchased substitutes. (These points also are covered in Haugerud 1988.)

28 Sixteen percent of the 82 sample households were polygynous in 1980.

29 Sample households include members of from one to four different generations, with 43 percent consisting of two generations and 45 percent of three generations. About half of the two-generation households are nuclear or elemental families consisting of only a husband, one wife, and their unmarried children.

30 A divorced woman and her children who occupy and farm a portion of her brother's land may do so as fully participating members of the brother's household or as a separate matrifocal segment of that household (both of which occur in household 41). An estranged co-wife may (as in household 5) occupy her husband's land, but live in a separate compound and cultivate and consume the products of a portion of his farm independently of him and his other wife. The degree and forms of separation or integration of such household segments shift frequently as interpersonal relations and conflicts alter the extent of economic cooperation practicable among household members at different times and for varying purposes.

31 Nearly one-quarter of the sample households include a separated, divorced, or never-married daughter's children; of these households, nearly two-thirds (17 percent of the total sample) include children of daughters who have not married and the remaining third are children of divorced or separated daughters who have left their husbands' homes. These children tend to fall under the care of their grandmothers when their mothers are employed or when they

remarry and leave children behind. Strangers are likely to be told that such a child's grandmother is its mother.

32 Six of the eighty-two sample households are headed by widows without resident married sons, and another seventeen by married sons with a widowed mother resident.

33 What determines which families and households are riven by conflict and which are peaceable is as likely to be the product of the social structural position of individuals as of psychological or personality differences that affect the way individuals respond to what S. F. Moore (1975: 128) terms "structurally loaded positions."

34 See, for example, Hart 1982, Tully 1984; on Kenya, see Moock 1978.

35 *Aka airi ni nyungu ciiri cia urogi.*

36 The term *nyomba*, as noted earlier, refers to one wife's sons and their descendants, to a woman's house within a homestead, and sometimes to a larger patrilineage with a demonstrated link to the apical ancestor (see Saberwal 1970). The term *nyomba* also is sometimes used interchangeably with clan or *muviriga*. Because when a homestead splits it is individual sons and not groups of brothers who found new homesteads, the *nyomba* tends not to persist as a residence group once a woman's sons begin to marry. Even after they have established separate homesteads elsewhere, however, the *nyomba* remains an important category in which one man's sons are bound together by obligations to one another's children and wives, as well as by their common interest in their father's heritable wealth (principally land and livestock).

37 This assistant was a very able student in her final year of secondary school (form six), who later completed a degree at Kenyatta University. Her home was in the western part of the district, she worked with me for about one year, and she was on excellent terms with about twenty survey families we visited repeatedly for interviews.

38 See Lonsdale's (1986: 142) discussion of the political significance of Kenyatta's words.

39 Material in this and the following paragraphs on pre-reform land tenure and moves toward privatization is drawn partly from Haugerud (1989a: 74–75).

40 In such transactions, rights to trees were negotiated separately and might require extra payment (see also Glazier 1985: 196–198; Kenyatta 1965).

41 See Sorrenson (1967: 56–61), Coldham (1978b: 95), Fleuret (1988), and Shipton (1988).

42 Official processes of land adjudication and issuing individual title deeds were undertaken first in central Kenya during the 1950s, and since have been extended to other parts of the nation. In the late 1980s they were still underway in places such as Taita (see Fleuret 1988).

43 Both letters are from File 86, Embu North Land Control Board, January 1979. The second letter I also quote in Haugerud (1989a).

44 For further discussion of such conflict see Haugerud (1989a: 80–81).

45 The following discussion of characteristics of food "surplus" producers is summarized in Haugerud 1989b.

46 In the study sample, 12 of the 82 households produced maize or beans or both in excess of consumption requirements in at least 6 of the 8 crop seasons monitored (here counting 4 rainfall seasons × two crops – maize and beans –

each season). Another 56 occasionally produced surpluses (in at least 1 and fewer than 6 of the 8 crop seasons monitored). And 14 did not produce crop surpluses in any of the 8 seasons monitored.

47 Such collective labor arrangements include both work parties organized by principles of generalized reciprocity (Sahlins 1972), and, less common, those whose membership and reciprocity are more regularized. The latter (*rutua*) consist of anywhere from two to six or more members (women in the cases I encountered). Work parties whose participants do not practice precise reciprocity (often termed *irima*, from *kurima*, "to cultivate") may work on crops destined for both home consumption and market. Such work parties are organized as well for non-crop tasks such as applying mud to a new house, grinding gruel for a special occasion, or constructing a cattle enclosure. A work party host prepares foods such as beer, tea, gruel, and *githere* (staple maize and beans dish) for guests, and sometimes the latter also contribute such items. Wealthier households are expected to better feed their guests than are poorer ones. About one-third of the recorded occasions on which sample households provided others cooperative labor between August 1979 and March 1980 were to assist kin and two-thirds to assist non-kin. (See W. Allan 1965, Erasmus 1956, and M. P. Moore 1975 on cooperative labor institutions in Africa.)

48 This relationship, however, is not significant at the 0.05 level or better (see table 6A).

49 As the table shows, for cooperative labor *received*, $p = 0.01$ and 0.05; but p is greater than 0.05 in the case of cooperative labor given. See also Donham (1981), who found a net transfer of cooperative labor from poorer to wealthier households in an Ethiopian market village.

50 The correlation between hired labor expenditure and use of cooperative labor is positive and significant ($p = 0.05$), while that between hired labor expenditure and cooperative labor contributed to other households is negative and significant ($p = 0.02$). Cooperative labor use and land ownership are positively related, and cooperative labor use and household dependency ratio are unrelated (see table 7).

51 The phrasing is James Dow's (1977), quoted in Wolf (1986: 327).

52 Cf. Parkin's (1978) fine study of political culture and language among Luo in Nairobi.

53 In addition, disagreements about the direction and scale of differentiation processes are connected to contradictory assumptions about the political roles and "revolutionary potential" of peasants, workers, or peasant/worker alliances.

54 These are summarized by Harriss (1982b: 37–49).

55 Consequences must be kept separate from intentions of course. Individuals may diversify with the intention of stabilizing subsistence, or of accumulating more wealth. But there is no necessary correspondence between intention and outcome.

56 See Scott (1985: 244): "The very complexity of the class structure in Sedaka militates against collective opinion and, hence, collective action on most issues."

57 The phrase is from Tilly (1984: 76).

58 An example is a situation of land scarcity in which a smallholder "might not do quite so well as a large-scale tenant in a given season, [but] his claim to the product of the land he holds is far stronger and therefore his subsistence is generally more secure." Likewise, social distinctions *within* categories such as tenant and wage laborer were "largely predicated on the security of tenure or work and the degree of social insurance the owner or employer customarily gave" (Scott 1976: 36, 38).

59 Excellent overviews include Chege (1987) and Kitching (1985).

60 The contribution of Cowen's earlier work, as Kitching (1985: 137) aptly summarizes it is as follows: "The whole thrust of this work, on precolonial patterns of accumulation, on the role of the *athomi* or *asomi* (literate individuals) in land accumulation and consolidation and in agricultural commodity production in the pre-Swynnerton period (with its central focus on the straddling process), radically undermined earlier conceptions of the Kikuyu peasantry as a uniformly impoverished mass of subsistence farmers forcibly subordinated to settler labor demands."

61 See Kitching (1985: 135–136) on contrasting political implications of positions that emphasize or downplay the scale of differentiation of the Kenyan peasantry. See the 1981 special issue of *Review of African Political Economy* (no. 20), on "The Peasant Question in Kenya," which includes articles by Mukaru Ng'ang'a, P. Anyang' Nyongo, Apollo Njonjo, S. B. O. Gutto, Michael Cowen, Michael Chege, and John Mulaa. See also Kaplinsky 1980, Langdon 1977, and Swainson 1980. Little (1992) and Ensminger (1992) are recent examples of studies that explore issues of differentiation and diversification processes among Kenyan pastoralists.

62 Higher densities (over 1,500 persons per square mile, or 575 per square kilometre) were recorded over fifteen years earlier in the southern Gikuyu district of Kiambu, and in North Nyanza District in western Kenya (Kenyan government 1962).

63 For the statistics, see note 16 in chapter 1.

64 Since the mid-1970s Kenya's annual agricultural growth rates have fluctuated, but on average have fallen below the population growth rate.

65 Future growth strategies emphasized by the World Bank and other donors focus on improved yields among small-scale farmers. Official statistics show that yield increases historically have contributed little to Kenya's agricultural growth. In Kenya, as elsewhere, the Bank's current emphasis is on increasing the role of the private sector in agriculture, and improving technology, rural infrastructure, and agricultural education.

66 "0.1 percent of farm holdings (2,227 large farms and plantations) contain 14 percent of the arable land area (800,000 ha.), 2.4 percent of farm holdings (including 40,000 gap farmers) contain 32 percent of arable land area" (Livingstone 1981: 12.25, quoted in Hunt 1984: 252). About 80 percent of the country's 2.7 million smallest farms (under 31 acres or 12.5 hectares) are under 5 acres (or 2 hectares) in size. Farms of under 50 acres (or 20 hectares) in size account for about two-thirds of the arable land (omitting exclusively pastoral and ranching areas) (Greene 1983: 338).

67 In the late 1980s agriculture contributed nearly 30 percent of GDP and 66 percent of export earnings (World Bank 1990: 9–10). Smallholders (holdings

under 31 acres or 12.5 hectares) dominate production: "smallholders account for about 75 percent of the value of agricultural output (including livestock), 55 percent of marketed output, about 80 percent of utilized arable land (excluding pastoral and ranch areas), and over 85 percent of agricultural employment" (World Bank 1990).

68 See Berman and Lonsdale (1992c) on how, in the first two decades of this century, differentiation among Kenya's African farmers both grew out of and shaped the productive expansion of settler capitalism.

69 Scholars of Kenya again have advanced contradictory arguments on whether proletarianization may be proceeding faster in other parts of Kenya, and if so, whether this is due to more or less commercialization than one finds in central Kenya (compare Njonjo 1981 and Cowen 1981, 1982).

70 See chapter 4 above, and Haugerud 1983 and 1989a.

71 With farm size shrinking for many people, the importance of off-farm incomes grew. Increasing output and income per unit of land presumably also became advantageous, though there is little official statistical evidence to suggest that higher yields have significantly raised Kenya's overall agricultural output. Instead increased output has come from expansion of cultivated area in new zones.

72 Among land purchasers in the Embu study sample who owned more than 15 acres (or approximately 6 hectares) in the early 1980s, one had seven separate parcels, another had six, another had four, two had three, one had two, and none had a holding consolidated into a single large parcel (see Haugerud 1989a: 77–78).

73 In both instances, chi-square is significant at the 0.001 level. The gamma correlation coefficient is 0.83 for land acreage owned and ownership of some purchased land, and 0.66 for the relationship between wealth rank and owner- ship of some purchased land. (These figures are for the early 1980s.)

74 This paragraph draws on Haugerud (1989a).

75 This sentence and all but the last in the rest of the paragraph are drawn from Haugerud (1989b).

76 The conceptualization and phrasing in this and the previous three sentences are drawn from remarks Sara Berry offered in a seminar discussion of this chapter at Johns Hopkins University. I am grateful to her, and to Gillian Feeley-Harnik, Elizabeth Sheehan, Michel-Rolph Trouillot and other seminar participants for helping to clarify some of these issues.

77 Berry (1993: 180) also states that agricultural employment in Kenya "has been ... more differentiated along lines of gender and class" than it has in cocoa economies of southern Nigeria and Ghana.

78 Again, thanks to one of the manuscript's anonymous reviewers for this notion.

6 CONCLUSIONS

1 Von Hohnel 1968 (1894): 310–311.

2 Indeed the Moi regime's political and fiscal crisis was worsened by coincident drought and food shortages in the early 1990s (see chapter 4). As I suggested in chapter 2, however, I do not propose a reductively "economistic" explanation of Kenya's early 1990s political upheavals.

3 *Utonga ni kigunyi.* Gikuyu proverb no. 952 in Barra (1960).

4 The term "bubble millionaire" occurs in Nairobi's *Finance* magazine (July 31, 1992: 16).

5 See Haugerud 1989a, 1983, and chapter 5 above.

6 See Africa Watch 1991: chapter 14, "Kenya's Land Crisis."

7 The phrase comes from Thucydides, *The History of the Peloponnesian War (431–413 BC)*, bk. I. sec. 1.

8 See, for example, a front-page headline in the *New York Times*, "Somali Warlord Agrees to Allow UN to Protect Its Relief Supplies," August 13, 1992; and in the same paper, August 18, 1992 (in an editorial titled "Finally, Help for Somalia"), a reference to "Somalia's capricious warlords," and to "a senseless clan war" and drought as the causes of the present "disaster."

9 The latter phrase is from Roseberry (1989: 223).

10 Early 1990s opposition political cultures were elaborated as well through institutions such as the church and professional law society.

11 Murray Edelman (1988: 10) makes the general point: "Affirmations bring to consciousness evidence for the contrary position, which the affirmations try to blunt, a form of inversion and self deception that is especially pervasive in political language."

12 On the Constitution as perceived obstacle, see Githu 1992.

13 This paragraph is drawn from Haugerud (1989b).

14 He adds that many regimes also have "neglected the peasants on whose labours they depend" (Lonsdale 1986: 155).

15 The April 1992 manifesto of one opposition group (FORD) "only broaches the idea of discussing land ceilings, productivity requirements, and distributing the land of some state farms to the tillers of those farms. There is also no reference to appropriate government emphases between the largeholder and smallholder sectors" (Holmquist and Ford 1992: 17).

16 Holmquist and Ford (1992: 17).

Bibliography

BOOKS AND ARTICLES

Abdulaziz, M. H. 1979. *Muyaka*. Nairobi: Kenya Literature Bureau.
Abrams, Philip. 1982. *Historical Sociology*. Ithaca: Cornell University Press.
Abu-Lughod, Lila. 1990. "The Romance of Resistance: Tracing Transformations of Power Through Bedouin Women." *American Ethnologist* 17(1): 41–55.
Abwunza, Judith M. 1990. "*Nyayo*: Cultural Contradictions in Kenya Rural Capitalism." *Anthropologica* 32: 183–203.
Achebe, Chinua. 1958. *Things Fall Apart*. London: Heinemann.
   1966. *A Man of the People*. New York: Anchor Books/Doubleday.
   1987. *Anthills of the Savannah*. New York: Anchor Books/Doubleday.
Africa Watch. 1991. *Kenya: Taking Liberties*. New York and Washington, DC: Africa Watch.
   1993. *Divide and Rule: State-Sponsored Ethnic Violence in Kenya*. New York and Washington DC: Africa Watch.
Allan, William. 1965. *The African Husbandman*. London and Edinburgh: Oliver and Boyd.
Ambler, Charles H. 1988. *Kenyan Communities in the Age of Imperialism: The Central Region in the Late Nineteenth Century*. New Haven and London: Yale University Press.
   1991. "Drunks, Brewers, and Chiefs: Alcohol Regulation in Colonial Kenya, 1900–1939." In *Drinking: Behavior and Belief in Modern History*, Susanna Barrows and Robin Room (eds.), pp. 165–183. Berkeley and Los Angeles: University of California Press.
   1992. "'What the World is Going to Come to': The Prophetic Tradition in Colonial Central Kenya." Manuscript (34 pp.).
Amin, Samir. 1994. "Africa: Beyond Crisis and Adjustment." *CODESRIA Bulletin* no. 1: 5–8.
Anderson, Benedict. 1991 (1983). *Imagined Communities: Reflections on the Origin and Spread of Nationalism*. London and New York: Verso.
An-Na'im, A. A. and Deng, Francis (eds.). 1990. *Human Rights in Africa: Cross-Cultural Perspectives*. Washington DC: The Brookings Institution.
Anyang' Nyong'o, P. 1981a. "What 'The Friends of the Peasants' are and How They Pose the Question of the Peasantry." *Review of African Political Economy* 20: 17–26.
   1981b. "The Development of a Middle Peasantry in Nyanza." *Review of African Political Economy* 20: 108–120.

Appadurai, Arjun. 1986. "Theory in Anthropology: Center and Periphery." *Comparative Studies in Society and History* 28(2): 356–361.

1991. "Global Ethnoscapes: Notes and Queries for a Transnational Anthropology." In *Recapturing Anthropology: Working in the Present*, Richard G. Fox (ed.), pp. 191–210. Santa Fe: School of American Research Press.

Appadurai, Arjun and Breckenridge, Carol A. 1988. "Why Public Culture?" *Public Culture* 1(1): 5–9.

Appiah, Kwame Anthony. 1992. *In My Father's House: Africa in the Philosophy of Culture*. Oxford: Oxford University Press.

Asante, Molefi Kete. 1987. *The Afrocentric Idea*. Philadelphia: Temple University Press.

Atieno-Odhiambo, E. S. 1987. "Democracy and the Ideology of Order in Kenya." In *The Political Economy of Kenya*, Michael Schatzberg (ed.), pp. 172–202. New York: Praeger.

Bailey, F. G. 1981. "Dimensions of Rhetoric in Conditions of Uncertainty." In *Politically Speaking: Cross-Cultural Studies of Rhetoric*, Robert Paine (ed.), pp. 25–38. Philadelphia: Institute for the Study of Human Issues.

1991. *The Prevalence of Deceit*. Ithaca and London: Cornell University Press.

Barber, Karin. 1987. "Popular Arts in Africa." *African Studies Review* 30(3): 1–78.

Barkan, Joel. 1984. "Legislators, Elections, and Political Linkage." In *Politics and Public Policy in Kenya and Tanzania*, Joel Barkan and John J. Okumu (eds.), pp. 71–101. New York: Praeger.

1987. "The Electoral Process and Peasant-State Relations in Kenya." In *Elections in Independent Africa*, Fred M. Hayward (ed.), pp. 213–237. Boulder and London: Westview.

1991. "The Rise and Fall of a Governance Realm in Kenya." In *Governance and Politics in Africa*, Goran Hyden and Michael Bratton (eds.), pp. 167–192. Boulder and London: Lynne Rienner.

1993. "Kenya: Lessons From a Flawed Election." *Journal of Democracy* 4(3): 85–99.

Barkan, Joel and Chege, Michael. 1989. "Decentralising the State: District Focus and the Politics of Reallocation in Kenya." *The Journal of Modern African Studies* 27(3): 431–453.

Barkan, Joel and Holmquist, Frank 1989. "Peasant-State Relations and the Social Base of Self-Help in Kenya." *World Politics* 41(3): 359–380.

Barra, G. (ed.) 1960 (1939). *1,000 Kikuyu Proverbs*. Nairobi: Kenya Literature Bureau.

Barth, Fredrik. 1959. *Political Leadership Among Swat Pathans*. London: Athlone.

Bates, Robert. 1989. *Beyond the Miracle of the Market: The Political Economy of Agrarian Development in Kenya*. Cambridge and New York: Cambridge University Press.

Bayart, Jean-François. 1992. "Introduction." In *Le politique par le bas en Afrique noire. Contributions à une problematique de la démocratie*, Jean-François Bayart, Achille Mbembe, and C. Toulabor (eds.), pp. 9–32. Paris: Karthala.

1993. *The State in Africa: The Politics of the Belly*. London and New York:

Longman. (First published in French as *L'Etat en Afrique: La politique du ventre*, 1989, Librairie Arthème Fayard.)

Beeman, William O. 1993. "The Anthropology of Theater and Spectacle." *Annual Review of Anthropology* 22: 369–393.

Beinart, William and Bundy, Colin. 1987. *Hidden Struggles in Rural South Africa.* London: James Currey. Berkeley and Los Angeles: University of California Press. Johannesburg: Ravan Press.

Berman, Bruce and Lonsdale, John. 1992a. "Introduction: An Encounter in Unhappy Valley." In *Unhappy Valley: Conflict in Kenya and Africa, Book One: State and Class*, Bruce Berman and John Lonsdale (eds.), pp. 1–10. London: James Currey.

1992b. *Unhappy Valley: Conflict in Kenya and Africa, Book Two: Violence and Ethnicity.* London: James Currey.

1992c. "Coping with the Contradictions: The Development of the Colonial State, 1895–1914." In *Unhappy Valley: Conflict in Kenya and Africa, Book 1: State and Class*, Bruce Berman and John Lonsdale (eds.), pp. 77–100. London: James Currey.

Berry, Sara. 1983. "Agrarian Crisis in Africa? A Review and Interpretation." Paper prepared for the Joint African Studies Committee of the Social Science Research Council and the American Council of Learned Societies, presented at annual meetings of the African Studies Association, Boston, December 1983.

1985. *Fathers Work For Their Sons: Accumulation, Mobility, and Class Formation in an Extended Yoruba Community.* Berkeley and Los Angeles: University of California Press.

1988. "Concentration Without Privatization? Some Consequences of Changing Patterns of Rural Land Control in Africa." In *Land and Society in Contemporary Africa*, R. E. Downs and S. P. Reyna (eds.), pp. 53–75. Hanover and London: University Press of New England.

1993. *No Condition is Permanent: The Social Dynamics of Agrarian Change in Africa.* Madison: University of Wisconsin Press.

Besnier, Niko. 1989. "Information Withholding as a Manipulative and Collusive Strategy in Nukulaelae Gossip." *Language and Society* 18: 315–341.

1990. "Language and Affect." *Annual Review of Anthropology* 19: 419–451. Bernard J. Siegel (ed.). Palo Alto: Annual Reviews Inc.

Biersteker, Ann and Njogu, Kimani. 1991. "Multilingualism in Kenya." In *International Perspectives on Foreign Language Teaching*, Gerald L. Ervin (ed.), pp. 63–74. Lincolnwood: American Council of Teachers of Foreign Languages.

Bledsoe, C. 1980. *Women and Marriage in Kpelle Society.* Palo Alto: Stanford University Press.

Bloch, Maurice (ed.). 1975. *Political Language and Oratory in Traditional Society.* London and New York: Academic Press.

Bourdieu, Pierre. 1977. *Outline of a Theory of Practice.* London and New York: Cambridge University Press.

Bratton, Michael and Van de Walle, Nicolas. 1991. "Toward Governance in Africa: Popular Demands and State Responses." In *Governance and Politics in Africa*, Goran Hyden and Michael Bratton (eds.), pp. 27–55. Boulder and London: Lynne Rienner.

Braun, H. M. W. 1980. *Kenya Soil Survey.* Nairobi: Ministry of Agriculture.

Brenneis, Donald L. 1987. "Talk and Transformation." *Man* 22: 499–510.

1988. "Language and Disputing." *Annual Review of Anthropology* 17: 221–237. Bernard J. Siegel (ed.). Palo Alto, California: Annual Reviews Inc.

1990. "Shared and Solitary Sentiments: The Discourse of Friendship, Play, and Anger in Bhatgaon." In *Language and the Politics of Emotion*, Catherine A. Lutz and Lila Abu-Lughod (eds.), pp. 113–125. Cambridge University Press.

Brenneis, Donald L. and Myers, Fred R. (eds.). 1984. *Dangerous Words: Language and Politics in the Pacific*. New York and London: New York University Press.

Brett, E. A. 1973. *Colonialism and Underdevelopment in East Africa: The Politics of Economic Change, 1919–1939*. London: Heinemann Educational Books.

Brokensha, David and Glazier, Jack. 1973. "Land Reform Among the Mbeere of Central Kenya." *Africa* 43(3): 182–206.

Brokensha, David and Nellis, John. 1974. "Administration in Kenya – A Study of the Rural Division of Mbere." *Journal of Administration Overseas* 13(3): 510–523.

Brokensha, David and Riley, Bernard W. 1980. "Introduction of Cash Crops in a Marginal Area of Kenya." In *Agricultural Development in Africa: Issues of Public Policy*, R. H. Bates and M. Lofchie (eds.), pp. 244–274. New York: Praeger.

1988. *The Mbeere in Kenya*. Lanham: University Press of America.

Brown, Penelope and Levinson, Steven. 1978. "Universals in Language Usage: Politeness Phenomena." In *Questions and Politeness: Strategies in Social Interaction*, Esther N. Goody (ed.), pp. 56–89. Cambridge: Cambridge University Press.

Brush, Stephen. 1977. *Mountain, Field, and Family: The Economy and Human Ecology of an Andean Valley*. Philadelphia: University of Pennsylvania Press.

Bujra, Janet M. 1973. "The Dynamics of Political Action: A New Look at Factionalism." *American Anthropologist* 75(1): 132–152.

Burke, Kenneth. 1966. *Language as Symbolic Action*. Berkeley and Los Angeles: University of California Press.

Chabal, Patrick. 1986. "Introduction: Thinking about Politics in Africa." In *Political Domination in Africa*, Patrick Chabal (ed.), pp. 1–16. Cambridge: Cambridge University Press.

Chayanov, A. V. 1966. *The Theory of Peasant Economy*. D. Thorner, B. Kerblay, and B. Smith (eds.). Homewood, Illinois: Irwin.

Chazan, Naomi, Mortimer, Robert, Ravenhill, John, and Rothchild, Donald. 1992. *Politics and Society in Contemporary Africa*. Boulder, Colorado: Lynne Rienner.

Chege, Michael. 1981. "Electoral Politics in Mathare and Dagoretti." *Review of African Political Economy* 20: 74–88.

1987. "The Political Economy of Agrarian Change in Kenya." In *The Political Economy of Kenya*, Michael G. Schatzberg (ed.), pp. 93–116. New York: Praeger.

Clark, Carolyn. 1980. "Land and Food, Women and Power, in Nineteenth Century Kikuyu." *Africa* 50(4): 357–370.

Clough, Marshall. 1990. *Fighting Two Sides: Kenyan Chiefs and Politicians, 1918–1940*. Niwot, Colorado: University Press of Colorado.

Cohen, Abner. 1974. *Two-Dimensional Man: An Essay on the Anthropology of*

Power and Symbolism in Complex Society. Berkeley and Los Angeles: University of California Press.

Cohen, D. W. 1983. "Food Production and Food Exchange in the Precolonial Lakes Plateau Region." In *Imperialism, Colonialism, and Hunger: East and Central Africa,* Robert I. Rotberg (ed.), pp. 1–18. Lexington and Toronto: Lexington Books.

Cohen, D. W. and Atieno-Odhiambo, E. S. 1989. *Siaya: The Historical Anthropology of an African Landscape.* London: James Currey. Athens: Ohio University Press.

Cohen, Ronald. 1988. "Introduction: Guidance and Misguidance in Africa's Food Production." In *Satisfying Africa's Food Needs: Food Production and Commercialization in African Agriculture,* Ronald Cohen (ed.), pp. 1–30. Boulder and London: Lynne Rienner.

1991. "Endless Teardrops: Prolegomena to the Study of Human Rights in Africa." Manuscript.

Coldham, Simon F. R. 1978a. "Land Control in Kenya." *Journal of African Law* 22(1): 63–77.

1978b. "The Effect of Registration of Title upon Customary Land Rights in Kenya." *Journal of African Law* 22(2): 91–111.

Collier, Paul and Lal, Deepak. 1980. *Poverty and Growth in Kenya.* Washington DC: World Bank Staff Working Paper, no. 389.

Comaroff, Jean and Comaroff, John. 1991. *Of Revelation and Revolution: Christianity, Colonialism, and Consciousness in South Africa,* vol. I. Chicago and London: University of Chicago Press.

1992. *Ethnography and the Historical Imagination.* Boulder, Colorado: Westview Press.

Cooper, Frederick. 1988. "Mau Mau and the Discourses of Decolonization." *Journal of African History* 29: 313–20.

Cowen, Michael. 1981. "The Agrarian Problem." *Review of African Political Economy* 20: 57–73.

1982. "Some Recent East African Peasant Studies." *Journal of Peasant Studies* 18(1): 252–261.

Cox, Pamela. 1984. "Implementing Agricultural Development Policy in Kenya." *Food Research Institute Studies* 19(2): 153–176.

Crowder, Michael. 1987. "Whose Dream was it Anyway? Twenty-five Years of African Independence." *African Affairs* 86(342): 7–24.

Davis, Gerald L. 1985. *I Got the Word in Me and I Can Sing It, You Know: A Study of the Performed African-American Sermon.* Philadelphia: University of Pennsylvania Press.

Donham, Donald. 1981. "Beyond the Domestic Mode of Production." *Man* 16: 515–541.

1990. *History, Power, Ideology: Central Issues in Marxism and Anthropology.* Cambridge and New York: Cambridge University Press.

Dow, James. 1977. "Religion in the Organization of a Mexican Peasantry." In *Peasant Livelihood,* Rhoda Halperin and James Dow (eds.), pp. 215–226. New York: St. Martin's Press.

Dreyfus, Hubert L. and Rabinow, Paul. 1982. *Michel Foucault: Beyond Structuralism and Hermeneutics.* Chicago: University of Chicago Press.

Durkheim, Emile. 1938. *The Rules of Sociological Method.* Glencoe, Illinois: The Free Press.

Eastman, Carol (ed.). 1992. Special issue on code-switching. *Journal of Multilingual and Multicultural Development.*

Edelman, Marc. 1993. "Introduction: Debt Crisis, Social Crisis, Paradigm Crisis." In *Defying the Invisible Hand: Peasant Politics and the Free Market in Costa Rica.* Manuscript.

Edelman, Murray. 1988. *Constructing the Political Spectacle.* Chicago and London: University of Chicago Press.

Ekeh, Peter P. 1990. "Social Anthropology and Two Contrasting Uses of Tribalism in Africa." *Comparative Studies in Society and History* 32(4): 660–700.

Ensminger, Jean. 1992. *Making a Market: The Transformation of an African Society.* New York: Cambridge University Press.

Erasmus, C. 1956. "Culture, Structure and Process: The Occurrence and Disappearance of Reciprocal Farm Labor." *Southwestern Journal of Anthropology* 12: 444–69.

Evans, Peter B., Rueschemeyer, Dietrich, and Skocpol, Theda (eds.). 1985. *Bringing the State Back In.* Cambridge and New York: Cambridge University Press.

Fallers, L. A. 1955. "The Predicament of the Modern African Chief." *American Anthropologist* 57(2): 290–305.

1956. *Bantu Bureaucracy.* London: W. Hefer and Sons.

Fatton, Robert. 1992. *Predatory Rule: State and Civil Society in Africa.* Boulder and London: Lynne Rienner Publishers.

Feierman, Steven. 1990. *Peasant Intellectuals: Anthropology and History in Tanzania.* Madison: University of Wisconsin Press.

1993. "African Histories and the Dissolution of World History." In *Africa and the Disciplines: The Contributions of Research in Africa to the Social Sciences and Humanities*, Robert H. Bates, V. Y. Mudimbe, and Jean O'Barr (eds.), pp. 167–212. Chicago: University of Chicago Press.

Ferguson, James. 1990a. *The Anti-Politics Machine.* Cambridge: Cambridge University Press.

1990b. "Mobile Workers, Modernist Narratives: A Critique of the Historiography of Transition on the Zambian Copperbelt." *Journal of Southern African Studies* 16(3–4): 385–412, 603–621.

1992. "The Country and the City on the Copperbelt." *Cultural Anthropology* 7(1): 80–92.

Firth, Raymond. 1959. *Social Change in Tikopia: Re-study of a Polynesian Community After a Generation.* London: George Allen and Unwin.

1975. "Speech Making and Authority in Tikopia." In *Political Language and Oratory in Traditional Society*, Maurice Bloch (ed.), pp. 29–43. London and New York: Academic Press.

Flanagan, James G. 1989. "Hierarchy in Simple 'Egalitarian' Societies." *Annual Review of Anthropology* 18: 245–66.

Fleuret, Anne. 1988. "Some Consequences of Tenure and Agrarian Reform in Taita, Kenya." In *Land and Society in Contemporary Africa*, R. E. Downs and S. P. Reyna (eds.), pp. 136–158. Hanover and London: University Press of New England.

Ford, Michael and Holmquist, Frank. 1988. "Review Essay: The State and Economy in Kenya." *African Economic History* 17: 153–163.

Fortes, Meyer and Evans-Pritchard, E. E. (eds.). 1940. *African Political Systems*. London: Oxford University Press.

Foster, Robert J. 1991. "Making National Cultures in the Global Ecumene." *Annual Review of Anthropology* 20: 235–60. Bernard J. Siegel (ed.). Palo Alto, California: Annual Reviews Inc.

Foucault, Michel. 1980. *Power/Knowledge: Selected Interviews and Other Writings, 1972–1977*. Colin Gordon (ed.). Sussex: The Harvester Press.

Fox, Richard. 1990. "Introduction." In *Nationalist Ideologies and the Production of National Cultures*, pp. 1–14. Washington DC: American Ethnological Society Monograph Series, no. 2.

Fox, Richard, (ed.) 1991. *Recapturing Anthropology: Working in the Present*. Santa Fe, New Mexico: School of American Research Press.

Furedi, Frank. 1989. *The Mau Mau War in Perspective*. London: James Currey.

Gal, Susan. 1989. "Language and Political Economy." *Annual Review of Anthropology* 18: 345–367.

    1991. "Bartok's Funeral: Representations of Europe in Hungarian Political Rhetoric." *American Ethnologist* 18(3): 440–458.

Geertz, Clifford. 1963. *Agricultural Involution: The Processes of Ecological Change in Indonesia*. Berkeley: University of California Press.

    1973a. "After the Revolution: The Fate of Nationalism in the New States." In *The Interpretation of Cultures*, pp. 234–254. New York: Basic Books.

    1973b. *The Interpretation of Cultures*. New York: Basic Books.

    1981. *Negara: The Theatre State in Nineteenth Century Bali*. Princeton: Princeton University Press.

    1984. "Social Change in Indonesia." *Man* 19(4): 511–532.

Gerhart, John D. 1975. *The Diffusion of Hybrid Maize in Western Kenya*. Mexico City: CIMMYT.

Gertzel, Cherry. 1970. *The Politics of Independent Kenya 1963–8*. Evanston: Northwestern University Press.

Giddens, Anthony. 1979. *Central Problems in Social Theory: Action, Structure and Contradiction in Social Analysis*. Berkeley and Los Angeles: University of California Press.

Githu, Muigai. 1992. "From the Governor to the Imperial President: Constitutional Transformation and the Crisis of Governance in Kenya." Paper presented in Nairobi, June 1992 at a meeting of University of Florida (Gainesville) Program on Governance in Africa.

Gladwin, Christina (ed.). 1991. *Structural Adjustment and African Women Farmers*. Center for African Studies, University of Florida, Gainesville: University of Florida Press.

Glazier, Jack. 1984. "Mbeere Ancestors and the Domestication of Death." *Man* 19: 133–147.

    1985. *Land and the Uses of Tradition Among the Mbeere of Kenya*. New York: University Press of America.

Gluckman, Max. 1940. "The Kingdom of the Zulu of South Africa." In *African Political Systems*, M. Fortes and E. E. Evans-Pritchard (eds.), pp. 25–55. London: Oxford University Press.

1958. *Analysis of a Social Situation in Modern Zululand.* Rhodes-Livingstone Papers, no. 28.

Godia, George. 1984. *Understanding Nyayo: Principles and Policies in Contemporary Kenya.* Nairobi: Transafrica.

Goffman, E. 1974. *Frame Analysis: An Essay on the Organization of Experience.* New York: Harper and Row.

1981. *Forms of Talk.* Philadelphia: University of Pennsylvania Press.

Goody, Esther N. 1978. "Towards a Theory of Questions." In *Questions and Politeness: Strategies in Social Interaction*, Esther N. Goody (ed.), pp. 17–43. Cambridge and London: Cambridge University Press.

Greene, David C. 1983. *Kenya: Growth and Structural Change, Volume II (Issues in Kenyan Agricultural Development).* Washington DC: World Bank.

Gregory, R., Maxon, R. and Spencer, L. 1969. *A Guide to the Kenya National Archives.* Syracuse, New York: Eastern Africa Bibliographical Series, no. 3, Kenya.

Guillet, David. 1981. "Land Tenure, Ecological Zone, and Agricultural Regime in the Central Andes." *American Ethnologist* 8(1): 139–156.

Gumperz, J. J. 1982. *Discourse Strategies.* Cambridge: Cambridge University Press.

Gupta, Akhil. 1993. "Blurred Boundaries: The Discourse of Corruption, The Culture of Politics, and The Imagined State." Manuscript.

Gutto, S. B. O. 1981. "Law, Rangelands, Peasantry, and Social Classes." *Review of African Political Economy* 20: 41–56.

Guyer, Jane. 1981. "Household and Community in African Studies." *African Studies Review* 24(2–3): 87–138.

Harriss, John. 1982a. "General Introduction." In *Rural Development: Theories of Peasant Economy and Agrarian Change*, John Harriss (ed.), pp. 15–34. London: Hutchinson University Library.

1982b. "Introduction." In *Rural Development: Theories of Peasant Economy and Agrarian Change*, John Harriss (ed.), pp. 37–49. London: Hutchinson.

1992. "Does the 'Depressor' Still Work? Agrarian Structure and Development in India: A Review of Evidence and Argument." *Journal of Peasant Studies* 19(2): 189–227.

Hart, Keith. 1982. *The Political Economy of West African Agriculture.* Cambridge and New York: Cambridge University Press.

Harvey, David. 1989. *The Condition of Postmodernity: An Inquiry into the Origins of Cultural Change.* Cambridge, Massachusetts: Blackwell.

Haugerud, Angelique. 1983. "The Consequences of Land Tenure Reform among Smallholders in the Kenya Highlands." *Rural Africana* 15/16: 65–89. Special issue on Land Use in Kenya, P. O'Keefe and C. Barnes (eds.).

1988. "Food Surplus Production, Wealth, and Farmers' Strategies in Kenya." In *Satisfying Africa's Food Needs: Food Production and Commercialization in African Agriculture*, Ronald Cohen (ed.), pp. 153–190. Boulder/London: Lynne Rienner.

1989a. "Land Tenure and Agrarian Change in Kenya." *Africa* 59(1): 61–90.

1989b. "Food Production and Rural Differentiation in the Kenya Highlands." In *Food and Farm: Current Debates and Policies*, Christina H. Gladwin (ed.), pp. 59–83. New York: University Press of America and Society for Economic Anthropology.

Haugerud, Angelique and Njogu, Kimani. 1991. "State Voices in the Country-side: Politics and the Kenyan *Baraza*." Boston University Working Paper, no. 159.

Heller, M. (ed.). 1988. *Code-Switching: Anthropological and Sociolinguistic Perspectives*. Berlin: Mouton de Gruyter.

Hewitt de Alcantara, Cynthia. 1984. *Anthropological Perspectives on Rural Mexico*. London and Boston: Routledge and Kegan Paul.

Heyer, Judith, Roberts, P. and Williams, G. (eds.). 1981. *Rural Development in Tropical Africa*. New York: St. Martin's Press.

Hobsbawm, Eric. 1990. *Nations and Nationalism Since 1780*. New York and Cambridge: Cambridge University Press.

Hobsbawm, Eric and Ranger, Terence (eds.) 1983. *The Invention of Tradition*. Cambridge: Cambridge University Press.

Hohnel, Ludwig von. 1968 (1894). *Discovery of Lakes Rudolf and Stefanie: A Narrative of Count Samuel Teleki's Exploring and Hunting Expeditions in Eastern Equatorial Africa*. Tr. Nancy Bell, 2 volumes. London: Frank Cass.

Holmquist, Frank and Ford, Michael. 1992. "Kenya: Slouching Toward Democracy." Forthcoming in *Africa Today*.

Holmquist, Frank W., Weaver, Frederick S., and Ford, Michael D. 1993. "The Structural Development of Kenya's Political Economy." Forthcoming in *African Studies Review*. Manuscript.

Hornsby, Charles and Throup, David. 1992. "Elections and Political Change in Kenya." *Journal of Commonwealth and Comparative Politics* 30(2): 172–199.

Human Rights Watch. 1991. *Human Rights Watch World Report*. New York: Human Rights Watch.

Hunt, Diana. 1984. *The Impending Crisis in Kenya: The Case for Land Reform*. Brookfield, Vermont: Gower.

Hyden, Goran. 1991a. "Governance and the Study of Politics." In *Governance and Politics in Africa*, Goran Hyden and Michael Bratton (eds.), pp. 1–26. Boulder and London: Lynne Rienner.

    1991b. "The Efforts to Restore Intellectual Freedom in Africa." *Issue: A Journal of Opinion* 20(1): 5–13.

Hyden, Goran and Bratton, Michael. 1991. "Preface." In *Governance and Politics in Africa*, Goran Hyden and Michael Bratton (eds.), pp. ix–xii. Boulder and London: Lynne Rienner.

Imanyara, Gitobu and Maina, Wachira. 1991. "What Future Kenya?" *Nairobi Law Monthly* 37: 19–21.

International Republican Institute. 1993. Kenya: The December 29, 1992 Elections.

Irvine, Judith. 1979. "Formality and Informality in Communicative Events." *American Anthropologist* 81(4): 773–90.

    1982. "Language and Affect: Some Cross-Cultural Issues." In *Georgetown University Roundtable on Languages and Linguistics*. H. Byrnes (ed.), pp. 31–47. Washington DC: Georgetown University Press.

Isaacman, Allen. 1990. "Peasants and Rural Social Protest in Africa." *African Studies Review* 33(2): 1–120.

Ita, Silas. 1972. "The Changing Role Expectations of the Chiefs in Mbere Division, 1900–1971." BA Thesis, Department of Government, University of Nairobi.

Jaetzold, R. 1982. *Farm Management Handbook*. Nairobi: Ministry of Agriculture.

Johnson, Frederick. 1939. *A Standard Swahili–English Dictionary*. Inter-Territorial Language Committee for the East African Dependencies. Nairobi: Oxford University Press.

Johnston, B. and Kilby, P. 1975. *Agriculture and Structural Transformation*. London: Oxford University Press.

Joseph, Richard. 1987. *Democracy and Prebendal Politics in Nigeria: The Rise and Fall of the Second Republic*. Cambridge: Cambridge University Press.

Kanogo, Tabitha. 1987. *Squatters and the Roots of Mau Mau*. London: James Currey.

Kaplinsky, Raphael. 1980. "Capitalist Accumulation in the Periphery: The Kenyan Case Reexamined." *Review of African Political Economy* 17: 83–105.

Karimi, Joseph and Ochieng, Philip. 1980. *The Kenyatta Succession*. Nairobi: Transafrica.

Karp, Ivan. 1980. "Beer Drinking and Social Experience in an African Society." In *Explorations in African Systems of Thought*, Ivan Karp and Charles S. Bird (eds.), pp. 83–119. Bloomington: Indiana University Press.

     1986. "Agency and Social Theory: A Review of Anthony Giddens." *American Ethnologist* 13(1): 131–137.

     1992. "Development and Personhood." Chicago, Illinois: Red Lion Seminar, Northwestern University Program of African Studies and University of Chicago Committee on African and African-American Studies. 23 pp.

Katz, Stephen. 1985. "The Succession to Power and the Power of Succession: Nyayoism in Kenya." *Journal of African Studies* 12(3): 155–161.

Keenan, E. 1975. "A Sliding Sense of Obligatoriness: The Polystructure of Malagasy Oratory." In *Political Language and Oratory in Traditional Society*, Maurice Bloch (ed.), pp. 93–112. London and New York: Academic Press.

Keller, Edmond J. 1991. "Political Change and Political Research in Africa: Agenda for the 1990s." *Issue: A Journal of Opinion* 20(1): 50–53.

Kelly, William W. 1991. "Directions in the Anthropology of Contemporary Japan." *Annual Review of Anthropology* 20: 395–431.

Kenyan government. 1962. *Population Census*. Nairobi: Government Printer.

     1969. *Population Census*. Nairobi: Government Printer.

     1979. *Population Census*. Nairobi: Government Printer.

     1992. *Report of the Parliamentary Select Committee to Investigate Ethnic Clashes in Western and Other Parts of Kenya, 1992*. Nairobi: Government Printer.

     1993. *Economic Survey*. Nairobi: Government Printer.

Kenyatta, Jomo. 1965. *Facing Mt. Kenya: The Tribal Life of the Gikuyu*. New York: Vintage.

     1968. *Suffering Without Bitterness: The Founding of the Kenya Nation*. Nairobi: East African Publishing House.

Kertzer, David I. 1988. *Ritual, Politics, and Power*. New Haven and London: Yale University Press.

Kinyatti, Maina wa (ed.). 1980. *Thunder From the Mountains: Mau Mau Patriotic Songs*. London: Zed Press.

Kitching, Gavin. 1980. *Class and Economic Change in Kenya*. New Haven: Yale University Press.

 1985. "Politics, Method, and Evidence in the 'Kenya Debate'." In *Contradictions of Accumulation in Africa*, Henry Bernstein and Bonnie K. Campbell (eds.), pp. 115–151. London: Sage.

Kopytoff, Igor (ed.). 1987. *The African Frontier: The Reproduction of Traditional African Societies*. Bloomington and Indianapolis: Indiana University Press.

Krapf, L. 1882 (1969). *Dictionary of the Swahili Language*. New York: Negro Universities Press, Division of Greenwood Publishing Corporation.

Krasner, Stephen D. 1984. "Approaches to the State: Alternative Conceptions and Historical Dynamics." *Comparative Politics* 16(2): 223–246.

Ladurie, Emmanuel LeRoy. 1976. *The Peasants of Languedoc*. Urbana: University of Illinois Press. Tr. John Day.

Lambert, H. E. 1950. *The System of Land Tenure in the Kikuyu Land Unit, Part I: History of the Tribal Occupation of Land*. Communications from the School of African Studies, University of Cape Town.

Lancaster, Carol. 1992. "Democracy in Africa." *Foreign Policy* 85 (Winter 1991–92): 148–165.

Landau, Misia. 1984. "Human Evolution as Narrative." *American Scientist* 72: 262–268.

Langdon, Steven. 1977. "The State and Capitalism in Kenya." *Review of African Political Economy* 8: 90–98.

Latham, M. C. 1981. *Human Nutrition in Tropical Africa*. Rome: FAO.

Leach, E. R. 1954. *Political Systems of Highland Burma*. Boston: Beacon Press.

Leakey, L. S. B. 1977. *The Southern Kikuyu Before 1903*. 3 vols. London: Academic Press.

Lemarchand, René. 1972. "Political Clientelism and Ethnicity in Tropical Africa: Competing Solidarities in Nation-Building." *American Political Science Review* 66(1): 68–90.

 1988. "The State, the Parallel Economy, and the Changing Structure of Patronage Systems." In *The Precarious Balance: State and Society in Africa*, pp. 149–170. Boulder and London: Westview Press.

 1991. "The Political Economy of Informal Economies." Paper presented at Program in Agrarian Studies, Yale University, November 22, 1991.

Lenin, V. I. 1964. *The Development of Capitalism in Russia*. Moscow: Progress Publishers.

Lentner, Howard H. 1984. "The Concept of the State: A Response to Stephen Krasner." *Comparative Politics* 16(3): 367–377.

Leo, Christopher. 1984. *Land and Class in Kenya*. Toronto: University of Toronto Press.

Leonard, David. 1991. *African Successes: Four Public Managers of Kenyan Rural Development*. Berkeley: University of California Press.

Leys, Colin. 1971. "Politics in Kenya: The Development of Peasant Society." *British Journal of Political Science* 1(3): 307–337.

 1975. *Underdevelopment in Kenya: The Political Economy of Neo-Colonialism*. London: Heinemann.

1976. "The 'Overdeveloped' Post-Colonial State: A Reevaluation." *Review of African Political Economy* 5: 39–48.

1978. "Capital Accumulation, Class Formation and Dependency: The Significance of the Kenyan Case." *Socialist Register* 241–66.

Link, Perry. 1991. *Evening Chats in Beijing: Probing China's Predicament.* New York: W. W. Norton.

Little, Peter D. 1992. *The Elusive Granary: Herder, Farmer, and State in Northern Kenya.* New York: Cambridge University Press.

Livingstone, I. 1981. *Rural Development, Employment, and Incomes in Kenya.* International Labour Organization.

Lofchie, Michael. 1986. "Kenya's Agricultural Success." *Current History* May: 221–331.

1990. "Kenya: Still an Economic Miracle?" *Current History* (May): 209–212 and 222–224.

Lonsdale, John. 1981. "States and Social Processes in Africa: A Historiographical Survey." *African Studies Review* 24(2/3): 139–225.

1986. "Political Accountability in African History." In *Political Domination in Africa: Reflections on the Limits of Power,* Patrick Chabal (ed.), pp. 126–157. Cambridge and London: Cambridge University Press.

1990. "Mau Maus of the Mind: Making Mau Mau and Remaking Kenya." *Journal of African History* 31: 393–421.

1992. "The Moral Economy of Mau Mau: Wealth, Poverty and Civic Virtue in Kikuyu Political Thought." In *Unhappy Valley: Conflict in Kenya and Africa.* Vol 2: *Violence and Ethnicity,* Bruce Berman and John Lonsdale (eds.), pp. 315–468. London: James Currey.

Lonsdale, John and Berman, Bruce. 1979. "Coping with the Contradictions: The Development of the Colonial State in Kenya, 1895–1914." *Journal of African History* 20: 487–505.

Lukes, Steven. 1975. "Political Ritual and Social Integration." *Sociology* 9: 289–308.

MacDonald, J. R. L. 1897. *Soldiering and Surveying in British East Africa, 1891–1894.* London and New York: Edward Arnold.

Macharia, Kinuthia. 1992. "Slum Clearance and the Informal Economy in Nairobi." *Journal of Modern African Studies* 30(2): 221–236.

Maina, Paul. 1977. *Six Mau Mau Generals.* Nairobi: Gazelle Books.

Mair, L. 1965. *An Introduction to Social Anthropology.* New York and London: Oxford University Press.

Malinowski, Bronislaw. 1965 (1935). *Coral Gardens and Their Magic, vol. 2: The Language of Magic and Gardening.* New York: American Book Company.

Marx, Karl. 1990 (1869). *The Eighteenth Brumaire of Louis Bonaparte.* New York: International Publishers.

Mbaabu, Ireri. 1978. *Proverbs, Idioms, and Poetry in Kimeru (Methali, vitendawili na mashairi ya kimeru).* Nairobi: Kenya Literature Bureau.

Mbembe, Achille. 1992. "Provisional Notes on the Postcolony." *Africa* 62(1): 3–37.

McCann, James C. 1991. "Review Article: Agriculture and African History." *Journal of African History* 32: 507–513.

Meinertzhagen, Richard. 1983 (1957). *Kenya Diary (1902–1906).* London: Eland Books.

Middleton, John and Kershaw, G. 1965. "The Central Tribes of the Northeastern Bantu." In *Ethnographic Survey of Africa*, Part 5. D. Forde (ed.). London: International African Institute.

Miers, S. and Kopytoff, I. 1977. *Slavery in Africa*. Madison: University of Wisconsin Press.

Miller, Christopher. 1993. "Literary Studies and African Literature: The Challenge of Intercultural Literacy." In *Africa and the Disciplines*, Robert H. Bates, V. Y. Mudimbe, and Jean O'Barr (eds.), pp. 213–231. Chicago: University of Chicago Press.

Mintz, Sidney. 1960. *Worker in the Cane: A Puerto Rican Life History*. New Haven: Yale University Press.

Mitchell, Tim. 1991. "America's Egypt: Discourse of the Development Industry." *Middle East Report* (March–April): 18–34.

Moi, Daniel T. Arap. 1986. *Kenya African Nationalism: Nyayo Philosophy and Principles*. London and Basingstoke: Macmillan.

Moock, Joyce. 1978. "The Content and Maintenance of Social Ties Between Urban Migrants and their Home-based Support Groups: The Maragoli Case." *African Urban Studies* 3: 15–31.

Moore, Barrington. 1966. *Social Origins of Dictatorship and Democracy*. Boston: Beacon Press.

Moore, M. P. 1975. "Cooperative Labor in Peasant Agriculture." *Journal of Peasant Studies* 2: 270–9.

Moore, S. F. 1975. "Selection for Failure in a Small Social Field: Ritual Concord and Fraternal Strife among the Chagga, Kilimanjaro, 1968–69." In *Symbol and Politics in Communal Ideology*, Sally Falk Moore and Barbara G. Myerhoff (eds.), pp. 109–143. Ithaca and London: Cornell University Press.

  1977. "Political Meetings and the Simulation of Unanimity: Kilimanjaro 1973." In *Secular Ritual*, Sally F. Moore and Barbara G. Myerhoff (eds.), pp. 151–172. Amsterdam: Van Gorcum.

  1986. *Social Facts and Fabrications: Customary Law on Kilimanjaro, 1880–1980*. Cambridge and New York: Cambridge University Press.

  1987. "Explaining the Present: Theoretical Dilemmas in Processual Ethnography." *American Ethnologist* 14(4): 727–736.

Moore, S. F. and Myerhoff, Barbara G. 1977. "Introduction: Secular Ritual: Forms and Meanings." In *Secular Ritual*, Sally F. Moore and Barbara G. Myerhoff (eds.), pp. 3–24. Amsterdam: Van Gorcum.

Moris, Jon. 1970. *The Agrarian Revolution in Central Kenya: A Study of Farm Innovation in Embu District*. PhD thesis, Department of Anthropology, Northwestern University. Ann Arbor: University Microfilms International.

Mueller, Suzanne. 1984. "Government and Opposition in Kenya, 1966–69." *Journal of Modern African Studies* 22(3): 399–427.

Mukaru Ng'ang'a, D. 1981. "What is Happening to the Kenyan Peasantry?" *Review of African Political Economy* 20: 7–16.

Mulaa, John. 1981. "The Politics of a Changing Society: Mumias." *Review of African Political Economy* 20: 89–107.

Mungeam, G. H. 1966. *British Rule in Kenya, 1895–1912: The Establishment of Administration in the East African Protectorate*. Oxford: Oxford University Press.

Muriuki, Godfrey. 1974. *A History of the Kikuyu, 1500–1900*. Nairobi and New York: Oxford University Press.

Murphy, William P. 1990. "Creating the Appearance of Consensus in Mende Political Discourse." *American Anthropologist* 92(1): 24–41.

Murphy, William P. and Bledsoe, Caroline H. 1987. "Kinship and Territory in the History of a Kpelle Chiefdom (Liberia)." In *The African Frontier*, Igor Kopytoff (ed.), pp. 123–147. Bloomington: Indiana University Press.

Murra, John. 1970. "Current Research and Prospects in Andean Ethnohistory." *Latin American Research Review* 5(1): 3–36.

Murray, Colin. 1981. *Families Divided: The Impact of Migrant Labour in Lesotho*. Cambridge: Cambridge University Press.

Mwaniki, H. S. K. 1971. *Ndai, nthimo, na ng'ano iri ukuwa wa Aembu*. Nairobi: East African Literature Bureau.

1973a. *A Political History of the Embu: CAD 1500–1906*. MA Thesis, Department of History, University of Nairobi.

1973b. *The Living History of Embu and Mbeere to 1906*. Nairobi: East African Literature Bureau.

1974. *Embu Historical Texts*. Nairobi: East African Literature Bureau.

1986. *Categories and Substance of Embu Traditional Folksongs and Dances*. Nairobi: Kenya Literature Bureau.

Myers, Fred R. and Brenneis, Donald L. 1984. "Introduction." In *Dangerous Words: Language and Politics in the Pacific*, Donald L. Brenneis and Fred R. Myers (eds.), pp. 1–29. New York: New York University Press.

Myers-Scotton, Carol. 1983. "The Negotiation of Identities in Conversation: A Theory of Markedness and Code Choice. *International Journal of the Sociology of Language* 44: 115–136.

National Election Monitoring Unit (NEMU). 1992. *The Multi-Party General Elections in Kenya December 29, 1992*. Nairobi: NEMU.

1993. "Courting Disaster: A Report on the Continuing Terror, Violence, and Destruction in the Rift Valley, Nyanza, and Western Provinces of Kenya." Nairobi: NEMU (Council of Elders).

Nellis, John. 1973. "Three Aspects of the Kenyan Administrative System." *Culture et developpement* 5(3): 541–570.

Nelson, Joan (ed.). 1990. *Economic Crisis and Policy Choice: The Politics of Economic Adjustment in the Third World*. Princeton: Princeton University Press.

Netting, Robert. 1964. "Beer as a Locus of Value Among the West African Kofyar." *American Anthropologist* 66: 375–384.

1976. "What Alpine Peasants Have in Common: Observations on Communal Tenure in a Swiss Village." *Human Ecology* 4: 135–146.

1977. *Cultural Ecology*. Menlo Park, California: Cummings.

Newbury, Catharine. 1994. "Introduction: Paradoxes of Democratization in Africa." Forthcoming in *African Studies Review* 37(1).

Ngugi wa Thiong'o. 1964. *Weep Not, Child*. Nairobi: Heinemann.

1977. *Petals of Blood*. New York: E. P. Dutton.

Njogu, Kimani. 1990. "Code-Switching and Negotiation among Kiswahili–English Bilinguals in Kenya." Yale University, Dept. of Linguistics, manuscript.

1991. "Discourse in Kiswahili Dialogue Poetry: Sociolinguistic Evidence from *Gungu*." Paper presented at annual African Linguistics Conference, July 1991, University of Nairobi.

1993. *Dialogic Poetry: Contestation and Social Challenge in East African Poetic Genres*. PhD thesis, Department of Linguistics, Yale University.

1994. "Witiire na Gicandi." *Mutiiri* 1(1): 115–122. Department of Comparative Literature, New York University.

Njonjo, Apollo. 1981. "The Kenya Peasantry: A Reassessment. *Review of African Political Economy* 20: 27–40.

Njururi, Ngumbu (ed.). 1983 (1968). *Gikuyu Proverbs*. Nairobi: Oxford University Press.

Nowrojee, Eruch. 1992. "Kenya: Political Pluralism, Government Resistance, and United States Responses." Forthcoming in *Harvard Human Rights Journal*.

O'Barr, William M. and O'Barr, Jean F. (eds.). 1976. *Language and Politics*. The Hague: Mouton.

O'Brien, Jay and Roseberry, William. 1991. *Golden Ages, Dark Ages: Imagining the Past in Anthropology and History*. Berkeley and Los Angeles: University of California Press.

Okoth-Ogendo, H. W. O. 1976. "African Land Tenure Reform." In *Agricultural Development in Kenya*, Judith Heyer et al. (eds.), pp. 152–186. Nairobi: Oxford University Press.

Ooko, Ombaka. 1982. *Political Justice in Kenya: Prolegomena to an Inquiry into the Use of Legal Procedures for Political Purposes in Post-Kenyatta Era*. Verfassung und Recht in Ubersee.

Orans, M. 1966. "Surplus." *Human Organization* 25: 24–32.

Orlove, Benjamin. 1977. "Integration Through Production: The Use of Zonation in Espinar." *American Ethnologist* 4(1): 84–101.

Ortner, Sherry. 1984. "Theory in Anthropology Since the Sixties." *Comparative Studies in Society and History* 26: 126–66.

Paine, Robert (ed.). 1981. *Politically Speaking: Cross-Cultural Studies of Rhetoric*. Philadelphia: Institute for the Study of Human Issues.

Parkin, David. 1975. "The Rhetoric of Responsibility: Bureaucratic Communications in a Kenya Farming Center." In *Political Language and Oratory in Traditional Society*, Maurice Bloch (ed.), pp. 113–140. London and New York: Academic Press.

1978. *The Cultural Definition of Political Response: Lineal Destiny Among the Luo*. London and New York: Academic Press.

1984. "Political Language." *Annual Review of Anthropology* 13: 345–365.

1990. "Eastern Africa: The View from the Office and the Voice from the field." In *Localizing Strategies: Regional Traditions of Ethnographic Writing*, Richard Fardon (ed.), pp. 182–203. Washington DC: Smithsonian Institution Press.

Pearson, J. J. 1957. "The Economy Has No Surplus." In *Trade and Markets in the Early Empires*, K. Polanyi, C. M. Arensberg, and H. W. Pearson (eds.). Glencoe, Illinois: Free Press.

Pick, Vittorio Merlo. 1973. *Ndai na gicaandi: Kikuyu Enigmas*. Bologna: Editrice Missionaria Italiano (EMI).

Presley, Cora Ann. 1986. "Kikuyu Women in the Mau Mau Rebellion." In *In Resistance: Studies in African, Caribbean, and Afro-American History*, Garry Y. Okihiro (ed.), pp. 53–70. Amherst: University of Massachusetts Press.

Rebel, Herman. 1989. "Cultural Hegemony and Class Experience: A Critical Reading of Recent Ethnological-Historical Approaches." *American Ethnologist* 16(1): 117–136 (part 1) and 16(2): 350–365 (part 2).

Richards, Audrey. 1939. *Land, Labour and Diet in Northern Rhodesia: An Economic Study of the Bemba Tribe*. London: Oxford University Press.

Richards, Audrey and Kuper, Adam (eds.). 1971. *Councils in Action*. Cambridge: Cambridge University Press.

Richards, Paul. 1982. "Ecological Change and the Politics of African Land Use." Paper commissioned by the Social Science Research Council, presented at annual meetings of African Studies Association, Washington DC. (Also published in *African Studies Review*, 1983, 26(2): 1–72.)

Robinson, Pearl T. 1994. "Democratization: Understanding the Relationship between Regime Change and the Culture of Politics." Forthcoming in *African Studies Review* 37(1).

Roeder, Philip G. 1984. "Legitimacy and Peasant Revolution: An Alternative to Moral Economy." *Peasant Studies* 11(3): 149–168.

Rosaldo, Michelle. 1973. "I Have Nothing to Hide: The Language of Ilongot Oratory." *Language and Society* 2(2): 193–223.

Rosberg, Carl and Nottingham, John. 1966. *The Myth of "Mau Mau": Nationalism in Kenya*. New York: Praeger.

Roseberry, William. 1988. "Political Economy." *Annual Review of Anthropology* 17: 161–185.

   1989. *Anthropologies and Histories: Essays in Culture, History, and Political Economy*. New Brunswick and London: Rutgers University Press.

   1991. "Potatoes, Sacks, and Enclosures in Early Modern England." In *Golden Ages, Dark Ages: Imagining the Past in Anthropology and History*, Jay O'Brien and William Roseberry (eds.), pp. 19–47. Berkeley and Los Angeles: University of California Press.

Ryle, Gilbert. 1970. *The Concept of Mind*. Harmondsworth: Penguin Books.

Saberwal, Satish. 1970. *The Traditional Political System of the Embu of Central Kenya*. Nairobi: East African Publishing House.

Sahlins, Marshall. 1972. *Stone-Age Economics*. New York: Aldine.

Sandbrook, Richard. 1990. "Taming the African Leviathan." *World Policy Journal* 7(4): 673–701.

Sapir, J. David and Crocker, J. Christopher (eds.). 1977. *The Social Uses of Metaphor*. University of Pennsylvania Press.

Saul, Mahir. 1983. "Work Parties, Wages, and Accumulation in a Voltaic Village." *American Ethnologist* 10(1): 77–96.

Schama, Simon. 1992. *Dead Certainties (Unwarranted Speculations)*. New York: Vintage Books/Random House.

Schatzberg, Michael G. 1988. *The Dialectics of Oppression in Zaire*. Bloomington: Indiana University Press.

   1991. *Mobutu or Chaos? The United States and Zaire, 1960–1990*. Lanham and New York: University Press of America.

Schmidt, Steffen W., Guasti, Laura, Lande, Carl H., and Scott, James C. (eds.).

1977. *Friends, Followers and Factions*. Berkeley and Los Angeles: University of California Press.

Schneider, Jane and Schneider, Peter. 1976. *Culture and Political Economy in Western Sicily*. New York: Academic Press.

Scott, James. 1972. "Patron–Client Politics and Political Change in Southeast Asia." *American Political Science Review* 66(1): 91–113.

1976. *The Moral Economy of the Peasant*. New Haven and London: Yale University Press.

1985. *Weapons of the Weak: Everyday Forms of Peasant Resistance*. New Haven and London: Yale University Press.

1986. "Everyday Forms of Peasant Resistance." *Journal of Peasant Studies* 13(2): 5–34.

1990. *Domination and the Arts of Resistance: Hidden Transcripts*. New Haven: Yale University Press.

Shanin, Teodor. 1982. "Polarization and Cyclical Mobility: the Russian Debate over the Differentiation of the Peasantry." In *Rural Development: Theories of Peasant Economy and Agrarian Change*, John Harriss (ed.), pp. 223–245. London: Hutchinson University Library.

Shipton, Parker. 1988. "The Kenyan Land Tenure Reform: Misunderstandings in the Public Creation of Private Property." In *Land and Society in Contemporary Africa*, R. E. Downs and S. P. Reyna (eds.), pp. 91–135. Hanover and London: University Press of New England.

Shipton, Parker and Goheen, Mitzi. 1992. "Introduction. Understanding African Land-Holding: Power, Wealth, and Meaning." *Africa* 62(3): 307–325.

Simmel, Georg. 1950. *The Sociology of Georg Simmel*. Ed. and tr. Kurt H. Wolff. Glencoe, Illinois: The Free Press.

Siu, Helen. 1990. "Recycling Tradition: Culture, History, and Political Economy in the Chrysanthemum Festivals of South China." *Comparative Studies in Society and History* 32(4): 765–794.

Smith, Gavin. 1991. "The Production of Culture in Local Rebellion." In *Golden Ages, Dark Ages: Imagining the Past in Anthropology and History*, Jay O'Brien and William Roseberry (eds.), pp. 180–207. Berkeley: University of California Press.

Sorrenson, M. P. K. 1967. *Land Reform in the Kikuyu Country: A Study in Government Policy*. Nairobi and London: Oxford University Press.

Spear, Thomas. 1981. *Kenya's Past: An Introduction to Historical Method in Africa*. London.

Spear, Thomas and Waller, Richard (eds.). 1993. *Being Maasai: Ethnicity and Identity in East Africa*. London: James Currey.

Staniland, Martin. 1986. "Democracy and Ethnocentrism." In *Political Domination in Africa: Reflections on the Limits of Power*, Patrick Chabal (ed.), pp. 52–70. Cambridge: Cambridge University Press.

1991. *American Intellectuals and African Nationalists, 1955–1970*. New Haven and London: Yale University Press.

Swainson, N. 1980. *The Development of Corporate Capitalism in Kenya, 1918–1977*. London: Heinemann.

Swynnerton, R. J. M. 1954. *A Plan to Intensify the Development of African Agriculture in Kenya*. Nairobi: Colony and Protectorate of Kenya.

Thomas-Slayter, Barbara P. 1985. *Politics, Participation, and Poverty: Development Through Self-Help in Kenya.* Boulder and London: Westview Press.

 1991. "Class, Community, and the Kenyan State: Community Mobilization in the Context of Global Politics." *International Journal of Politics, Culture and Society* 4(3): 301–321.

Thompson, E. P. 1966. *The Making of the English Working Class.* New York: Vintage Books.

 1971. "The Moral Economy of the English Crowd in the Eighteenth Century." *Past and Present* 50: 76–136.

Throup, David. 1987a. *Economic and Social Origins of Mau Mau, 1945–1953.* London: James Currey.

 1987b. "The Construction and Destruction of the Kenyatta State." In *The Political Economy of Kenya*, Michael G. Schatzberg (ed.), pp. 33–74. New York: Praeger.

 1993a. "Elections and Political Legitimacy in Kenya." *Africa* 63(3): 371–396.

 1993b. "Elections and Political Legitimacy in Kenya: The Githunguri Case." Paper presented at Kenya Elections Workshop, Hampshire College (Amherst, Massachusetts), August 1993.

Throup, David and Hornsby, Charles. *The Triumph of the System: The Kenyan Struggle for Multi-Party Democracy* (forthcoming).

Tignor, Robert L. 1971. "Colonial Chiefs in Chiefless Societies." *Journal of Modern African Studies* 9(3): 339–359.

 1976. *The Colonial Transformation of Kenya: The Kamba, Kikuyu, and Maasai from 1900 to 1939.* Princeton, New Jersey: Princeton University Press.

Tilly, Charles. 1984. *Big Structures, Large Processes, Huge Comparisons.* New York: Russell Sage Foundation.

Tosh, John. 1980. "The Cash-Crop Revolution in Tropical Africa: An Agricultural Reappraisal." *African Affairs* 79(314): 79–94.

Tully, Dennis. 1984. *Culture and Context: The Process of Market Incorporation in Dar Masalit, Sudan.* Doctoral dissertation, University of Washington (Seattle). Ann Arbor: University Microfilms International.

Turner, Victor. 1957. *Schism and Continuity in an African Society.* Manchester: Manchester University Press.

Vail, Leroy. 1989. "Introduction." In *The Creation of Tribalism in Southern Africa*, Leroy Vail (ed.), pp. 1–19. London: James Currey and Berkeley: University of California Press.

Van de Walle, Nicolas. 1993. "Economic Ideas and Structural Adjustment in Francophone Africa." Paper presented at annual meeting of the African Studies Association, Boston, December 4–7, 1993.

Van Zwanenberg, R. M. A. with King, A. 1975. *An Economic History of Kenya and Uganda 1800–1970.* Nairobi: East African Publishing House.

Vincent, Joan. 1968. *African Elite: The Big Men of a Small Town.* New York and London: Columbia University Press.

 1977. "Colonial Chiefs and the Making of a Class." *Africa* 47(2): 140–159.

 1978. "Political Anthropology: Manipulative Strategies." *Annual Review of Anthropology* 7: 175–94.

 1982. *Teso in Transformation: The Political Economy of Peasant and Class in Eastern Africa.* Berkeley: University of California Press.

1990. *Anthropology and Politics: Visions, Traditions and Trends*. Tucson: University of Arizona Press.

1991. "Engaging Historicism." In *Recapturing Anthropology: Working in the Present*, Richard G. Fox (ed.), pp. 45–58. Santa Fe, New Mexico: School of American Research.

Wanjau, Gakaara wa. 1988. *Mau Mau Author in Detention*. Translated from Gikuyu by Ngigi wa Njoroge. Nairobi: Heinemann.

Wanjiku, Mukabi Ireri. 1983. *The Oral Artist*. Nairobi: Heinemann.

Wanjiku, Mukabi Kabira and Mutahi, Karega. 1988. *Gikuyu Oral Literature*. Nairobi: Heinemann.

Wasserman, Gary. 1976. *Politics of Decolonization: Kenya Europeans and the Land Issue, 1960–1965*. London: Cambridge University Press.

Watson-Gegeo, Karen Ann and White, Geoffrey M. (eds.). 1990. *Disentangling: Conflict Discourse in Pacific Societies*. Palo Alto: Stanford University Press.

Watts, Michael. 1989. "The Agrarian Question in Africa: Debating the Crisis." *Progress in Human Geography* 13: 1–41.

Weber, Max. 1946. *From Max Weber: Essays in Sociology*. Ed. and tr. H. H. Gerth and C. Wright Mills. New York: Oxford University Press.

1947. *The Theory of Social and Economic Organization*. A. M. Henderson and Talcott Parsons (eds.). New York: The Free Press.

White, Luise. 1990a. "Separating the Men from the Boys: Colonial Constructions of Gender in Central Kenya." *International Journal of African Historical Studies* 23/1: 1–26.

1990b. *The Comforts of Home: Prostitution in Colonial Nairobi*. Chicago: University of Chicago Press.

Whiteley, Wilfred. 1969. *Swahili: The Rise of a National Language*. London: Methuen.

Whiteley, Wilfred (ed.). 1974. *Language in Kenya*. London: Oxford University Press.

Widner, Jennifer. 1992. *From Harambee! to Nyayo!: The Rise of a Party-State in Kenya*. Berkeley: University of California Press.

Widner, Jennifer (ed.). 1994. *Economic Change and Political Liberalization in SubSaharan Africa*. Baltimore: Johns Hopkins University Press.

Williams, David. 1993. Review article: "Liberalism and 'Development Discourse'." *Africa* 63(3): 419–429.

Williams, Raymond. 1973. *The Country and the City*. New York: Oxford University Press.

Wilson, G. 1941. "The Economics of Detribalization in Northern Rhodesia." Rhodes-Livingstone Institute Paper no. 5.

Wolf, Eric. 1956. "Aspects of Group Relations in Complex Society." *American Anthropologist* 58: 1065–1078.

1966. "Kinship, Friendship, and Patron–Client Relations in Complex Societies." In *The Social Anthropology of Complex Societies*, Michael Banton (ed.), pp. 1–22. London: Tavistock.

1982. *Europe and the People Without History*. Berkeley: University of California Press.

1986. "The Vicissitudes of the Closed Corporate Peasant Community." *American Ethnologist* 13(2): 325–329.

Wolpe, H. 1972. "Capitalism and Cheap Labour Power in South Africa."
    Economy and Society 1(4): 425–456.
World Bank. 1981. *Accelerated Development in Sub-Saharan Africa*. Washington
    DC: World Bank.
    1982. *Growth and Structural Change in Kenya*. Washington DC: World Bank.
    1989. *Sub-Saharan Africa: From Crisis to Sustainable Growth*. Washington DC:
    World Bank.
    1990. *Second Agricultural Sector Adjustment Operation*. Washington DC:
    World Bank.
Young, Tom. 1993. "Elections and Electoral Politics in Africa." *Africa* 63(3):
    299–312.
Zimmerman, Erich W. 1972. *World Resources and Industries*. New York: Harper
    and Row.

NEWSPAPERS AND NEWS JOURNALS

Daily Nation (Nairobi)
Standard (Nairobi)
Weekly Review (Nairobi)
Kenya Times (Nairobi)
Nairobi Law Monthly
Finance (Nairobi)
Economic Review (Nairobi)
Monthly News (Nairobi)
New York Times
Independent (London)
Washington Post
Manchester Guardian Weekly
Christian Science Monitor

ARCHIVES

Embu District:
    Local Native Council (LNC) Minutes
    African District Council (ADC) Minutes
    Ministry of Agriculture: Monthly Divisional Reports, and District Annual
        Reports.
    Handing Over Reports
    Land Registry, divisional files and district records

Index

Abdulaziz, Vittorio Merle, 69
Abrams, Philip, 58
Abwunza, M. H., 83
academic research, in Kenya, 7
accountability, 11
  and colonial government, 74–5
  demands for, 19, 26, 50
  and development projects, 62
  and economic crisis, 137, 138, 192
  for economic policy, 54
  and multiparty politics, 21–2
  and patron–client politics, 46–7, 96–9
Achebe, Chinua, 199, 200, 225, 226
administrative units, and Embu
    neighbourhoods, 113
Africa Watch, 33, 41, 42
agrarian change, 111
  and Embu households, 182–90
agrarian ecology, in Central Kenya, 115–17
agricultural exports, 34, 235
agricultural improvements, and wealth in
    Embu households, 153
agricultural production
  colonial regulation of, 129–30
  and Embu household economy, 154–8
  see also farmers
aid donors, and politics, 20–2, 50
Allan, William, 154, 156
Ambler, Charles H., 40, 86–7, 112, 117,
    119, 120, 123, 124, 126, 223
Amin, Idi, 76, 79
Amin, Samir, 20
Amnesty International, 20
Anderson, Benedict, 1, 5, 85, 102
Appadurai, Arjun, 6, 7, 9, 57
Appiah, Kwame Anthony, 43
assemblies, *see baraza*
assistant chiefs
  baraza, 148
  and "sublocations", 113
  place in administrative hierarchy, 216
athomi (literate people), 123, 143, 163
Atieno-Odhiambo, E. S., 17, 121

Bailey, F. G., 14, 58, 66, 85
bananas, cultivation of, 156
banks
  Central Bank of Kenya, 34
  Western, and debt recovery, 20
  see also World Bank
baraza, 2–4, 54, 56, 57, 60–71, 102–5, 196,
    197
  audiences at, 14, 58, 59, 69, 85–6, 87–91,
    96–9, 103
  and the ban on home-brewed beer,
    88–91, 103
  coffee cooperative society and, 96–9,
    103, 139
  and colonial administration, 73–4
  dissident voices at, 3, 96–9
  and district commissioners (DCs), 143–5
  and district officers (DOs), 8, 58, 88, 89
  and a Durkheimian "common spirit",
    12, 56
  and images of Kenya, 7, 102, 105, 195
  importance in state-building, 8, 99–100,
    136
  languages spoken at, 62–4
  meanings of term, 61
  media coverage of, 2, 85, 102
  and moral contract between citizens and
    state, 10, 72
  national political culture and local
    realities, 8–9, 10
  and opposition politics, 16, 59, 67–8, 196
  and patron–client politics, 68, 95, 100
  and President Moi, 12–13, 55, 58, 61,
    81–2, 84
  and requests for government assistance,
    66, 92–4
  rhetorical clashes played out at (1990s),
    16
  and social structure/culture, 59–60
  speakers and speeches at, 3, 10, 64–8,
    85–6
  speaking style at, 68–71
  successful, 14

258

Other recent books in the series